C0-FZV-904

THE SPIRIT OF LIFE

THE HOLY SPIRIT IN THE LIFE OF THE CHRISTIAN

BT
121.2
.B47
1987

LUIS M. BERMEJO, S.J.

THE SPIRIT OF LIFE

THE HOLY SPIRIT
IN THE LIFE OF THE CHRISTIAN

1987
GUJARAT SAHITYA PRAKASH
ANAND, GUJARAT 388 001
INDIA

Imprimi Potest: Julian Fernandes, S.J.
Provincial
New Delhi, 27th March 1987

© 1987 Luis M. Bermejo, S.J.
Pune, India

ALL RIGHTS RESERVED. NO PART OF THIS BOOK MAY BE REPRODUCED OR TRANSLATED, IN ANY FORM OR BY ANY MEANS, WITHOUT THE PREVIOUS PERMISSION OF THE AUTHOR.

American printing produced in 1989 and distributed by
Loyola University Press, 3441 North Ashland Avenue,
Chicago, Illinois, 60657, with permission of the publisher.

ISBN: 0-8294-0603-4

Published by X. Diaz del Rio, S.J., GUJARAT SAHITYA PRAKASH, P.B.70,
ANAND, Gujarat, 388 001, India.

57094

CONTENTS

INTRODUCTION

At the very start one has to note regretfully that after twenty long centuries of Christianity the Holy Spirit means next to nothing to the average Christian. We are all proud of and glory in the name of Christ, but this profound attachment to Christ — undoubtedly legitimate and most fundamental — seems to have had the regrettable result of almost ousting the Holy Spirit from our spiritual field of interest. Maybe our Catholic liturgy is to some extent both a sign and a partial cause of this situation. The entire liturgical year is brightly studded with innumerable celebrations in honour and commemoration of Christ: Christmas, Holy Week and Easter are traditionally considered as the peak feasts of the year; the daily, or at least weekly, eucharistic liturgy is centered on the death and resurrection of Jesus; when reading and reflecting on the Scriptures our attention is oftener than not riveted on the four gospels which recall the early tradition about Jesus; Christian buildings, whether churches, schools or hospitals are clearly distinguishable because of their oversized crosses....Need I continue? The memory of Christ is gone down deep into the very lifestream of our religious consciousness, spreading far and wide to all spheres of our Christian life.

As compared to this myriad of christological reminiscences and signs of our all-pervading attachment to Jesus Christ, what does the Holy Spirit mean to most of us? The Spirit seems to be nothing but an impersonal abstraction, either wrongly identified with the mentality, frame of mind and values of Jesus of Nazareth, or turned into an abstract belief of only academic interest. We all know, of course — every catechism kid does — that there are three persons in God, but has the reality of the Holy Spirit gone beyond the realm of a merely theoretical tenet of our Christian faith? Do we value and loudly proclaim the person and activity of the Holy

Spirit as a positive and distinct force in our Christian life to be reckoned with? Briefly stated: in our religious enterprise the lion's share goes surely to Jesus, with only a passing nod — if at all — to the Holy Spirit. We seem to forget that the Spirit is the supreme gift of Easter, that the pentecostal outpouring of the Holy Spirit is but the fruit of Christ's death and resurrection, that if the Spirit is the gift the glorified Jesus is the giver, and to leave a gift untouched and unappreciated is an insult to the giver himself.

Several reasons could immediately be pointed out which account for this deplorable situation: the peculiar manner in which the Spirit makes his appearance in the gospels, always under impersonal symbols like water, fire, breath or wind; the obvious visibility and tangibility of Christ, in contrast with the invisibility and elusiveness of the Holy Spirit, of whom not a single word is recorded in the gospels; the disastrous schism of 1054, when the two sister Churches of East and West, which had imperceptibly but steadily been drifting apart for centuries, finally broke off communion with each other, with the result that the rich spiritual tradition of the Holy Spirit, typical of the East, was to a large extent lost to the West, whose attention centred increasingly and almost exclusively on Christ; etc....

The present situation in this respect, unsatisfactory as it surely is, has however improved somewhat due mainly to two important realities of the contemporary Church: Vatican II and the present Charismatic Renewal. Vatican II has as many as 258 scattered references to the Holy Spirit, but lacks a unified body of doctrine on the Spirit. During the Council critical voices were heard — mostly from the Oriental, non-Catholic observers — which pointed out that all these references were no more than a sprinkling, the external icing on the conciliar cake, making it undoubtedly colourful and somewhat attractive, but without penetrating into its substance. The Holy Spirit, though repeatedly mentioned, was certainly not a prominent theme in Vatican II.

This has been implicitly acknowledged by John Paul II in his recent encyclical on the Holy Spirit, in which he quotes approvingly a passage from Paul VI: "The christology and particularly the ecclesiology of the Council must be succeeded by a new study of and devotion to the Holy Spirit, precisely as the indispensable complement to the teaching of the Council".[1] These words were

1. Quoted by John Paul II in his recent encyclical *Dominum et Vivificantem*

originally pronounced by Paul VI at a general audience in 1973, and one has ruefully to acknowledge that fourteen years afterwards the legitimate wishes of that Pope seem to have been hardly fulfilled.

Thank God two years after the conclusion of the Council the Holy Spirit himself intervened and shook the Catholic Church — he had done the same with other Christian Churches a few years earlier — out of her slumber, as far as her interest in the Holy Spirit was concerned, by making her experience the fruit of the so-called Charismatic Renewal. Not only the rank and file of the Catholic laity, but the Church's hierarchy as well has of late sanctioned and approved, even if somewhat cautiously, this new movement which, on the whole, seems to bear the unmistakable signs of the Holy Spirit's action, as I shall succintly explain in the concluding chapter of the book.

The present work resembles an ellipse with two foci, the person of the Holy Spirit and the Christian. I am not particularly interested in the eternal and internal life of the trinitarian family, in the mysterious way the Spirit proceeds from the Father and the Son and is related to both of them. This is an area of awesome majesty and mysterious splendour which demands almost reverential silence. My aim is more modest, more down-to-earth: to explain, under the unfailing light of the New Testament and the authentic Christian tradition, the inexhaustible riches of the Spirit's activity in the heart — in the body, rather, as I shall repeatedly point out in the course of the present work — of the Christian. For the two foci of the ellipse, namely, the two persons of the Spirit and the Christian, are closely interlocked in a permanent dialogue which takes place within man.

All the theological and spiritual themes developed in the course of the book turn around this double centre, around this unbelievable reality which is the real presence of the Holy Spirit in the sanctuary of the sanctified Christian. A few years ago the controversial Dutch Catechism put it well: "We receive divine life, we are children of God, we are in Christ, God dwells in us...we receive grace. In each case light is thrown from different angles on the one truth, that the Holy Spirit is in us".[2]

This is perfectly correct, but on the other hand an excessive unification of themes may result in a regrettable loss of the riches

of 18th May 1986; cf. *Osservatore Romano*, English ed., 9 June 1986, p. 1.
2 *A New Catechism* (New York 1987), p. 287.

contained in any comprehensive treatise on the Holy Spirit. I shall deal first with the profound transformation which the baptized Christian undergoes at the hands of the Holy Spirit dwelling inside him, the Spirit he has received as the result of his baptismal immanence or incorporation into the person of the glorified Jesus. The Christian becomes thereby a new creature, radically altered, deeply transformed and sanctified in the very core of his being. And he emerges from this transformation as a child of the Father, empowered to address him with childlike confidence and trust as his *Abba*.

If the Christian is so completely changed, this newness of life is bound to overflow into his activity; he has to *act* as a new person because he *is* a new person — and this will be the second part of the book. "If we live by the Spirit, let us also walk by the Spirit" (Gal 5,26). But if the Christian is active in keeping with his newly acquired potentialities, so is also the Spirit who certainly does not lie idle in the heart of the Christian; rather the Spirit makes him the object of his promptings, inspirations and touches, all of which probably occur much more frequently than we imagine. And because the Spirit is so active — restlessly active, I am tempted to say — the Christian cannot but experience his touch, hear his voice and feel his presence. Faith is surely fundamental, but most of us find it very hard to accept all these wondrous ralities that take place in the person of the Christian exclusively on the basis of dark faith; a minimum of personal experience as a prop to faith is certainly welcome, it is even necessary.

The trinitarian life poured so lavishly into the Christian by the Holy Spirit is no dead capital of any sort, for it grows and keeps growing, whether we realize it or not, until its final consummation after death, when it will blossom into the fullness of life everlasting, when the Christian will finally not only contemplate face to face, but also — and specially — plunge into the very source of this blessed life: the Holy Spirit himself.

But let us return to earth. During his pilgrim state the Christian leads a life in the Spirit which is already exhilarating because it is deeply marked by two characteristics that thrill the heart of man: freedom and charisms, both typical of the Spirit. To a contemporary Christian these two realities are bound to be heady wine, both exceedingly attractive but also difficult to handle well.

These are the main themes expounded in the course of the

present work. Since the book itself is fairly long — I have tried to make it truly comprehensive — I should cut this introduction short or I will try the reader's patience. I am certainly not a defender of male chauvinism in any form, but I must confess that at times I found it very difficult to avoid entirely language that may seem discriminatory. I only request all feminine readers to transcend the inadequacies of all human speech and to see themselves represented and honourably included in the innumerable references they will find to the word "man", which should always include both man *and* woman.

A genuine, sincere word of thanks to my two main collaborators: Fr. P. Kehres, S.J., indefatigable and exceedingly accurate proofreader of the entire manuscript; and Mrs. Anne Drego, who with characteristic professional competence typed the entire book twice over. I am conscious of thanking both a man and a woman, so as to dispel all accusations, however slight, of favouring my own male sex.

I would like to conclude by making my own the words of Y. Congar, the great French theologian who combines in his person so remarkably both scholarly competence and religious spirit. In the first of his two volumes on the Holy Spirit he says: "The Spirit is breath. The wind sings in the trees. I would like, then, to be an Aeolian harp and let the breath of God make the strings vibrate and sing. Let me stretch and tune the strings — that will be the austere task of research. And let the Spirit make them sing a clear and tuneful song of prayer and life!".[3]

3. *I Believe in the Holy Spirit,* I (New York-London 1983), p. x.

Chapter One

NEW LIFE IN CHRIST JESUS

If there is a word that has acquired right of citizenship in our Christian vocabulary, a word that is constantly used in religious circles, it is that of "sanctity" or "sanctification". Terms that are indiscriminately used, however, run the risk of losing much of their original lustre. When is a Christian sanctified and — especially — what does this term imply? It is often implied or even explicitly asserted that sanctification can be reduced to good moral behaviour, the practice of Christian virtue, an upright, honest and sincere way of life. Yet the reality goes far deeper than that, for sanctification does imply all this, to be sure, but also a good deal more. Sanctification, from the biblical point of view, cannot possibly be reduced to the external aspect of virtue and behaviour, of amiable demeanour and agreeable conduct. The reality lies much deeper.

A Christian is profoundly sanctified in the very core of his personality when he or she is incorporated through living faith and the waters of baptism into the glorified Christ. The Christian thereby becomes a new creature, acquires something he did not have before, drinks in the very paschal life of the risen Lord. He receives an inflow of new life in Christ Jesus. The Lord of Easter, bathed in paschal splendours, shares his own personal life with the Christian, thereby profoundly transforming him, truly sanctifying him deep down to the last recesses of his person.

This new reality that so radically transforms and sanctifies the Christian is obviously rooted in faith, not in experience. It is something exceedingly rich, for it implies a most intimate, vital union with the transfigured Christ, the indwelling or personal possession of the person of the Holy Spirit and the all-pervading reality of sanctifying grace. It is this marvelous triple gift that will sanctify the Christian, making him the child of the Father, and thereby draw him into the inner circle of the trinitarian family. This, in a nutshell, is the wonder of the Christian's sanctification. Moral virtues and upright ethical behaviour will follow, no doubt, but it would be a serious mistake to reduce the enormously rich content of sanctification to the external dimension of the moralizing practice of virtue. Right conduct and correct behaviour flow from sanctification, but right conduct cannot simply be identified with sanctification, which in itself is a profound mystery of shared trinitarian life, not merely the correctness of ethical behaviour.

1) The transforming power of faith

The root cause of this profound transformation experienced by the Christian is simply faith, living faith in Christ Jesus. And this vivifying faith cannot be reduced to a mere intellectual grasp of an abstract truth that is apprehended by man's mind while his heart remains cold and unaffected. Faith, according to the biblical conception (which is ultimately the only one that matters), is the warm, intimate, deeply personal self-commitment of man into the hands of the risen Christ. Faith bespeaks warmth and surrender, affectivity and trust. Through faith, the Christian gives over to Christ his mind and his will, his heart and affections, his body and soul, the totality of his person. Faith is the vital link that connects a Christian with the glorified Jesus, the channel of transmission through which Christ's own life pours down into the heart of man, flooding him with the very life of God, gently drawing him into the inner sanctuary of the trinitarian family. In the words of the reputed Catholic exegete F. Prat, for Paul "faith is not a mere intellectual apprehension of a revealed truth, but rather man's wilful entrance into the economy of the Gospel, *a total gift of self* whereby man surrenders himself to God and shares, in an anticipated manner, the plenitude of the divine gifts".[1]

This transforming faith contains necessarily an element of trust, for it is strongly coloured by confidence in the divine promises, an all-pervading assurance that these promises, once made, will be fulfilled, for God is faithful, he is truthful. Divine fidelity is the ultimate basis of man's faith. We believe because God is faithful to himself, because he cannot deny himself. He is a rock of stability and firmness on which man can rest assured. Through faith, man simply leans on God and he is certain that God will not withdraw, for then, deprived of support, man would fall. Man knows that God is trustworthy and as a consequence he puts his trust in him, certain that he will not be deceived.

This trust, which is an essential element of faith, is all-pervading, for it embraces not only the past salvific events already accomplished (particularly Jesus' death and resurrection) but also future realities yet to be realized. The fulfillment of past promises is a firm guarantee for man's trustful confidence in the future. Man, through faith, draws trust and certainty from the past and projects it into the future. Man's faith is a present reality that exists here and now, but its roots lie in the past and its projection extends into the future. And so the entire life of the Christian, past, present and future, is gathered up in a movement of trustful faith that thrusts man into the very person of God. This is vivifying faith, the source of the new life in Christ Jesus.

Yet this same faith does not operate in isolation, for it is embodied in the externally visible sacrament of baptism. Absolutely speaking, faith, even apart from baptism of water, can bring down torrents of divine life on man (and this will explain the possibility of salvation for non-Christians), but baptism necessarily presupposes faith. For a Christian, both these realities, faith and baptism, are inextricably bound together and thus joined they produce the marvel which is man's sanctification.

It is most unfortunate that nowadays for most Christians the day and fact of their baptism means next to nothing. They know of course that they were baptized in childhood,

1 F. Prat, *The Theology of St. Paul*, 5th ed. (London 1945), p. 236, with emphasis added.

but this is an event that lies hidden in the remote past. For all practical purposes it is both taken for granted and almost forgotten. Most of us celebrate joyfully every year our own birthday and that of our friends, and we are right in doing so. We thank God and our parents for the wonderful gift of life we received from them so many years ago — and pass over in silence the far more precious gift of divine life we received in baptism. We all know the day that we were born, but do we remember the day when we were baptized, the day when our gates were thrown wide open to a veritable invasion of trinitarian life? the day we became brothers and sisters of Christ, temples of the Spirit and children of the Father? Who remembers that day? We all regularly celebrate important dates which punctuate our entire life, like our wedding anniversary, the date of our first communion, religious profession, silver or golden jubilees in married or religious life. But who has ever heard of anybody celebrating the anniversary of his baptism?

It is the combination of both these salvific realities, faith and baptism, or, better still, the one reality of baptismal faith, that brings down on the Christian the wonder of his personal sanctification. If baptismal faith can be compared to the root, then man's sanctification becomes the fruit. Faith and baptism are like the two parents that, joined, bring forth the child called sanctification. This kind of fruitful marriage has taken place in all of us, parents and child are both doing well, they are healthy and in good shape. It might be worthwhile now to examine a little more closely this wonder child which is our personal sanctification.[2]

2 The explanation that follows in the text is but a condensed summary of the Pauline notion of justification. This concept is fundamental in Pauline theology, but the term itself "justification", through the wear and tear of centuries, has lost in common English the sharp, technical meaning it had in Paul. For us now "justification" means usually something very different from what it meant for first-century Christians. After some hesitation I have opted for "sanctification" as a term that is roughly equivalent to the Pauline "justification" and is certainly clearer to the average modern reader. At times technical accuracies are to be sacrificed so as to make the reality pastorally more understandable. The first of the liturgical readings at Mass is often taken from Paul, with his frequent references to justification or the justice or righteousness of God. These dry, terse, somewhat unappealing and hardly understandable expressions are likely to become more palatable if reset within the context of man's sanctification. We cannot change Paul's expressions, but we should definitely try to grasp their meaning by having recourse to other terms which are roughly synonymous.

a) *A radical, gratuitous transformation*

The salvation of man was a key issue hotly controverted at the time of Paul. Perhaps we do not sufficiently realize nowadays how exceedingly difficult it was for the first generation of Christians to cut themselves free from the moorings of Judaism that kept them firmly tied to the revered prescriptions of their ancestors. The Law was for them simply the embodiment of Yahweh's saving will, something sacred to be observed unquestioningly. Adherence to the Law was for them the only way to be sanctified now and eventually saved later. The prescriptions of the Law were not juridical fetters, constricting bonds that curtailed man's freedom, but rather blessed means of salvation given to man by a merciful God.

And yet, that passionate character that was Paul of Tarsus opposed the Law fiercely. He was conscious of having attained a new, Christ-given freedom which made him intolerant of any outmoded prescriptions, even if they had been firmly sanctioned by Yahweh himself. A few years after Paul's conversion and after a prolonged, bitter struggle, it had been finally decided by the authorities in the mother church of Jerusalem that the prescriptions of the Law would no longer be binding on the new converts to Christianity. The Law had simply lost its saving power; it was no more than a temporary measure entirely superseded by faith in Christ. Yet old habits die hard. A group of Christian Judaizers, apparently unable to uproot themselves entirely from Old Testament soil, makes a bid for the restoration of the Law in a move that amounts to a compromise: man, they claimed, will be sanctified now and saved later by believing in Christ *and* by obeying the Law. What they proposed was not a substitution but an addition: not Christ instead of the Law, but rather Christ along with the Law. One could thereby be faithful to both his newly acquired Christian identity and his previous Jewish heritage. One need not cease to be a Jew in order to become a Christian.

A fiery character like Paul was not particularly fond of compromises. According to him, this cautious, "prudent" solution, on the surface reasonable and therefore acceptable, in reality strikes at the very root of the Christian faith. Paul will defend passionately till his last breath that the Christian can be saved *exclusively* by commiting himself to Christ through saving faith, quite independently of the prescriptions of the Law. Paul firmly refuses to accept means of sanctification and salvation which have grown obsolete, badly dated. Paul's contention is sharp and crystal clear: not the Law and Christ, but only Christ, without the Law. It was no secondary question, this. For on the satisfactory resolution of this problem depended the Christian's fundamental orientation. In Paul's view, absolutely nothing can be allowed to stand between the Christian and Christ, nothing should be tolerated that can call into question, however minimally, the centrality of Christ. It is a passionate man defending the most central truth of Christianity passionately, as befits his character.

Present sanctification and future salvation are closely linked; they are in fact governed by the same principles. But leaving aside for the time being the Christian's eventual salvation, Paul portrays his sanctification here and now as endowed with certain characteristics that make it exceedingly attractive. It is by patiently analysing each of these fundamental features that one can have a realistic, objective idea of what Christian sanctification is and how incredibly deeply it affects man.

To begin with, man is justified (that is, sanctified, according to our rough equivalent) when God *declares* that he is so sanctified. The framework utilized by Paul is definitely juridical, legal. It is as if man, guilty because of his sin, were brought before God who, like a judge, declares that hereafter man is free from guilt, he is innocent, he is righteous and in good standing in the eyes of God. The divine judge gives a formal assurance that man, so justified or sanctified, has been restored to a state of friendship with God, that God is pleased with him. The state of enmity between God and man becomes a thing of the past, man is now again basking in the sunshine of God's benevolence.

All this is certainly spiritually comforting, but the reality lies much deeper yet. A mere verbal declaration that man is sanctified is, by itself, rather superficial. God declares man sanctified, reconciled with him, and by doing so, makes him a new creature. It is not that by an act of divine generosity and benevolence God considers man as if he were sanctified, when in reality sin still clings to him; as if God, by means of a legal fiction, were to look upon man as cleansed when in reality he is still leprous, infected with sin; as if man were still covered with filth but God considered him as already cleansed, purified.

This is not at all the true reality of things. God declares man sanctified and reconciled to himself, and this divine declaration, accomplished by his word, is so powerful and effective that it produces what it signifies. God's own word is at work, and his word "is living and active, sharper than any two-edged sword, piercing to the division of soul and spirit, of joints and marrow" (Hebr 4,12). The word of God has, from the biblical point of view, an inbuilt power of its own, a strength that is simply irresistible. God's word is creative, it is powerful enough to draw creatures into existence out of the dark abyss of nothingness. "And God said, 'Let there be light' and there was light....And God said 'Let the waters under the heavens be gathered together into one place, and the dry land appear'. And it was so" (Gen 1,3.9): Our entire material universe, rich and variegated, is the result of God's efficacious word. And it is the same word that is operative when Jesus cleanses lepers: "And a leper came to him beseeching him...,'If you will you can make me clean'. Moved with pity...he said to him...'I will; be clean'. And immediately the leprosy left him and he was made clean." (Mk 1,40-42).

God's word, which created the world and cleansed lepers, is also operative in the process of man's sanctification. Not only does God declare man sanctified and just, he makes him so. On the part of God, it is a declaration, but it is an effective declaration that accomplishes what it announces. As a consequence, man is *radically transformed*, *profoundly altered*. He simply becomes a new creature, he is endowed with new potentialities, he is steeped in the very life of God that now streams into him, enveloping him, soaking him in the deepest recesses of his person. Maybe we shall begin to understand and appreciate the enormous potentialities of power and might hidden in the divine word when we consider the radical, almost incredible transformation that is effected in the sacraments by means of the divine word spoken through the priest:

"This is my body...this is my blood", and as a consequence, bread and wine are no longer what they were, they are transformed into the body and blood of Christ. "I absolve you in the name of the Father...", and the sinner becomes a new creature deeply cleansed, profoundly sanctified. Man, through faith, opens himself to the onrush of divine life which, propelled by the word of God, cascades down into him and engulfs him entirely. From this moment he enjoys a new life in Christ Jesus. Paul pithily speaks of "justification of life" (Rom 5,18), for the immediate principle that produces this radical change in man is precisely divine life, Christ's own life which is now abundantly shared with man.

As a consequence of this inflow of trinitarian life, man is transformed *here and now*. In virtue of this radical change which he experiences within himself, and provided he remains faithful to God, he will eventually be saved. His final salvation lies still in the future, somewhat blurred and hazy due to distance and the uncertainty of his sustained response to God; but his sanctification is already present, it is operative here and now. He truly has a share in God's own life already now, but this life will grow and eventually blossom into fullness when he is saved, when he encounters the justifying God face to face. "Justification is forgiveness in the full sense. It is not only a merely covering up of the past. Rather, it is the antedonation of the full salvation; it is a new creation of God's Spirit, it is Christ taking possession of the life already now, already here".[3]

Finally, this sanctification or radical transformation of man is in itself a *gratuitous* gift of God which cannot possibly be merited by man. That the onrush of transformative, divine life should be acknowledged to be a divine gift will, perhaps, be readily granted, for left to himself man cannot possibly have access to the treasures of divine life. This life is simply too high for man; he cannot, unaided, scale such heights, for the origin of this life, God's own life, lies hidden in the inner recesses of God's own heart, well beyond the grasp of man. Man has no access to his life; it is God himself who has to invite and gently draw him to the spring of life.

3 J. Jeremias, *The Central Message of the New Testament* (London 1965), p. 66.

All this is certainly reasonable, but the gratuitous, unmeritable character of man's sanctification is still deeper and more radical. In order to receive this bountiful gift of divine, sanctifying life, man has obviously to open up and let in the inflow of the divine outpouring. This opening on the part of man is precisely the gift, of faith. Now man, in a movement of total self-gift, opens the floodgates and God's life pours in. It would seem that man, through the opening of faith, has accepted the divine invitation to share God's own life and be thereby sanctified. God invites and man accepts, and thus the mystery of man's radical transformation at the hands of God is rendered perfectly understandable. For it is up to man to accept or to refuse the divine gift, his acceptance cannot possibly be forced. Man retains his freedom, and as a rational creature, free and responsible, he decides to open up, accept the divine gift and be thereby transformed.

All this sounds very persuasive and will readily be accepted by many. But there is one little snag: it is totally false. In fact, it dangerously borders on heresy. For Paul is explicit and emphatic: in order to be so transformed into a new creature, man has to surrender himself to God through faith, but *this opening of faith is itself a gratuitous gift from God.* Unaided, man cannot possibly open up to God. The very act of opening is God's gift. Man is simply powerless to believe in God without God's help. Man is therefore confronted, not with one but with two gifts from above: God invites him to share in his own life *and*, in order to achieve this, gives him the preparatory gift of faith! Faith is not man's personal contribution to his own salvation, faith is essentially a preparatory gift from above that disposes man to receive the participation in divine life. Without God's help man cannot believe, he cannot possibly open the floodgates, he is to be helped even in this. Paul writes to the Ephesians: "By grace you have been saved through faith; and this is not your own doing, it is the gift of God" (Eph 2,8). Similarly in another passage, often weakened by English translators: "For God has given you the grace, with regard to Christ, not only to believe in him, but even to suffer for him" (Phil 1,29). To believe in Christ is in itself an unmerited gift from God.[4]

This conception does not turn man into a robot. Even at the supreme moment of his sanctification he retains his freedom intact and unimpaired. God makes him a double offer, faith and divine life, and he, aided by God, accepts both: the radical transformation of man has taken place in a profoundly gratuitous atmosphere. Hence, man has absolutely no reason for useless boasting before God. Now man is soaked in divine life thanks to the opening of faith, but man, without God's help, would have been unable to open up. It is the realization of this deeply gratuitous character of his sanctification and therefore of his future salvation that will keep man truly humble in the eyes of God. In spite of his freedom man cannot save himself, he is to be saved only by God.

b) *Trinitarian sanctification*

Christians are legion today who unfortunately seem to be entirely satisfied with a narrow, exclusive concentration on the person of Jesus. This widespread attitude, in spite of certain appearances to the contrary, is certainly regrettable, for the simple reason that it is at odds with the genuine biblical conception. For all practical purposes we seem to have forgotten that Jesus is essentially the mediator to the Father and the immediate source of the bountiful outpouring of the Holy Spirit. This near obsession with the person of Christ sounds pious and very commendable, when in reality it is downright deplorable. There are many who oversimplify the rich New Testament spirituality to the point of distortion. Every spiritual dimension, every angle of our relationship with God is almost mechanically attributed to Jesus. For them Jesus really suffices.

Yet Paul and in general the New Testament writers speak a different language. It was certainly the risen Christ

4 Here all the four English translations consulted, the Revised Standard Version (RSV), the New English Bible (NEB), the New American Bible (NAB) and Today's English Version (TEV) are deficient, for Paul does not speak of a "privilege" (TEV, NEB, NAB) or of something "granted" to men (RSV). The French *Traduction Oecuménique de la Bible* renders perfectly the original by retaining the very word used by Paul when speaking of faith: "grace". And grace is obviously gratuitous or it is no longer grace. This is the translation I have followed in the text.

who turned Saul into Paul on the way to Damascus, and yet Paul is never narrowly obsessed with the person of Christ. For him the present sanctification and future salvation of the Christian are strongly marked by a profoundly trinitarian character. Paul will never stop at Jesus, Christ is for him an intermediary, a mediator who points higher up, to the person of his Father, besides being the dispenser of the Spirit. In other words, the reality of man's sanctification is for Paul decidedly trinitarian, not only christological.

This is forcefully brought out by Paul in two complementary passages from the two sister epistles, Romans and Galatians. *Romans 3,21-31* is a marvelous testimony of his largeness of views. Contrary to the opinion prevalent among his Jewish contemporaries, Paul proclaims, loud and clear, that the heart of the Father (whom according to custom he refers to simply as "God") is large enough to want the salvation of all, Jews and Gentiles. The exclusive election of the Jews as his chosen People does not at all mean that God wants to save only them. This may sound to a modern reader like a perfectly harmless platitude, but Paul had some difficulty in putting it across to his fellow Jews who had arbitrarily restricted God's love and salvation to the physical descendants of Abraham.

But Paul knows better. The Father, according to him, is fundamentally a just God, not however in the usual, modern sense of a person who is impartial in the administration of justice, somebody who cannot easily be swayed right or left, but who rather passes a judgment with cold objectivity. This is definitely *not* what Paul means by saying that God is just. He is just and justifying because he ardently wants the salvation of man. It is not legal, distributive justice that Paul has in mind, but rather saving or salvific justice. God is instinctively inclined to outstretch his arms to sinful men and women — all, Jews and Gentiles — and draw them all to himself: this is divine justice, namely, the Father's saving will, which extends far and wide to all humankind and excludes no one.

"All have sinned and fall short of the splendour of God" (v. 23). In typical Semitic fashion, Paul conceives the Father as bathed in his own splendour, the effulgence of his majesty.

and the brightness of his goodness. God is simply light, and his genuine desire is to sanctify and eventually save all men and women by drawing them with gentle force unto himself, to make them sharers of his own splendour, the splendour that shone on the face of the transfigured Jesus on Tabor. Sinners are deprived of his brightness, and the only way for them to be sanctified and deeply transformed is to pass, through living faith, from darkness to light, to open themselves to the onrush of the divine effulgence that streams down from the heart of the Father. Once drawn into the sphere of the divine brightness they will be profoundly altered, radically transformed, totally changed. In a word, they will de sanctified.

In a language which is almost forbidding by its dryness and even apparent severity, Paul continues to fathom the mystery of man's sanctification. This transition into the light is a reality today because the Father, moved by his will to save man, "put Christ forward as an expiation" (v. 25). We have reached the heart of the passage. Once we break through the outer crust of Paul's dry expressions we shall come to taste and relish the incredibly rich content of such a terse expression. The Jewish Christians in Rome, addressees of Paul's leter, certainly understood the implications of the phrase, but the passage of time and a radically changed culture have dimmed its meaning for us now.

In an implicit reference to the Jewish liturgy celebrated in the Temple of Jerusalem, Paul speaks of the "expiation", or rather the "expiatory" or "propitiatory", namely, the lid of the Ark kept in the Temple and made of solid gold according to the specifications received by Moses in centuries gone by: "You shall make the mercy seat (or propitiatory) of pure gold... and you shall make two cherubims of gold...on the two ends of the mercy seat" (Ex 25,17-18). It is this mercy seat or propitiatory, the dwelling place of Yahweh, that the high priest, dressed up in a resplendent white tunic, will sprinkle with blood on the solemn feast of *Yom Kippur* or Day of Atonement. This, for a Jew, is the solemn sacrifice of expiation. After the high priest, acting in the name of the people and for their benefit, has completed the complex ritual of blood-sprinkling, the sins of all, priest and people, are considered to have been forgiven by God. The expiatory sacrifice is over and their sins have been blotted out, they are no more.

This liturgical imagery which Paul and his readers in Rome knew only too well serves him as a platform from which to convey the kernel of his teaching. The real propitiatory, he tells the Romans, is not a gold covering sprinkled with the blood of animals, but the person of Christ hanging on the cross and covered with his own blood: this is the real propitiatory for the Christian. It is the bleeding Christ on the cross that the Father "put forward as an expiation" (v. 25) for man's sins. Even on Calvary — especially on Calvary — Christ is essentially a mediator, a stepping stone to go higher, to the person of his Father. For Paul Calvary is not only the supreme manifestation of Christ's love, but also the tangible proof of his Father's saving will with regard to humankind. For Paul it is as if the Father were behind the cross, offering us the broken and bleeding body of his Son. Man's sins are wiped out through blood. This is the highest and most eloquent testimony of the saving justice of the Father, the most convincing proof that he does want to save man. Now sinful humanity is reconciled to him through the broken body of the Son. It is a costly meeting between the Father and man, effected on the bleeding body of Christ. This is the price of man's sanctification. Now he is reunited with God, but it is a reunion sealed in blood. Sin is no more, and man, purified, has made his peace with God, he is justified, he is sanctified, he will be saved — provided he appropriates to himself through living faith the saving power of the cross. The transition from the darkness of sinful man into the splendour of the Father has been accomplished through the blood of Christ.

Undoubtedly all this is both enormously rich in doctrinal content and spiritually extremely comforting. Yet it is incomplete. The full reality of man's sanctification is so complex, it has so many different facets that one cannot possibly expect to exhaust all its riches in one single scriptural passage. Romans 3 — we have seen above — has trained a most powerful light on the event of Jesus' death, but other areas of man's sanctification still remain in darkness. Calvary is still the root of the transformation accomplished by God in man, but what is man's sanctification in itself, intrinsically?

Once the foundation of Calvary is presupposed, how is man actually sanctified, here and now, two full millennia after Golgotha?

In order to know this one should have recourse to Paul's complementary passage, *Galatians 3,1-6*. His Christians in Galatia were in serious trouble. Their faith in Christ had apparently been badly shaken, and Paul, on hearing of it, reacts strongly, almost angrily. The Jewish Law had been left behind, it had been substituted with faith in Christ, been apparently those new Christians in Galatia were again attracted by their past Jewish heritage. Their new Christian roots were still tender — they were new converts — whereas the pull of their ancestry proved too strong. The Law, whose splendour had been dimmed by the preaching of Paul, begins to shine again, enticing the Galatians not to give up its observance entirely. In proportion as the Law acquires a new lustre and starts to shimmer again, faith in Christ begins to fade, and it is this diminished splendour of the cross that accounts for Paul's strong reaction and polemical tone.

In order to prop up their wobbly faith in Christ, Paul portrays before them the case of their revered father Abraham, who was sanctified in the eyes of God not because of his deeds but because of his faith. This was undoubtedly a most powerful example to the readers of Paul's letter, but it is likely to leave most of us perfectly cold now. Our lack of the necessary Jewish background will probably render the figure of Abraham far less compelling for us than it was for Paul's Jewish Christians. Besides this, Paul handles a second argument which is likely to affect us much more directly, for it is not related to Jewish history. In order to drive his point home, Paul appeals to their personal experience. Paul is exceedingly annoyed that somebody had bewitched those foolish Galatians before whom Paul had portrayed Jesus as crucified. In Paul's contention, they will have to drop all forms of compromise and choose, once and for all, between the Law and faith in Christ: "Let me ask you only this: Did you receive the Spirit by works of the law or by hearing with faith? Are you so foolish? Having begun with the Spirit are you now ending with the flesh?" (Gal 3,2-3).

At the time of their conversion to Christianity they had

received the Holy Spirit, whom they are now foolishly ready to jettison. This, put across with his accustomed brevity of expression, is what sanctification or justification means for Paul: the interior reception of the person of the Spirit within the Christian. This is the immediate result of the Christian's living faith. And by the reception of the Spirit Paul most probably means both the personal indwelling of the Spirit and his charismatic effusion in the Christian community. We shall have ample opportunity to explain both these aspects later on, in two subsequent chapters. Suffice it for the moment to remark and forcefully underscore the fact that deep down, Christian sanctification implies, in its most intimate reality, the possession of the Holy Spirit, his abode in the sanctified Christian as in a temple.

The Spirit may be the deepest transforming principle, the sanctifier *par excellence*, but he is essentially the gift given by the Father. Paul speaks of "he who supplies the Spirit" (v. 5) — namely, the Father, who, however, remains unnamed. The Christian believes in Christ and as a consequence the Father sanctifies him deeply, to the very core of his being, by sending down into him as his supreme gift the person of the Holy Spirit. Now man's sanctification is accomplished, it is complete.

We are finally in a position to understand and appreciate in all its depth and beauty what the sanctification of the Christian really means. By joining both the Pauline passages, those namely from Romans and Galatians, as explained above, one can perceive the extraordinary richness as well as the essentially trinitarian character of Christian sanctification. The foundation lies on Calvary, where the benevolence and forgiving love of the Father gave us the fractured body of Jesus as the propitiation of our sins, as the necessary means to effect the passage from the darkness of sin to the splendour of God. Furthermore, and on the basis of Christ's saving action on Golgotha, the Father now completes the work begun there by giving us the precious. additional gift of the Holy Spirit who, by taking complete possession of the Christian, brings the work started by Christ to its completion. And so the sanctification of the Christian emerges in the New Testament as an essentially trinitarian event, performed by the benevolence of the Father, through the death of Christ, in the person of the indwelling Spirit. This is, in a nutshell, the reality of the Christian's sanctification.

A marvelous little passage, *Titus 3,4-8*, free from all polemical overtones, offers us an apt summary and confirmation of this trinitarian character of Christian justification or sanctification. The deepest root cause is always "the goodness and loving kindness" of the Father (v. 4), his "mercy" (v. 5) which becomes effective and tangible in the baptismal infusion of the Holy Spirit (v. 5), whom the Father imparts to us richly "through Jesus Christ" (v. 6). The purpose of all this munificence is that we may be sanctified "by his grace" (v. 7), namely, by his unmerited benevolence, and so be firmly set on the path that leads to eternal life.

When confronted with the fullness of this trinitarian conception, one realizes how dreadfully inadequate is the popular notion that reduces everything to the person of Jesus. As seen above, Christ has undoubtedly an essential role to play in the comforting reality of our sanctification, but to reduce everything to him is to act myopically, to restrict unduly the enormous riches revealed by God as present in the work of our sanctification. Any explanation of this reality which is not deeply trinitarian will be nothing but an arbitrary distortion of the biblical data, a pale ersatz of the rich biblical conception. Let us be convinced that Jesus alone does *not* suffice.

c) *Faith or concern for the poor?*

Already in his own lifetime and much more after his death down to the present day, Paul has undoubtedly enjoyed an unparalleled reputation. His personal views have left a deep imprint on the body of Christian belief, but Paul, no matter how high his prestige, is only one writer, not the entire New Testament. We have in the past perhaps taken for granted with a certain amount of naiveté that the New Testament offers us a perfectly coherent body of doctrine, harmonious and homogeneous, with no differing views and certainly no contradictions. Today, however, we know better. The Bible is the word of God expressed in the words of men, and this human dimension accounts for the considerable variety of views and opinions, sometimes hardly reconcilable, that we find within the pages of the New Testament.

This being the case, it will come as no surprise to learn that, regarding the same mighty theme of Christian sanctification, James, the brother of the Lord and leader of the Jerusalem church, held views entirely different from those espoused by Paul. It would seem that probably a few years before the death of Paul in Rome, his doctrine of justification, expounded above, had already begun to be distorted into a real caricature. His strong insistence on the centrality of faith in Christ in order to attain to the newness of life had been badly twisted and thoroughly misunderstood. Apparently there were Christians in Syria and Egypt who, on the strength of Paul's authoritative teaching, were claiming that what really matters, after all, is naked faith, that right conduct and exemplary behaviour as the overflow of this faith, are of no consequence. Deeds do not count, only faith does. Cling to Christ through faith and you can afford to disregard the importance of deeds.

If Paul had heard of such a distortion of his personal views, he would have turned in the grave. Yet such an opinion, no matter how foreign to Paul's real intention, did spread. It was the situation that made James intervene in writing. *James 2,18-26* will insist against this background that this kind of theoretical or abstract faith, devoid of good works, does not suffice in the least. The devil, too, has this sort of faith, for he "believes" in the existence of God, and yet shudders. This kind of naked faith will never save anyone, for "faith apart from works is barren" (v.20). Paul would have agreed wholeheartedly, but the following statement of James would have made him frown in utter disbelief: "Was not Abraham our father justified by works...? You see that a man is justified by works and not by faith alone" (vv.21.24). This is certainly puzzling, for Paul, in reference precisely to their common ancestor Abraham, had said exactly the opposite, namely, that the principle of Abraham's internal transformation was his faith, not his pious works. Now James asserts exactly the reverse. To buttress their respective contentions both of them appeal to the very same passage, Gen 15,6 (Abraham's case), and give two differing interpretations which are hardly compatible. How was Abraham justified before God, on account of his external works (James) or because of his faith (Paul)? Both the authors are obviously to be taken seriously, for both are part of the New Testament, yet the harmonious reconciliation of their views seems to be next to impossible.

It is true that the contexts in which they wrote were entirely different. For whereas Paul was fighting pharisaical self-righteousness and an inadmissible depreciation of the centrality of Christ, James was rather concerned with sheer laziness and especially with a scandalous indifference with regard to the poor. His puzzling statements, so different from Paul's, are to be understood within the larger context of his extreme concern for the poor, the downtrodden, the marginalized. For him, Christianity is above all love for one's neighbour, a love which is not only verbally proclaimed, but actually enfleshed in deeds, tangible and visible. Faith and deeds, what a Christian believes and the way he lives, form an unbreakable unit. Faith, if genuine, should overflow into external works which benefit the neighbour in need. Hence, faith is certainly a transforming principle provided it springs into action. Naked, abstract faith, not incarnate in deeds, is of no use. Man is not sanctified or justified before God only through faith or only through works, but rather through a harmonious blend of both.

Given the very different situation of the local churches in which Paul and James write, their divergent approaches are perfectly understandable. For whereas Paul is worried about orthodoxy, James is concerned about orthopraxis. Whereas Paul is wrestling with a doctrinal principle of the utmost importance, James, more down-to-earth, is concerned with a practical issue. After all, Jesus himself, in the so-called passage on the last judgment (Mt 25,31-46) also laid heavy stress on right Christian behaviour as the supreme criterion that will ultimately determine man's eternal fate. In this discourse of Jesus faith is certainly presupposed, but the accent falls rather on works. For "Paul has no more intention of substituting faith for works than James has of substituting works for faith".[5] Neither of the two can be neglected, for both are mutually complementary. Faith enlightens the Christian's deeds and his deeds manifest his internal faith. Ultimately, these are two different ways of looking at the mystery of Christ: James is oriented towards the compelling example of the earthly Jesus, who "went about doing good" (Ac 10,38), whereas Paul focuses rather on the risen Christ, present and active today in the life of the Christian who believes in him. The two approaches may be different, but ultimately the saving personal Jesus is the same. Two different perspectives of the same salvific reality.[6]

2) A VANISHING ECUMENICAL GAP

In the mind of many Catholics today, and despite the changed ecumenical atmosphere in which we live as a happy result of Vatican II, the name of Luther provokes an almost instinctive reaction of complete indifference coupled with ignorance, if not open hostility. All Catholics have of course heard of Luther and Lutherans, but if asked to voice, however briefly, their opinion of this Christian Church, the immense majority of them would probably keep deadly quiet. If the same request were made to many priests and even bishops, their reaction would likely be much the same as that of the faithful. They would either frown or shrug their shoulders with a gesture of dismissal. They would acknowledge that they know next to nothing, that they are not particularly interested in dispelling their ignorance As far as they are concerned, the revolutionary ecumenical opening effected by the latest Council remains largely academic, theoretical. It has simply not touched their lives.

As regards Luther, the only thing they may perhaps know is that he fiercely attacked the papacy, that he was a dangerous heretic who eventually had to be condemned and excommunicated, and that previously he had been a pious Augustinian monk turned rebel. Such a sketchy, stereotyped summary

5 H. Küng, "Justification and Sanctification according to the New Testament", in D. Callahan, ed., *Christianity Divided* (London 1962), p. 326.

6 For an excellent account and a very satisfactory solution of this classical discrepancy between James and Paul, see E. Schillebeeckx, *Christ. The Christian Experience in the Modern World* (London 1980), pp. 159-164.

of his life seems to put paid to all efforts at a sympathetic understanding of the Lutheran cause.

Luther was a passionate man, no doubt, and badly wrong in certain respects, but he has also been recently acclaimed by a reputable Catholic writer as a real theological genius. Extreme positions of either scathing condemnation or blind, uncritical admiration are seldom correct. One should try to detect, coldly and objectively, the lights and shadows — both extremely sharp and real — in this complex, fascinating religious personality.

Regarding the essential question of man's justification in the eyes of God, of the sanctifying transformation he undergoes when, through faith, he comes into contact with Christ, Luther had very definite opinions of his own which were strongly opposed by Roman Catholic authorities at that time, and which, nevertheless, have deeply influenced millions of his followers down to the present. The theme is absolutely fundamental, and without at least a cursory knowledge of Luther's own position we can neither understand what makes so many of our Lutheran brothers and sisters tick today, nor even have a clear, enlightened grasp of our own Catholic position, which was largely shaped as a reaction to the vicious Lutheran onslaught against the Roman citadel in the sixteenth century.

That momentous episode in the history of the Church is simply enthralling. Luther was a troubled man, anxious, fearful, almost scrupulous — but also incredibly passionate and strong-willed. On a certain occasion and when he was still but a youth, he was suddenly caught in a terrific storm and, plainly terrified, promised to God there and then that if he was saved from that mortal danger he would become a monk. The storm subsided, he survived, and, true to his promise, he became an Augustinian monk. For many years he lived as a devout religious, but in an atmosphere of terror and almost despair, partly due to his own psychological make-up, his family upbringing (his father was apparently exceedingly severe with young Martin) and partly to a dreadful misunderstanding of St Paul. Luther loved Scripture and exposed brilliantly in packed lecture halls the religious content of the word of God, particularly the Psalms and Paul. How he loved Paul! But an almost blind attachment to one man, even if he be of the gigantic stature of Paul, is always dangerous. Luther's religious and theological attitude was largely shaped by Paul, and within the corpus of Pauline writings by Romans, and within Romans by Romans 7. Solid, no doubt, but a trifle too narrow and, as such, dangerous.

Luther reads Paul's lapidary sentence: "The justice of God has been revealed" (Rom 1,17), and the man is simply terrified. He takes the expression to be equivalent to the wrath of God, severe and merciless, and this sends a shiver down his spine. He sees before him nothing but the gaping gates of hell. He is "in the presence of God . . . a sinner with the most unquiet conscience. If God is against man, who can be on his side? When this battle is joined and a man sees nothing but hell, there is no escape before his eyes . . . the wrath of an eternal God . . . can never have an end".[7] "Then God appears horrifyingly angry and with him the whole of creation. There can be no flight, no consolation, neither within nor without, but all is accusation".[8] Confronted with such a terrifying God, Luther's reaction is understandable: "I did not love, but rather hated this just God who punishes sinners, and if not in silent blasphemy, at least with huge murmurings I was indignant against God".[9]

It is not only God in general, but specifically Christ that inspires him such a terror: "I knew Christ as none other than a stern judge . . . from whose face I wanted to flee and could not. . . . Christ was for me not a mediator, but a judge. . . . I used to turn pale when I heard the name of Christ. . . . I have often been terrified by the name of Christ, and when I saw him on the cross, it was like a lightning stroke to me".[10]

Poor Luther knows no peace. Fear and terror keep pouring into him from three different sources: his fatal misunderstanding of Romans 1,17, which in reality has a meaning diametrically opposed to the one arbitrarily attributed to it by Luther, for what Paul expresses there is not God's

7 Weimar edition (1883-1961) of Luther's works, 61 volumes; vol. 5, p. 79. All quotes from Luther's works are taken from G. Rupp, *The Righteousness of God* (London 1953).

8 Weimar ed., vol. 1, p. 558.

9 *Ibid.*, vol. 54, p. 185.

10 *Ibid.*, vol. 38, 148; vol. 40, 136, 298; vol. 47, 590.

punishing justice but rather his saving mercy regarding the sinner; his psychological make-up, always prone to anxiety, scruples and fear; and finally his theological conception of man as excessively affected by the ravages of original sin. All three combined result in a spiritual climate, a theological atmosphere of pessimism, darkness and gloom.

Deeply bogged down in the morass of this triple reality that engulfs him, Luther sees faith in Christ as the only saving remedy. In spite of the fear that Christ instills into him Luther clings to him blindly and hopes thereby to be free from the encompassing reality that suffocates him. Only trustful faith in Christ can save man.[11] Finally, light pours into his tormented soul and he comes to realize that his former interpretation of Romans was totally wrong, that what Paul wanted to express in this fundamental passage was exactly the opposite of what he had originally thought. Now he takes the passage as "that passive justice by which the *merciful God* justifies us by faith".[12]

Once he has got hold of this solid foundation which is faith in Christ, Luther's expressions become warm, intense, almost mystical. Luther emerges as a man whose entire life is centred on Christ, a man who speaks of Christ with a passionate love worthy of Paul himself: "By faith you are *glued to Christ* to such an extent that you form with him one single person".[13] "He who believes in Christ is joined to Christ, is one with Christ and shares the same justice with him".[14] Faith is not just holding on to Christ but *being seized by and transformed into Christ.* "Because Christ lives in me, whatever grace, righteousness, life, peace and salvation there is in me is all Christ's; nevertheless it is mine as well by

11 "Only trustful faith in Christ": this sentence is loaded. During his sojourn at Wartburg, Luther translated Rom 3,28: "...man is justified...*only* through faith", for which he has been repeatedly accused by Catholics of arbitrarily distorting Paul's thought by adding the word "only". The criticism is pointless, however, for much before Luther reputable Catholic authors like Basil, Hilary, Thomas Aquinas and others did exactly the same in an attempt to bring out forcefully Paul's meaning.

12 Weimar, vol. 54, 179-180, with emphasis added.

13 *Ibid.*, vol. 20, p. 229.

14 *Ibid.*, vol. 2, p. 146.

the cementing and inherence that are through faith, in which we become as one body in the Spirit".[15]

Hence, the sanctification of man, according to Luther, is not something externally imputed, like a beautiful garment that merely covers up but does not heal the festered wound of sin. It is something much deeper than that. When a Christian is sanctified, it is not that God fictitiously declares him to be just and righteous; rather God makes him just by wiping away his sin and pouring into him, because of Christ, the person of the Holy Spirit. This is man's sanctification according to Luther, deep, personal and all-pervading. In this conception there is absolutely nothing a Catholic can object to. On the contrary, the depth, warmth, and accuracy of such a theology is highly commendable. It is neither Lutheran nor Catholic, it is simply Christian because it is biblical.

And yet, in spite of such a profound transformation, Luther holds the sanctified man to be simultaneously saint and sinner, a citizen of two worlds, at once enjoying the effulgence of God and sunk in the quicksands of sin. This is a typical case of Lutheran realism. Obviously the sanctified Christian cannot be at once in a state of grace and sin, cannot be at the same time surrounded by light and enveloped by darkness, he cannot be a son of God and a son of the devil, for these two realities are contradictorily opposed. Yet Luther does not mean that. He knows only too well that a man sanctified by Christ is no longer encumbered by the burden of sin. What he means is something else.

The Christian can be deeply changed as a consequence of his sanctification, but his sinful inclinations remain intact. The allurement of sin still persists and will continue to harass him as long as he lives. Faith in Christ never transforms the Christian so profoundly as to render him incapable of sinning. Man will always retain the possibility of betraying God again, for he stands on slippery ground where a fall is always possible. "At the same time the saints, while they are just, are sinners. They are just because they believe in Christ whose righteousness covers them and is imputed to them; sinners, however, because they do not fulfill the law and they are not without

15 *Ibid.*, vol. 40, p. 284.

concupiscence".[16] Inwardly, by themselves, they are sinners, but outwardly they are saints, for they draw life from a source that originally was external to them and has now been interiorized: Christ.

The Lutheran expression, to be "simultaneously just and sinner" may be, at first sight, shocking. However, it expresses a conception which is very traditional and profoundly Catholic. For, after all, it was the great St Augustine who, centuries before Luther, expressed the same idea in his inimitable manner by calling the Church a "chaste prostitute". There is no contradiction involved here, but rather marvelous depth, for, on the one hand, the Church has been rendered chaste and pure by the gratuitous, transforming love of Christ; but, on the other, she is temperamentally always inclined to sell herself out, like a prostitute, to the highest bidder. She delights in God and at the same time enjoys the caress of sin; she wants to be faithful to Christ and is always in danger of betraying him; she loves God, yet is enamoured of the surrounding creatures; she wants to fly to God unimpeded and yet is still fettered by sin. This is Augustine's extremely realistic conception of the Church; and let us not forget that Luther was for many years a pious Augustinian monk....

Lutherans have every reason to be annoyed by the shameful distortions of Lutheran doctrine presented in the past by Catholic authors. Luther's famous expression to his friend Melanchton, "believe strongly and sin more strongly", has been often enough lifted out of context, twisted and misunderstood by his Catholic opponents as if it offered irrefutable evidence of Luther's loose living. And the marriage of the ex-monk to Catherine, the ex-nun, seems to supply supporting evidence that his much vaunted faith in Christ was not really shown in his moral behaviour.

The reality, however, was poles apart from this facile, cheap oversimplification. A modern Lutheran who knows Luther extremely well, has recently stated: "Luther's conception is dynamic, and worlds apart from the caricature put forward (by Catholics) of an antinomian (i.e., a man unconcerned by the moral law) who sins behind the covering

16 *Ibid.*, vol. 56, p. 347, with emphasis added.

and external merits of Christ, or even the milder, but no less perverse view, which considers that Luther would encourage the Christian to slack or let up in the moral struggle".[17]

One should remember that Luther was a a prolific writer. Theological and pastoral treatises poured from his pen nonstop. It is but natural, therefore, that in such a copious production he should have been unable to avoid all contradictions. And besides being prolific, he is also a passionate author who often writes in the heat of controversy, not in the cold and calm atmosphere of a well-stocked library. He often delights in paradoxes and shocking expressions, but it would obviously be totally unfair to the man to lift one of these passing expressions, dropped carelessly in the heat of polemical wrangles, and contend arbitrarily that it conveys in summary form an essential element of his conception. It is always hazardous to summarize a complex author into a single sentence and parade it as if it were the exact, accurate portrayal of his views.

The isolated expression "believe strongly and sin more strongly" (found in an intimate, personal letter to Melanchtom, not in a theological treatise meant for the public) finds scanty support in other Lutheran writings. In reality, according to Luther, the Christian, sanctified and transformed by Christ living in him through faith, *is bound to produce* good works, which retain their extraordinary value as an overflow and external manifestation of a sanctification already achieved; but in themselves these good works do not increase man's inner sanctity. Good deeds are totally powerless to confer on man the supreme gift of sanctification. They flow from sanctification, they do not lead up to it: "It is not the case that a man becomes just by doing good works (as the foolish Jews, Gentiles, and self-justifiers arrogantly trust) but by being just, he does good deeds".[18] For faith in Christ is essentially dynamic, it is always active, bubbling, impelling the Christian to pour out his inner faith into external works. "The faith of none is so great that it cannot be, nor ought to be, increased. Thus for its increase *good works are to be done*

17 G. Rupp, *The Righteousness of God*, p. 177.
18 Weimar, vol. 56, p. 3.

and bad ones avoided".[19] These clear, unambiguous statements should lay to rest, once and for all, the false notion of Luther's lawlessness and unconcern about an upright moral behaviour.

Faced with this rich, complex doctrine, the risk of oversimplifying it is great. Many of the elements that make up this theological construction are entirely acceptable from the Catholic point of view: the living faith in Christ that transfers the sinner from darkness to light; the strongly christological nature of the Christian's sanctification, which implies necessarily a most personal, intimate union with Christ; the convincing realism of man's innate and ineradicable inclination to sin; the absolute necessity of showing one's faith in good works -- all these are extremely valuable contributions on the part of Luther towards the building up of a solid, coherent system of Christian living. So far so good. If Luther had said only that, he would not have been condemned by Rome, for there is nothing objectionable in all this.

But there are shadows too in his theology, and here and there also dark — very dark — corners. Luther's conception of original sin, which is the deepest root of man's present sinful inclinations, is far too pessimistic. Man has not been so grievously wounded by original sin as Luther contended. And this pessimism is no accidental feature in his system, for the alleged ravages of original sin cast a certain gloom over his entire theology. A healthy, if cautious, Christian optimism does not seem to be one of Luther's characteristic features. Closely akin to this is his deplorable misunderstanding of human liberty which, in his conception, is but an empty shadow without consistency. And so, deprived of his essential freedom, the Christian can hardly lay a claim to his eternal reward, for God has promised his reward to free and responsible persons who can take their destiny into their own hands. Heaven is not meant for robots. From the Catholic point of view this conception of man's nominal freedom remains entirely unacceptable. Even modern Lutherans refuse to follow their master on this point.

19 *Ibid.*, vol. 57, p. 70 with emphasis added.

And finally — though the point is probably of lesser importance — one should also point out Luther's regrettable refusal to accept the full vitality of the good works performed by the sanctified Christian. These good works, as an indispensable overflow of his faith in Christ, are not only the external manifestations of the new life he has acquired in Christ Jesus, they are also the cause of its further increase. This new life, present and operative in the Christian, grows incessantly precisely through his good works. Luther's understanding of this point, therefore, rather than false is incomplete. The Christian's good deeds are richer and more powerful than Luther seems to have imagined.

All this, though buried now in the remote past, has been a lasting wound in ecumenical relations between Lutherans and Catholics for more than four centuries. Mutual coldness and indifference, if not open hostility, have been the predominant features between the two great Christian Churches for far too long. It is as if, as the result of the Protestant Reformation, not an iron curtain or a bamboo curtain, but rather an ice curtain had been set up between Rome and Wittenberg, between Catholics and Lutherans. It is only recently that one can detect signs of a thaw. The wall of ice has not yet disintegrated, far from it, but one day it surely will.

As a practical result of the changed atmosphere ushered in by Vatican II, vigorous and cordial theological conversations have been going on between these two Christian families in the U.S. After some very remarkable achievements in other areas, the U.S. Roman Catholic/Lutheran Commission issued in 1983 a splendid document, precisely on the theme of man's sanctification, which had been for so long the main bone of contention between Lutherans and Catholics.[19a] The most important areas of agreement are the following:

19a The reader will probably notice an abrupt change of style in the following paragraphs, due to the fact that in them I am simply quoting and occasionally paraphrasing what the US ecumenical team expressed in somewhat dry technical language. After some hesitation I have decided to retain this short section in the hope that the reader's patience will not be excessively taxed by it. Cf C. Anderson-T. Murphy, eds., *Justification by faith. Lutherans and Catholics in dialogue, VII* (Minneapolis 1985).

1 — Internal sanctification is the necessary pre-condition to attain eternal salvation. In order to be saved, one must be judged to be just and must in reality be just.

2 — As a consequence of original sin all human creatures stand in need of this interior transformation called justification or sanctification, which remains an absolutely gratuitous gift of God's grace, beyond the possibility of human merit.[20] Even the beginning of any conversion or turning towards God, for instance, repentance, the petition for grace and the desire for forgiveness, is the work of God in us. This point should be stressed, for there are innumerable Christians who still fondly imagine that we, even apart from God's grace and help, can turn towards him and ask for his assistance. If our requests are granted, we feel a smug satisfaction that we have prayed well and therefore God has answered our prayer. This conception, however, is false and borders on the heretical, for the reality is that man, unless aided by God's grace, cannot turn to God. Even the initial steps of our sanctification are God's gift to us. When in perfect sincerity we turn to God to ask or thank him, it is he who has to inspire and sustain our prayer, or this prayer will be a hollow, empty gesture, full of sincerity, no doubt, but entirely devoid of efficacy.

3 — Justification (or sanctification), as a transition from the lack of grace to the grace of God, is entirely the work of God. In justification we are at the same time *declared and made just*. Therefore, justification is not a legal fiction, a pretense on the part of God who would consider us as if we were sanctified. There is no "as if". We are dealing here with realities, not with fictions. In justifying man, God makes his promise effective; he does forgive our sins and make us really just and internally holy, entirely acceptable to him.

4 — It is in sanctification that we receive, through faith, the effects of Christ's death and resurrection. Living faith

20 This notion of merit is very traditional in Catholic theology and spirituality, but it seems to stand in need of reconsideration. Let it suffice for the moment to point out that man's initial sanctification lies beyond the grasp of merit. A more extensive treatment of the idea of merit, however, will be given below in a subsequent chapter.

in Christ is not only historical knowledge or intellectual conviction affecting exclusively man's mind, but a total response to the Gospel full of trust, a response that engages the whole person by putting him in contact with the salvific events of Calvary.

5 — This living faith that so intimately transforms man cannot exist without hope and love; and it overflows necessarily into good works. Those sanctified, however, cannot rely on their own good works or boast of their own merits, as if they do not need any longer the divine mercy, for even the man so sanctified continues to be entirely dependent on God.

6 — Sin does not reign any more in the sanctified who, however, remain always subject to their sinful inclinations and the harassment of sin, in such a way that, left to their own resources, they fall incessantly. By themselves they are capable of losing their state of sanctification but, thanks to God's great mercy in Christ Jesus, they can firmly hope and believe that this sanctification, once lost, can be regained, and that God will bring them to final salvation.

All this undoubtedly constitutes a most remarkable ecumenical achievement which would have delighted Luther. In fact, it is quite possible that if such an agreement had been reached in the early 16th century, the Protestant Reformation might not have taken place at all. The six points given above, taken comprehensively, indicate a very considerable area of convergence and even agreement, though one must in all fairness acknowledge that all the differences in this domain have not yet been satisfactorily ironed out. The remaining points of disagreement, however, are of relatively little consequence, and in any case by themselves they cannot possibly justify the continuing separation of the two Churches. The ecumenical gap is fast closing up.

3) The Doctrine of the Church

The official Catholic position, which had been somewhat uncertain before the 16th century, crystallized in the Council of Trent as a recation against the Reformers in general and Luther in particular. Luther himself had died four months before the opening of the Council, and consequently could not react to the new body of Catholic doctrine on the question of man's relation with God, which had troubled him for so long.

The terminological tools available at that time lacked sufficient precision, aud this certainly did not make for clarity of thought, with the result that confusion and uncertainty at the popular level were noticeable almost everywhere. The Council's primary task was to sharpen and clarify the issue under discussion. And it did. A modern reader may find some of the conciliar terms somewhat abstract and obscure, but once we pierce through this outer shell of a partially dated terminology, we realize to what an extent the conciliar teaching is theologically solid, pastorally useful and spiritually nourishing.

The Secretary of the Council, the indefatigable Masarelli, seems to have been particularly fond of accuracy and precision: "As regards the name, justification means simply making just, and 'to justify' means to become just before God; with regard to the reality, justification is simply the remission of sins through grace".[21] On the basis of this fundamental clarification, the Council proceeds authoritatively to state the core and kernel of its teaching: when a man is justified or sanctified by God, a deep, radical change takes place within him, and as a consequence he becomes a new creature, profoundly altered. Sanctification does not consist in a superficial, fictitious covering up of man's sins which in reality would remain intact and unaffected. Sanctifying grace pours into man and wipes out his sins entirely, making him a resplendent creature agreeable to God. The root of this transformation is precisely the new reality of grace that — the Council says in a powerful expression — *inheres* in man, clings to him and goes into the marrow of his bones, as it were. Some of the Reformers — but almost certainly not Luther — had wrongly postulated a shallow sanctification which was in reality no more than the cover-up of sin, leaving man substantially untouched in his inner self. It is against this superficial and totally unsatisfactory conception that the conciliar Fathers react strongly and with perfect clarity: "Justification...is not only the remission of sins, but the

21 *Concilium Tridentinum,* V (Friburgi 1911), p. 279.

sanctification and renewal of the interior man through the voluntary reception of grace and of the gifts, whereby from unjust man becomes just, and from enemy a friend, that he may be 'an heir in hope of eternal life' (Tit 3,7)".[22]

This state of sanctification is deeply marked by the *influence of Christ*, who initiates, sustains and perfects it. "For Jesus Christ himself continuously infuses strength into the justified, as the head into the members (cf Eph 4,15) and the vine into the branches (Jn 15,5); this strength always precedes, accompanies and follows their good works which, without it, could in no way be pleasing to God and meritorious".[23] It would probably be an accurate rendering of the Council's mind to describe Christian sanctification as an act of christological vivification, for, through Christ, new life streams down into the sanctified Christian: "Hence, in the very act of justification, together with the remission of sins, man receives through Jesus Christ, *into whom he is inserted*, the gifts of faith, hope and charity, all infused at the same time".[24] And such an infusion of life obviously implies the total remission of sin, just as darkness is instantly dispelled by an infusion of light: "It is necessary to believe that sins are not forgiven and have never been forgiven except gratuitously by the divine mercy *on account of Christ*".[25] At the moment of his sanctification the Christian clings to Christ, and thus the transfusion of life takes place; he receives new life in Christ Jesus. Official Catholic doctrine on this point could hardly be more comforting and satisfying.

The Council, however, does not indulge in flights of fancy, it rather keeps its feet firmly on the ground, with a remarkable sense of realism. Luther's typical contention that even the person sanctified retains his concupiscence and

22 J. Neuner – J. Dupuis, *The Christian Faith*, 4th ed., (Bangalore 1982), n. 1932. Secretary Masarelli could be even more forceful: "Man is justified by God, not only by the mere imputation of the justice (or grace) of Christ, but *through inherent grace* which is given to him, is infused into him and becomes his own, so that by it he becomes just" (*Concilium Tridentinum* V, p. 280, with emphasis added).

23 Neuner-Dupuis, *The Christian Faith*, n. 1947.

24 *Ibid.*, n. 1933, with emphasis added.

25 *Ibid.*, n. 1936, with emphasis added.

innate inclination to sin, that man therefore is simultaneously just and sinner, is far from false, and hence it has been officially incorporated into the official Catholic position. One can be drenched in the new life derived from his or her incorporation into Christ, but the sinful roots are still there, ever ready to sprout into sin proper: "This holy council, however, knows and professes that concupiscence or the inclination to sin remains in the baptized (and therefore already sanctified); since it is left to us to wrestle with, it cannot harm those who do not consent and manfully resist it by the grace of Jesus Christ".[26] But in the long run some minor blemishes are simply unavoidable: "For although in this mortal life men, however just and holy they may be, fall sometimes at least, into those slight and daily sins which are also called venial, they do not on that account cease to be just. For the petition of the just, 'forgive us our debts' (Mt 6,12) is both humble and true".[27] Man has been truly sanctified, but even so he retains his feet of clay.

So far we have admired the beauty of the bright flower which is sanctification. It is time now to have a closer look at the root which has given birth to this flower, and this root is faith: "When the Apostle (Paul) says that man is justified through faith... (Rom 3,22), those words are to be understood in the sense... that we are said to be justified through faith because 'faith is the beginning of man's salvation' (St Fulgentius), *the foundation and root of all justification*, 'without which it is impossible to please God' (Hebr 11,6) and to come into the fellowship of his sons".[28] It is faith, full, vivifying faith, that brings down on man in torrents the new life in Christ Jesus.

Yet faith is such a complex reality and there are so many stages in its growth, that it would be a regrettable falsification of its full reality to claim that this faith is either present in full or not present at all. This sharp division of either/or is supported neither by the word of God nor by pastoral experience. After all, James' epistle is as much part of the

26 *Ibid.*, n. 512, in the discussion on original sin.
27 *Ibid.*, n. 1938.
28 *Ibid.*, n. 1935. with emphasis added.

New Testament as the writings of Paul, and therefore no one can glibly dismiss it, as Luther did, as "a straw epistle". Its intrinsic value is inferior to that of Paul's epistles, no doubt, but it is still part and parcel of the New Testament. And it is precisely James who speaks of that peculiar sort of faith which is reduced to a cold apprehension of a truth with hardly any practical implication for one's life. This, as seen above, is the devil's "faith", who believes that God exists and yet continues to be damned. This is simply loveless faith, weak faith, germinal faith which has not blossomed into the fulness of that complete surrender of the Christian into the hands of the risen Christ. This kind of faith, though very real, will by itself not save anybody. It is certainly good, but it is far too weak to bring down an infusion of new life into the Christian.

The existence of this type of faith, besides being biblical, is also attested to by pastoral experience. If a Christian lapses into grievous sin and thereby loses his sanctification, he is expected to recapture his pristine state of internal transformation by having recourse to the sacrament of reconciliation. This will be readily granted. And when he, sufficiently contrite, but still in sin, approaches the Church's minister with the request for absolution, what kind of faith does he have if not this meagre, loveless faith which by itself and apart from the efficacy of the sacrament will not be able to give him back the sanctification lost? Once truly absolved and reconciled to God, his faith will hopefully grow again unto the fulness of maturity. A sincere appreciation of the great worth and importance of full, living faith should not make us close our eyes to the early stages in its growth. The fulness of manhood is surely admirable, but the mature man of today is the weak child of yesterday.

In view of all this, the Lutheran "either full faith or no faith at all" is far too drastic and as such cannot be accepted. A truly grievous sin is like an octopus that tries to strangle man and nearly succeeds, leaving him half dead and gasping for breath, but still alive and able to recover. So also most grievous sins destroy man's living faith and reduce it to a

29 *Ibid.*, n. 1945.

shadow of its former self, but faith is not yet killed; it survives the onslaught to eventually recover and be restored to its former healthy condition. Grievous sin weakens faith considerably, but normally does not kill it altogether. Sin and faith (in its weaker form) can still coexist in uneasy truce. The teaching of Trent in this respect is terse and crystal clear: "The grace of justification, once received, is lost, not only by unbelief which causes the loss of faith itself, but also by any mortal sin, even though faith is not lost".[29] For the hardened sinner still believes in God, after all....

Bibliography

Rupp, G.: *The Righteousness of God* (London 1953).

Küng, H.: "Justification and sanctification according to the New Testament", in D. Callahan, ed., *Christianity Divided* (London 1962), pp. 309-333.

Lyonnet, S.: "Pauline soteriology", in A. Robert - A. Feuillet, *Introduction to the New Testament* (N. York 1963), pp. 821-837.

Küng, H.: *Justification* (N. York 1964), pp. 99-303.

Jeremias, J.: *The Central Message of the New Testament* (London 1965), pp. 51-70.

Cerfaux, L.: *The Christian in the Theology of St. Paul* (London 1967), pp. 373-468.

Rahner, K.: "Justified and sinner at the same time," *Theological Investigations*, 6 (London 1969), pp. 218-230.

Ziesler, J.: *The Meaning of Righteousness in Paul* (Cambridge 1972).

Haight, R.: *The Experience and Language of Grace* (N. York 1979), pp. 79-118.

Schillebeeckx, E.: *Christ. The Christian Experience in the Modern World* (London 1980), pp. 132-164

Reumann, J.: *Righteousness in the New Testament* (Philadelphia 1982).

Chapter Two

IMMANENCE IN THE RISEN CHRIST

"You exist in Christ" (1 Cor 1,30). This lapidary sentence of Paul conveys pithily what our Christian life is, but, as it happens with many of such Pauline expressions, its meaning is not immediately clear. When the Christian passes from darkness to light and receives a bountiful outpouring of new life in Christ Jesus, he is truly justified before God, he is deeply sanctified. Yet justification, sanctification and life are, in themselves, nothing but abstractions, and no human person will ever be satisfied with mere abstractions, for we all instinctively tend to a fullness of communion with another person, whether human or divine. It is only the intimacy of a personal presence and the plenitude of personal communion that will satisfy the human heart. God has made us all thirsty, and this innate, ineradicable thirst can be slaked only by another person.

At the moment of his transforming sanctification, man is drawn into the warm atmosphere of God's intimate friendship. But even this is not enough, for the New Testament demands that we be much more concrete, more specific. Deep down sanctification and new life in Christ Jesus imply that the Christian has entered into a new relationship, warm, intimate, and personal with the glorified Christ, his Father and their common Spirit. This triple reality, if well understood, is so enormously rich, so entirely satisfying, that each of these three personal relationships that mark the life of the sanctified Christian deserves a special, separate treatment.

In this chapter we shall concentrate exclusively on the person of the risen Christ, in whom we all exist.

I have been struck and somewhat dismayed more than once, when realizing how extremely few are the Christians — even among those enriched by special training, who, therefore, should know better — with a clear, firm grasp of what this personal relationship with Christ implies. By far the majority, both men and women, seem to be entirely satisfied with the aspect of an external imitation of Christ. We are all well acquainted with his selfless life and salvific work, we delight in bringing back to mind the example of the life poured out in magnanimous devotedness to all, with special preference for the socially poor and downtrodden. We all know and recall with hearts full of gratitude the events of his death and resurrection that gave us life. And confronted with and spurred on by such a remarkable example, we try hard to imitate Jesus and pattern our lives on his own.

All this is highly commendable of course — as commendable as it is unsatisfactory. For the true reality of things lies far deeper than that. If our relationship with Christ were reduced to this sort of pale, exterior imitation, he would be to us one more saint in heaven, whose exemplary life we cherish and whose aid and assistance we implore. Is that all Christ means to a Christian today? A model of imitation and a paragon of virtue? If so, where is the difference for us today between him and St Anthony or St Francis Xavier? It would be downright shameful to let our "devotion to Jesus" come down to such a deplorably low level. Jesus is to be imitated by all Christians, who has ever doubted that? But to reduce our relation to him to this external level of imitation is nothing short of a disgraceful travesty of the truth. Christ should mean to us more, infinitely more than that. For he is not only an external exemplar held up for imitation and reproduction, he is also *immanent* in us, living in us in a way which perhaps requires some explanation, for the reality is not immediately obvious.*

* One must acknowledge in honour of the truth that the deeper relationship with Christ proposed in the text is not entirely new, for already in the 17th century the French school represented by Condren, Olier, Lallemant, etc., as well as more recent writers like Columba Marmion and Raoul Plus had already

And this person present in us now is not simply Jesus, the earthly Jesus, but emphatically the perpetually transfigured, resurrected Lord of Easter, radiant with paschal splendours. When a Christian is sanctified, he is gently, yet powerfully drawn into this enveloping paschal atmosphere of warmth and splendour. It is not simply Jesus, but the *risen* Christ to whom we are linked and from whom we drink in Easter life in plentiful draughts.

Obviously, this peculiar kind of presence called immanence should not be confused with eucharistic communion. The reception of the risen eucharistic Christ is even more intense and intimate, but also fleeting, for it does not last, whereas the immanence that is the result of baptism, not of the Eucharist, is permanent, as an essential component of the Christian's total sanctification. A mere imitation of Christ is too pale, too weak; but eucharistic communion is too strong. The immanence of the risen Christ lies somewhere between these two extremes: it is surely far superior to our attempts at conformity to the exemplar which is Christ, but not so absorbing as the presence of the glorified Jesus in eucharistic communion.

1) Intimacy of Communion and Fullness of Life

One of the principles characteristic of Pauline theology is that the initiative of our salvation belongs not only to God in general, but specifically to the Father's gratuitous love. It is the Father who sets in motion the entire process that will eventually reach its culmination when he, gently but firmly, will draw man "unto himself" (Eph 1,5) in heavenly bliss. But this salvific plan of the Father has been historically realized in the person of Christ and, as a consequence, man's entire process of salvation is now deeply marked by a strongly christological imprint. The love of the Father, ultimate root cause of man's salvation, is manifested and concretized in the fact of the Christian's unmerited election, which has been

propounded a Christ-centred spirituality that goes well beyond the external aspect of mere imitation. However, in the pastoral ministry still one comes across today many men and women who seem to be unable to transcend this popular aspect of imitation.

effected "in Christ before the foundation of the world" (Eph 1,4). Our predestination by the Father is "to be conformed to the image of his Son" (Rom 8,29). The Father puts Christ forward as a propitiatory victim that we may attain redemption "in Christ Jesus" (Rom 3,24-25). The Father sanctifies now the Christian "by faith" in Jesus Christ (Rom 3,28). And at the end we shall be raised, and "in Christ shall all be made alive" (1 Cor 15,22). Election, predestination, redemption, sanctification, resurrection: the Christian's entire existence, from start to finish, is profoundly marked by Christ.

The extraordinary doctrinal and spiritual wealth contained in the Pauline expression "the grace of God" (comprising all the themes just enumerated) is now concentrated in Christ. Because the fidelity and grace of the Father have been enfleshed in Christ Jesus (Jn 1,14), we are always able to contemplate the splendour of the Father shining on the face of the transfigured Son (2 Cor 4,6). Now the dwelling place of the Father's love, in a fixed, permanent, indestructible manner, is the glorified humanity of Jesus. It is in him and through him that the love and grace of the Father pour into humankind.

Our immanence or vital union with the glorified Christ is briefly expressed by Paul by means of three expressions, deceptive in their simplicity, yet marvelously dense in content. The Christian is with Christ, he moves into Christ, he is in Christ. These three expressions, so closely related as to look almost synonymous, convey in reality three different moments of our *insertion into the glorified Christ;* or, differently put, they express our dynamic, vital union with the risen Christ. Saul, breathing murder against the infant Church and persecuting her savagely (Gal 1,13), had unexpectedly been confronted with the risen Lord on the way to Damascus, blinded by his effulgence, profoundly transformed and turned into a Christian. It is this ineffable, shattering experience, this incorporation into the glorified Jesus that Paul is trying to convey pithily by means of this triple expression.

a) *With Christ, into Christ*

Paul is surely not a man to be sidetracked by secondary, unimportant issues. He will rather zero in at once on the core of any problem that confronts him. And so, typical of the man, he never breathes one word about the earthly life of Jesus, which is usually our favourite object of reflection and imitation. He never as much as mentions any of the events in Jesus' life prior to the passion. He never refers to his mother by name. He is entirely silent about Jesus' virginal conception and birth, his hidden and public life, his baptism and his preaching. Paul is a man of the essentials, and for him the really essential event in Jesus' life is Calvary, understanding by this term, not only Jesus' death — as we unfortunately do — but both his death *and* his resurrection. That is, for Paul, Christ's life in a nutshell, all the other events that filled his earthly life being but preparatory, leading up to the final consummation of Golgotha.

Quite in keeping with this conception, therefore, Paul sees the Christian as already linked, in a highly mysterious, but real manner, with these salvific events that took place on Calvary. Paul lacked the terminological tools to express this profound, puzzling reality. Never mind, he will bend the language if need be, and daringly, defying all rules of grammar, invent new terms that can convey somewhat this absolutely unique, even baffling union of the Christian with the dying and rising Jesus. He will coin more than thirty new terms, totally unknown to his contemporaries, but extremely powerful and eloquent, all of them pointing to the same reality: the peculiar union of the Christian with the Christ of Calvary.

Thus he will daringly say that the Christian is to "co-suffer with Christ" (Rom 8,17); he is "co-crucified with Christ" (Rom 6,6); he is to be "co-raised with Christ" (Eph 2,6), to be "con-glorified with Christ" (Rom 8,17), etc.[1] The idea suggested is that the Christian was almost contemporaneous with these salvific events that took place so very long ago. But how a Christian, who existed only in God's mind and heart at the time of Jesus' death and resurrection, could be intimately united with him there and then, is a question

1 English translators usually polish up these clumsy Pauline terms so as to render them smoother to modern ears, but the force of Paul's intuition and expression is thereby weakened. In the text, I have opted for a literal, if crude, translation of these peculiar Pauline expressions.

that continues to baffle commentators. For it is not easily understandable how the Christian could leap backwards, as it were, over the centuries and be mysteriously present in Jerusalem at the time of Pontius Pilate. This huge time-lag can be bridged over to some extent by the sacramental reality of baptism, for usually Paul makes use of these strange expressions in baptismal contexts. Baptism for him is like an ambassador of the cross, making it present to the Christian here and now. "Baptism, without repeating or cancelling the time elapsed (between the cross and the reception of the sacrament) is the real event, here and now, laden with the weight of the cross".[2]

Consequently, it is not that the baptized Christian incomprehensively leaps backward to Calvary; it is Calvary, or rather its saving effects, that are propelled forward and made to connect with and transform the newly baptized. The salvific fruits of Calvary reach the Christian through the channel of baptism. The baptismal waters are not colourless: they are tinged crimson in the blood poured out on Golgotha; and similarly the paschal splendours of the first Easter stream out and envelop the newly baptized. In this sense, one can to some extent understand what Paul meant by saying that the Christian, thanks to his baptism, is both "co-buried" and "co-raised" with Christ.[3]

Into Christ: This second formula is more easily understandable, for it suggests a dynamic tendency towards, or rather into, the very person of the glorified Jesus. It is exceedingly powerful in its concise brevity. It indicates a "movement which brings us to Christ, *introduces us into him and keeps us in him*".[4] The reference is no longer to the salvific events of Calvary already dimmed by distance, but rather to the moment when the Christian comes for the first time into

2 M. Bouttier, *En Christ. Etude d'Exégèse et de Théologie Pauliniennes* (Paris 1962) p. 50.

3 Paul makes use of the very same compound expressions when speaking of our final heavenly glory. It all goes to show that the entire life of the Christian, from Christ's paschal mystery to the Christian's final union with him in glory, is profoundly christological. The Christian's existence bears already now this indelible christic stamp and will remain so for all eternity.

4 M. Bouttier, *En Christ. Etude d'Exégèse et de Théologie Pauliniennes*, p. 36, with emphasis added.

actual contact with the person of the glorified Christ through the total gift of self in the act of faith and baptism.

No leap over the centuries now, for both the risen Christ and the newly baptized Christian are really contemporaneous, both are alive to each other here and now. The Christian is now drawn into Christ. This is the beginning of his later existence "in Christ". Torn away from his previous condition "in Adam" (1 Cor 15,22), from his natural, sinful inclinations "in the flesh" (Rom, 7.5), he is now not only led up to, but really introduced into the Christ of Easter through faith and baptism. This second expression, therefore, connotes *a movement of incorporation* into the risen Christ.

b) *In Christ*

If there is a Pauline expression deceptive in its very simplicity, it is this. At times it is but another way of saying "Christian", for example, when Paul writes that "the churches of Thessalonika are...in the Lord Jesus" (1 Thes 1,1). But oftentimes the expression means a good deal more.

If to enter "into Christ" meant a dynamic movement of incorporation into him, the next obvious stage is that signified by "in Christ", as a permanent, lasting state of communion with the risen Lord. The Christian is no longer moving towards Christ or even into Christ; he simply is in Christ, he rests in Christ, he communes with Christ. He has been received into the Easter, enveloping atmosphere that radiates from the risen Christ, and now the ensuing union is emphatically with the person of the glorified Jesus, radiant with paschal splendours. As a consequence, something radically new takes place, the Christian becomes "a new creation" (2 Cor 5,17), "a new man" (Eph 2,15). Deep down, at the deepest level of his personality, man experiences a new communion of being, a new transfusion of life, a real symbiosis, almost a fusion of his own life with that of Christ. Some authors go so far as to speak daringly of a quasi-identification between the Christian and Christ. "These are bold formulae; they would be excessive, did we not allow them an enormous flexibility. But they correspond better than any other to the language of St Paul".[5]

5 F. Durrwell, *The Resurrection* (London-N.York 1960), p. 241.

In the past, this union with Christ as the result of baptism has been authoritatively explained as a psychological union of knowledge and love. Christ would know and love each and every future Christian, and this double movement of knowledge and love would be reciprocated by the Christian, who correspondingly knows and ardently loves Christ. This would be what Paul meant by the formula "in Christ". This union is surely not physical, like the one between the limbs and the rest of the human body, for in this case the Christian would lose his independent existence, he would be, in a way, absorbed into Christ to the detriment of his own individual, distinct personality; in a word, this type of union would be too strong. But on the other hand, neither can we water down the Pauline "in Christ" to a merely moral union, like the one binding the members of a human society through a common aspiration and purpose; this kind of union would be too weak. The reality — it is said — lies midway between these two extremes of a strong, overpowering physical union, on the one hand, and a weak, diluted moral union on the other. The union of the Christian with Christ would be neither physical nor moral, but rather mystical.[6]

The reality, however, lies elsewhere, namely, in a better understanding of the very writings of Paul himself. The nature of this peculiar union with Christ is best understood by putting together the extremely forceful comparisons used by Paul himself to describe it. This union is directly opposed to, but strictly on the line of, a man's union with a prostitute (which some of the Corinthian Christians knew only too well

6 The above is a faithful summary of the position defended by Pope Pius XII in 1943 in his famous encyclical *Mystici Corporis*. However, his explanation of the Pauline "in Christ" is not very satisfactory, for it seems to unduly dilute the strength of the Pauline expressions. The Pope claims, in support of his contention, that Jesus "by means of the beatific vision which he enjoyed from the time when he was received into th womb of the mother of God, has forever and continuously had present to him all the members of his Mystical Body, and embraced them with his saving love.... In the manger, on the cross... Christ sees and embraces all the members of his Church and sees them far more clearly, embraces them far more lovingly than does a mother the child of her bosom" (*Mystici Corporis*, CTS ed., n. 74). This form of pious fiction will hardly be accepted by any reputable theologian today. A really convincing explanation of the Pauline "in Christ" cannot be made to rest on such a precarious basis.

from personal experience): "Do you not know that your bodies are members of Christ? Shall I therefore take the members of Christ and make them members of a prostitute? Never! Do you not know that he who joins himself to a prostitute becomes one body with her?....But he who is united to the Lord becomes one spirit with him" (1 Cor 5, 15-16).

Similarly, Paul also says that he is in travail until Christ be formed in them like an embryo (Gal 4, 19). Christians grow up into the full stature of Christ (Eph 4, 13). Christians are united with Christ in the unity of a single flesh (1 Cor 6, 16), they are limbs of "one body in Christ" (Rom 12, 5). Prostitute, embryo, bodily growth, flesh, limbs: all of them comparisons of the *physical* order, taken, all of them, from the physical reality of the human body. The force of all these comparisons is obviously lost when we arbitrarily, and so as to make them more understandable, reduce them to the psychological sphere of knowledge and love. Paul meant that, surely — but also much more than that. The great Oriental doctor St Athanasius displayed a remarkable grasp of Paul's mind when he said that "the Christian is 'christified' by christ, he is made one with the Word, he is 'wordified' ". "Christified" end "wordified": despite their awkwardness these neologisms seem to express prescisely what Paul had in mind.

Romans 6, 2-11. With Christ, into Christ, in Christ: the totality of Paul's doctrine concerning the Christian's vital communion with the glorified Lord is conveyed by these three terse expressions, and all three are present in this text which is as controversial in meaning as it is rich in doctrinal content. The passage is a true theological jewel, bright and sparkling. Paul is instructing the Roman Christians about the inexhaustible richness contained in the sacrament of baptism. He waxes eloquent, but as often happens with him, some of his expressions are so very pithy, so incredibly rich in their concise brevity, that the average reader is likely to miss their profound meaning altogether. A merely literal translation will fail to convey the depth of Paul's thought.

The baptismal liturgy offers Paul a convenient platform from which to expose his doctrine. Let us not forget that at that time the person of the baptized did not have his forehead sprinkled with a few drops of water, rather he was entirely immersed in the baptismal pool, to emerge out of it a new man, an entirely sanctified Christian endowed with the very life of Christ. In reaitly — Paul tells the Romans — to be baptized, immersed in water, is only the external symbolism; in reality we are "baptized into Christ Jesus" (v. 3) because the baptismal waters are endowed with the sanctifying power of his death, which becomes operative through the sacrament. In fact, we are buried, submerged, "with him, by baptism, unto death" (v. 4): an extremely dense formulation pregnant with meaning. As a consequence of the baptismal immersion, we are "with Christ" and at the same time enter "into Christ", so as to live hereafter "in Christ". The neophyte sinks into the pool, and this act is but an eloquent symbolism of death; and subsequently he emerges out of the water raised, as it were, to a new life: the entire paschal mystery, the death and resurrection of Jesus, is operative through the effective symbolism of baptism laden with the power of Calvary.

And now Paul comes to the climax of verse 5. This verse, which, because of its brevity borders on the cryptic, has been traditionally a crux of both translators and commentators.[7] It should probably be rendered as follows: "If it is *one single being with Christ* that we have become because of a death similar to his...". Paul is making use of a very forceful term, *symphythos*, from the root *symphyein*, meaning "to grow together". The idea suggested is that of two plants growing together, like the thorns and the seed in the parable of the sower (Lk 8, 7). Or better still, like the unborn baby, the foetus (from the very same Greek root, *phytos*) growing in the mother's womb. It is hardly possible to imagine a more intimate form of union between two living persons than that suggested here by Paul. The mother surrounds, envelops completely the unborn baby, which grows within her; the baby draws life and sustenance from the mother and, according to modern gynecology, were the mother to die, the baby would also perish unless it was

7 Most English translations weaken and obscure considerably Paul's original thought. Probably the best of the translations consulted is the original French Jerusalem Bible, which comes very close to the one given in the text.

taken out of the womb within ten minutes. To such an extent is the foetus dependent on the mother. But this dependence is non-mutual, for whereas the baby literally lives and depends completely on the mother, the mother does not in any way depend on the baby. Life flows down from the mother to the baby, not the other way around.

So far the imagery. The reality is even more beautiful. As the result of the baptismal regeneration the neophyte (the very word is reminiscent of the Pauline *phytos*) begins to grow within the "womb" which is Christ. It is the transfigured, Easter Christ that envelops the Christian and constantly pours life, Easter life, into him. Baptism has taken him "into Christ", and now, once the vivifying contact has been established, Christ grips the Christian who begins to grow, so enveloped and surrounded, into the fullness of Christ. In the light of this, it makes absolutely no sense to restrict the union between the Christian and Christ to a kind of imitation, to a psychological union through knowledge and love. The unborn baby cannot imitate anybody; yet he draws life into himself in plentiful draughts. The union is certainly not only moral, it is plainly physical, linking up, as it does, two human bodies. Keeping this forceful comparison in mind, one can grasp the fullness of meaning implied in Paul's concluding sentence: "So you must consider yourselves... alive to God in Christ Jesus" (v. 11). After baptism we are alive to the Father, certainly, but this is because we are *in Christ Jesus.* The "mother" continues to feed her baby. This is our Christian life.

It should be transparently clear by now, against the above background, how intimate is the communion between Christ and the Christian. Even at the risk of exaggerating we are justified in speaking of an existential communion, almost an identification of two living persons, the Christian and Christ, one of whom — Christ — assumes the other into himself so as to make him share a life that is common to both. This is obviously a strictly supernatural reality based exclusively on faith, with no human parallels anywhere. It is not only in the psychological order of knowledge and love that this communion takes place, but far deeper than that, in the very order of being, as befits living persons. This union affects the very root of the human person.

Often enough one comes across people who are quite satisfied with the ideal of knowing Christ ever more deeply and loving him ever more ardently. They seem to be fully contented with this, they aspire to nothing more. Yet Paul would be the first to react against such an unscrupulous weakening of the true Christian life. We know and love Christ, no doubt, but knowledge and affection are only the twin flowers that attract us by their external beauty. A mature Christian will surely appreciate the delicate beauty of the flowers, but he should not stop there, he should rather go deeper and examine the very root that has given birth to such flowers, and this hidden but vital root is precisely our being "in Christ", as explained above.

Let us have a closer look at the root now. We are and live in Christ as persons, and a person is essentially characterized by a necessary openness to another. A person closed in upon himself, folded up and withdrawn within himself hardly deserves the name of person, for this withdrawal goes counter to the very core of his being, which is clamouring first for an opening, and then, based upon it, for a total gift of self to another person. And so, true to his own nature as man, Jesus was open both to his Father and to his fellow men and women, and this double opening of his person resulted in his self-gift to God and to humankind. He gave himself to others because deep down he was open to others, he was fully a man.

Similarly now the Christian, as a human person — man or woman, it does not really matter — is open to Christ, but even before Christ comes into his life, man is necessarily open to other persons, to his fellow beings. For the human person cannot possibly reach perfection unless in communion with another, and this enjoyable, satiating communion is necessarily built upon a previous opening of the person. A rejection of this essential, radical opening and the ensuing personal communion would unavoidably have a crippling effect on the fulness of the human person. A man half open is only half a man.

It is this natural opening of man that is raised and transformed by the transfigured Christ. The risen Christ enters into man through that opening and possessess him fully: this is christic communion. Man's natural openness and innate capacity of self-gift is not thereby destroyed, on the contrary, it is respected and built upon. The greater the natural openness and self-gift of the human person (both of which admit of degrees and the possibility of growth) and the greater the person or Person to whom he is united, the greater will his personal fulfillment be, both as Christian and as man.

But let us return to Paul. That man is so full of Christ that, apart from the triple pregnant expression explained above, and besides what he so tellingly wrote to the Christians in Rome, he comes back to the same reality from a different angle, viz, that of the *pleroma* (Greek, for fullness) of Christ. The Christian, according to Paul, enjoys the intimacy of a personal communion with Christ and receives from him the fullness of life.

This Pauline notion of *pleroma* is probably best understood if we keep in mind the following descending scheme: (a) the Father fills Jesus with the plenitude of the divinity, hence he becomes the *pleroma* of the Father, he is full of the Father; (b) the risen Christ in turn fills up the Church and therefore she becomes the *pleroma* of Christ, she is simply filled with Christ; (c) each and everyone of the faithful acquires this divine plenitude as he or she is incorporated into the Church through baptism. The Church acts now as an intermediary, a channel of transmission through which the fullness of God streams down into the Christian. This is an immanence of plenitude and growth.

This descending scheme becomes externally visible in the episode of Jesus' transfiguration, a mystery which is so very dear to Orientals. "This is my beloved Son, listen to him", said the Father on that occasion. But it would be wrong to imagine that the Father is the origin only of the voice heard. The very effulgence of Jesus is a descending effulgence, for it is the splendour of the Father that shines on the face of Christ. The Father lives in unapproachable light, he is light and in him there is no darkness, and this divine brightness is rendered now externally visible on the face of the transfigured Son, Jesus. And from Jesus it cascades down to the three sleepy disciples who are assumed, along with Jesus, into the bright cloud covering them all. On Tabor we witness the divine effulgence pouring down from the Father to Jesus and from Jesus to the disciples.

It is exactly the same descending pattern that obtains when we are made to be the receptacles of God's *pleroma.* Yet this technical word is nothing but an abstraction — and a Greek abstraction at that. What is it, in the concrete, that descends from the Father to Christ and from Christ to the Christian? What is it that the Christian receives when he is filled with Christ? Opinions among Pauline specialists differ, but it would seem that it is Christ's vivifying presence that fills the Church and therefore the individual Christian also. Or, better still, it is Christ's own *paschal life* that, originally proceeding from the Father and filling the transfigured Lord of Easter, pours down into the Church which is progressively being filled with this Easter life. "For in him (Christ) the whole fullness of deity dwells bodily, and you have come to the fullness of life in him" (Col 2,9). It is not only Christ as the Son but specifically the humanity of Jesus born of Mary that is so filled with life, and therefore it is Jesus man, transfigured and glorified, that is the immediate source of life for the Christian. Baptism plunges him into an ocean of life which is Christ, and it is this fullness of life that possesses him now entirely.

But whereas in Jesus this fullness was complete, without the possibility of increase, in the Christian it is relative and always subject to growth. We receive this divine life according "to the measure...of the fullness of Christ" (Eph 4,13), until we reach mature manhood. The process of growth is slow, and it is continuous. Let it suffice for the moment to point out and stress that this infusion of life is markedly christological in its origin, for it proceeds from Christ into whom the Christian is inserted. Just as Jesus and the Christian are both sons of God, but in a different sense, so also the divine fullness communicated by the Father through Christ is to be compared to, but not to be identified with, the fullness that the Church receives from Christ in a limited manner which is always subject to growth.

2) The vine and the branches

John 15, 1-11. If there is a passage which has become really popular and highly appreciated in Christian spirituality it is this. John puts it in the mouth of the historical Jesus in the context of the Last Supper, when he is fast approaching the end of his life. However, we all know that John is not particularly concerned about chronology and the ordered flow of events. In spite of this concrete historical framework it is the Easter Christ, the glorified Jesus that speaks throughout the passage. The constraints of that particular moment and the limitations of that particular place drop out of sight. Now it is the risen Christ who conveys the message that transcends both space and time.

"I am the true vine...", namely, the stalk or the root from which all the branches draw their sap. The branches live by being physically linked to the root; so also by being almost physically united with the risen Christ the disciple lives with Christ's own life. The very comparison utilized by John makes it plain that this union with Christ certainly includes, but cannot be reduced to, a mere psychological bond of love and affection; it goes much deeper than that. The disciple is united with Christ not only through love but also through life, and it is especially the latter that runs throughout the entire passage. For the vine is not only fruit-producing, it is also life-bearing; it produces fruit because it is bursting with life. Just as the sap flows uninterruptedly from the stem into the branches, so also Christ's life pours unceasingly into the disciple united with him.

"You are already made clean by the word which I have spoken to you" (v. 3). This saying points to the essentially cleansing, purifying power of the word, namely, the entire message of Jesus received and interiorly assimilated through living faith. But the disciple is cleansed, not only through the word, laden with the purificatory power of God, but also and primarily through his Word. It is the spoken word and the living Word that purify the disciple. Hence, the glorified Jesus, incarnate Word of God, both vivifies and purifies the Christian. The very life of God courses through the disciple, thereby cleansing him. A fresh infusion of life means a higher degree of purity, for both the realities, life and purity, are always subject to growth.

"He who abides in me and I in him. . . ." This is, clearly expressed, the state of mutual immanence between Jesus and the disciple. It is a mutual abiding in each other, mutual clinging to each other, mutual, reciprocal adherence. It is the intimacy of a mutual possession. This abiding is either mutual or does not exist at all. This mutual inherence is necessarily based upon the previous, mutual openness to each other. Jesus is open to the disciple united to him and the disciple is also open to Jesus, so that through this double opening, a torrent of life may pour from Jesus to the disciple. For reception of divine life necessarily presupposes a previous opening, so that the stream of life may pour in, and on the part of the Christian this is the openness of living faith. He, through faith, opens up and clings to the glorified Christ, and by clinging to him, he lives.

Furthermore, it should also be noted that this union, which by its very nature is both permanent and vital, is profoundly suffused with an atmosphere of love. Actually there are two distinct streams flowing between the risen Christ and the disciple, namely, those of life and love. But there is a remarkable difference between the two, for love bespeaks reciprocity, whereas life does not. The disciple loves Jesus and is loved by him, the stream of love flows in both directions, whereas in the domain of life the disciple can only receive from Christ, he cannot possibly return life to him. But even in the case of love, which allows for reciprocity, for giving and receiving, the disciple can only react to the initiative taken by Jesus. The first step, the setting in motion of the entire process of love depends on Christ, not on the Christian. This is clearly exemplified in the gospel episode of the sinful woman in the banquet hall who wiped Jesus' feet with her hair. It is not she that starts the process; rather, Jesus gratuitously forgives her many sins, and then she, full of loving gratitude, reacts to Jesus' initiative. It is Jesus who loves first; her love for Jesus is only a response to the divine initiative. The disciple is simply unable to begin the process of love, he can only react to it.

The disciple is, in reference to Christ, like a suckling baby at the mother's breast. The baby can cling to the mother and receive the life-giving streams of the nourishing milk, unable to return any form of life to the mother; in the domain of life he can only receive, not give, he is but a permanent receiver. Whereas in the area of love the mother pours out her tender affection on the baby and the baby, in return, by smiling and flailing his puny arms and legs, makes a clumsy attempt at reciprocity. It is the mother that, by her own initiative, awakens the budding affection of the baby towards her.

The baby, in order to live, depends entirely on the mother — and so does the disciple depend absolutely on Christ if he wants to live. "Apart from me you can do nothing" (v.5). Despite its naked simplicity, this is an enormously powerful statement. The great St Augustine used to remark and stress that the Lord had not said that without him we can do very little or next to nothing, but *absolutely nothing*. And this shows not only the absolute dependence—non-mutual dependence—of the disciple with regard to Jesus, but also the complete gratuitousness of the gift of life, which we can only receive in gratitude. If we cannot possibly bestow this gift of life on ourselves, much less can we increase it in us. Therefore, both in the initial reception and in the further increase of this life the dependence of the disciple on Jesus is total, it is complete. We can live apart from Christ no more than the branch torn away from the central stem can go on living — it will soon dry up and die.

If, on the contrary, the branch remains attached to the stem, not only will it live, it will also develop and grow. For a branch it is impossible to become simply stunted, though alive; lack of growth indicates lack of life, and lack of life is a sure sign of impending death. The christic life poured into the disciple has to grow, and it is with a view to this growth that Jesus adds: "Ask what you will, and you shall have it" (v. 7). It is true that the offer on his part is unrestricted, it is a sort of a blank cheque signed by him and handed to us: "whatever you will". But the context is somewhat restrictive, for without in any way curtailing the universality of the promise, it seems to be primarily — though not exclusively — directed precisely towards the growth of divine life. Do we ever take this broad promise seriously and do we especially ever think of asking for an increase of Christ's life in us? Does this ever constitute the object of our petitionary prayer? Maybe a deeper conviction, a more profound realization that neither the origin nor the increase of this life lies within our power, would result in a pointed petition to the risen Jesus to make his own life grow within us. For stagnation and lack of growth would be a sure sign of approaching death.

The entire passage ends on a note of joy: "That my joy may be in you" (v. 11). The disciple is now confronted with an outpouring of gifts: it is not only love and life that he receives from the glorified Jesus, but also a share in his own joy, "*my* joy". This intimacy of mutual possession between the transfigured Christ and the disciple draws the disciple into the soft glow of Tabor, makes him not only contemplate but also radiate the effulgence of the Lord. He feels enveloped in an atmosphere of mutual love and mutual joy prompted by this reception of the gift of Easter life. Christ gives generously of his love, his life and his joy, and the disciple can only respond by acknowledging that his returning joy and love are but a shadow of Christ's love for him, a pale reflection of that love. He is acutely conscious of being unable to return life for the life received, but is at the same time pervaded by intense joy for being able to return love for love. Undoubtedly, the deepest and most precious of the three gifts received from Christ, love, life and joy, is life, and with regard to life the disciple is bound to be but a continuous receiver. The imagery of the baby and the mother conveys the true reality: the mother gives unreservedly to the baby life, love and joy, and rejoices in the giving; whereas the baby on its part can only show feeble signs of joy and love, for it truly rejoices in receiving.

We spoke above of the intimacy of the mutual possession between the resurrected Christ and the disciple. It is this intimacy that is beautifully described by an unknown thirteenth-century monk:

> In me, in my most interior, Jesus is present. All outside of our heart is to discover the treasure hidden

> interiorly in the heart. There is found that sepulchre of Easter and there the new life. "Woman, why do you weep? Whom do you seek?" Whom you seek you already possess and you do not know him? You have the true, eternal joy and still weep? It is more intimate to your being and still you seek it outside! You are there outside, weeping near the tomb, your heart is my tomb. And I am not there dead, but I repose there, living always, your soul is my garden...your tears, your love, your desire, all this is my work. *You possess me at the most intimate level of your being* without knowing it, and that is why you seek me outside. It is then outside also that I appeared to you and also that I made you to return to yourself, to make you find at the intimacy of your being him whom you seek outside.[8]

John is not a very logical or systematic writer, he rather delights in coming back on the same theme repeatedly, looking at it from different angles and explaining it from different perspectives. This is precisely what he does with his favourite notion of immanence in Christ. One would believe that, after the fairly lengthy section on the vine and the branches, there is nothing left to be said on the matter; yet this is not so. In typically Johannine fashion he returns to this fundamental idea and deepens it beautifully: *John 17,20-23* is a marvel of conciseness and depth. In it John takes the reader to dizzying trinitarian heights, or — to reverse the metaphor — to unsuspected depths. In the midst of his lengthy prayer to his Father, where he is constantly making use of the plural, Jesus says: "That they (the disciples) may be *in us*....I *in them* and you *in me*" (Jn 17,21.23).

The internal, trinitarian unity binding together Father and Son is proposed, in a way, as a model of imitation, and a good deal more. No closer union can be thought of than the one binding together Father and Son; in fact, this type of union is clearly beyond reach for the disciples, it is far too high. The disciple is simply unable to scale such heights of union and intimacy. And yet the trinitarian model is there, high in the sky, as a supreme exemplar to be striven for.

8 Quoted by G. Maloney, *Invaded by God* (Denville 1979), p. 137, with emphasis added.

But, over and above the aspect of imitation, there is also the deeper and more satisfying aspect of insertion. It is not only that the disciple contemplates in awe and amazement the unity of Jesus with his Father, he is simply *drawn into it*, he is immersed in it. The disciple, immanent in the glorified Christ, is introduced into the intimacies of the trinitarian family to which he now, in a certain way, belongs. He is drawn into the torrent of life that flows ceaselessly from the Father to the Son and back. He is made to feel at home in such exalted surroundings. This trinitarian angle, more than anyting else, discloses the fact that the Easter life, abundantly imparted by Jesus to the disciple immanent in him, is originally not Jesus' own, for he received it from his Father. Once again Jesus is essentially an intermediary of divine, trinitarian life. He is himself soaked in this life, and as if unable to contain the flood within himself, he pours it out on the disciple, who, as a consequence, receives in reality not so much Jesus' own life as the life of his Father, supreme and ultimate fountainhead of this trinitarian torrent. The disciple is certainly in Christ, and by being in Christ he is also in his Father. In a way, we could perhaps speak of a double immanence, in the risen Christ and in his Father. For now Christ gives to the disciple whatever he has, not only his own personal life but even the ultimate source of this life, namely, his Father. "Divine unity is implanted in the disciples by Jesus being in them and the Father being in Jesus".[9]

Nor should we fail to pause and reflect on the purpose and goal of this divine munificence: "...that they may be one, even as we are one" (Jn 17, 22). Since all the disciples are in the very same *milieu*, namely, in Jesus and his Father, and since all of them receive the very same life from both, it is obvious that, linked among themselves by this powerful binding force, they have to be one and appear to be one, united by the same stream of trinitarian life that draws and keeps them together. In other words, unity in the community is the result of this immanence in Christ.

Now John changes the metaphor slightly to express once more the very same reality: "The effulgence that you have

9 R. Schnackenburg, *The Gospel according to St John*, III, (New York 1982), p. 193.

given me I have given to them" (Jn 17, 22). John is taking us right up to Tabor again, where the three disciples find themselves subsumed into the luminous cloud, bathed in the very splendour that cascades down from the Father through the transfigured Jesus. This is the effulgence John speaks of, which is but the result of the disciple's immanence in Christ. The disciple is now in the midst of light and splendour because he is in Christ. All the disciples obviously share the same brightness because they are all in the same risen Christ. The idea is both profound and exceedingly suggestive: the vision of the entire community bathed in the soft glow of the Easter Christ....

Conclusions. From this brief consideration of the disciples' immanence in the glorified Christ as expressed by Paul and John, several consequences flow, common to both, that can conveniently be summarized as follows:

a) This peculiar kind of union we called immanence should in no way be reduced to the psychological level of knowledge and love, as if it could be sufficiently accounted for by the fact that Jesus knows and loves the disciple, and in return, the disciple knows and loves Jesus. This is perfectly true, but also clearly insufficient. In order to be faithful to the New Testament, this union should be explained rather as a bond which is almost *physical*, not only psychological. The strong, almost crude, bodily comparisons utilized by Paul, and the agricultural simile of the stem and the branches used by John seem to admit of no other description but the physical.

b) The metaphors used by both these authors imply the reality of *growth:* it is an unborn baby growing in the mother's womb, and an equally living and growing branch that draws life from the central stem. For ultimately immanence is a mystery of shared life, and life necessarily implies development and growth.

c) This union with Christ is not fleeting but *permanent,* it lasts. Eucharistic communion offers a type of union which is even more intense, more intimate and absorbing, but also much shorter, for it does not last, it is transitory. Although this immanence in Christ which is the result of baptism may be weaker, it is much more durable. It lasts as long as grievous sin is avoided, and in this sense it is permanent.

d) Furthermore, immanence implies a radical *dependence* of the disciple on the risen Lord, a dependence that is profound and non-mutual, for whereas the disciple, in order to live and fructify, depends entirely on Christ, Christ does not in any way depend on the disciple. Love is mutual, but life and dependence are not.

e) Finally, there is a deep *trinitarian* colouring that pervades this immanence, for in addition to making the disciple share in his own life, Jesus invites him to drink at the very source of his own life: his Father. It is only now that the disciple is entirely satiated.

At the end one cannot but be stunned when realizing in awe and wonder to what an incredible extent we depend on Christ. For the fact is that, as a consequence of our baptism, not only are we immanent in Christ, sanctified and transformed into him; not only, looking behind our baptism, were we co-buried with Christ and co-raised with him, but further back still and much before the vivifying paschal mystery of Calvary took place, we were also "created through Christ" (Col 1,16), for "all things were made through him" (Jn 1,3). Our dependence on Christ goes right back to the very moment of our creation.

And so, out of all these considerations and as a fitting conclusion to this section, an awesome picture of christological dependence emerges clearly: we were all created in Christ (Col 1, 16), elected in Christ (Eph 1, 4), predestined in Christ (Eph 1,5), redeemed in Christ (Eph 1,7), justified in Christ (Rom 8, 30), baptized into Christ (Rom 6, 4), and shall be glorified in Christ (Rom 8, 30). We simply live in Christ (Rom 6, 5), Christ is the alpha and omega, the beginning and the end of every Christian. We are, from the moment of our creation, simply enveloped in a dense christological atmosphere. Without this essentially christological dimension we would cease to exist. No man can exist without air, and the air we breathe, consciously or not, is Christ.

3) Living tabernacles?

Given the extremely close, intimate nature of this union between the glorified Jesus and the Christian sanctified by baptism, and given especially some of the forceful expressions utilized by both John and Paul, it is quite possible — in fact, I think it is quite likely — that at this juncture the reader will come to a wrong conclusion.

At first sight Paul's expressions seem to be conclusive: "That Christ may dwell in your heart through faith" (Eph 3, 17); "Christ lives in me" (Gal 2,20); "Christ is in you" (Rom 8, 10). Christ dwells, Christ lives, Christ is in you. Could Paul have been any clearer? Does he not mean to say— and the reality is so very comforting — that the transfigured humanity of Jesus is permanently in us, namely, that we are living tabernacles, endowed with the wonder of Jesus' continuous presence within us in a physical manner, almost as he is present in the Eucharist?

That may be spiritually consoling, no doubt, yet in reality it is nothing but a golden statue with feet of clay, a colourful soap-bubble that will disintegrate at the slightest pressure. The true reality of things may be disappointing to some, but the fact is that the glorified humanity of Jesus is *not* physically present in the person of the baptized Christian. This kind of presence, the so-called substantial presence of Christ, is reserved exclusively to the Eucharist. The very substance of Christ's person, the transfigured humanity of the son of Mary, definitely does not dwell in us as in a temple, this kind of presence belongs rather to the Holy Spirit, as we shall see in the next chapter.

It would be extremely hazardous to build up a beautiful and consoling theory by making it rest on such precarious foundations. In these matters it is futile to argue a priori, for we have no other means to know the truth except by examining what God himself has revealed to us in the Bible. If the scriptural foundations of such an extraordinary opinion cannot be discerned with certainty anywhere, then we had better abandon the entire enterprise. If the triple Pauline expression quoted above (Christ dwells, lives, is in you) were lifted out of context, understood literally and taken in isolation, apart from the entirety of our Christian revelation, we could perhaps come to the astonishing conclusion that we are actually carriers of Christ, just as the consecrated bread is the vehicle of his presence. We may not, however, act this way, for it would be not only arbitrary, but also exceedingly dangerous to pick and choose, to select a couple of expressions — no matter how forceful and apparently clear in themselves — as the only basis of such an artificial construct. Paul did not mean to say that Jesus' humanity abides perpetually in us; there is no trace of such an opinion in the rest of the Christian revelation.

When Paul, writing to the Galatians, says so very pointedly that "Christ lives in me" (Gal 2, 20), he means something quite different from his physical presence in us. J. Fitzmyer, a scriptural scholar of international reputation, comments on the above text as follows: "Faith in Christ does not substitute a new norm or goal of action; rather it reshapes man anew internally, supplies him with a new principle of activity on the ontological level of his very being. A symbiosis results of man with Christ, the glorified *Kyrios*, who has become...the vital principle of Christian activity".[10] Which is a far cry from saying that after his resurrection Jesus dwells permanently in the justified.

Several years ago there were theologians inclined to hold this opinion of Christ's quasi-physical presence in the person of the baptized Christian. The matter was deemed serious enough to justify Pope Pius XII's authoritative intervention, who declared unambiguously in his encyclical "*Mediator Dei*" (1947): "Beware also lest there be any spread of the false doctrine that the glorified humanity of Christ really and perpetually abides in the justified".[11] And it would be of little use to claim that this encyclical is already forty years old, that in the meantime further theological progress has clarified and deepened the issue, and that as a consequence now, in 1987, we may hold the opinion Pius the XII rejected in 1947. This is nothing but futile escapism, for this alleged "progress" is not visible anywhere. It is better to acknowledge in all sincerity that such a "consoling" doctrine is nothing but a pious fantasy.

Besides, it is not easy to see what meaning the Eucharist would have if, as a consequence of baptism, the Christian were

10 *The Jerome Biblical Commentary,* II (Bangalore 1968), p. 241.
11 CTS edition, London 1947, n. 216.

already endowed with this intimate personal presence of Jesus' humanity. Such a presence would sound the death toll of the Eucharist, at least of certain forms of eucharistic cult cherished by Catholics. In fact, why keep up the salutary custom of visits to the Blessed Sacrament if the very person we long to encounter in the chapel is perpetually living within us? Wouldn't such a presence render all visits plainly superfluous? Wouldn't Christ's presence in the tabernacle be but a useless duplication, a sort of eucharistic replica of his physical presence within the Christian as a result of baptism? Why should God give us two different sacramental means to secure the same kind of presence?

These brief reflections show that both the sacraments, baptism and the Eucharist, are productive of Christ's presence within us, but in a completely different manner. The substantial presence of Jesus' humanity is not a common effect of baptism and the Eucharist, it is rather the exclusive privilege of the Eucharist. We should never confuse the immanence of Christ in us as a result of baptism with his substantial presence under bread and wine. And eucharistic visits remain highly meaningful precisely because there is something, there is a surplus in the eucharistic presence which goes beyond the baptismal presence we have called immanence. Both are presences of the very same Christ, obviously, but these two types of presence should not be identified. They are both surely precious, but it would be an unworthy depreciation of God's wondrous gift if we were to reduce these two distinct kinds of presence to just one. We would thereby be surely simplifying things, but this simplification would be obtained at the cost of an impoverishment of the sacramental reality.

It is only now, after all the above clarifications, that we are finally in a position to grasp how very mysterious is this presence of Christ called immanence. Perhaps a homely example will throw some further light on the question. I love ardently my mother who happens to be hundreds of miles away from me. In a very real manner and in spite of her physical absence she is present to me by means of my fond memories of her, and especially because of my intense love for her. Fond memories and love bring her close to me, I really feel her presence — and yet she is physically absent, not present. This is a kind of psychological or moral union, not physical. But there is a friend of mine, also very dear to me, who is physically present to me here and now, a person I can see, hear and touch, a person from whom I can receive and to whom I can give physical expressions of love. Our mutual love is being fed by our physical proximity. This intimate friend of mine is physically present to me, whereas my mother is physically absent. My love for my absent mother is true and genuine and real, but her absence reduces this love to a psychological union; whereas the bodily proximity of my friend places our mutual love rather on the physical level.

To speak of a physical, bodily union with a person who is here, close to me, is not a particularly mysterious reality. Similarly, to speak of a psychological union with a person who is absent makes sense, and there is nothing particularly obscure about it either. Both these types of union fall within the area of our own personal experience. But can you imagine an exceedingly intimate, almost physical union with a person who is physically absent? Can physical intimacy and physical absence go together? Are they not almost contradictory?

Yet, this is precisely what happens with this peculiar type of union we call immanence. The glorified Jesus is not physically present in us as in a temple, he is rather physically absent. And yet, according to the authoritative testimony of the New Testament, the union of the Christian with Christ should almost be described as physical. To equate this union with that between my mother and me is to minimize, to water down unduly the rich doctrine given to us by John and Paul. The baptized Christian is permanently united with the Christ of Easter in a manner and with an intimacy that far exceeds the intimacy he can feel towards his absent mother. The union with the risen Christ is of a superior kind, it belongs to an incomparably higher level of closeness and intimacy. And yet Christ is physically absent, not present. It is the reconciliation, the simultaneous existence of these two qualities, on the one hand an intense, almost physical intimacy with him, and on the other his physical absence, that renders the immanence of Jesus in us so very mysterious.

This union is so baffling, so peculiar, that in our human experience we seem to completely lack anything similar. In a way the presence of Christ in the Eucharist and the presence of the Holy Spirit in the baptized are easier to grasp. Once the indispensable basis of faith is presupposed — for without this basis none of these supernatural realities makes any sense at all — both these types of presence are perhaps not so very difficult to understand; but to be so intimately close to a person who is not physically present — here lies the core of the mystery. Our immanence in Christ can be explained soberly and reflected upon lovingly, but its full reality will always escape us. In the best of cases we shall perceive this mysterious reality always in a somewhat blurred, indistinct manner, enveloped by a cloud of incense, as it were. The veil of mystery will never be entirely lifted. We rejoice in the living presence of Christ in us, but we are definitely not his living tabernacles.

4) The glorified Christ, fountainhead of the Holy Spirit

The Christian, regenerated by baptism, is present, immanent in Christ, and Christ is immanent in him: it is a mutual, unifying immanence. It cannot be sufficiently emphasized that this intimate, vital union is not with the earthly Jesus, but specifically with the glorified Lord of Easter. The baptized Christian enters the luminous atmosphere that radiates from the risen Jesus, and it is from him, transfigured and glorified, that he will drink the Holy Spirit. Surely the Spirit was no stranger to the earthly Jesus, but whereas Jesus always had the Spirit within himself, it is the risen Christ that imparts the same Spirit to us, it is the Christ of Easter that is the spring of living water, the source of the Holy Spirit.

There stands today in Nazareth a majestic, beautiful two-storeyed basilica in the nave of which one finds the awesome inscription: "Here the Word became flesh". There, somewhere in Nazareth, where one breathes a subtle, undefined, but very real Marian atmosphere, the young mother of Jesus was overshadowed by the Holy Spirit at the moment of Jesus' conception. No sooner had Jesus been conceived than the Spirit was already with him. Furthermore, it has often been remarked that the same Spirit seems almost to hover about the persons that play such an important role in the infancy narratives: it is announced that John the Baptist, the precursor, "will be filled with the Holy Spirit even from his mother's womb" (Lk 1,15), and both his parents, Elizabeth and Zechariah too, were "filled with the Holy Spirit" (Lk 41.67); Mary and Joseph take the baby Jesus to the Jerusalem Temple and there they encounter the old man Simeon, of whom it is said that "the Holy Spirit was upon him" (Lk 2,25). Mary, Elizabeth, Zechariah, John, Simeon: all those surrounding the infant Jesus are explicitly said to be under the influence of the Holy Spirit.

This being the spiritual atmosphere in which Jesus moved from his early days, it will come as no surprise to hear that he, acting upon an inspiration, an internal impulse of the Spirit, leaves the quiet surroundings of Nazareth and begins his public life. He walks to the banks of the Jordan, plausibly to a bend of the river not far from the extremely beautiful oasis which is Jericho, and there undergoes the momentous experience of his baptism, when, just as he "was praying, heaven was opened and the Holy Spirit descended upon him in bodily form" (Lk 3,21-22). Soon after his baptism, "Jesus, full of the Holy Spirit, returned from the Jordan and was led by the Spirit for forty days in the wilderness" (Lk 4,1-2). From the soothing, almost idyllic surroundings of Jericho, with its swaying palm trees and orange groves in full bloom, Jesus proceeds to the forbidding solitude of the wilderness which lies within walking distance from the Jordan. This episode of Jesus' baptism will later on make a deep impression on the apostolic Church, which will refer to it lovingly as the moment when "God anointed Jesus of Nazareth with the Holy Spirit and with power" (Ac 10,38). For a Hebrew, a body anointed with oil gains in strength, health, joy and beauty, for oil penetrates deep into the body. Similarly now, Jesus is metaphorically anointed with the Holy Spirit, who penetrates and possesses him fully. Then he returns to Galilee "in the power of the Spirit" (Lk 4,14).

a) *The feast of Tabernacles*

In the time of Jesus one of the most solemn feasts in the Jewish liturgical calendar was that of Tabernacles, very closely associated with the Jerusalem Temple, whose dedication under Solomon had taken place on such a feast day. It has been estimated that for the feast of the Passover the population of Jerusalem swelled from 30,000 to about 150,000 and, given the special solemnity of the feast of Tabernacles, probably the population flocked from the countryside to Jerusalem also in huge numbers. The feast lasted for eight continuous days, when the pilgrims would dwell outside the walls of the city, in "tabernacles or tents or booths", constructed with leafy tree branches in remembrance of the time when they lived in tents during their forty-year long trek through the desert under the leadership of Moses.

At that time the imposing structure of the Temple stood out prominently on the Jerusalem skyline. Enormous in size, massive, lovingly built with multicoloured marble, gold and the finest woodwork, it was the very centre of Israel's religious life, the sacred shrine where Yahweh dwelt. It was there that the feast of Tabernacles was celebrated every year at the end of September or early October. The feast was marked by a double symbolism of light and water, and the liturgical ceremonies were performed accordingly. Four huge lampstands, standing 13 metres tall, were placed on the so-called women's court or outer part of the Temple. As a consequence, there was hardly a house in Jerusalem which did not reflect the stream of light radiating from the Temple precincts. For the Temple was the house of Yahweh who "is light" (1 Jn 1,5), "lives in unapproachable light" (1 Tim 6,16), and "wears a mantle of light" (Ps 103, 2). At night the Temple illumination made the whole of Jerusalem sparkle like a jewel.

As rich as the symbolism of light is that of water. On the morning of the first seven days of the festival, a golden pitcher was filled with water from the pool of Siloam, to the joyous singing of Is 12, 3, "With joy you will draw water from the wells of salvation". The faithful, gathered by the thousands, would wind their way up to the Temple in a joyful procession and enter it by the Water Gate. Then the priest would stand in front of the altar of holocausts and pour the water into a silver funnel from which it would flow down onto the ground. It almost looked like the fulfilment of the prophecy of old: "Behold water was issuing from below the threshold of the temple towards the east" (Ez 47, 1); "on that day living waters shall flow out from Jerusalem" (Zech 14,8).

Mixed with the crowd, Jesus and the Twelve went up to the Temple. It was probably on the seventh day, when the festival was drawing to a close, that Jesus uttered that magnificent prophecy: "If anyone thirsts let him come to me; and let him drink who believes in me. As the scripture says, 'from within him shall flow rivers of living water'. Here he was referring to the Spirit, which those who came to believe in him were to receive. For the Spirit had not yet been given, because Jesus was not yet glorified" (Jn 7, 37-39). Earlier on Jesus had identified his own body as the real Temple: "Destroy this temple and in three days I will raise it up" (Jn 2, 21), and now he promises that the Holy Spirit, symbolized by the stream of living water, will flow from within his body. "In the desert wanderings which this feast recalled, Moses had satiated the thirst of the Israelites by striking a rock from which he brought forth rivers of living water. Now those who thirst need only come to Jesus, and through belief the water of life will be theirs".[12]

According to John it is almost certainly not the believer, but the glorified Jesus who is to be the source of the Spirit.[13] Streams of living water will flow out from his heart (literally, from his belly), that is, from within himself. Once Jesus is glorified, the Spirit will overflow from the pure receptacle of his transfigured humanity into those who believe in him.

12 R. Brown, *The Gospel according to John*, I (London 1971), p. 327.

13 The point, however, is debatable. A very ancient Oriental tradition which goes back to St Polycarp, disciple of St John, favours this interpretation. It is also the opinion of most modern commentators and translators, based on the probable punctuation of the text; cf R. Brown, *The Gospel according to John*, I, p. 320; R. Schnackenburg, *The Gospel according to John*, II, p. 54. The Jerusalem Bible, the New English Bible, the New American Bible, and the French *Traduction Oecuménique de la Bible*, all four opt for the punctuation that makes Jesus the source of living waters.

Once again, living faith as the total commitment to Jesus is the gateway to the plentiful reception of the Holy Spirit. Believe and you will live.

b) *The crucifixion*

We have already seen above that John is particularly fond of coming back, over and over again, to certain central themes of the gospel. Given, on the other hand, the extraordinary importance he attaches to the bestowal of the Holy Spirit by the glorified Christ, it is but natural to expect a repeated promise of this final outpouring. Already at the feast of Tabernacles the promise had been made explicitly under the imagery of living water, and now, with the dying Jesus hanging on the cross, John returns to the very same theme.

Each of the Synoptics describes the death of Jesus in its own way. For Matthew, Jesus "yielded his Spirit" (27,50). Mark states flatly that he "breathed his last" (15,37). Luke, on the other hand, has the crucified Jesus entrust his spirit to his Father, "Into your hands I commend my spirit" (Lk 23,46). John is peculiar. He presents Jesus at this supreme moment as turned, not towards his Father, as Luke had done, but rather towards the infant Church that he is about to leave behind, represented by his mother and the beloved disciple standing at the foot of the cross. It is within these peculiar perspectives that the Johannine Jesus "handed over the Spirit" (Jn 19, 30) — presumably to the Church, though this is not said explicitly.

Yet, important and meaningful though it is, this is but a repeated, final promise of the bestowal of the Spirit. It is a promise depicted as anticipated realization, for the actual outpouring of the Holy Spirit will take place two days later on Easter Sunday: "If such an interpretation of 'he handed over the Spirit' has any plausibility, we would stress that this symbolic reference is evocative and *proleptic*, reminding the reader of *the ultimate* purpose for which Jesus has been lifted up on the cross".[14]

14 R. Brown, *The Gospel according to John*, II,p. 931, with emphasis in the original. Substantially the very same interpretation and reference to the Spirit in R. Schnackenburg, *The Gospel according to John*, III, p. 285 and C. Vawter in *The Jerome Biblical Commentary*, II, p. 462.

John, on the other hand, is not particularly concerned about chronology. His main interest lies in explaining to the reader the nature of the gift and the person of the giver, rather than the exact moment when the imparting of the gift takes place. For John *doxa* (glory) is a crucial term, signifying at once the death and the exaltation of Jesus. And this exaltation, according to John's conception, begins already on the cross. Gone is the dramatic description of the crucifixion characteristic of the Synoptics: John omits the scoffing remarks of the passers-by, the blasphemies of the people, the insults of the robbers crucified with Jesus. His death is presented not as that of a man deformed by suffering and tortured by physical pain, but rather as that of a real king who majestically, in full peace and serenity, surrenders his spirit to God. Already the Gethsemane episode at the beginning of the Passion illustrates this inner attitude of the Johannine Jesus, his unruffled calm and compelling majesty. Now, at the end, the very same attitude shines through. His real exaltation, the exaltation of a king, begins already on the cross; for John death and glorification are but two inseparable facets of one single movement of exaltation. The dying, but triumphant Jesus hands the Spirit over. Now "it is accomplished" (Jn 19,30), the task entrusted to him by his Father has been brought to a successful conclusion.

As if all this were not clear enough, John has the dead Jesus pierced by a lance, "and at once there came out blood and water" (Jn 19, 34).[15] It has been debated for a long time whether this episode is really historical or merely symbolic. In view of the heavy stress laid by the author on the presence of an eye-witness, it is more plausible to assume that the narrative is substantially historical. Assuredly John is primarily interested in its deeply symbolic meaning, but this interest does not render it fictional. Either water or a colourless liquid resembling water did come out of Jesus' dead body as the result of the lance's thrust. John, in typical fashion, builds his symbolism on this historical basis.

15 This verse surprisingly appears in some manuscripts at the end of Mt 27,49. According to this localization the lance's thrust comes *before* Jesus' death. Then it would be "either a *coup de grâce* or a final act of hostility" (R. Brown, *Gospel*, II, p. 935, with emphasis added).

In order to grasp fully the import of this symbolic interpretation, one should view it within the totality of John's gospel. Jesus had already promised to the Samaritan woman in veiled form the outpouring of the Spirit. To this woman standing by the well Jesus had promised that "whoever drinks of the water that *I shall give him* will never thirst; the water that *I shall give him* will become in him a spring of water welling up to eternal life" (Jn 7,14).[16] Later on, on the occasion of the feast of Tabernacles, Jesus reiterates the promise, as we saw above. And now, for the third and last time, the dead Jesus is once again presented by John as the source of living water. It is worth remarking that at Tabernacles, Jesus had promised that streams of living water would flow "from within him" (or from his heart or belly). This acquires added significance in view of the cavity opened in his side by the lance. from which opening water flowed out. In Johannine theology water often stands as a symbol of the Spirit. In keeping with this symbolism and echoing the same theology, the author of the Apocalypse speaks in his description of heaven of "the river of the water of life, bright as crystal, flowing from the throne of God (the Father) and of the Lamb (the risen Christ)" (Apoc 22,1)

When projected against this Johannine background, the profound, symbolic meaning of the flow of water from Jesus' open side becomes clear. The actual giving of the Holy Spirit will take place later, but when presented as an anticipated symbolism on the cross it shows graphically that the outpouring of the Spirit is the final outcome, the fruit of the entire salvific process of Jesus' passion, death and exaltation.

At the end we see that in narrating the salvific events of Calvary, John has twice expressed the same truth, first verbally and then graphically; first, by presenting the dying Jesus as handing over the Spirit to the Church, and then by referring to the outflow of water from his pierced side as a symbol of the Spirit. For John, Jesus dead and risen is the fountainhead of the Spirit.

16 Notice the stress in the wording: twice in the same verse Jesus is presented as the proximate source of this mysterious water; the emphasis is obviously added.

c) *Easter Sunday*

Finally, all prophecies and symbolic announcements of the bestowal of the Spirit come to an end on Easter day, when the Spirit begins to overflow, as it were, from the risen Christ into the disciples.

It is not easy for us to visualize the glorified Christ. Maybe we have grown accustomed to think of him as popularly depicted in the post-Easter appearances of the Synoptics, without even realizing how exceedingly difficult it is to reconcile those legendary accounts [17] with the sober description given by Luke in Acts. Paul's experience on the way to Damascus was nothing but an encounter with the risen Christ, and we will do well to remember that he perceived no human figure, but only a flash of blinding light and a voice — nothing else. Paul seems to be the only New Testament writer who put down in writing for the benefit of posterity his vision/experience of the glorified Jesus. For it is a curious fact that those who describe the Easter appearances in the gospels never saw the risen Jesus; and those who saw him never described their vision. The only exception seems to be Paul himself.

For, writing to his Corinthian Christians about eighteen years later[18] Paul, in a passage often quoted, (1 Cor 15, 42-45) gives in a few bold strokes the description of our future glorified body, and it is more than likely that the only source of information at his disposal for this esoteric knowledge was precisely his personal Damascus experience. According to this reasonable suggestion, Paul is describing the exalted qualities of our glorified body against the backdrop of his personal experience; he applies to the Christian what he himself saw in the risen Christ, for according to his own principles, our future glorified body will be patterned on Jesus' own body. He says explicitly that at the end Christ "will transfigure the body belonging to our humble state and

17 The accounts may be legendary, but they do embody an objective experience of the risen Lord. I have developed this at some length in my previous book, *Life Beyond Death* (Anand 1985), pp. 130-135.

18 Namely, the time between his Damascus experience (usually dated 38 A.D.) and the writing of 1 Cor in the year 56.

give it the form *like that of his own resplendent body*".[19] What Paul saw was Jesus' luminous body, literally "a body of light" (Phil 3,21), of splendour and brightness—in a word, the transfigured body of Tabor, with the "effulgence of God shining on the face of Christ" (2 Cor 4,6).

For the body of Jesus, no less than that of any deceased Christian, "was sown in humiliation, it is raised in *splendour;* sown in weakness, it is raised in *power*" (1 Cor 15,42). For Paul what stands out at the resurrection of Jesus is precisely the incredible power of God. The empty tomb is for him the most telling testimony of God's power. In a classical passage, short, dense and compelling, he speaks of "the strength of the might of the power (of God), powerfully exercised" (Eph 1,19) at Christ's resurrection.[20]

Jesus, therefore, was raised in splendour and in power, and the last and deepest reason for this double quality of his body is precisely that his body was, like that of the Christian, *spiritual*, though not spiritual in the sense in which we take his word now, for through the wear and tear of centuries it has lost much of its original force. For Paul "spiritual" should almost be capitalized, for it means possessed, entirely penetrated by the Spirit, the Holy Spirit. Easter Sunday is the culmination of whatever has preceded. The Spirit begins to pour out through the pure, resplendent channel which is the perpetually transfigured Jesus. It is Christ who is the giver and the Spirit is the gift — a splendid, magnificent Easter gift of Jesus to his Church.

It is the same glorified Jesus who, on Easter Sunday, appears to his terrified disciples behind closed doors and bestows on them the supreme gift of the Holy Spirit: "Peace be with you...He then breathed on them, saying, 'Receive the Holy Spirit' " (Jn 20,22). Jesus, at his resurrection, is so entirely penetrated by the Spirit, so thoroughly imbued with the Spirit of God that he becomes "a life-giving spirit" (1 Cor 15,45). He is the source of Easter life, precisely because he is

19 Phil 3,21, with emphasis added.

20 This is the somewhat clumsy and inelegant but accurate rendering of Eph 1,19, which most translators, apparently more concerned about the purity of the language than about Paul's thought, weaken considerably.

the fountainhead of the Spirit of life: the waters of the Spirit begin to flow out from that pure reservoir which is his transfigured, resplendent body. He breathes on the disciples in a symbolic action which at the same time both signifies and effectively imparts the Holy Spirit. But before breathing on them "he showed them... his side" (Jn 20,20), possibly as a reminder that, two days earlier, from the very same side, water, as a symbol of the Spirit, had flowed out. At the feast of Tabernacles Jesus only promised, but did not communicate, the Spirit, "because he had not yet been glorified" (Jn 7,39). Now he is finally glorified, now he imparts to others the Holy Spirit he had himself possessed from the beginning.

"Thus the two Apostles (John and Paul) agree in making the bodily humanity of the Saviour the point from which the divinizing Spirit gushes out for us".[21] Jesus had himself received the Holy Spirit bountifully from his Father, for "it is not by measure that he (the Father) gives the Spirit" to Jesus (Jn 3,34). Now, on Easter Sunday, Jesus shares his own Spirit with his disciples. The glorified Jesus of Easter becomes the fountainhead of the Holy Spirit.

BIBLIOGRAPHY

Wikenhauser, A.: *Pauline Mysticism* (New York 1960), pp. 17-109.

Durrwell, F.: *The Resurrection* (London-N.York 1960), pp. 78-108; 209-227.

Bouttier, M.: *En Christ, Etude d'Exégèse et de Théologie Pauliniennes* (Paris 1962).

Spicq, C.: *St Paul and Christian Living* (Dublin 1964), pp.38-56.

Fitzmyer, J.: *Pauline Theology* (Englewood Cliffs 1976).

Cerfaux, L.: *The Christian in the Theology of St Paul* (London 1967), pp. 321-373.

Dunn, J.: *Baptism in the Holy Spirit* (London 1970), pp. 23-27.

Guillet, J.: "Spirit of God", in Léon-Dufour, F., ed., *Dictionary of Biblical Theology*, 2nd ed. (Bangalore 1973), pp. 569-576.

21 F. Durrwell, *The Resurrection*, p. 106.

Green, M.: *I Believe in the Holy Spirit* (London 1975), pp. 32-47.

Harrington, W.: *Spirit of the Living God* (Wilmington 1977). pp. 17-36; 97-117.

Malatesta, E.,ed.: *The Spirit of God in Christian Life* (New York pp. 113-145.

Vellanickal M.: *Studies in the Gospel of John* (Bangalore 1982), pp. 124-145.

Congar, Y.: *I Believe in the Holy Spirit*, I (London 1983), pp. 15-62.

Chapter Three

TEMPLES OF THE HOLY SPIRIT

"Do you not know that you are God's temple and that God's Spirit dwells in you"? (1 Cor 3,16). The Christian, sanctified at baptism, is immanent in Christ and the temple of the Holy Spirit. There are modern authors who, presumably prompted by their desire to simplify matters and avoid unnecessary complications, seem to consider these two relationships as practically equivalent, for the place of the ascended and absent Christ — they contend — has now been taken over by his Spirit. It is he who now performs the function and role exercised before by Jesus. According to this conception, the Holy Spirit would be a kind of vicar of Christ, rendering his presence active and effective in the midst of the Church. Consequently, these authors speak indiscriminately of the indwelling of Christ and the indwelling of the Spirit.[1]

I think that this is a mistake which could have been avoided by adhering more closely to scriptural terminology. According to the New Testament we are all temples of the Holy Spirit rather than temples of Christ. It is the Holy Spirit that substantially and almost physically dwells in us, not Jesus of Nazareth with his glorified humanity. As a rule and with only one exception (Eph 3,17) Paul never says that Christ dwells in the Christian; this function is reserved to the Spirit, and we would do well to follow Paul and not to fuse

1 This trend is noticeable, for instance, in two recent books by G. Maloney, *Invaded by God, Mysticism and the Indwelling Trinity* (Denville 1979) and *Called to Intimacy. Living the Indwelling Presence* (Bombay 1984).

and confuse two spiritual relationships that should remain essentially distinct, though inseparable.

The Spirit dwells in us as in a temple *because* we are immanent in Christ, rather than the other way around. Jesus proclaimed in the Jerusalem Temple, as we saw above, "If any man is thirsty, let him come to me and drink. This he said of the Spirit" (Jn 7,37). The Christian, already incorporated into Christ and immanent in him, drinks in the waters of the Spirit from that Easter source. He comes to Jesus through living faith and receives from him the bountiful outpouring of the Holy Spirit. The indwelling of the Spirit is but the natural result, the fruit, of our immanence in the glorified Christ.

1) Suggestive foreshadowings: close presence and loving intimacy

The comforting doctrine of God's indwelling in man should be seen against the general backdrop of God's presence to his People. Though manifested through externally visible signs, this presence is that of a spiritual person whose love envelops and vivifies man, in order to make him his living witness. This remarkable closeness of God to his People is brought out already in the Old Testament, mainly by two different but closely related themes: a presence of God that is almost tangible, localized, and his familiarity or loving intimacy with men.

The Hebrew certainly knows and loudly proclaims that Yahweh is present everywhere, that his salvific activity cannot be restricted to one particular place: "Whither shall I go from thy Spirit? Or whither shall I flee from thy presence? If I ascend to heaven, thou art there! If I make my bed in sheol thou art there! If I take the wings of the morning and dwell in the uttermost parts of the sea, even there thy hand shall lead me..." (Ps 139, 7-10). The Israelite simply cannot hide from the enveloping presence of God.

And yet, in spite of this universal presence, the Hebrew also knows that certain privileged places are endowed with a special kind of God's presence, perhaps more solemn, less diffuse, more intimate and permanent. In their 40-year long wanderings in the desert, the Israelites perceive sometimes in the so-called Tent of Meeting a cloud and a fire, or a certain bright effulgence, as visible signs of God's presence: "Then the cloud covered the tent of meeting and the glory (that is, the splendour or effulgence) of the Lord filled the tabernacle. And Moses was not able to enter the tent of meeting, because of the cloud that abode upon it, and the glory of the Lord filled the tabernacle....For throughout all their journeys the cloud of the Lord was upon the tabernacle by day, and fire was in it by night" (Ex 40, 34-38). The Lord is similarly present in the mercy seat of the Ark, from where he speaks to Moses: "There I will meet you, and from above the mercy seat, from between the two cherubims...I will speak to you" (Ex 25,22). Yahweh, though present everywhere, intensifies his presence, as it were, both in the Tent and in the Ark, which as a consequence become revered shrines hallowed by his person.

But, once the weary journey across the desert is finally over and the Israelites settle down in the Promised Land, it is very specially in the Jerusalem Temple that the Lord is said to dwell; it is the Temple that becomes the privileged witness of his presence, filled with the brightness of God: "And when the priests came out of the holy place a cloud filled the house of the Lord so that the priests could not stand to minister because of the cloud; for the glory (or effulgence) of the Lord filled the house of the Lord....Then Solomon said...'I have built thee an exalted house, a place for thee to dwell in forever' " (1 Kings 8,10-13). The Lord dwells in his Temple and fills it with his light. It is a kind of luminous presence in the Temple, the heart of Jerusalem. The city of David is enveloped in the gentle glow radiating from the inner recesses of the Temple, where Yahweh dwells.

On the other hand, friendship and intimacy with God are also expressed, if somewhat crudely, by the metaphor of physical proximity: if the Lord is pleased, he is said to be near; if he is displeased, he is far: "Why, oh Lord, do you stand aloof? Why hide in times of distress?" (Ps 10,1). Contrariwise, the Lord draws near to the just: "He is near to uphold my right....See, the Lord is my help" (Is 50,8-9).

This is the indescribable nearness of God to certain holy

places, sanctuaries of his presence. But there is a second trend, another line of thought that is primarily concerned, not with material places, but rather with living persons, who enjoy the comfort of the divine familiarity. So for instance, Abraham, the man of faith, is called simply "the friend of God" (Jn 2,23); similarly Moses is addressed by Yahweh as "my intimate friend", as a man to whom God speaks "face to face" (Ex 33,11), a man who enjoys always the company of God: "My presence will go with you" (Ex 33,14). On the other hand, divine wisdom, subtle and powerful, enters the person of the just: "Wisdom passes into holy souls and makes them friends of God" (Wis 7,27).

But friendship is not enough. God's intense love for his People is touchingly described in rather anthropomorphic images which may seem crude and clumsy, but are also capable of conveying powerfully the intensity of God's love. God is compared to a father who pours love and affection on his child: "I took my people up in my arms...I drew them to me in affection and love. I picked them up and held them to my cheek; I bent down to them and fed them" (Os 11,3-4). Yahweh carries Israel "as a man carries his child" (Deut 1,31). The Lord is "like an eagle that stirs up its nest, that flutters over its young, spreading out his wings..,bearing them on its pinions" (Deut 32,11). "Even if a mother should forget her child I will not forget you. I have written your name on the palms of my hands" (Is 49, 15-16). These images express eloquently God's passionate love for man and the incredible closeness of his presence to the person he loves. But a return of love is the response expected from man to such a divine initiative: "You shall love the Lord" (Deut 6,5). Mutual love tends instinctively to mutual proximity and physical closeness: it is divine love that will produce the intimacy of the indwelling.

The pious Israelite yearns, thirsts for Yahweh and delights in his presence: "As a hind longs for the running waters, so my soul longs for you, O God. Athirst is my soul for God, the living God" (Ps 42,2). "My soul thirsts for you like a parched land" (Ps 142,6). Only the intense presence of Yahweh in the Temple of light can slake the Israelites' longing:

"How I love your temple, Almighty God! How I want to be there! I long to be in the Lord's temple. With my whole being I sing for joy to the living God. . . . How happy are those who live in your temple" (Ps 84, 1-4).

The process of yearning and longing is finally over. Now the Hebrew has found his dwelling place and rests in the Lord, who is for him a fortress, a shield, a rock, a stronghold. These rugged metaphors, however, strongly suggestive of closeness and protection, are quickly toned down by the coziness of protective wings and the refreshment offered by a cool stream. All this and much more is Yahweh to the Israelite, as we can see magnificently brought out, for instance, in Ps 72: "I always stay close to you and you hold me by the hand. . . . Since I have you, what else could I want on earth? . . . . God is my strength . . . . As for me, how wonderful to be near God, to find protection with the sovereign Lord!" Now delightful rest ensues: "In the shadow of your wings I shout for joy. My soul clings fast to you, your right hand upholds me" (Ps 63,7-8). The proximity of God makes his light fall and reflect on the worshipper: "Look to him and be radiant. . taste and see how good the Lord is. Happy the man who takes refuge in him" (Ps 34,5.8).

And so, these two Old Testament streams, namely, those of physical nearness and of loving affection, run parallel for centuries and occasionally intermingle. God makes his presence felt in both places and persons. It is an intimate presence steeped in familiarity and affection. The Lord is near and the Lord is loving. Both these trends, once joined, will produce the marvel of the indwelling.

2) A LIVING PERSON DWELLS IN THE BODY

We shall have to start by squarely facing the fact that today the Holy Spirit means next to nothing to most Christians. When they think of God (if they think of him at all), it is usually as personalized in Jesus; rarely do they think specifically of the Father, and practically never of the Spirit. For them the Spirit is an intellectual superfluity that certainly exists "up there" somewhere, but who does not touch their lives in any way. The Holy Spirit is simply expendable. If one day -- if I am allowed to make use of an absurd parable-- we were told that the Holy Spirit has expired, that he is no more, it is more than likely that most of us would dismiss the news with an indifferent shrug of the shoulders: "He is dead — so what?" But the sudden disappearance of Jesus' eucharistic presence would undoubtedly deal a mortal blow to traditional, popular Catholicism. We simply cannot imagine our Church without any form of eucharistic worship. It is plainly unthinkable. But the Holy Spirit? Whether he is alive and well or diseased and dying, not to say dead, who cares?

The parable is obviously absurd and far too crude, and yet, it surely contains an element of truth in as much as it conveys a prevailing attitude of many of our Christian faithful, who really love Jesus Christ, are satisfied with a barely discernible nod to the Father and clearly forget about the Spirit. As the reputed Catholic theologian K. Rahner puts it, we are, by and large, no better than Old Testament Jews. They only knew of Yahweh, and their entire religious life turned around their strictly monotheistic God. For them there was only one God and only one person in God. Are we any better now? We have only to substitute Jesus for Yahweh and the result is much the same for many Christians. Jesus is the incarnation of God, he is God personified and rendered visible, he draws all our loving attention. We are called Christians and are deeply attached to Christ, certainly, but anything beyond Christ is shrouded in obscurity, it is enveloped in darkness — the darkness of ignorance and indifference. Our trinitarian faith is largely academic, abstract, theoretical, having no practical impact on our lives. Jesus suffices, the rest is nothing but an unnecessary complication. We ought to be congratulated for having so marvelously simplified our lives.[2]

2 This kind of practical reluctance to move beyond Jesus and specially to let the Holy Spirit enter and grip our lives is not restricted to the rank and file of the faithful, for the hierarchy too seems to a large extent to suffer from the same debilitating disease. It is embarrassing to recall that, compared to the endless flow of papal encyclicals on almost any topic, religious or secular, in the last 150 years we have had only one —*just one*! — encyclical on the Holy Spirit, *Divinum Illud*, and even that as far back as the reign of Pope Leo XIII in 1897.

Maybe part of the blame for this deplorable situation rests heavily on the New Testament itself. That both Jesus and the Father are living and distinct persons is something that nobody will doubt, for the gospels convey this at every turn; hence, to try and prove it would be labouring the obvious. But the same can hardly be said of the Holy Spirit. In a way it is most unfortunate that neither the biblical writers nor modern theologians seem to have been able to find a better term to refer to him than the unsatisfactory "Spirit". For in most languages this word seems to have an inbuilt vagueness that renders it so very elusive, so difficult to grasp. We usually speak of the spirit of this association, the mentality and spirit of that religious congregation, the spirit of the times and so forth. The meaning remains rather unspecified, somewhat blurred and undefined. As a consequence of this usage, we seem to unconsciously transfer the same lack of precision to the Spirit of God when we encounter him in Scripture — and this is a fatal mistake, for this sort of imprecision acts like a screen which prevents us from seeing that behind such an abstract, unappealing and generic term lies a living and loving person throbbing with life. It is not the spirit of God we often encounter in the New Testament, but rather the Spirit, capitalized, the Holy Spirit.

The present Pope, John Paul II, has very recently tried to somewhat make up for this shocking and protracted silence by issuing a new encyclical on the Holy Spirit, *Dominum et Vivificantem*, of 18 May 1986. It is reliably reported that, unlike his predecessors, he wrote the entire encyclical himself, personally. It shows. For, on the whole, it is a rather disappointing piece of work, at times excessively philosophical, unnecessarily long, rambling and repetitious. A keen observer will immediately detect three glaring omissions: nothing is said (apart from two or three biblical references without the slightest comment) on the climax of the Spirit's activity in the life of the Christian, namely, on his indwelling in the person of the baptized; then there is not a trace of the Oriental tradition which is so very rich as regards the doctrine of the Holy Spirit (apart from a few references to Oriental sources artificially added in the footnotes, almost certainly by a different hand); and finally, it is hard to understand why a modern encyclical on the Spirit does not breathe one word on the contemporary charismatic movement. This being the case, it is more than likely that the encyclical will not have much impact on the contemporary Christian world and will soon lapse into oblivion. The neglect of the Spirit, both at the popular and the official levels unfortunately continues.

Biblical authors, of course, did not make matters any easier by giving us such dull, colourless and specially such impersonal similes as wind or breath, fire, water and — worst of all — the dove. For the average Christian, unless he or she be very alert, is not likely to transcend these mediocre images and detect behind them the heart of a living person. Besides, we ought to remember that these biblical symbols do not primarily refer to the person of the Holy Spirit but rather to his function, his activity. When you pause and think of it, it is not easy to understand why the person of God should be compared to such impersonal elements as wind, water and fire. And what has the Almighty to do with such an insignificant creature as a pigeon?[3]

The cumulative damage of all this to the Christian has been serious. If the name "Spirit" is rather unsatisfactory, the biblical images associated with him are much worse still. As a result and for all practical purposes, the Holy Spirit has been rendered largely impersonal, as elusive as the symbols themselves, as difficult to grasp and retain as wind and water.

Precisely because the name "Spirit" is so imprecise, many Christians seem to reduce him to God in general or — specially — to Jesus himself. When Paul, for instance, speaks of the "Spirit of Jesus", many seem unconsciously to twist the meaning of the expression so as to identify it with the mentality, the interior disposition, the frame of mind of Jesus. They fail to understand that often enough, nearly always in fact, the expression refers, not to the interior attitude of Christ, but rather to another person, *distinct from Christ*. In their distorted view, to speak of the Spirit of Jesus is simply to speak of Jesus. The Holy Spirit, as a distinct person, has simply vanished, he has been swallowed up by Christ.

3 The meaning of this particular symbolism of the dove remains exceedingly obscure. The latest commentator of Luke's gospel, J. Fitzmyer, states dryly in connection with the scene of Jesus' baptism: "The precise significance of the dove has been the subject of much discussion. . . . There is no passage in the older literature in which the dove would be a clear and distinct symbol of the Holy Spirit" (*The Gospel according to Luke*, New York 1982, pp. 483-484). The origin of the symbol remains as obscure as its meaning. Twenty centuries of exegesis have been unable to dispel the darkness surrounding the famous dove. It is astonishing that Christianity has been using this symbol almost blindly, without even knowing what it really means.

In reality, the Spirit (with or without the adjective "Holy" attached to it, for this is secondary) is not Jesus, and Jesus is not the Spirit. Our desire for simplicity and fear of unnecessary complications should not drive us so far as to reduce both persons to one. For what right have we to arbitrarily distort the biblical message, which speaks of Christ *and* the Holy Spirit? Didn't Jesus himself, shortly before his departure to the Father, promise his disciples that he would send them "*another* Paraclete" (Jn 14,16), therefore different from Jesus himself? Are we so blind as to identify the gift with the giver? We usually experience no difficulty in grasping the full implications of the much-quoted passage from John's gospel: "God (the Father) so loved the world that he gave his only begotten Son" (Jn 3,16). Here the Father is the giver and the incarnate Son is his personal gift to us. Similarly, when the risen Christ fulfilled his promise on Easter Sunday and gave the Church the person of the Spirit, Christ was the giver and the Holy Spirit was the gift — both of them equally loving, divine and personal, certainly, but *distinct*. To practically identify the two (as many still do) would be as absurd as to reduce Christ and his Father to one single person.

There stands in old Goa the ancient Augustinian monastery of Sta. Monica, built by the Portuguese in the early 17th century. In one of the rooms of that massive building there is a rather peculiar painting of the Trinity as theologically significant as it is artistically mediocre. The passing of time and the moisture of many monsoons have not succeeded in obliterating the painting, still clearly discernible today: the Father is in the center, depicted, as usual, as a venerable old man with a white, flowing beard. To his right, a young man in his early thirties, well built and carrying a cross — obviously Jesus. To the Father's left and contrary to expectations, no dove, no gust of wind, no rushing waters, but another young man, similar to Jesus, but carrying no cross: the Holy Spirit. I love that painting.

One can, of course, object loudly to such a pictorial representation on the ground that this way of portraying the third person is false, for he never took up human flesh, as the second did. This is certainly correct, but then exactly for the same reason we should also object to the grossly anthropomorphic painting of the Father, who never appeared in human form either. There are obvious dangers in such artistic representations, no doubt, probably the greatest being that such paintings turn the one God into three distinct Gods, and this is plainly heretical. But the alternative seems to be equally bad, if not worse, namely, to reduce the triplicity of persons to one abstract God, undifferentiated and living alone in his majestic solitude. This may be almost the Old Testament Yahweh, but certainly not the Christian God revealed in the New Testament. Human language is and will always remain imperfect and clumsy, unable to grasp and express the infinite riches of God. Obviously, our inadequate literary expressions have to undergo a process of refinement and purification before they are applied to God. But what else can we do if not utilize the terminological tools at our disposal, no matter how imperfect in themselves? When speaking of God we can only stumble and stammer, but must we, as an alternative, keep silent?

Conscious, therefore, that our human speech will always fall far short of expressing accurately the divine reality, we should nevertheless explicitly believe, grasp and proclaim the existence of not just one or two but three distinct persons in God. The person of the Holy Spirit has a right to be included in the inner circle of God's family.

Furthermore, the Holy Spirit is far from being a remote person living in the inaccessible heavenly regions, behind the clouds and beyond reach. Far from it. On the contrary, the person of the Spirit *dwells within the sanctified Christian*, is continuously present in the most intimate recesses of his being. It is this astonishing, almost unbelievable proximity to man that goes under the name of indwelling. The Spirit breathes, lives and loves inside man. This is the wonder of baptismal sanctification. Not only has the glorified Christ given the Christian a share in his own personal life — the life he himself draws from the Father — but, far better still, Christ makes the Holy Spirit live within the person of the sanctified Christian.

A brief comparison with the Eucharist might be helpful here. For a long time now it has been an object of amazement to me to realize, on the one hand, how deeply attached the

Catholic faithful usually are to the mystery of the Eucharist, particularly to the belief that the glorified Christ is really and substantially present in the Eucharist; and to see, on the other, how ignorant and indifferent they generally are to the equally marvelous reality that God is continuously dwelling in them, within them, inside them. They are certainly not living tabernacles of Christ, as if they were carrying within themselves the glorified Christ of Easter, but they are in truth the temples of the Holy Spirit. Christ does not dwell in them with his own substance and person, but the Holy Spirit does.

Both these forms of presence, in the Eucharist and in the indwelling, are equally real, equally genuine, equally precious. I have often wondered why the immense majority of the faithful are so very appreciative of one and so neglectful of the other; why they love and cherish the presence of Jesus in the tabernacle and at the same time remain perfectly cold and indifferent as regards the presence — real, substantial presence — of the Holy Spirit within themselves. Is this neglect due to faulty catechetical instruction? Is it due to the fact that deep down they are not convinced that the Spirit is as living and loving a person as Christ himself? Is it that they find it difficult to believe in such an intimate presence within themselves? Whatever the reason — probably a mixture of all three — the fact remains that for the plain, unsophisticated faithful, the eucharistic Jesus is very close, as close as his mysterious Spirit is remote. Deplorable but true.

This widespread attitude of unaffected indifference with regard to the indwelling of the Spirit in man is all the more astonishing that, in a certain way, this form of presence surpasses in intensity and especially in duration the eucharistic presence. At the moment of eucharistic communion the intensity of union between the risen Christ and the communicant is very high, certainly, it is intimate and absorbing, but it does not last, it is fleeting and transitory; whereas the presence of the Holy Spirit within man is equally intense — even if usually not appreciated — and much more lasting, more permanent and durable. At least from the viewpoint of duration, the indwelling presence is therefore still more precious than Christ's eucharistic presence, even when the latter is interiorized through communion. Jesus is present in the tabernacle. The Holy Spirit is present within us. Both are divine, living persons, whose astonishing nearness to man is to be received with equal gratitude, equal thankful appreciation.

But there is more to it yet. Not only is the Spirit a distinct person, not only does he dwell in man, he specifically dwells in the *body of man.* It used to be said, not so very long ago — and one still sees traces of this mentality here and there — that the Spirit is "the guest of the soul", that he dwells in the soul of man. This insistence on the soul as the seat or dwelling place of the Spirit is certainly not very biblical, it seems to be rather Greek, that is, pagan, in origin. A slightly less objectionable, but still unsatisfactory expression is to say that God dwells "in the heart of man". Why not adhere more closely to biblical terminology and say instead that the Holy Spirit dwells in the body of man? It is not a soul or even the heart of man that is the hallowed shrine of the Spirit, but rather the totality of man with a special emphasis on the materiality of the body.

Man, the whole man, is the temple of the Spirit, the body included. This is but a touch of Hebrew realism from which the New Testament, particularly Paul, does not fail to draw important ethical conclusions. Given the rampant vice of debauchery in Greek society at that time, Paul lays heavy stress on the fact that it is precisely the body, seat of passion and lust, that is sanctified by the permanent presence of the Spirit. Paul makes use of this fundamental truth to convince his Corinthian Christians that the human body — one's own body or that of the neighbour, whether man or woman, for homosexuality was apparently as widespread as fornication — is sacred, sanctified by the Holy Spirit of God and carrier of the divine presence. Hence, improper use of the human body — any human body — amounts to a shameful desecration of God's temple. Let it suffice for the moment to point out this significant aspect of the Spirit's indwelling in man. We shall not fail to return to it later on and draw from it some important conclusions.

3) The fullness of the indwelling

The Holy Spirit is a living person who abides permanently

in the body of the baptized. But the question is sometimes raised as to the moment when God imparted his marvelous gift to humankind. We do have the gift now, that is sure, but does the indwelling of the Spirit begin with the Christian era? How were God's friends in the Old Testament sanctified? Were they also temples of the Holy Spirit, just as we are? Does the gift of the indwelling Spirit have a kind of retroactive effect that reaches far back into salvation history? Did the divine Spirit dwell in those mighty figures that strode the Old Testament scene like Abraham and Moses, David and Samuel, Amos and Isaiah?

This is a remarkably obscure question, and hence the solution offered cannot go beyond the realm of probability. It would seem, if we are to judge from certain scattered but significant references in the Bible, that the indwelling of the Spirit in man is a gift of the risen Christ to the Church, unknown before him. Those giants that stud the Old Testament sky like bright luminaries were certainly the friends of Yahweh, pleasing to him and acceptable in his sight, but it is not at all likely that they enjoyed the personal presence of the Spirit as we do now. There is a substantial, radical difference between their mode of sanctification and ours, with Christ's paschal mystery lying between them and us as the dividing line.

Certain scriptural indications point in this direction. Several important biblical themes develop gradually, from external beginnings to an interior consummation. The Old Testament knew the starting point of the gradual process of evolution, but not the climax. The important theme of sanctity, for instance — which will be expounded more fully in a later chapter — has originally only the meaning of separateness, of something or somebody cut off from the surrounding world and consecrated to God. At a much later stage, however, the very same notion is deepened and interiorized so as to convey the idea of an internal, personal transformation which was not noticeable in the early stages. The very same evolution is also discernible in the theme of divine filiation, which shifts from the original meaning of a communitarian and somewhat external relationship to God, to the strongly individual and internal sense the same word acquires in the New Testament. Other examples could be adduced, but it would be unnecessary, for the general trend of the evolution is always the same, from external foreshadowings to internal consummation.

Quite in keeping with this conception, the epistle to the Hebrews refers to the Law as a stage of growth and incompletion. There was something in the old economy of salvation that was still missing, a kind of unfulfilled promise: "The Law contains only the shadows of those blessings which were still to come, not the full expression of their reality" (Hebr 10,1). "They (the Old Testament saints) never saw the promise fulfilled; for us God had something better in store. We were to make the history of their lives complete" (Hebr 11,39-40).

The Old Testament is essentially the stage of an unfulfilled promise, straining towards the future but unable to grasp it. It is a forward movement with an elusive goal, a longing without satiation, a promise without fulfilment. And, in sharp contrast to all this, the New Testament speaks explicitly of the Holy Spirit as "the Spirit of the promise" (Eph 1,13), almost as if the Spirit, promised earlier, had been given only after Jesus' death and resurrection. It is only now that the long, drawn-out process comes finally to an end: the Spirit is not only promised but given, not only desired but enjoyed, no longer absent but present. This is the fullness of the indwelling which seems to be an exclusive privilege of the New Testament, a glorious gift reserved only for those who are born after the death and resurrection of Jesus. Calvary remains the source and origin of the indwelling.

a) *The inwardness of the Spirit's presence: Paul*

The mentality and personal opinions of an author can best be known from a careful study of the terms he uses. Words are pointers to ideas, they are an indication of what the author has in mind. So, in order to detect Paul's conception of the indwelling Spirit, one can do no better than scrutinize his language carefully, for his theological system is likely to be manifested in his expressions.

We usually are far too rough and lacking in the necessary nuances when speaking of God. As remarked above, we instinctively tend to attribute everything to Christ. Redemption, sanctification, salvation, grace, friendship, help, support, regret, repentance: the entire gamut of our spiritual attitudes is narrowly centred on Christ, or at most, on God in general. In itself, this is not a serious mistake, but on the other hand it does disclose a certain spiritual roughness, a lack of sensitivity to delicate nuances that are far from superfluous — unless we want to accuse the Bible of indulging in superfluities. A certain intellectual and spiritual finesse may be necessary to grasp these delicate shades of meaning, these tiny gleams of light that will ultimately illumine the entire landscape. The effort demanded in the enterprise is likely to prove extremely rewarding in the end.

When speaking of the indwelling Spirit, Paul makes use of a set of terms apparently so very trivial, so unimportant that, unless we are forewarned, we are likely to discard them as irrelevant. The Spirit is said *to dwell* in the Christian: "The Spirit of God really dwells in you" (Rom 8,9). "Don't you know that you are God's temple and that God's Spirit dwells in you?" (1 Cor 3,16). "The Holy Spirit... dwells within us" (2 Tim 1,14). Apart from Eph 3,17, which is but a solitary exception, Paul never says that Jesus dwells in the Christian; this function of permanent presence, this activity of hallowing by his personal presence the human body is reserved to the Holy Spirit. Let us not speak of Christ dwelling in us, for this is inaccurate and jarring to sensitive ears which are attuned to Pauline melodies. Let us not confuse persons or even functions that should remain clearly distinct, even if inseparable. It is the Spirit that dwells, not Christ.

The arrabhon or pledge. Here is another peculiar word which is not easy to render accurately in English. It signifies an assurance, a guarantee, or, better still, a partial down payment with the promise of a full payment to come later. If you intend buying a new house for a total sum of $50,000, you begin the transaction by putting down in hard cash, say, $10,000 as a tangible assurance that you mean business and that the rest of the payment will come later. Those $ 10,000 are the *arrabhon*, your pledge to the present owner of the house that you are serious about the whole transaction. Similarly, the Father, according to Paul, has given us the *arrabhon* of the indwelling Spirit wrapped in faith as a proof that eventually he will give us the fullness of the same Spirit, no longer enveloped in faith, but rather bathed in the splendours of a vision face to face that will be the payment of the full sum. And so the Holy Spirit is "the Spirit of the promise" (Eph 1,13) already fulfilled, certainly, but this peculiar fulfilment includes yet a further promise, the promise of the final and definitive completion.

In order to convey all this wealth of meaning, Paul says pithily: "You also, who have believed in him (Christ), were sealed with the promised Holy Spirit who is the guarantee (*arrabhon*) of our inheritance until we acquire full possession of it" (Eph 1,13-14). Similarly, Paul is tantalizingly putting before the Corinthians their future "building" in heaven, namely, their resurrected body, which lies yet in the future; then he adds: "He who has prepared us for this very thing is God (the Father) who has given us the Spirit as a guarantee (*arrabhon*)" (2 Cor 5,5). The presence within the Christian of this personal *arrabhon* which is the Holy Spirit necessarily thrusts the Christian forward, making him look ahead to his personal fulfilment in heaven. It is the indwelling Spirit that leads us towards our final destiny. He is our *arrabhon* and only he, not Jesus, nor his Father.

The seal, or *to seal*. "Do not grieve the Holy Spirit, by whom you were sealed for the day of redemption" (Eph 4,30). "You...were sealed with the Spirit of the promise" (Eph 1,13). Another peculiar function of the Spirit and one extremely suggestive. According to this imagery, somewhat crude but extremely powerful, the Father seals us by applying the Holy Spirit directly to us, just as you imprint a seal on a piece of soft wax. We bear the image of God in us precisely because of the seal imprinted on us, namely, the Holy Spirit. Now we are marked, branded for eternity as the clear possession of God. Paul will never say that we are sealed either by the Father or by Jesus, but always and only by the Holy Spirit.

Finally, not to make this list of peculiar Pauline terms too long, *to sanctify*—a very common word, much used and abused in some spiritual circles. As we shall see later more in detail, this is one of the biblical terms that through constant repetition and thoughtless use has lost much of its original lustre. As regards the person who is said to sanctify us, Paul is rather flexible: if he is speaking of the Passion in general he will attribute our sanctification to Christ, but in the context of the indwelling it is not Christ but the Spirit who is said to sanctify the Christian. "We are bound to give thanks to God... because God chose you...to be saved through sanctification by the Spirit" (2 Thess 2,13). Paul is a "minister of Christ Jesus to the Gentiles...so that the offering of the Gentiles may be...sanctified by the Holy Spirit" (Rom 15,16). After all, it is not for nothing that the Spirit is known in Christian tradition as the *Holy* Spirit, namely, the sanctifier *par excellence*. Jesus laid the foundation through his Passion, but here and now, in the concrete, it is the Spirit that sanctifies the Christian.

To dwell, to pledge, to seal, to sanctify: four different expressions, all of them pregnant with meaning and extremely suggestive, which Paul applies exclusively to the indwelling Holy Spirit. By itself this is enough to show that there is something very distinctive, though difficult to grasp and express accurately, in this presence of the living Spirit in the Christian. In the biblical passages quoted above Paul uses indiscriminately three expressions: "The Spirit of God (the Father)", "the Spirit of Christ" and "the Holy Spirit". All three are perfectly synonymous expressions that should not puzzle the reader, for all of them refer to one and the same Holy Spirit. Richness and variety of expression in the writer should not produce confusion in the reader.

But how did Paul come to this perfectly astounding notion, that the very person of God dwells in man as in a temple? Is this really credible, or was Paul dreaming? For he seems to have been the first biblical writer to state this doctrine explicitly. Is he echoing previous Jewish tradition or breaking new ground?

Paul was a profound thinker, not a fanciful dreamer. He was thoroughly conversant with previous biblical conceptions, but in the light of his personal Damascus experience he deepens and interiorizes the patrimony of his ancestors. As regards the question under consideration, Paul seems to have been heir to a twofold tradition. He benefits from two streams that run throughout the Old Testament, streams that are eventually crystallized into two themes: the temple and the covenant.

Writing to the Corinthians, Paul recalls a thought that apparently belonged to the first Christian catechesis. It was part of the Jewish tradition that in the last times God would erect a new, glorious and perfect temple in which he would dwell: "See how I lay in Sion a stone of witness, a precious cornerstone, a foundation stone; the believer will not stumble" (Is 28, 16). For the pious Jew the Jerusalem Temple is the house of God, the place where he dwells in the midst of his People. Within the Temple, the holy of holies, and particularly the mercy seat on top of the Ark, is the tabernacle of his presence. The Jerusalem Temple will eventually be razed to the ground by the invading Roman legions, but at the time of Paul it still stood, tall and majestic, as a constant reminder to the Israelites that Yahweh had not deserted them, that, in fact, he was dwelling in their midst.

All this was common knowledge at that time. But primitive Christianity regarded the prophecy concerning the future temple as already fulfilled. On the other hand, a man-made temple is impossible for the last times. A very ancient oral tradition, which probably can be traced back to Jesus himself, proclaimed openly that God was no longer interested in material temples of brick and mortar. The real temple, the dwelling place of God, is not a dead structure but living man. In his long speech before his execution (witnessed and approved by Saul) Stephen, the first Christian martyr, told the surrounding Jews that "it was Solomon that built the house for him (God). Yet the Most High does not dwell in houses made with hands; as the prophet says, 'Heaven is my throne and earth my footstool. What house will you build for me, says the Lord...?' " (Ac 7,47-49). Hadn't Jesus himself said, as reported by Mark, that the real temple was not the one built by Solomon, but rather his own body, to be raised three days after his death?

The process, therefore, which aimed at personalizing and interiorizing the imagery of the temple was already afoot when, approximately a quarter of a century after Jesus, Paul wrote to his Christians in Corinth as a reminder of something that they already knew: "Don't you know that *you are God's temple* and that God's Spirit dwells in you?...For God's temple is holy, and that temple you are" (1 Cor 3,16-17). Paul seems to have attached considerable importance to this doctrine, for in the same letter he comes back to the same idea even more pointedly: "Do you not know that your body is a temple of the Holy Spirit within you, whom you have from God?" (1 Cor 6,19). A few years later he will insist again on the same point: "We are the temples of the living God" (2 Cor 6,16). It matters little that sometimes for Paul it is rather the Christian community that is the temple of the Spirit, whereas at other times he will consider the body of the single Christian as the place where the Holy Spirit dwells. The shift is now complete: it is not so much the material structure of the temple that is the shrine of God, but rather the person of the baptized Christian.

Along with the idea of the temple, it is the all-important theme of the covenant that will eventually lead Paul, through a gradual process of interiorization, to the indwelling of the Spirit in man. When writing to the Corinthians for the second time (2 Cor 6,16), Paul is echoing the Old Testament Covenant which had originally been made by Moses by sprinkling blood on the altar, representing Yahweh, and on the People. The blood of animals, as a telling symbol of life, unites the People to Yahweh with a permanent bond of fidelity and submission: "My dwelling shall be with them; I shall be their God.... Ever present in your midst, I shall be your God, and you will be my people" (2 Cor 6,16, quoting the Old Testament). The intimate connection between the presence or dwelling of God and the Covenant was well known centuries before Paul. But he now takes up this connection and deepens it: God will be their God and they shall be his People not because of the symbol of blood as vehicle of God's own life poured on the People, but rather because *God himself will dwell in them.* The link between God and his People is no longer blood or even life, but rather the very person of God dwelling in them. This is the real Covenant, based on the intimacy of God's personal presence within the People, namely, on the indwelling. The Covenant has been deepened and interiorized.

This framework of the Covenant between Yahweh and his People explains the remarkable ecclesial or communitarian dimension of the indwelling in Paul. Already in the Old Testament the outpouring of the Spirit had been promised primarily to the community of Israel, and now Paul keeps up the very same ecclesial, social dimension. It is primarily the Church that is the recipient and beneficiary of the indwelling, and the individual Christian only in as far as he belongs to the ecclesial body.

The Old Testament, therefore, supplies Paul with the raw materials, the granite blocks with which he will build this magnificent conception of the Spirit's indwelling. No, Paul is definitely not a dreamer, but a builder who receives his materials from the past, chisels and polishes them up and makes them fit into a new structure which is solid, attractive, impressive: the dwelling presence of the Holy Spirit within the person of the sanctified Christian. This is the real temple where God dwells.

Paul is absolutely firm on this, he does not waver. Many, perhaps most, of his letters bear the stamp of a concrete situation to which the letter is addressed, but when he writes to the Roman community, which he has never visited, he has obviously to rise above the level of local problems. It is in his letter to the Romans that we find the fullest expression of his teaching on the indwelling Spirit. The eighth chapter of this Pauline epistle is a real gem on the subject of the Holy Spirit, and every single author will have later to refer to it as to a guiding star to illumine his faltering steps on this fascinating subject.

Romans 8,1-11 especially is a very dense passage which has given rise to a variety of translations, some of them no more than fairly inept paraphrases of Paul's thought. Paul has just described in the previous chapter man's dramatic struggle before being sanctified by Christ. On the one hand, man knows only too well where his obligations lie, for his mind is sharp and clear. But he lacks the necessary strength to fulfill them. And nobody, apart from Christ, will supply him with the strength that he so badly needs. He feels fettered by the power of sin, innate in him, which drags him down. He would honestly like to submit to God's law but is unable to do so. He is inexorably sliding down on the path of sin that eventually might lead him to death and damnation.

He feels constrained by a strange force that dwells within him and overpowers him. Much against his will he submits to this extraneous force that is firmly lodged in him. He sees nothing but darkness, engulfed as he is by the gloomy atmosphere of his natural weakness, enveloping sin and eventual death. And so he bursts out desperately, "Wretched man that I am! who will deliver me from this body of death?" (Rom 7,24).

But now suddenly the oppressive gloom vanishes, the dark cloud disappears. Instead of darkness there is light, the blinding light of the Spirit. In sharp contrast to the depressing atmosphere of Romans 7, with nothing but a constant, futile struggle without respite, Romans 8 is bathed in light, life and peace. The transition has been sudden and totally unexpected. Now it is no longer the damning power of sin that dwells in man, pulling him down, but rather the strength of the Holy Spirit, who has taken possession of him and acts from within him. The very strength of God wipes out his weakness, and the light of God dispels his darkness. Now there is no anxiety, but quiet assurance, no fear but hope, no death but life. The root of this radical transformation is the fact that now the Holy Spirit dwells within man. The struggle is over and peace ensues.

Christians "are in Christ Jesus" (v.1) and "Christ is in you" (v.10): it is a mutual immanence in the glorified Lord, as we saw above. But this engrafting, this incorporation into the risen Christ results in the intimate presence within the Christian of "the Spirit of life" (v. 2), the Holy Spirit that infuses divine life in torrents. Now the Christian breathes and lives the very life of God which becomes his own possession. Because he is controlled by the Spirit, no longer by sin, he experiences within himself "life and peace" (v.6).

Paul is certainly optimistic, for, addressing people he does not know personally — except a handful lovingly mentioned at the end of the latter — he assumes that they live according to the Christian principles and that therefore the Holy Spirit continues to dwell in them: "But you are not in the flesh, you are in the Spirit, since the Spirit of God really dwells in you" (v. 9), suffusing your life and guiding your conduct. Now the Holy Spirit has dislodged the power of sin and consequently the regenerate Christian is no longer subject to an impersonal power of sin, but to the person of the Spirit, living and acting within him. This inner presence of the Spirit means a "settled, permanent, penetrative influence"[4] which reaches to the last recesses of man.

Without in any way indulging in unnecessary hair-splitting, one should remark that Paul in this passage of Romans uses two distinct expressions when referring respectively to the Spirit and to Christ. He says that "Christ (is) in you" (v.10), but the Spirit "dwells in you" (vv. 9.11). Obviously, in the work of men's sanctification the glorified Christ and the Holy Spirit act in perfect unison, but each of them performs a different function. Christ is in the Christian, but the Spirit *dwells* in him (repeated emphatically three times in three verses). If the functions of Christ and the Holy Spirit are identical, as some pretend, why does Paul reserve a special term for the Spirit? Does not this carefully selected and consistent phraseology rather strongly suggest that our relationships with Christ and with the Spirit, though intimately connected, remain distinct? Christ does not dwell, but the Spirit does. The difference may look somewhat subtle to the reader, but it is certainly important, and when confronted with the post-biblical tradition this difference in roles, far from being abolished, will rather be confirmed.

"The *Spirit is your life* because of righteousness" (v.10). We have seen before that Paul refers to the Spirit as "the Spirit of life" (v. 2), and now, quite logically, since the Spirit dwells within the Christian, he becomes the principle of the Christian's life. The baptized Christian has within himself the very source of life: divine life, gushing forth from within him, spreads out in an irresistible flood throughout his whole being; his entire person is penetrated, soaked in life, the life of the Spirit. The Christian has attained righteousness, namely, he has been sanctified by the Holy Spirit taking full and complete possession of him. In this sense, his sanctification is a mystery of life. Now he is gripped from within by the Spirit of life — and so he lives with the very life of God.

4. C. Cranfield, *The Epistle to the Romans. International Critical Commentary* (Edinburgh 1975), p. 388.

Paul's thought and expression can be compact, but Rom 8,11 is an extreme case of conciseness. As Paul dictated his letter — he never wrote the letters himself except possibly the salutations and final greetings — thoughts seem to come tumbling out one upon the other, creating in the reader an impression of bewilderment: "If the Spirit of him who raised Jesus from the dead dwells in you, he who raised Christ Jesus from the dead will give life to your mortal bodies also through his Spirit who dwells in you".

A solid, meaty verse if there ever was one. Paul's thought here is entirely trinitarian, for the circumlocution "he who raised him from the dead" obviously refers to the Father, whereas Christ and the Spirit are mentioned explicitly and repeatedly. The Father raised Jesus from the dead, and since the Holy Spirit dwells in you (repeated here for the fourth and fifth time), the Father will also raise your mortal bodies just as he raised Jesus'. Palu's original expression is somewhat ambiguous, but he seems to say, not only that our bodies will be raised because they are now the temples of the Spirit (and this, when viewed against the totality of his doctrine would certainly make perfect sense), but deeper than that, that our resurrection will be effective precisely *through* the Spirit. In other words, the Holy Spirit, who hallows our bodies now, will be the personal agent of our future resurrection. The Father will bring us back to life by means of the Spirit almost as if he had commissioned the Spirit to perform in his name this miracle of final vivification. Hence, according to Paul, the role of the Spirit with regard to our personal bodies is twofold: he sanctifies them now by dwelling in them; and he will vivify them later by resurrecting them. The present sanctification and the future vivification of man are both the work of the Spirit. This shows to what an extent man is suffused with, penetrated by the Spirit. Once possessed by the Spirit of life, he will live, he will not die. The indwelling is a mystery of God's own life shared with man.

Rome, the capital city of the Empire, may have been unknown to Paul at the time he wrote his letter to the Romans. but Corinth certainly was not. A maritime centre of the first rank and the necessary crossroads of all commerce between the eastern and the western Mediterranean, Corinth could hardly have been a paragon of virtue. In fact, the very word *korinthiazesthai*, to live like a Corinthian, was synonymous with drunken immorality and pagan debauchery. Overlooking the city, right on top of the hill of the Acropolis, there stood the temple of Aphrodite, the goddess of love. To this temple were attached more than a thousand priestesses or sacred prostitutes who regularly swooped down on the lustful Corinthians to ply their carnal trade.[5]

The Corinthian Christians, living in an atmosphere that connived at and even encouraged sexual license, certainly knew from personal experience what riotous living was. Paul's list of the Corinthians' sins makes grim reading: idolatry, greed, robbery, drunkenness, fornication, prostitution, homosexuality. The Corinthian Christians came from such a morass of vice. Many of the above sins were committed in the body, and the body should be the temple of the Spirit, rather than the seat of sexual pleasure. The libertinism of the Corinthians was based on the principle that nothing done in the body really matters, therefore anything and everything may be done. They contended that, just as the transient, ephemeral character of food justified complete freedom from dietary laws as regards physical appetite, so also sexual appetite could be satisfied by the indiscriminate use of one's sexual powers.

This is the necessary background to understand the stinging rebuke contained in *Corinthians 6,12-20.* The root cause of the problem is the misuse of the body, and it is therefore on the body that Paul will centre his attention. Paul's language is sharp and direct to the point of bluntness: "Do you not know that your bodies are members of Christ? Shall I therefore take the members of Christ and make them members of a prostitute? Never! Do you not know that he who joins himself to a prostitute becomes one body with her?" (vv. 15-16). Fornication and prostitution desecrate the human body, whose owner is Christ, not a prostitute. One should physically cling to the risen Christ, not to a harlot.

5 For a more detailed description of the rampant immorality prevailing in Corinth at the time of Paul, see my previous book, *Body Broken and Blood Shed* (Anand 1986), pp. 192-3.

These two extremes presented by Paul could hardly be more contradictorily opposed.

Yet Paul is not satisfied. As if afraid that his message was not clear enough, he tackles the same problem from a slightly different angle, and makes use of a line of argument even more compelling. The Christian who indulges in such shameful behaviour not only dishonours Christ, but acts against the Spirit of Christ. "Every other sin which a man commits is outside the body; but the immoral man sins against his own body. Do you not know that your body is *the temple of the Holy Spirit within you*, whom you have from God?" (vv. 18-19). In other words, sexual licenciousness desecrates the very shrine where the Spirit dwells. The prostitute is preferred to the Holy Spirit, and the Spirit's temple is handed over to a whore. This is the absurdity of the Corinthians' behaviour. On the contrary, their sexual control should be motivated and based upon the fact of the Spirit's indwelling. An upright moral behaviour in the area of sexuality should rest on the presence of the Holy Spirit within the Christian.[6]

b) *The warmth of the Spirit's presence: John*

The other New Testament author who sheds considerable light on the comforting doctrine of the indwelling of the Spirit is John. But whereas Paul was heir primarily to the Old Testament trend that emphasized God's quasi-physical proximity to man conveyed by metaphors like dwelling and temple, John echoes rather the other Old Testament theme of divine

6 In the above section I have prescinded entirely from the technical problem still debated among exegetes, whether Paul had a clear idea of the Holy Spirit's distinct personality. Did he conceive the Spirit as a distinct, divine person, or merely as a poetic personification in the light of the Old Testament? The question remains open and debatable, but, despite Paul's fluid notion of personality, it would seem that he did perceive the Spirit as a distinct person. Numerous passages in which he enumerates in the same breath the Father, Jesus and the Spirit seem to support this contention. One such text, for instance, is our familiar introduction to the Mass, "The grace of Our Lord Jesus Christ, the love of God (the Father), and the fellowship of the Holy Spirit be with you all" (2 Cor 13,14). There are many other such passages, like 2 Cor 1,21-22; 1 Cor 6,11; Rom 5,1-5; Gal 4,4-6, etc.

familiarity and intimate affection. Paul conceived the indwelling along the lines of physical nearness, whereas for John it is rather a personal relationship with God suffused with love. Probably a full, comprehensive understanding of the doctrine requires that we fuse both the conceptions into one. Proximity without love and affection would clearly be as unsatisfactory as intense love without presence would be insufficient. An extraordinary inwardness of the Spirit within man steeped in an enveloping atmosphere of intimacy and loving affection: this is the comprehensive description of the indewlling of the Spirit.

It is the month of Nisan, and Jesus together with the Twelve is celebrating the Passover banquet in grateful commemoration of the Israelites' deliverance from Egypt under the leadership of Moses many centuries earlier. It was on that occasion that, according to John, Jesus respectively promised and gave to his disciples his best two parting gifts: the Holy Spirit and the Eucharist.

John 14,15-23 is an extremely rich section deceptive in its apparent simplicity. The language is simple enough, but this simplicity of expression covers a wealth of meaning. The future sending of the Spirit is presented as the result of Jesus' petitionary prayer to his Father. His prayer is always efficacious; hence, such a prayer now is, for all practical purposes, equivalent to a promise. Whereas for Paul the giver of the Spirit is the Father, for John it is Christ who bestows the Spirit on the Church. Jesus will reiterate the promise: "When the Counsellor comes, *whom I shall send to you*" (Jn 15,26). "If I do not go away, the Counsellor will not come to you; but if I go *I shall send him to you*" (Jn 16,7). For John, the Spirit is the gift of Jesus to his disciples.

Counsellor? It is rather unfortunate that there seems to be no exact English rendering of the Greek term *Parakletos*. This is John's favourite term to signify the Spirit, and all the different shades of meaning conveyed by the term can hardly be captured by one single word. *Parakletos* covers at least three different meanings: attorney, advocate or counsellor in a court of law; intercessor, mediator or spokesman, and hence, helper or friend; and finally, comforter or consoler. Since no single English word can convey this wealth of meaning, it might be better to retain the original word and refer to him simply as the Paraclete.[7]

He is "the Spirit of truth" (v. 17), Jesus says, both because he is truth personified and because he imparts truth to the disciples, just as Jesus said he is the bread of life both because he is himself life and especially because he is the source of life for others. In the Johannine conception, "Spirit of truth" seems to imply, on the one hand, the idea that the Spirit is the fullness of revelation, the means by which the disciples will avoid falling into the trap of error: "By this we know the Spirit of truth and the spirit of error" (1 Jn 4,6). The Spirit is the channel through which light pours into the Church. The Spirit of truth illumines, radiates light and dispels darkness. With the Spirit of truth in her midst, the Church glows and glitters. He is the Spirit of genuineness and discernment that will help the disciple to distinguish the solidity of truth from the fickleness and mutations of untruth, the genuine product from a fake and a counterfeit.

But, on the other hand, the Spirit of truth, in typically biblical fashion, implies also the idea of firmness, stability, fidelity. He is a Spirit that can be leaned upon, trusted, because he is reliable and trustworthy. He is the personification of God's own unshakable faithfulness and persevering permanence. The Spirit is simply a rock of stability. Hence, Jesus was promising the disciples a Spirit of light and strength, of discernment and stability, of illumination and firmness. He is the Spirit of truth.

The world may not know the Spirit, but the disciples "will know him" (v. 17), not in the trite, superficial sense of a theoretical intellectual knowledge, as we know chemistry or astronomy. Biblically, to know somebody means to experience, touch, taste, relish him. For instance, "Adam knew Eve, his wife, and she conceived" (Gen 4,1). The expression means, not only conceptual apprehension but also experiential affection; not only an infusion of light but also an onrush of

7 I said, deliberately, "to refer to *him*", for as regards the personality of the Spirit in John there is no dispute. All exegetes agree that John did conceive the Holy Spirit as a distinct person, not merely as a personification of God along Old Testament lines.

love. The Hebrew knows with his mind and with his heart; it is a knowledge that includes both mental grasp and — specially — affective experience. Not only the mind, but the whole of the person "knows". It is affective knowledge pervaded by love. And this is the way the disciples of Jesus will know the Holy Spirit: they will love, taste and relish him, they will experience his presence deep down inside themselves, not up there beyond the clouds. Let it suffice for the moment to point this out briefly but clearly; further on we shall not fail to draw some important conclusions that flow from this notion of biblical knowledge.

Now John gives us the real foundation, the fundamental reason which explains this marvelous experiential knowledge of the Spirit, and he does it with astonishing simplicity: "...for *he will be in you*" (v. 17). How much John has given us in this simple sentence! The Spirit is not next to the Christian as a counsellor whispering to him what to do and what to avoid; he is not just very near to him, though outside him. The Spirit is *in* him, inside him, dwelling in him, occupying, possessing the most intimate recesses of his person. Now the Christian becomes the bearer of the Holy Spirit, his living temple. "The Spirit of truth fills them inwardly....The disciples know him because they possess him inwardly".[8] This is the wonder of the indwelling, which makes us living tabernacles, consecrated, sealed by God's personal presence.

Perhaps a familiar liturgical simile will clarify this fundamental truth further. In certain parishes where the Easter vigil ceremonies are performed by three ministers, shortly before midnight they, together with the faithful, assemble just outside the church or temple which is kept in darkness. After the blessing of the fire and the lighting of the Easter candle, the procession is formed and, to the joyous singing of the traditional "Light of Christ", the congregation marches into the church, with the three ministers bringing up the rear. Once the three ministers — three distinct persons — are inside the temple, the lights are switched on and the temple is suddenly flooded with light. Now the temple is both illumined and — of particular importance to us now —

8 R. Schnackenburg, *The Gospel according to St John*, III, p. 75.

indwelt by three living persons. Need I explain the imagery further? So also, through faith and baptism, the disciple of Jesus has the three divine persons in him, inside him, dwelling in him. He has become the temple of God, flooded with grace and sanctified by a triple divine presence.

But let us return to John. The disciples "know" the Spirit because the Spirit is in them. The intimate presence is the foundation of experiential, affective knowledge. This is the way things should be, not the way things are. Unfortunately, given the general, widespread ignorance of this doctrine of the indwelling among Christians, the reality in most cases is but a travesty of the truth, almost a caricature of what John — and Jesus — wanted the disciples to be. The disciple is expected to know and understand and then relish the presence of the Spirit within him. In reality he does have the indwelling, but he is totally unaware of its existence, blissfully ignorant that he is the temple of the Spirit of God living inside him. There is presence without knowledge, and therefore without relish and conscious experience. The truth of the divine indwelling has made absolutely no impression on him, he seems to be entirely unaffected by it. The Spirit is there, all right, he lives within the Christian, but the Christian, foolishly, thinks — if he thinks at all — that all this is but a fairy tale, a poetical imagery not to be taken literally.

The real presence of Jesus under bread and wine, that is a most solid, consoling tenet of our Christian faith; but a real presence of the Holy Spirit within the disciple can be safely put aside as poetical license. It would seem that Jesus has wasted his time in promising and giving us a gift that is not appreciated because it is not known. Most Christians are in this respect no better than the original disciples on the first Easter Sunday, unable to believe, for the news conveyed to them is simply too good to be true. By and large, the indwelling of the Spirit in the person of the disciple is not taken too seriously; it is hardly believed.

And so the Spirit, though present and dwelling in the Christian, continues to be ignored and pushed aside, like a guest who is physically present inside the house, but neglected by all and attended by none. The indwelling of the Spirit remains for most Christians an unknown — and therefore unappreciated and unloved — treasure. Exceedingly precious in itself, no doubt, but who knows about it? This indifferent attitude of the average Christian would make John wince.

John's message has been imparted in words whose simplicity is matched by their depth, and now he returns once again to the same theme: "If a man loves me...my Father will love him and we will come to him and *make our home with him*" (Jn 14,23). The indwelling again, under a slightly different imagery. Notice that, as repeatedly stated above, the indwelling is promised here enveloped in an atmosphere of mutual love between the Father and Jesus, on the one hand, and the disciple on the other. It is warmth and affection that surrounds the Spirit's presence in the Christian. It all seems to hinge on the disciple's love for Jesus, for this love is said to produce the indwelling; but this is highly deceptive, for the disciple's love for Jesus has been preceded by the Father's love for the disciple: "This is what love is: it is not that we have loved God (the Father) but that he loved us..." (1 Jn 4,10). The indwelling of God may be preceded by the love of the disciple for God, but the disciple's love is in turn preceded by the Father's gratuitous love for him. The disciple does not initiate the process of love that leads to the indwelling; he can only react to the initiative taken spontaneously by the Father. Hence the disciple — even the loving disciple — can only receive the indwelling with a grateful heart, he cannot possibly bring it about.

It is the Father and the Son that, in the midst of this surrounding atmosphere of love and affection, come to the disciple to dwell in him. The plural used ("*we* shall come") is deceptive: here John has in mind only the Father and the Son — the Spirit is not referred to, possibly because his indwelling presence has already been mentioned earlier on.

According to John, the Holy Spirit remains necessarily and emphatically the *Spirit of Christ*, not only because he proceeds from the Son, but also because he is given to the Church by the risen Christ and leads the disciples to Christ. The Holy Spirit has rightly been called the Spirit of self-effacement that points to Christ, rather than to himself. "He will teach you all things" (Jn 14,26), says Jesus. He will not teach you new things but rather help you to deepen, interiorize and assimilate the teachings of Christ. He will not teach you in extension but in depth, he will not impart to the disciple a string of truths, but rather a thorough penetration and personal assimilation of the message of Christ. The Spirit's activity will not be sidewise but depthwise, for he is and remains the Spirit of truth, of genuineness and depth, opposed to fickleness and superficiality. He is like John the Baptist, a pointer to Christ, a messenger who makes the disciple attached to Christ. If a disciple claims to be indwelt and led by the Spirit and yet does not grow deeply attached to Christ, he may be guided by some other spirit, but certainly not by the Holy Spirit, who is essentially the Spirit of Jesus Christ.

One thing should stand out clearly now, at the end of this fairly long scriptural exposé: the strictly personal character of the indwelling. It is always a divine Person (or Persons, as in John) that turns the believer into a temple of God. It is a person receiving a Person, and a Person possessing a person. Later theology will make these sharply personalistic features somewhat blurred and hazy by speaking of the indwelling of the "Trinity". In the New Testament it is not the Trinity — the term is not scriptural — but rather the Father, the Son and their common Spirit, three living and loving persons, who delight in coming to the believer and turning him into their personal temple, their dwelling place.

4) The voice of the East

Quoting the contemporary French theologian Y. Congar, the present Pope has more than once spoken of the "two lungs of the Church" universal, namely, the East and the West. In a healthy body both the 'lungs' are of equal size and equal importance, and man breathes with equal ease through both. When applied to the body of the Church, however, the analogy limps, for the two 'lungs' happen to be of equal importance in theory, but of very unequal size in reality. The western lung is almost overdeveloped, whereas its eastern counterpart at times gives the impression of having collapsed. Nowadays the western or Latin Church is certainly massive in size, structure and organization, whereas the eastern Church looks tiny indeed by comparison.

In the early centuries, however, it was certainly not so. Already at that time the West witnessed the increasing claims of superiority on the part of Rome, but this self-assertion was kept in check by an extremely independent eastern spirit. Oriental writers would claim that both the Churches, East and West, were sisters of equal worth in the eyes of God, and that therefore there should be no question of juridical superiority of one over the other. The undeniable Latin genius might have proved of considerable help to Rome to develop its claims in other domains, but as regards the doctrine of the Holy Spirit it is rather the West that has to bow to the East, for the latter could rightly boast of profound developments and penetrating insights that were not matched by corresponding perceptions in the West. With regard to the Holy Spirit and his function in the person of the Christian, one has to acknowledge that the East reigns supreme.

It is most unfortunate that such treasures of theology and spirituality seem to be hardly known by the rank and file of the faithful of the Latin Church, even by those born and brought up in the East, who therefore should know and appreciate their eastern roots better than they actually do. The early Oriental writers are second to none when expounding the marvels connected with the indwelling of the Holy Spirit. Their doctrine in this regard can be summarized under three headings: the Spirit as link of union; the Spirit and the sanctification of the Christian; and the Spirit as engraver of the divine image.

a) *The Spirit, link of union*

When seeing this heading very likely the reader will have the impression that he or she knows all about it. For, is it not common knowledge repeated over and over again in most of the spiritual and even technical literature on the subject, that the Holy Spirit is like a golden link uniting Father and Son? Is he not, after all, the link of love between the other two divine persons, the solidified, as it were, personalized torrent of love flowing from the Father to the Son and back?

All this is commonly asserted, but this is not at all what the Oriental writers mean by the expression "Spirit, link".

Through constant, and to some extent thoughtless, mechanical repetition we have come to associate the Holy Spirit with love, primarily because — we contend — it is he who brings about a union of love between Father and Son in the internal life of the Trinity. As a consequence, we keep up the very same contention when referring to the activity of the Spirit on the Christian. He simply continues to be the Spirit of love, like a channel through which the love of God pours out on humankind.

Very plausible, no doubt, and in itself possibly correct, this conception of the person of the Spirit is hardly biblical and certainly not very Oriental. The Latin Church to which most of us belong has been influenced in this regard by St Augustine to a considerable degree, and Augustine is a western, not an eastern author. The connection between the Spirit and love has surely become exceedingly popular nowadays, and echoes of it are found even in the Church's official liturgy, but this connection is only mildly biblical. According to the entire Bible, the Spirit is primarily a Spirit of power, strength and might rather than the Spirit of love. The characteristic of the Holy Spirit is not so much love as power. The biblical passages connecting the Spirit with love are extremely few, outnumbered by far by those making him rather the vehicle of divine power operative in man. St Augustine builds up an impressive trinitarian scheme based on the connection Spirit-love, but at the end he ruefully acknowledges: "Scripture does not tell us 'The Spirit is love'. If it had, the present inquiry would be considerably shortened".[9]

Therefore, the popular conception that almost automatically links the Holy Spirit with love may be theologically correct and even reasonable, but it is certainly not "catholic" in the sense of universal, for this conception seems to have flourished almost exclusively in the West, not in the East. Eastern writers, when speaking of the Holy Spirit, seem to have a conception of their own which is possibly closer to the biblical line than that of the West. The Spirit, according to them, is not so much the internal bond of love in the unfathomable bosom of the Trinity, as rather the link between God

9 *De Trinitate*, XV, 17.

and man. The Spirit is not turned inwardly to God's own trinitarian life, but outwardly towards men. The linking function performed by him is not that of connecting Father and Son, but rather that of joining both of them to the Christian.

This conception can best be characterized by the pattern of the straight line, a descending line that goes from the Father, passes through the Son and terminates in the Spirit. Most of the beautiful comparisons used by these eastern writers become perfectly clear if we keep in mind this vertical scheme. For instance, one of the most renowned Oriental thinkers, St Gregory of Nyssa, makes use of a delightful simile: "It is as if a man were to see a separate flame burning on three torches: we will suppose that the third flame is caused by that of the first being transmitted to the middle, and then kindling the end torch".[10] It is almost like the imagery of the Easter vigil mentioned above: the main celebrant lights his own candle first, and then passes the flame to the second minister who in turn transmits it to the third. The light is passed on in a straight, descending line. Similarly, "a transmission of power, beginning from the Father advancing to the Son and completed in the Holy Spirit....For like grace flows down in an unbroken stream from the Father through the Son and the Spirit..."[11] It is a perpendicular cascade of life that gushes out from the Father and passing through the Son reaches the Holy Spirit and eventually the Christian.

Obviously, the three divine persons invade the body of the believer simultaneously, but from the logical point of view it is the Spirit who comes first, it is he who is the first occupant of the heart of man. The Spirit is poured down by the Son who is the immediate source of the Spirit. This is voiced eloquently by one of the most prestigious Oriental writers, St Cyril, bishop of Alexandria, in Egypt: "It is for this end that Christ says the disciples had to be sanctified by the Father, who causes the Holy Spirit to dwell in them through the Son....For the Spirit does not flow to us in any other way except from the Father through the Son".[12]

10 *On the Holy Spirit*, in *Nicene and Post-Nicene Fathers*, Vol. V (Oxford 1893), p. 17.
11 *Ibid.*, p. 233.
12 *In Joannem*, XI, 10; XII, 1; *Patrologia Graeca* (PG) 74, 540 and 711.

Elsewhere Cyril is even more eloquent: "Wiping out the sins of the one who clings to him, the Son anoints him with his own Spirit, *whom he inserts into the believer*...and whom he pours out on us from his own substance".[13] This passage is marvelously compact. The Son anoints the Christian, pours, inserts the Spirit into him. The Spirit is like the ointment used by the Son on the Christian; the ointment cools, refreshes, soothes the receiver, and imperceptibly penetrates him: this is precisely the function of the indwelling Spirit. Making use of a plethora of telling comparisons, Cyril conveys always the same message, namely, that we receive the Holy Spirit from the fullness of the Son, from his own substance. This mysterious effusion of the Spirit on men is compared to the rain issuing from a cloud, which is the Son; or to the steam rising from the water. So also the Son waters us with the vivifying and joyful gift of the Spirit. As a consequence of this munificence, we are filled to the brim with the person of the Holy Spirit, soaked in the Spirit. The Father is obviously not absent from this entire process, yet his function in the indwelling is difficult to describe precisely. He is the ultimate giver, no doubt, and he himself is present in man, but he does not seem to be very active. It is almost as if he were looking on from a distance, obviously pleased with the work being accomplished by the Son in the heart of man. This presence, however, is detected in a manner that is blurred, somewhat diffused and, one could say, as if enveloped by mist. The immediate giver of the Spirit is the Son rather than the Father.

Now, once the Spirit has descended into the Christian and taken full possession of him, his linking function begins. That is to say, he places the Christian, already entirely transformed by him, into the hands of the Son and the Father. The Spirit becomes like a mediator through whom the believer is joined to the Son and to the Father. The Spirit is the golden link between God and man. We should listen to Cyril again: "If, when we receive the Spirit of Christ, *we are taken by him to God the Father* as sharers of his own nature, how can he be a creature through whom...we are united to

13 *De Incarnatione Unigeniti:* PG 75, 1241.

God?"[14] It is the Spirit who, once he is firmly lodged within the Christian, takes him by the hand, as it were, and leads him to the Father.

Much the same should be said of the person of the Son whom the Spirit brings down to us. After all, he is rightly called the Spirit of the Son, and therefore when the Spirit fills and saturates the believer the Son cannot be very far. It is impossible for us to possess the Spirit so intimately without at the same time possessing the Son, who is his source and immediate origin: "The Son took up our human nature... he himself is in us,...for *we have him in us through the Spirit*... and similarly, we have in us also the Father through the Son".[15]

Now the Spirit's linking function is complete: he descends into us through the Son and after making his abode within us, he brings down and fills us with the persons of the Son and the Father. We now possess all three within us thanks to the Spirit. In the words of yet another prominent eastern writer, St Basil, the Spirit is like a first link in a golden chain of three: it is the first we grasp and by pulling it we bring down the other two as well.

This function performed by the indwelling Spirit is certainly not the result of wild imaginings, as if the mind of those eastern writers had run riot and they had given us a beautiful but artificial construct, flimsy and without foundation anywhere. For the gist of all this, obviously in an undeveloped form, is clearly found in the writings of Paul. In 1 Cor 2,10-12, for instance, he says that "the Spirit searches everything, even the depths of God (the Father)....Now we have received...the Spirit who is from God, that we may understand the gifts bestowed on us by God". Namely, the Spirit is here portrayed as a mediator who first scrutinizes the heart of the Father and then is sent to us. Consequently, he is a kind of intermediary between the Father and men, a link between both.

Again, but from a slightly different angle, Paul calls the Spirit our intercessor before the Father. We normally associate this title of intercessor exclusively with Jesus, who

14 *Thesaurus* 34: PG 75, 612.
15 *In Joannem*, IX, 1: PG 74, 280.

pleads for us before God. It is precisely this function that, according to Paul, the Holy Spirit performs before the Father: "The Spirit himself intercedes for us with sighs too deep for words...the Spirit intercedes for the saints according to the will of God" (Rom 8,26-27). The Spirit prays for us and pleads our cause. Is not the notion of intercessor, helper or mediator, included in the very name of Paraclete? And what does intercessor mean if not a kind of link between God and man? Therefore, the conception of the Spirit as link was born in scriptural soil, not in the fertile imagination of the eastern writers. The full tree grows in the Oriental garden, but its roots are clearly biblical.

b) *The Spirit and sanctity*

If there is a term in popular Christian literature that is often used, and yet so little understood, it is that of holiness or sanctity. We normally associate sanctity with the practice of heroic virtue, and any new saint canonized in Rome is immediately held up as a paragon of upright Christian behaviour, a person who throughout his or her life practised the Christian virtues to a heroic degree. It is precisely because of this exemplary conduct that he or she is put on a pedestal for all the world to see.[16]

If we proceed along this line, we shall never have a correct understanding of what sanctity is. In this regard most of us are shallow, superficial rather than wrong. It is the price we have to pay for ignoring the immensely rich eastern tradition, which has so much to give us, and yet is so little known. According to the profound eastern understanding, sanctity cannot in any way be reduced simply to the practice of virtue; it lies far deeper than that. Sanctity consists in the direct and immediate union between

16 Even the bishops in the course of Vatican II seem to have wrongly identified sanctity with an upright moral life. When *Lumen Gentium* was still in the melting pot one episcopal speech after another reduced sanctity to the practice of virtue. Thanks to Cardinal Bea's decisive intervention, however, this trend was stopped, and the conciliar draft modified and deepened, but even in its final version the text is not entirely satisfactory. A better acquaintance with the Oriental tradition would have enriched the text considerably.

the Spirit indwelling and the Christian indwelt. The Spirit, as a consequence of the indwelling, is already present with his own substance in man, and no creature, even of the supernatural order, stands between the two. The possession of man by the Spirit is immediate, it is total, with the Spirit penetrating and pervading the inner sanctuary of man, filling him up with his own divine person, leaving no recess in man which is not invaded by the indwelling Spirit. The Spirit grips man from within, completely. We witness now a direct fusion, a coalescence of the Holy Spirit and man, a real divinization effected by the Spirit himself.

Water, wind, fire — the three biblical symbols of the Spirit. When the Spirit, who is sanctity personified, dwells in man, he cannot but diffuse his own sanctity into man. He pours out lavishly his own personal sanctity into the privileged receptacle which is the heart of man. As water soaks thoroughly a sponge, or the lungs are filled with air, or fire burns and transforms a log of wood into glowing embers — so does the Holy Spirit communicate his own sanctity to man who, as a consequence, is sanctified, transformed, penetrated by the very person of the Holy Spirit. Water, fire and wind may be rather poor, unsatisfactory symbols to designate the personal character of the Spirit, but at least they prove useful to give us an idea to what an incredible degree he soaks, burns, fills the living temple which is man. Man is penetrated with the Spirit, entirely possessed by him, fused with him — and thereby he is radically sanctified with the very sanctity of God himself.

Keeping in mind the pattern of the straight line mentioned above, so dear to the eastern tradition, we can more clearly understand why these Oriental Fathers so emphatically insist that the work of human sanctification should not be attributed to God in general or indiscriminately to any of the divine persons, for such a work is an exclusive privilege of the Holy Spirit. We have already met St Cyril of Alexandria, who surely surpasses himself when expounding the subject of man's sanctification at the hands of the Spirit: "And they, honest and just, with a heart stripped of all holy desires, *introduce the Paraclete further down into themselves*, and once received, they keep him... For he sanctifies them".[17] Perhaps one could reverse Cyril's formula without in any way distorting his throught: it is the Spirit who introduces man further down into himself, into the very person of God, and keeps him there, rendered substantially holy by the very substance of the Holy Spirit. Cyril gives us a terse, limpid definition of sanctity which is, according to him, "the participation in (or inclusion into) the Holy Spirit".[18] Similarly, in another powerful passage he says:

> It is untrue to say that we cannot be one with God except by union of will. For above that union there is another, more sublime and far superior, which is effected by the communication of the divinity to man, who, while keeping his own nature, is, so to speak, transformed into God, just as iron plunged into fire becomes fiery, and while remaining iron seems changed into fire... .Union with God cannot be achieved in anybody unless by participation in the Holy Spirit, who *inserts his own sanctity into us*.[19]

But for short, pithy expressions, St Basil is really unbeatable: "The Holy Spirit is the fountainhead of sanctity".[20] "The Spirit is a living substance, the Lord of sanctity".[21] Sanctity is simply the quality or characteristic that marks the Spirit off from the other two divine persons: "The essence is common, like, e.g., goodness, divinity and other similar things; but the person is something proper, like paternity, filiation, or the power of sanctification".[22] Basil's fellow bishop and intimate friend, St Gregory of Nazianzen, is equally emphatic: "Truly the Father is Father, much more than other human fathers among us...the Son is truly Son....Truly the Holy

17 *In Joannem*, IX, 1: PG 74, 290.
18 *In Joannem*, IV, 2: PG 73, 566.
19 *In Joannem* X, Introd.: PG 74, 293; and *ibid.*, XI, 2 PG: 74, 553. A similar expression recurs elsewhere: "The Holy Spirit works in us by himself, truly sanctifying us and joining us to himself; and by this coalescence and union of ourselves with him he makes us sharers in the divine nature" (*Thesaurus* 34: PG 75, 958).
20 *Adversus Eunomium*, 3,2: PG 29, 660.
21 *De Spiritu Sancto*, 16, 28: PG 32, 136.
22 *Epistola* 214: PG 32, 789.

Spirit is holy. There is no saint like him: for he does not have acquired sanctity but is himself sanctity".[23]

Just as the Spirit's linking function has deep scriptural roots, as remarked above, so also, and much more so, his sanctifying power is a constant biblical datum. Paul is acutely conscious of having been called by God to spread Christ's message among the Gentiles, "so that the offering of the Gentiles may be acceptable sanctified by the Holy Spirit" (Rom 15, 16. Peter too, in reference to his vocation states that he has been "chosen and destined by God the Father and sanctified by the Spirit" (1 Pet 1,2). The eastern Fathers are definitely not dreaming dreams when they so emphatically and insistently attribute the work of human sanctification to the Spirit — they are rather echoing pure scriptural doctrine.

c) *The Spirit, engraver of the divine image*

This is the third and last aspect which throws light on the wonder of the indwelling. The sanctified Christian is sunk into the Holy Spirit, who impregnates and pervades him entirely, and as he does so, he leaves on man the features of the Son of God. As the result of the indwelling, man acquires a divine resemblance which he did not have before. And the Spirit performs this, not like a painter who remains somewhat extrinsic to the painting and at a certain distance from it, but rather by joining himself to the believer, by pressing himself on his surface, as it were, like a seal that is pressed on a piece of soft, receptive wax. The seal may be withdrawn but its features are clearly left on the wax. Or, to change the imagery, the Spirit chisels the image of the Son on the Christian according to the divine model.

We often speak of imitating Jesus, and this is undoubtedly correct and very rewarding, but not particularly profound, all the more so that in most cases we reduce this christological imitation to a moralizing process. Maybe we could deepen this to a remarkable degree by listening to the voice of the East. The external imitation of Jesus is based upon the much more solid and fundamental fact of the indwelling of

23 *Oratio* 25,10.

the Spirit. For it is the Spirit of Jesus that, drawing the sanctified Christian deep down into himself, turns him into "another Christ", bearing on himself the features of the Son of God.[24] Our christological resemblance is not due to our own efforts at reproducing in our daily lives the divine model, it is rather the result of the Spirit's own activity within us. It is he who shapes us into a replica of the Son by submerging us into himself, by steeping us in his own person. The Spirit makes us reflect in ourselves the features of Christ, the Son of God, as an image is reflected in a mirror. There is a marvelous little passage tucked away in the Old Testament that could throw light on this aspect of the indwelling: "She is a reflection of eternal light, a spotless mirror of the working of God and an image of his goodness" (Wisdom 7,26). The light of God which is the Spirit falls on the transparent surface of the divinized Christian and, as a consequence, the image of the Son begins to be visible in him.

Here again Cyril, the Alexandrian doctor, is incomparable. Commenting on Gal 4,19, he says: "My little children, with whom I am again in travail until Christ be formed in you. If Christ is formed in us only through the Spirit, who impresses on us his own features, beautifying human nature with the splendour of the divinity...".[25] "We are sealed by the Holy Spirit with the image and similitude of the Father's face, that is, of the Son".[26] "And Christ will never be formed in you in any other way except through the participation in the Spirit".[27]

24 In ordination ceremonies it is traditional for the preacher to speak eloquently of the new priests as "other Christs". The expression is, however, misleading. It is not the sacrament of Orders that turns the Christian into another Christ, but rather, much more fundamentally, the sacrament of baptism. It is not at the time of his ordination, but rather at the moment of his baptism that he begins to resemble Christ, precisely because baptism marks the beginning of the indwelling. The stress on ordination is clearly misplaced. Besides, one should also remark that if our configuration to Christ were the exclusive result of the sacrament of Orders, women — half of Christianity! — could not resemble Christ in any way, whereas baptism extends the divine resemblance to all, regardless of sex.

25 *Thesaurus*, 34: PG 75, 609.

26 *De Trinitate*, 5: PG 75, 945.

27 *In Joannem*, XII, 1: PG 74, 716.

This seems to have been quite a common doctrine in the illustrious see of Alexandria, for even before Cyril the great St Athanasius gave voice to the very same idea: "The Spirit is called unction and he is also the seal.... If therefore the Spirit is the unction or ointment and the seal, through whom the Word anoints and seals all things.... And the seal bears the image of Christ who seals, to which image all those are conformed who participate in him".[28]

The above conception of both the Alexandrian doctors is nothing but a further development of pure scriptural doctrine, as found particularly in Paul. At the end of that remarkable chapter devoted to the Holy Spirit, Romans 8, he says: "For those whom he (the Father) foreknew he also predestined to be conformed to the image of his Son, in order that he might be the first-born among many brethren" (Rom 8,29). For Paul, the very word "seal" seems to bring to mind the person of the Holy Spirit: "And it is God (the Father)...who has put his seal upon us and given us his Spirit in our heart as a guarantee" (2 Cor 1,22). "You also...who had believed in him (Christ) were sealed with the promise Holy Spirit" (Eph 1,13). The colourful flower of the indwelling will blossom on the Alexandrian shores of the Mediterranean centuries later, but the roots of the tree were already discernible in Paul.

5) Special, intimate relations with the Father and the Son

This strong emphasis on the person of the indwelling Spirit, however, can be misleading. As a matter of fact, it has misled some into fancying that the indwelling is an exclusive privilege of the Holy Spirit, that this form of vivifying presence cannot be extended to the other two persons. Obviously, such a conception would be totally wrong and plainly heretical. The baptized Christian houses within himself all the three divine Persons, inseparably linked among themselves and intimately united to the Christian. Origen, one of the most brilliant and original Oriental thinkers of early Christianity, put it forcefully: "I know what is a soul inhabited and a soul

28 *Ad Serapionem*, 1, 23: PG 26, 584.

deserted. If she does not have God, if she does not have Christ, who said 'I and my Father shall come to him and make our abode in him'; if she does not have the Holy Spirit she is deserted. She is inhabited when she is filled with God (the Father), when she has Christ, when the Holy Spirit is in her".[29]

All three persons dwell within the baptized person, and thus he enjoys a special, intimate relation with each and everyone of them. It is like a human family of three members, all three dwelling in the same house under the same roof. Yet it is just not possible to be equally related to your father, mother and sister. You may enjoy and appreciate the company of all three, you may deeply and tenderly love all three, but each of these three relationships is special, it is unique. There is something undefinable in your relation with your father which definitely cannot be extended to your relationship with your mother or sister. These relationships are definitely not interchangeable, for each one of them is special and unique.

It is much the same with the three relations that have flowered in the Christian as a consequence of the indwelling. He is now the temple of the Holy Spirit who sanctifies him deeply and engraves on him the image of Christ. He becomes Christ-like, a genuine replica of Christ, in a word, a brother (or sister) of Christ. And precisely because he is a brother of Christ, because he is another Christ, he instantly becomes a child of the Father. The Father of Jesus becomes his own father in the proper and real sense of the word, just as really as Jesus is his brother. These two relations, respectively of filiation with regard to the Father, and of brotherhood with regard to Christ, are surely not interchangeable. We are the sons and daughters of the Father, and of the Father only, not of an abstract Trinity. And our relation with Christ, our elder brother, is equally sharp and exclusive. Three loving relationships within the same family of God.

This of course does not mean that, from the psychological point of view, the Christian's affection is equally directed towards all three. This is next to impossible. Just as, within one's own family, one has legitimate choices and

29 *In Jeremiam*, 8: *Griechischen Christlichen Schriftsteller*, vol. 3 (Leipzig 1935), pp. 55-56.

justifiable preferences, so also in the family of God one may be particularly inclined to one or the other of the three Persons, whereas an absolutely equal love for all three is almost impossible. Much will depend on one's own degree of spiritual progress towards the summit. Nor is it rare to come across excellent Christians who have, in the course of their lives, imperceptibly shifted their allegiance from one to the other of the divine Persons. Obviously, no rules of universal application can be given in this regard. The Holy Spirit, acting from within the Christian, may well lead him along paths which are different from those of his neighbour. Choices cannot be imposed and preferences cannot be forced. Yet it is good for all to remember the foundation of the triple indwelling, solid like a granite rock. Diversity can only be built on such a solid foundation.

The distinctive character of these three loving, intimate relationships, is ultimately based on the New Testament. There are certain delicate biblical nuances that we can ignore to our own detriment. The reader will remember that, as explained above, Paul has a set of special terms that he applies exclusively to the Holy Spirit, and to nobody else, which goes to show that for him the Christian's relation to the Spirit is characterized by something special, something peculiar that is definitely not common to all three. Paul does not use those terms indiscriminately, rather he uses them exclusively in reference to the Holy Spirit. Similarly, when Jesus prayed to his Father and taught his disciples so to pray; when on Easter Sunday he gave his disciples the comforting message that from that moment on he and they had a common Father, he was obviously thinking exclusively of his own *Abba*. Is he not the person to whom we address the most common of all prayers, the Our Father? This scriptural way of speaking should be taken seriously and as literally as possible, and not reduced to grey generalities. In this regard K. Rahner can be trenchant: "We must take Scripture and the expressions it uses in as exact a sense as we possibly can".[30]

30 "Some implications of the scholastic concept of uncreated grace", *Theological Investigations*, I (London 1963), p. 346.

It is a real pity that subsequent theology has to a large extent lost these fine scriptural nuances by referring almost everything to an abstract, grey, undefined God or — worse still — to a mysterious and unappealing Trinity high above. But not all theologians are guilty of such a loss of biblical perspectives. There is something in the eastern mentality, as we saw above, that prevents such generalizations. The voice of the East should be taken more seriously than has hitherto been the case. The few remarkable testimonies quoted above clearly imply or openly state that the Christian is the brother of Jesus, the son of the Father and that he is sanctified by the Holy Spirit. To speak of a baptized person as the brother of the Spirit and the son of the Trinity would certainly be jarring to those sensitive eastern ears. Theologically this would simply make no sense. Our distinct relations with the three indwelling persons should be taken more seriously.

Nor should we forget, finally, that our present condition, which includes the indwelling, is not substantially different from that of our final, heavenly glory. The spotlight of our final destiny should be trained on the indwelling, and immediately its distinct, personalistic features will come into focus. For heaven is essentially nothing but a warm, personal, intimate communion of love between the three divine persons and man. The blessed do not contemplate a cold divine essence or an abstract Trinity. They are rather drawn into a fully satiating relationship with their Father whom they will not only contemplate face to face, but into whom they will also sink; with their brother Jesus transfigured and eternally glorified, who will beckon them come forward to drink from the fountain of life, which is himself, the pure waters of the Spirit. The face of God, the light of Christ, the crystal-clear waters of the Spirit: the glorified Christian is now drawn into three distinct, perfectly distinguishable, fully absorbing relations. It is not a colourless, unappealing trinitarian essence that irresistibly draws him out of himself, but rather Jesus, his Father and their common Spirit, three loving persons throbbing with life, who gently beckon the Christian to come forward and daringly enter into themselves: now the roles have in a way been reversed, the Christian is no longer their temple, they have become his temple, the house where he dwells.[31]

Our present pilgrim condition is much the same, thanks to the indwelling, which has rightly been called heaven anticipated. For whom do we possess in the warm intimacy of the indwelling if not the Father of Jesus and our Father, his Son and their common Spirit? We are now the temple of all three, before they become our temple in heaven. We already have within ourselves, but do not yet see, whom later we shall have and see. Our present possession is necessarily enveloped in the thick cloud of faith, which as long as we live cannot possibly be dispelled. We possess the three persons now as if surrounded by a cloud of incense. But when the powerful light of the afterlife is focussed on the cloud, it becomes to some extent translucent, we can see through it our heavenly, satiating relationships with all three which will not start when we die, because they have already started now. After death, once the surrounding cloud of faith disappears, the three Persons will be directly grasped, intuitively apprehended, more intensely loved. But the fact remains that heaven will be the crowning and completion, not the beginning, of this blessed triple relationship. The light of heaven is beckoning us forward, but now, thanks to the indwelling, heaven has already started. The full floweiing is still left, but the seed has already been planted. This is the marvel of the indwelling.

6) Full members of the Trinitarian family

It has already been remarked above that the Bible testifies to two different kinds of God's presence in the world, which, for the sake of convenience and for want of a better term, we shall call ubiquity or omnipresence and indwelling. The question as to where the divide between them lies is far from academic. God is surely present everywhere, and therefore, also in the person of the sinner. God's presence is all-pervading, like the air of the atmosphere, which cannot possibly be restricted to this or that place. The sinner does

31 For a fuller, more comprehensive description of our heavenly glory, see my previous book *Light Beyond Death* (Anand 1985), pp. 161-188.

have this general presence, but he certainly does not have the indwelling, he is not God's temple. The reception of the sacrament of reconciliation may be the privileged moment when the sinner passes from one kind of God's presence to the other, when omnipresence loses its vagueness and becomes the indwelling. "I absolve you...", and he becomes God's temple again.

To explain satisfactorily the difference between these two forms of God's presence is far from easy, hence the variety of attempts that have been made in order to solve the problem. Perhaps a solution can be attempted along strictly personalistic lines, in the hope that some light will be thrown on this obscure, but important question.

The notion of presence is exceedingly rich and variegated, it admits of almost innumerable degrees of intensity and perfection. The lowest form of presence is spatial or local, which is characterized by a mere extension or material juxtaposition of bodily parts. Persons can well be spatially present to one another while remaining perfect strangers; there is perhaps physical proximity and even physical touch, but there is no interpersonal contact, there is no mutual current of warmth and loving affection. The two persons are spatially very near each other, yet they are not at all close. In reality, juxtaposition and physical nearness without mutual influence is not presence but absence. Material things influence one another through action and reaction; persons by giving themselves to one another in openness and freedom: this is personal presence. The former physical proximity or spatial presence may still continue, but now it has become the sign of a much deeper, strictly personal presence. So, for instance, a tight embrace is in itself nothing but a form of physical touch and spatial proximity, but when effected between two persons deeply in love, it becomes the external, visible sign of a profound, warm, intimate personal presence.

Now God's general presence to a sinner, or omnipresence, is a kind of spatial presence, whereas the indwelling is rather a form of intimate, personal presence. Already in God's omnipresence and prior to the indwelling, his love for all men and women is certainly present — for, as St Thomas says, there are two things in God that can never change:

his joy and his love — but previous to the indwelling this love is not reciprocated by the sinner, the torrent of God's love flows only in one direction. God's love, though undoubtedly real, is also inefficacious, powerless to bring about any transformation in the sinner on account of the lack of reciprocity on the part of man. The sinner remains closed to the inrush of divine love, and hence God's love cannot penetrate and transform him, God's presence is only one of omnipresence, there is no indwelling.

Yet this kind of dull physical proximity on the part of God can become the sign of a deeper transforming personal presence when man, under the influence of grace, finally opens up to the inflow of God's persistent love, and then omnipresence becomes indwelling. Man's open reciprocity has produced the change. Now God's love for man is not new — it has always been there, whispering, knocking, enticing, attracting — but the transforming character of this love is new. Now God can, not only love, but also deeply change man.

A waterfall, rushing down in an endless, continuous stream, is a breath-taking spectacle, a telling testimony of God's power and might. If a man were to stand under the waterfall entirely covered by a metallic armour he would surely stand dry, very dry. The metallic protection would prevent the thunderous waterfall from reaching him. The rushing waters are there, descending in a mighty torrent against him, enveloping him entirely — and yet they cannot penetrate him, he stays dry. It is much the same with God's omnipresence and love for the sinner. As long as he is surrounded by the hard shell of his own selfishness, the waters of God's love cannot penetrate him, they simply bounce off; they may fall all around him, but they do not penetrate him. It is only when the external crust or protective shell is removed that the onrushing waters will soak and drench him to the bone. Now he is deeply changed, profoundly transformed, radically altered. The rushing waters are not only splashing all around him, they are entering him. God's love is now reciprocated, for man has finally opened up to the irruption of God's love which has the power to make of him a new person: omnipresence has become indwelling and spatial presence has turned into personal presence.

The Old Testament offers us another, and possibly better, analogy. I have already referred more than once to the awesome Temple that at the time of Jesus stood, tall and majestic, overlooking the holy city of Jerusalem. The Temple structure was enormous in size, and access to it was terraced, built at different levels, with its courts opened respectively to Gentiles, Jewish women, men and priests. The higher the dignity of the person the deeper the degree of penetration into the Temple. But only the high priest had access to the holy of holies, the very heart of the Temple where the mercy seat was kept, a sign of Yahweh's presence to his People. Access to this holy of holies, therefore, was severely restricted to one man, the high priest, and to one single occasion, the solemn feast of *Yom Kippur* or Day of Atonement. Throughout the year God was present, certainly, but at the same time kept his distance. Access to the inner sanctuary was a privilege not to be easily taken for granted. It was only God himself, not sinful man, that could open his own residence and invite man to come closer.

This is exactly what happens in the mystery of the indwelling. God is no longer satisfied with keeping man — as he did in the days of old — on the outer fringes of his Temple, satisfied with a vague, general omnipresence. God himself comes forward and gently leads man into the inner holy of holies where he dwells — and this is the indwelling. Now God opens up to man the inner, most secret recesses of his own person, of his own trinitarian family. He takes man be the hand, as it were, and kindly invites him to move in, not to be satisfied any longer with the outer courts of his Temple, to go deeper into the very heart of God. Now man finds himself, in wonder and amazement, right in the centre of God's own mansion, in the inner chamber where he dwells in majesty and splendour. Man is now admitted into the family of God, made a full member of the trinitarian family; no longer a stranger but a son, he is shown the secrets of God's own life to which formerly he had no access — this is precisely the indwelling. Now man is no longer sustained by a distant Creator, but by a loving Father, present in him. Now there is in him an overwhelming sense of awe and reverence, no doubt, but also, and primarily, a vivid consciousness of deeply reciprocated love. God is not only present in man, he dwells in him. Man has entered into the very person of God himself, and God has occupied and filled the sanctuary of man. The greyness of omnipresence has yielded to the warm intimacy of the indwelling.

BIBLIOGRAPHY

Wikenhauser, A.: *Pauline Mysticism* (New York 1960), pp. 80-92.

Burrell, D.: "Indwelling presence and dialogue", *Theological Studies* 22 (1961), pp. 1-17.

Gribomont, J.: "L'Esprit sanctificateur dans la spiritualité des Pères", *Dictionnaire de spiritualité* 4 (1961), col. 1257-1272.

Gleason, R.: *Grace* (New York 1962), pp. 123-173.

Congar, Y.: *The Mystery of the Temple* (Staten Island 1966), pp. 21-38.

Cerfaux, L.: *The Christian in the Theology of St Paul* (London 1967), pp. 295-312.

Rondet, H.: *The Grace of Christ* (Westminster 1967), pp. 265-377.

Fransen, P.: *The Life of Grace* (London 1969), pp. 40-57.

Montague, G.: *The Holy Spirit: Growth of a Biblical Tradition* (New York 1976).

Malatesta, E.: "Covenant and indwelling", *The Way* 17 (1977), pp. 23-32.

Congar, Y.: *I Believe in the Holy Spirit*, II (London 1983), pp. 73-90.

Chapter Four

CHILDREN OF THE FATHER

As the result of the interpenetration between the Holy Spirit and the Christian at the moment of the indwelling, the latter bears in himself the image of the Son and becomes thereby a brother of Jesus, and consequently a child of the Father. Such an intimate relationship with the Father had already been vividly foreshadowed many centuries before the Christian era. As a matter of fact, some of the most touching biblical passages in this connection belong not to the New but to the Old Testament. The all-important historical episode of the Exodus from Egypt under the leadership of Moses marked the beginning of the People of God and at the same time the beginning of the Israelites' filial relation to Yahweh. "When Israel was a child, I loved him, and out of Egypt I called my son" (Os 11,1). It is the entire People of Israel, rather than the single Israelite, that is the son of God, and as such, it is on the entirety of the People that the most astonishing signs of divine tenderness and love are poured out: "I myself taught Ephraim to walk, I took them in my arms...I led them with the reins of kindness, with leading-strings of love. I was like someone who lifts an infant close against his cheek; stooping down to him I gave him his food" (Os 11,3-4).

Yahweh's tender solicitude for his People continues unabated during the long trek across the desert. In spite of its frequent infidelities and wayward behaviour, Israel was still loved by God as his own child. There is a very vivid contrast between the People's shameful behaviour, on the one hand, and Yahweh's stubborn, persevering love on the other: "They are no longer his children because of their blemish...they are a perverse generation, children in whom there is no faithfulness" (Deut 32,5.20). Against this sombre backdrop Yahweh's gratuitous love shines out all the more: "Is he not your father who created you...? Like an eagle that stirs up its nest, that flutters over its young, spreading out its wings, catching them, bearing them on its pinions" (Deut 32,6.11). Care, concern, solicitude: this is the attitude of Yahweh towards his recalcitrant child.

Marvelous, yet incomplete. Glimpses of light are not yet the full light, just as the pale light of dawn cannot match the fullness of the midday sun. This warm relationship between Yahweh and Israel is yet to be deepened and interiorized; from social and communitarian it has to become individual and intimately personal. With Paul and John it is not only the People, the community of Israel, that will be the son of God, but also — and primarily — each individual Christian that will be privileged to address the Father of Jesus as his own *Abba*.

1) The reality of our divine sonship

The notion of filiation or sonship (the two terms are synonymous and interchangeable) is so very fundamental for Paul that he, in a certain way, reduces to it the entire economy of salvation. From the scattered references spread throughout his writings, the following picture emerges: Originally and in its earliest stage, our filiation amounts to a sort of blueprint, an ideal plan in the Father's mind (or, shall we say, in the Father's heart?) which will later assume historical visibility: "He (the Father) chose us in him (Christ) before the foundation of the world...he destined us in love to be his sons through Jesus Christ" (Eph 1,4-5). The Father wants to have sons and daughters, but his plan is not yet fulfilled. Then comes the second step in the realization of this plan, namely, the Incarnation, which is specifically viewed by Paul as the means to confer the gift of filiation on humankind: "But when the time had fully come,

God sent forth his Son, born of a woman. . . so that we might receive adoption as sons" (Gal 4,4-5). The Son has appeared in human form as the first-born of many future brothers and sisters. The Father's plan begins to take shape, it is no longer hidden in his heart, for with the Incarnation it has already begun to acquire some historical visibility.

Approximately thirty-six years roll by and the incarnate Son, after being put to death and raised again to life, sends the Spirit to his Church — the plentiful effusion of the Spirit has begun. It is the same Spirit of the risen Christ that, at baptism, enters into and takes possession of the Christian, making him or her the son or daughter of God. This is the full flowering of our filiation, the moment when the Father's plan becomes finally effective in each one of us. Baptism turns us into children of the Father in the proper sense of the word. Even so, this is not yet the full realization of the Father's plan, which will reach its fourth and final stage only at the end of history (or possibly at the end of each one's earthly life?) when man's corruptible body will be raised in splendour, like that of Jesus on Mount Tabor. Then, and only then, will the Father's design be fully realized, when he draws his beloved sons and daughters, entirely glorified, "unto himself" (Eph 1,5). Then the Father's effulgence will envelop all his children into the one family of God.

This is but a bird's-eye view of the entire unfolding of our sonship. With this overall perspective in mind, it is worth focussing our attention on the third and most fundamental stage of the evolution, namely, on the Christian's filiation which becomes a reality at the moment of baptism. A close look at this stage of growth will disclose its extraordinary theological and spiritual riches, as expounded primarily by Paul in two related passages from Romans and Galatians.

We shall have to turn our attention again to *Romans 8*, whose central theme, as the reader will surely remember, is that of the living presence of the Holy Spirit within the Christian. In the first verses of the chapter Paul has spoken in glowing terms of the Spirit's indwelling, and now he draws from it the unavoidable conclusion that, since the Spirit we have received is the Spirit of the Son, we are truly sons of God. For it is the Holy Spirit, the Spirit of Jesus, that shapes us into sonship by making us brothers or sisters of Jesus and children of the Father.

"For all who are led by the Spirit of God are sons of God" (Rom 8,14). True sonship leads to fidelity to the Spirit but, leaving the aspect of fidelity for a subsequent section, this may be the right time to make a remark which, though apparently nothing but a harmless platitude, seems in reality to be forgotten by many, with spiritual consequences which are certainly not trivial. For many Christians — even for those who are fairly well instructed in religious matters and who, therefore, ought to know better — the Father means next to nothing. The obsession with Jesus seems to leave no room for anybody else. They seem — unconsciously perhaps— to be somewhat afraid that to go beyond Jesus is dangerous and unsafe. They cling fiercely to Jesus and are blind to anything or anybody that cannot be identified with or reduced to the son of Mary. The Father is there, to be sure, but did not Jesus say that "the Father and I are one" (Jn 10,30)? They find comfort in this Johannine passage, which seems at first sight to confirm their opinion that Jesus is enough. They give one the impression that their sight has been impaired, almost as if they were wearing "christological blinkers", which hinder both their peripheral and their frontal vision.

It may be that biblical language — or rather our deficient way of understanding it — is partly responsible for this attitude, which is as widespread as it is regrettable. In the passage under consideration, and in typical biblical fashion, Paul refers to the Father as God — nothing else. This is very misleading to a modern reader, for most of us fail to realize that this term does not refer to God in general, but specifically and exclusively to the Father, and that is precisely what Paul meant. An accurate, though clumsy and jarring English rendering of Paul's Greek should speak rather of "*the* God", with a definite article. For Paul, "God" does not at all mean the triune God, as if the name were but a common designation covering the three divine Persons. Nothing of the sort. For Paul "*the* God" means exclusively the Father. The expression is not an umbrella concept under which the Son and the Spirit could also take shelter; it is rather the distinctive and exclusive name of the Father. If, whenever we come across the name of God in the New Testament — for this is not a peculiarity of Paul, we were to mentally refer it specifically to the Father, we would come much closer to what the biblical writer had in mind, and gradually move beyond that narrow concentration on Christ.

But let us now return to the passage of Romans under scrutiny. "We are the sons of God" (v. 14), namely, the sons of the *Father*. "For... you have received the *Spirit of sonship*" (v. 15).[1] It might be of some importance to place this typically Pauline notion of sonship in the correct perspective. As is often the case with Paul, he is here using a non-biblical word which was entirely unknown in the Old Testament (though the same idea was at times expressed under different names). By itself, the term "sonship" meant at the time of Paul the act of adopting somebody as son or, at times, the status gained by such an act. The notion itself, therefore, is certainly juridical, but it would be a serious distortion of Paul's thought to reduce the very profound and highly spiritual idea of sonship to the merely juridical notion of adoption. Paul borrows the term from the legal world, but attaches to it a markedly religious significance. The husk may be highly juridical but the content is definitely religious. Hence, to speak unguardedly of adoption in this context would be rather misleading, for Paul, despite the legal overtones of the term, means much more than a legal fiction.

The essential background to this Pauline usage of the term is the historical episode of the Israelites' election as the People of God at the time of the Exodus, as we saw briefly above. And that was certainly not a legal, but rather a creative and deeply transformative act. The election of the People of God was not an act of law but an act of love. This is the absolutely necessary background in order to grasp in all its fullness the Pauline notion of sonship. God chose the Israelites freely, pulled them out of their degrading Egyptian slavery and made them into his People — into his

1 The original expression used by Paul in v. 15 remains ambiguous, for "spirit" might refer either to man's own spirit or to the Holy Spirit, and it is not easy to dispel the ambiguity. Today's English Version, for instance, renders v. 15: "The Spirit makes you God's children", with a clear reference to the Holy Spirit.

son, according to the prophets — by a gratuitous and entirely unmerited act of love to which they had no right and on which they could lay no claim. For Paul, therefore, sonship spells love, not legal rights of any sort. The general atmosphere is one of warm, personal relationships, rather than the stiffness of a court of law.

"When we cry 'Abba! Father!' it is the Spirit himself bearing witness with our spirit that we are children of God" (v. 6). *Abba* seems to be the only word from Aramaic, Jesus' mother tongue, to have been retained by the early Christian community. It is obviously reminiscent of the Gethsemane scene narrated in the gospels, when Jesus in agony prayed to his Father. This term was used at the time of Jesus — and it is still used today in Israel — by children, as an endearing form of address when speaking to their natural father. Hence, a better translation than the solemn "father" would probably be "daddy", with a ring of close familiarity and intimate affection. The Holy Spirit himself both effects and bears witness to this filiation. It is he who makes of the baptized Christian a child of the Father, and who testifies to this new familiar relationship.[2]

If we are true children of God, then we can have a share in the paternal inheritance: "If children, then heirs, heirs of God and fellow heirs of Christ" (v. 17). The term "inheritance" immediately evokes in the mind of the contemporary reader the unavoidable atmosphere of juridical rights and legal claims to paternal property. However, nothing could be further from Paul's mind. If the very notion of sonship was for him evocative of Moses and the Exodus, that of the inheritance brings back to mind something even older and more fundamental: the gratuitous promise originally made to Abraham, the father of the nation, and granted

2 Actually Paul uses two different terms, *tekna* and *uioi*, both rendered in English as "children", for the actual difference between the two is very slight: *tekna* contains the idea of origin of descent as well as that of the personal relationship arising therefrom, characterized by bonds of love, friendship and trust between father and son. *Uioi*, in addition to all this, includes also the recognized status of sons. *Tekna* is possibly more tender, *uioi* more solemn. John never calls Christians *uioi*, for him they are only *tekna*, whereas Paul seems to use both the terms indiscriminately.

to his descendants. Hence, the notion of our supernatural filiation is to be seen against the biblical background of the promise and the election, both equally gratuitous and unmeritable. When reflecting on the fundamental fact of our sonship, one should be able to discern in the remote past, blurred by distance and hazy with the passage of time, the two mighty figures of Abraham and Moses. It is they that frame our present sonship and, as beneficiaries respectively of the divine promise and the election, give to sonship its full meaning and significance. Just as Moses and Elijah appeared Mount Tabor flanking the transfigured Jesus in the luminous cloud, so also now Abraham and Moses are a vivid reminder to Paul of the utterly gratuitous character of our Christian filiation.

The above doctrine of Paul on the reality of our filiation is undoubtedly attractive and solid, but if we were to stop here it would rather resemble a torso or an unfinished symphony. As often happens with Paul when dealing with realities of such extraordinary richness and depth, he cannot be expected to convey a full picture at one shot, as it were. The above passage of Romans 8 is rich, no doubt, but it needs the compliment supplied by Paul's sister epistle to the Galatians, written about three years before Romans.

The role played by the Holy Spirit in our filiation is left somewhat in the shadows by Romans 8, whereas it comes strongly to the fore in a little passage of Galatians, which is a model of density and concise thought. We are certainly getting used by now to Paul's sobriety of language and economy of expression; he is not a man to waste words in empty rhetoric. The very purpose of the Incarnation, Paul tells the Galatians, was precisely to enlarge the trinitarian family, to receive more sons and daughters into the family of God. And then he is suddenly caught up by the idea of our sonship, and in one single stroke fathoms its very depths: "The proof that you are sons is that God (the Father) has sent the Spirit of his Son into our hearts: the Spirit that cries 'Abba, Father', and it is this that makes you a son...and if God has made you son, then he has made you heir" (Gal 4,6-7).[3]

3 Once again the original Greek of Paul is ambivalent, for it could also be trans-

Apparently the Galatians accepted the fact of the indwelling as a fundamental article of their faith, but had some nagging doubts about the reality of their supernatural filiation. Now Paul leads them from the accepted basis to the removal of their doubt. The Holy Spirit himself effects our filiation, it is he who, by possessing the Christian thoroughly and by imprinting on him the features of Christ, renders him similar to the Son, and therefore a child of the Father. The indwelling of the Spirit and our baptismal filiation are two distinct but inseparable faces of the very same reality which cannot possibly be dissociated. It is the Spirit of Jesus that makes us children of the Father.

2) Living faith and gracious love, the twofold root of sonship

Our divine filiation may be compared a prism. You turn it round, the light impinges on it from different angles and, as a consequence, the prism reflects different colours not visible before. In a way, Paul has just given us the rich content of filiation, what it is and in what it consists. John will now complete the picture by turning the prism around so as to make us see a new colour, a new dimension. He will give us, not so much the content of filiation as its root, its origin, the principle from which it proceeds, which is faith in Christ.

In the very prologue, which is the quintessence of his gospel, John already states that "to all who received him (Christ), who believed in his name, he gave power to become children of God" (Jn 1,12). In typically Hebrew fashion, here "name" stands for the very person of Christ; hence, to believe in his name is simply to believe in Christ, to entrust oneself to him, to adhere and cling to him with the totality of one's mind, heart, and affectivity. The whole person goes

lated: "And because you are sons, God has sent the Spirit of his Son...", as found in the RSV. The translation of the Jerusalem Bible given in the text, whichis generally favoured by most modern commentators, probably conveys better Paul's thought. It is not that the indwelling is the consequence of our filiation (implied in the RSV translation) but exactly the opposite: it is the indwelling of the Spirit that effects our filiation.

over to Christ in a movement of self-surrender: this is living faith in Christ, this is "to believe in his name", this is the attitude that bestows on the Christian the dignity of sonship. Christ's name, in which one believes, is precisely "the only begotten Son of God" (Jn 3,18). Through faith, therefore, one commits himself, not only to Christ in general, but specifically to the Son of God, and thereby appropriates to himself Christ's divine sonship as a life-giving principle. It is through the gateway of faith that man enters the realm of divine sonship.

This living faith in the Son imparts to man "the power to *become* children of God", a power given to them by the Father as a gift. They cannot claim it by right, nor do they have the natural ability for it; this power is rather a gracious gift of the Father who makes them participate in the very sonship of Jesus. We are not born sons and daughters of God, we receive the power to become such, not in birth but after birth. The principle and root of sonship is *not natural birth but supernatural faith in Christ.* Our parents made us their children, not the children of God. The latter was done only by the Father of Jesus and our Father. Our parents were utterly powerless to bestow on us this new dignity, this supernatural sonship. We receive from the Father the gratuitous gift of faith in Christ, and along with it, the concomitant gift of sonship. The Father, through faith, introduces us into the trinitarian family.

Assuredly faith in Christ is a life-giving principle, the immediate origin of our filiation, but it is not the deepest root. Ultimately, our filiation proceeds, not only from the gift of faith, but also — and specially — from the gift of love. It is not man's faith but rather God's love that is the ultimate foundation of our sonship. "See what love the Father has given us, that we should be called the children of God; and so we are.... Beloved, we are God's children now" (1 Jn 3, 1-2). "The Father loved the Son" (Jn 3,35); "you (Father) have loved them (the disciples) even as you have loved me" (Jn 17, 23); "God so loved the world..." (Jn 3,16). The Son, the disciples, the world; this is the triple object of the divine love which, like a torrent, descends from the Father and encompasses the whole of humankind. It is this gratuitous love of the

Father that is the deepest root, the ultimate principle of our sonship. We are sons of the Father because we believe in Jesus, and we believe in Jesus because we are loved by the Father. Now the circle is complete: it is not our faith in God, but God's love for us that has produced the wonder of our filiation. Its deepest root lies in God, not in man, who can only receive the gift, but never produce it.

This is a love that "the Father has given us" — as an unmerited gift. Our sonship is a heavenly endowment proceeding from the Father's munificence for his children. It is the Father that gives us both undeservedly and unreservedly a participation in his own life, since sonship is nothing but a mystery of participated divine life.

And this divine life in us, result of our sonship, springs into eternal life: "We are already the children of God, but what we are to be in the future has not yet been revealed; all we know is, that when it is revealed we shall be like him because we shall see him as he really is" (1 Jn 3, 2). The seed of eternal life has already been planted in us. Our present sonship will eventually blossom into the vision of the Father face to face. It is our present filiation that will produce our future vision of God. Then we shall really be like God himself, similar to him; and we shall be like him because we shall see him; and we shall see him because we are already now his children. Our filiation will yield a harvest of eternal life.

At the end, after this brief exposé of Pauline and Johannine doctrine, one realizes with a sense of amazement to what an incredible extent we are caught up in an unbroken chain of gratuitous gifts. Directly and immediately it is the person of the Holy Spirit that, acting from within us, makes us children of God; but the presence of the indwelling Spirit in us is due to our living faith in Christ Jesus, for it is this faith, exteriorized in baptism, that draws the Spirit down to us; and, on the other hand, this faith which opens for us the gate to God's inner life is his supreme gift to us. Hence, our sonship is imbued, steeped in an atmosphere of gratuitousness, graciousness and gifts. We are simply destined to receive all along the line. A deeply felt gratitude for such divine liberality is the only possible answer.

3) Sons in the spirit of the son

It is commonly said that we are "sons in the Son", that our sonship is but a participation in Jesus' own. This is surely correct provided it is properly understood, for not only the Son, but the Spirit of the Son too has an essential role to play in our filiation. Short formulas can be expressive and catchy, but at times they run the risk of leaving out elements which are essential.

The humanity of Jesus is essentially filial, for outside the flow of life linking it to the Father, it simply cannot exist. An endless stream of life proceeds from the Father to the Son, and from the Son to the humanity of Jesus. Life gushes forth continuously from the Father and it streams down into the Son, into Christ, who drinks this divine life in plentiful draughts. Jesus simply draws life from his Father, he lives by the very life of his Father and it is into this ceaseless flow of divine life, linking up Father and Son, that the Christian is inserted, plunged. The Son is irresistibly drawn to the Father, and outside this necessary orientation, this dynamic movement towards the Father, the Son cannot exist. Similarly, the Christian cannot be the son of God unless in the centre of this ceaseless flow, in the midst of this mutual torrent of life between Father and Son. In order to be the son of God one must necessarily be in God.

Furthermore, the Christ who communicates his own personal relation to man is not the earthly Jesus but emphatically the Easter Christ. Hence, our present filiation is essentially an Easter filiation, a filiation of light and glory. It is the radiant splendour of the glorified Son that draws and envelops the sons: "And we all, who, with unveiled faces, contemplate and reflect as in a mirror the splendour of the Lord, we are transfigured into his own image with an ever growing splendour" (2 Cor 3,18). Not only do we contemplate from afar, as it were, but we also *reflect* the radiance of the Son, and this necessarily implies a certain proximity, a certain nearness. The transfigured Son draws his own brothers and sisters into himself, for he is much more than a merely external model. We, through our filiation, are inserted into him and therefore bathed in the very same Easter effulgence that envelops him: we are "sons in the Son".

This being the true reality of things, it should be obvious by now how very pale and unsatisfactory is the comparison commonly used, which likens our filiation to the act of adopting a child in a human family. The couple's inability to have a child of their own is in a way compensated by the legal act of adopting a stranger. In the eyes of the law, after all the formalities have been gone through, the child is considered to be the true son or daughter of the couple, with a right to their inheritance. Similarly — it is said — God adopts us gratuitously into his own family, we are his adopted children.

A very common comparison — as common as it is inadequate. For in the above example the legal fiction does not really make up for the lack of common life. The adopted child was born of different parents and, therefore, the very life by which he lives is *not* the life of his adopting parents. Deep down he remains a stranger, brought into the world by somebody else, by another couple. An exceedingly poor model to understand the reality of our supernatural filiation, which goes far beyond the human example proposed. For in our case we do share a common life with God. God is our Father and Jesus is our brother precisely because we have a share in the very same life that irresistibly draws him to his Father. Easter Sunday was the great day of our filiation, a day when the risen Christ and his disciples began to have a common Father: "I am ascending to my Father and your Father" (Jn 20,17). No legal fiction of any kind is involved here. Baptism and faith in Jesus bestow on the Christian a share in God's very life, which wells up in the Father, and after filling to the brim the risen humanity of Christ, now plunges down to the Christian. Like Jesus, he too lives by the very life of God. But obviously he is not God's natural son as Jesus is. Jesus is the eternal Son, whereas we have "become sons" in the pregnant expression of John. Despite this unbridgeable, essential difference, the fact remains that our sonship is built upon a participation, a sharing in God's own life. It is therefore to the risen Lord's natural sonship that we should compare our own sonship, rather than to the pale pattern of a merely human adoption. In view of all this, perhaps we should drop from our religious vocabulary the term "adopted sonship", which, though correct in a certain way, is likely to be misunderstood and weakened in pastoral usage.

Hence, the pattern should be Christ's own filiation, for "we are predestined to be conformed to the image of the Son" (Rom 8,29). We bear the image of Christ, we are Christ-like already now, just as Christ himself "is the image of the invisible God (the Father)" (Col 1,15). It is remarkable that Scripture uses the very same word to express both the relations, that of Christ to his Father and that of the Christian to Christ. We are the image of Christ just as Christ is the image of the Father. We mirror Christ just as Christ mirrors the Father. Yet in a way the word "image" is somewhat misleading, for by itself it seems to suggest only an external resemblance of extrinsic similititude, like a model that is reproduced by a painter. In this case Christ would be no more than an exemplar to be reproduced, and we would slip down once again into the area of moralizing imitation. Fortunately, however, the scriptural *eikon*, image, means much more than that. It is not only likeness between the original model and its reproduction that is included here, but also the idea of union. Therefore, between the glorified Christ and the Christian there is a similitude that is reproduced, that is sure, but also an intimate union that is effected. In a certain way, the glorified model is interiorized, it lives in the Christian. It is precisely this union that produces the resemblance. We are like Christ (similititude) because Christ is in us (union). "We are transfigured into his image" (2 Cor 3,18), Paul said. We become his transfigured image because he is the transfigured model, a model which is not external, but rather immanent in the Christian, as explained above.

This image is a dynamic reality, a reality that bespeaks development and growth. For we are being transformed into the image of Christ "with an *ever growing* splendour" (2 Cor 3,18). The image of the risen Christ is not duplicated in us in all its fullness from the beginning; it rather grows gradually, imperceptibly. Here all our poor human comparisons break down, for in a human family it is hardly possible to increase and perfect one's own filiation. We are children of our earthly parents and this relationship existed in all its fullness from the time of our birth; whereas our supernatural sonship began at baptism, certainly, when the link was first established between the Son and the sons, but this filial and fraternal relationship keeps growing "with an ever growing splendour". As the effulgence of the risen Christ in us grows, so does the reality of our filiation. We should not lose sight of the fact that, as stated above, the full perfection of our filiation lies in the future, for it includes as a necessary element the final glorification of the body. We are sons already now, but our sonship has still to grow unto the fullness of the glorified Christ. Then, and only then, shall we completely be sons in the Son, when the glory of Tabor will be finally our own.

The formula "sons in the Son" has gained currency in Christian literature, but after taking the teaching of the New Testament into consideration it would probably be more accurate to say that we are sons in the Spirit of the Son. For, when everything is said and done, Jesus does not make us sons of God by himself, but only by means of the Spirit, the Holy Spirit dwelling in us. He is the Spirit of the Son, proceeding from him, resting on him, dwelling in him and drawing the sons to him. This Spirit imprints himself directly on the baptized, and since, according to a typical Oriental conception, he is the image of the Son, he, by being fused with the Christian, makes him the brother of Jesus and the son of the Father.

The Holy Spirit accomplishes this work of filiation directly by himself, rather than through the reality of sanctifying grace, as is often unguardedly said. The work of making ordinary men and women into sons and daughters of God is too delicate to be 'delegated' to anybody. Rather, given the extraordinary importance of the task, the Spirit accomplishes it himself in the inner recesses of man. In the very depths of his person man receives the Spirit of the Son who confers on him this new status that enables him to cry "Abba, my Father". As the Church's liturgy sings with touching simplicity: Christ "ascended above all the heavens, and from his throne at your right hand poured out into the hearts of your adopted children the Holy Spirit of your promise".[4]

At the end, our filiation resembles an imposing structure of great beauty which rests solidly on two pillars: faith in Jesus and the indwelling of the Spirit. Both of them support the structure, but both are in turn supported by something that lies even deeper: the Father's unmerited love that prompts him to make of sinful human persons children of his own family.

4) Sonship and prayer

That sonship tends to express itself in prayer was already stated by Paul. After having reminded the Roman Christians that it is the Holy Spirit who bestows on us our sonship, he says: "Likewise the Spirit helps us in our weakness; for we do not know how to pray, but the Spirit himself intercedes for us" (Rom 8,26). The Spirit of sonship makes the sons of God pray to their Father.

Jesus was the first to give expression to this intimate relationship with his Father in prayer. As remarked above, it is from Jesus' own mode of addressing his Father as *Abba* that the same word passed on to the early Christian communities of Galatia and Rome. The gospels testify to Jesus' passion for prayer, to his custom of spending at times entire nights in converse with his *Abba*. It is certainly remarkable that, "whereas there is not a single instance of God being addressed as Abba in the literature of Jewish prayer, Jesus *always* addressed him in this way"[5] — with the exception of his cry of dereliction on the cross, when the form of address was fixed by Ps 22 which he was quoting.

Abba was at the time of Jesus — and continues to be in modern Israel — a babbling sound used originally by small children when addressing their natural father, but later it came to be used also by adult persons when addressing their father. However, no Jew would dare use this mode of

4 Preface of the Holy Spirit.
5 J. Jeremias, *The Prayers of Jesus* (London 1967), p. 57.

address when praying to Yahweh, for this would have seemed unbecoming, excessively familiar, as if he were trespassing the boundaries of dignity and respect which are due to God. An innate sense of awe and reverence demanded that in prayer they use the term "God" or "Yahweh", not the familiar *Abba*.

And yet Jesus always used this intimate form of address in his prayer life, not only in Gethsemane. This simple fact is already a pointer to that unfathomable mystery of filial union and intimacy, to that mutual current of love that bound Jesus to his Father. His natural sonship was externally manifested in this unusual way of addressing God in prayer. This is something so characteristic and so exclusive of him that, when reflected upon and deepened out, it permits us to glimpse, in a blurred and hazy manner, the profound mystery of his divinity. Extreme familiarity with God without the undercurrent of a very special, inner relationship with him would hardly justify this intimate mode of address. His spontaneous *Abba* is the window through which we begin to look into the deep mystery of his personal relation with his Father. The Gethsemane episode lifts the curtain somewhat, and by looking through the tiny opening we begin to surmise what lies beyond.

When compared to his contemporaries, Jesus stands out as entirely different. He completely breaks with past tradition by taking a step that is unheard of in Judaism. For him Yahweh is not only his God, he is his dear Father, his *Abba*: "He spoke to God like a child to his father, simply, inwardly, confidently; Jesus' use of Abba in addressing God reveals the heart of his relationship with God".[6] The use of the word by Jesus implies an extraordinary familiarity in his prayerful converse with God, but it is a familiarity steeped at the same time in a deep sense of reverence and submission: "Abba, Father...not what I will, but what you will" (Mk 14,36). His intimacy springs from the consciousness of his sonship, but is tempered by a deep sense of reverential submission to his Father. Familiarity and reverence fused together in a harmonious blend: this is the inner attitude of Jesus in prayer.

6 J. Jeremias, *The Prayers of Jesus*, p. 62.

It is more than probable that this intimate but reverential relation with his Father is an attitude Jesus learnt from his mother, for he belonged to a devoutly religious family, faithful to the best traditions of Judaism. At the time of Jesus all Jews were expected to recite twice a day the so-called *Shema*, namely, Deut 6,4-9: "Love the Lord your God with all your heart, with all your soul and with all your strength. Never forget these commandments.... *Teach them to your children.* Repeat them when you are at home, and when you are away, when you are resting and when you are working". Teach them to your children. So Jesus was taught at home by his parents. His daily prayer nurtured his sense of filiation, for in it he addressed God as his *Abba.* In his case familiarity did *not* breathe contempt; on the contrary, it fostered and deepened the reverential intimacy he had been taught at home.

If the use of *Abba* by Jesus in his prayer life was absolutely unique among his contemporaries, part of this uniqueness overflowed into the early Christian communities. The retention of Jesus' own Aramaic term *Abba* by Greek-speaking communities like those of Galatia and Rome shows clearly that they were conscious that something new had been given them. The *Abba* used by the Christians in Rome is but an echo of Jesus' prayer in Jerusalem. By authorizing and encouraging them to address his Father just as he himself did, he was giving them "a share in sonship, (for) only he who, through Jesus, lets himself be given the child-like trust which resides in the word *Abba* finds his way into the kingdom of God".[7]

Paul consistently connects the use of *Abba* with the presence of the Holy Spirit in the believer. It is the Spirit that enables him to address God as his *Abba*, and this shows

7 J. Jeremias, *The Prayers of Jesus*, p. 97. It is this child-like trust in God that pervades the following beautiful passage from Newman in its quaint English: "He (the Father), has numbered the very hairs of thy head and the cubits of thy stature. He compasses thee round and bears thee in his arms. He takes thee up and sets thee down. He notes thy very countenance, whether smiling or in tears, whether healthful or sickly. He looks tenderly upon thy hands and feet; he hears thy voice, the beating of thy heart and thy very breathing. Thou do not love thyself better than he loves thee" (*Parochial and Plain Sermons*, III, p. 126).

that the relation of filiation expressed in this use of the term is beyond human capabilities. Without the Spirit dwelling in him the Christian would not possibly pray this way. It becomes possible only when, through the Spirit of Jesus, men and women share in his own filial relation with the Father. The Spirit is both the cause and the witness of this filiation, which means that whenever Christians address God as their *Abba* in the Spirit, they can be absolutely certain that they are his children. For the earthly Christian communities the prayerful use of *Abba* amounted to a partial fulfilment of the Old Testament promise, "I will be your father and you will be my sons and daughters" (2 Sam 7,14).

5) And non-christians?

In the present Indian context where Christians constitute an insignificant minority, the pertinent question can be raised whether filiation is an exclusive privilege of the baptized or, on the contrary, can be extended to the mass of non-Christians surrounding us. An almost instinctive answer to the question is likely to be that all men and women, regardless of colour, caste and creed, are truly God's children; that it would be intolerable and conceited narrow-mindedness to restrict this privilege to baptized Christians. Are not Hindus and Muslims, Jews and Jains, Buddhists and Parsees equally children of the Almighty, and as such, loved by him?

Yet, the answer is not half as simple as that. When confronted with this question — as well as any other question pertaining to the Christian faith — the first thing to do is search for an answer in the Scriptures, scrutinize carefully the word of God in search for light. And Scripture does give an answer to our question, even if it is not precisely the sort of answer we had anticipated. The pertinent source of information is the body of Pauline and Johannine writings which deal explicitly with our filiation. As seen above, according to Paul our sonship is beyond our human capabilities, beyond our human grasp. Man, by himself, cannot possibly become the son of God. This peak is far too high for him to scale alone and unaided. To accomplish this feat he absolutely needs the help of the Spirit of the Son. Without the Holy Spirit dwelling and acting within us, our supernatural filiation would be an absolute impossibility, for it is the Spirit that not only witnesses to, but, even more fundamentally, effects our filiation. We become the children of the Father through the Spirit of Jesus, not through our own spirit. This is plainly Paul's teaching.

Nor is John any different, for according to him — as seen above — our filiation, as an act of sharing in God's own life, is not the result of natural birth but of supernatural faith in Jesus Christ. It is an explicit belief in Jesus that brings about our sonship. Given his strong emphasis on faith, John seems to be saying that apart from this faith filiation is inconceivable. And since, on the other hand, only a fraction of humanity has explicit faith in Jesus Christ — approximately 30 percent of the present world population — it would seem that, on the basis of John's premises, we should unavoidably come to the shocking conclusion that the immense majority of men and women are *not* the sons and daughters of God.

When confronted with this unpalatable reality, one could of course make a desperate attempt to try and go beyond both Paul and John, to the very origin of the Christian message, namely, to Jesus himself. Jesus is known to have praised on occasion the strong faith of non-Jews, which could put the feeble faith of some of the Jews to shame. This appealing broad-mindedness of Jesus, however, does not seem to tally with his use of *Abba* as a filial designation of God. For, according to the earliest strands of tradition embodied in the Synoptics, Jesus recommended addressing God as "your Father" only to his disciples, never to outsiders. "This indicates that Jesus did not see the fatherhood of God as something to be taken for granted, a common possession of all men, *but as a privilege enjoyed by his disciples*".[8]

Therefore, our way of proceeding from John and Paul back to Jesus seems to have only strengthened the negative conclusion we had reached earlier. Neither Jesus nor Paul nor John seem to have extended the reality of our supernatural filiation to non-Christians. The solution may be harsh, difficult to accept and even more difficult to justify before

8 J. Jeremias, *The Prayers of Jesus*, p. 81.

our non-Christian friends, but that is the way it is. The New Testament seems to give us little hope in our generous and large-hearted endeavour to extend our filiation to all and sundry, regardless of religion. It would seem that we can embrace the generous solution (that is, filiation for all) only at the cost of betraying our Christian faith — an exceedingly heavy price to pay, indeed.

But now it would appear that the prospects are not so dark, after all. We have only to turn to the very origins of humankind, centuries and even millennia before Christ's arrival divided the world into Christians and non-Christians. In the very first pages of the Bible we find God's decision recorded: "Let us make man in our image, after our likeness" (Gen 1,26). If a man is made according to the divine model, he should be God-like, bearing in himself the divine resemblance, and therefore, for all practical purposes, he is God's own son. And this applies — let us repeat it again — to absolutely all men and women, it simply refers to the entirety of the human race.

Yet this is nothing but a mirage, a reality without consistency, a soap-bubble full of colour but empty of substance. The real meaning of this statement of Genesis has nothing to do with our supernatural filiation, and the use of the word "image" is deceptive. The real sense of the passage seems to be that man has a divine origin, for Adam was fashioned by God himself, according to the Genesis narrative; and, especially, that he is made God's representative and as such exercises dominion over nature. He is made in God's image because he is an intelligent creature, endowed by God himself with intellect and will, and thus he mirrors the very nature of the Creator himself. But we are still miles away from the doctrine of our supernatural filiation in Christ. Man, as a creature, certainly reflects in himself the nature of his Creator, but this is something quite different from saying that he has God as his Father. Genesis is dealing with the theme of creation, not with that of filiation. The notion of image may be common to both, but this is a rather precarious, flimsy link which may soon snap. All men are made in God's image, but this is not to say that they are all God's children. A facile transition from the realm of creation to that of filiation would be totally unwarranted.

And yet the horizon is not too dark, nor is Christian theology as pessimistic as the reader might have thought. It is true that within the limited perspectives of Paul and John the answer to the question should be negative, but what prevents us from enlarging these views to a broader horizon? In the latter half of the first century — when most or all of the New Testament was written — the Christian communities known to Paul and John were surrounded by and almost drowned in, the overwhelming mass of the non-Christian population, and yet, the question we are trying to answer — viz., whether our sonship can be extended to non-Christians — does not seem to have occurred to them, or, if it did, neither of the two seems to have answered it. Both of them write exclusively to Christian communities, and directly say not a word on the possible extension of our sonship to non-Christians. As regards this question they are simply silent and therefore neutral, neither favouring nor opposing such an extension.

We certainly may not go *against* Scripture, which for a Christian remains normative and binding, but what is there to prevent us from going *beyond* Scripture, namely, why cannot we try to give tentative answers to legitimate questions which are not found in the written word of God? As a matter of fact, the New Testament does offer us some solid foundation on which we can build. If so, our answer may not be immediately and directly scriptural, but it would be in keeping with the spirit of Scripture.

In order to be the son of God, one should have the Spirit of the Son (Paul) or faith in Christ (John). And what guarantee do we have that an unbaptized non-Christian lacks both? Since when is baptism of water the only way to be in fellowship with God and gain the companionship of the indwelling Spirit? The gates of the eternal kingdom are certainly not open only to Christians, but to non-Christians as well, provided they act according to their conscience. Paul is explicit on the matter: "For he (God) will render *to every man* according to his works: to those who by patience and well-doing seek for glory and honour and immortality, *he will give eternal life*... ;glory and honour and peace *for every-*

one who does good, the Jews first and *also the Greek*. For God shows no partiality" (Rom 2,6-11).

On the other hand, access to eternal life is simply impossible to those who are not reconciled with God at the supreme hour of their departure from this life; and we know that reconciliation implies the internal presence of the Holy Spirit. If a man, Christian or not, is to hope for eternal life, he must sooner or later be in a state of friendship with God, namely, he must possess, or rather, be possessed by, the Spirit of the Son who is the Spirit of sonship. If the non-Christian is indwelt by the Spirit, he is already son of God, whether he is conscious of it or not. The indwelling of the Spirit of sonship is by no means the exclusive privilege of baptized Christians.

In addition to the Spirit, the non-Christian must also have at least faith, living faith in God. For a Christian this faith is concretized as faith in Jesus, but a non-Christian who lacks explicit faith in Christ may still have a living, transforming faith in God. John insists that faith in Christ is the gate to sonship, yet the same John also states that "he who hears my word and believes him who sent me, has eternal life; he does not come into judgement, but has passed from death to life" (Jn 5,24).

This is further confirmed by the famous text in Matthew's gospel which is known in Christian literature as the scene of the last judgement (Mt 25, 31-46). The passage is simple in appearance but rich in doctrine. It deals specifically with the harrowing problem of the possibility of salvation for non-Christians, and the conclusion is astonishingly broad: some of the "nations", namely, the non-Christians, who have not acknowledged Christ explicitly in their lives, will hear, to their own amazement, "Come, O blessed of my Father, inherit the kingdom prepared for you...;for I was hungry and you gave me food....When you did it to one of the least of these my brethren, *you did it to me*" (Mt 25, 34-40). They lacked explicit faith in Christ, and yet this faith was in a way present, manifested and rendered tangible in their ethical behaviour, in their service to the poor.[9] Nothing else is needed

9 For a more detailed treatment of this passage in Matthew's gospel, see my previous book *Light Beyond Death* (Anand 1985), pp. 49-52.

for their salvation, for their saving faith in God was already present and operative in them, even if explicit faith in Christ was missing. In other words, if at the end they are saved, they must necessarily have been in a state of friendship with God: their explicit faith in God and implicit faith in Christ has made them children of God and heirs of eternal life.[10]

BIBLIOGRAPHY

Marchel,W.: *Abba, Père! La Prière du Christ et des Chrétiens* (Rome 1963).

Scheuberg,N.: "St Paul's notion on the adoptive sonship of Christians", *The Thomist* 28 (1964), pp. 51-75.

Von Rad, G. - Kittel,G.: "Eikon", *Theological Dictionary of the New Testament* 2 (1964), pp. 381-397.

Rey B.: *Créés dans le Christ Jésus* (Paris 1966), pp. 157-231.

Rondet, H.: *The Grace of Christ* (Westminister 1967), pp. 65-88.

Jeremias, J.: *The Prayers of Jesus* (London 1967).

Baumgartner,C.: "Filiation adoptive", *Dictionnaire de Spiritualité* 4 (1967), pp. 715-722.

Blinzler, J.: "Sonship", in J. Bauer, ed., *Encyclopedia of Biblical Theology* 3 (1970), pp. 862-869.

Ternant, P.: "Fathers and Father", *Dictionary of Biblical Theology*, 2nd ed., (Bangalore 1973), pp. 169-173.

Dunn, J.: *Jesus and the Spirit* (London 1975), pp. 21-26.

Schillebeeckx, E.: *Christ. The Christian Experience in the Modern World* (London 1980), pp.463-714.

Marchel,W.: "Paternité de Dieu", *Dictionnaire de Spiritualité* 12 (1984), pp. 413-429.

10 Hopefully the doctrine exposed above will not take the reader by surprise, for Vatican II states explicitly: "Those also can attain to eternal salvation who through no fault of their own do not know the gospel of Christ or his Church, yet sincerely seek God, and moved by grace, strive by their deeds to do his will as it is known to them through the dictates of their conscience" (*Lumen Gentium*, n.16: W. Abbott, ed., *The Documents of Vatican II*, New York 1966, p. 35). If eternal salvation is not restricted to Christians, neither is sonship.

Chapter Five

THE CHRISTIAN, GRACED BY GOD

The Christian enjoys within himself both the personal, transforming presence of the Holy Spirit and the mutual immanence with the risen Christ. This new double relationship cannot but effect deep down in man a radical change, a complete transformation. He has become "a new creature" (2 Cor 5,17). Now the Father looks on him with benevolent complacency; he has become the object of God's loving kindness. For the ultimate reason which accounts for his newness in man is the Father's gratuitous love, namely, his grace. Now man stands "in the sunshine of his benevolence".[1] enveloped in his loving kindness.

Christian catechisms usually make much of sanctifying grace, a divine reality distinct from Christ and the indwelling Spirit, which — it is alleged — is responsible for all that is new in man. It is due to sanctifying grace that man is transformed into a new creature, that the Spirit dwells in him, that he becomes the son of God, that he gains a participation in the divine nature, that he will eventually be admitted to the facial vision of God. It all seems to hinge on the reality of grace which covers him like a wide, resplendent mantle. This claim, however, seems to be somewhat exaggerated, for in this regard it is important that we take the Bible as our centre of gravity, rather than a later tradition of doubtful value. A gift of God to man, concomitant to that of the indwelling Spirit, is certainly to be admitted, we do have

1 H. Küng, *Justification* (New York 1964), p. 221.

sanctifying grace. Yet the widespread conception that considers this grace both as the most fundamental reality in the baptized Christian and — specially — as somewhat disconnected from the person of the Spirit, is to be shunned as foreign to Scripture. For we are sanctified primarily by the person of the Holy Spirit himself, not by an impersonal sanctifying grace. Scriptural perspectives should always be kept, not sacrificed in the interest of a later systematization. Our sanctification now and our salvation later depend on deeply personal relationships, rather than on impersonal realities, no matter how precious. Grace should accompany the gift of the personal Spirit, not dislodge him from the inner sanctuary of man.

1) God's covenanted loving kindness

Yahweh's attitude towards Israel is hardly understandable. Here is an insignificant nation of slaves, subject to the mighty Egyptian empire, whose only title of glory is a remote, obscure promise made to one of their ancestors, that one day God would come to their rescue, make them into his People and multiply them like the grains of sand on the seashore. Empty promises dimmed by the relentless passage of time? The tiny flame of the original promise is kept alive and passed on incessantly from one generation to the next. The harsh inhuman conditions in which the Israelites lived could only foster despair rather than hope. Disorganized and disunited, they are simply crushed by the yoke of the oppressor which lies heavy on their shoulders.

When the darkness is almost total, a flash of light as radiant as it is unexpected: Moses, who had seen their plight many years earlier, before he became a murderer and a fugitive from justice. In order to fulfil his promise, God, incomprehensibly, chooses an old man whose only concern was to pasture his flock in the inhospitable region of Sinai, and sends him to make of that batch of slaves his own beloved People, the People of God. A new nation of free men is born, due exclusively to God's utterly gratuitous love for them. For God is a rock of fidelity, stubbornly persistent and bountifully generous. He has not forgotten his earlier promise after all. He remembered, and here is Moses the shepherd, as the embodiment of his loving fidelity for his People. The Sinaitic Covenant is made, and thereby Yahweh binds the Isrealites to himself with bonds of love and fidelity: the People of God is born. Memories of the recent past, the situation of near despair in which they lived, and God's gracious intervention in their favour have left an indelible mark in their collective memory. Specially Yahweh's merciful intervention on their behalf is branded forever into their consciousness; they know – and they know from personal experience — that their newly acquired human dignity, their nationhood and their liberation are due exclusively to God's own initiative, to his grace and to his love.

It is the reality of this national experience that they encapsulate in one single word of difficult translation: *hesed.* It primarily means God's steadfast love in making and keeping the terms of the Covenant, freely established by him with Israel. After the experience of Sinai and the making of the Covenant, the Israelite can ask God to remember his favours and to act in keeping with them, namely, he can always appeal to God's *covenanted loving kindness*, to his gratuitous, faithful love embodied in the terms of the Covenant. The warming rays of God's fidelity and love embrace the whole of Israel, for it is the entire nation that has entered into a Covenant. Now the People of God basks in the sunshine of his goodness and the comforting presence of his fidelity. Love and fidelity cover them like a protective mantle and, so enveloped, they feel cozy, they feel secure. God loves them.

This wealth of spiritual meaning enclosed in the divine *hesed* is further strengthened by an allied term, *hen*, which etymologically comes from a root meaning "to approach, to bend over". And Yahweh, because of this *hen*, does bend over Israel, like a father bends over his child to bring him to his cheek and offer him food, in the touching imagery of Osee. *Hen* means that someone is pleasing to Yahweh, as the husband is pleasing to his wife or the subject is pleasing to his king. This is simply God's grace to his People, his subjective disposition of loving benevolence. The epitome of God's gracious attitude towards his chosen People is partially portrayed in Ex 34, 6 7: "Yahweh, Yahweh, God of tenderness and of grace (*hen*), slow to anger, rich in kindness (*hesed*) and in fidelity, showing kindness (*hesed*) to the thousandth generation...." Little wonder that this passage will be subsequently treasured by Jewish religious tradition as the deepest revelation of God's personality made to Moses. Years later the prophet Osee will sing in lyrical terms and under the familiar imagery of marriage: "I will betroth you to me for ever; I will betroth you to me in righteousness and in justice, in steadfast love (*hesed*) and in mercy. I will betroth you to me in faithfulness and you shall know the Lord" (Os 2,19-20). Israel, united to Yahweh by a marital bond of love and fidelity, will "know", that is, will have a deep personal experience of God's faithful love for her. Hereafter, God's grace towards her will no longer be the object of academic instruction, but the object of experiential perception; she will feel, taste and relish the grace of Yahweh.

Yet, no sooner was the Covenant made than it was torn to shreds. The wife proved unfaithful and turned to men other than her husband, who, however, doggedly kept up his efforts in an attempt to entice her back. She broke the terms of the Covenant, but Yahweh will not give up, for her infidelities have been unable to quench his *hesed* for her. A new covenant is promised, and this time, so as to make sure that the very root of her infidelity and wayward behaviour is plucked out, Israel will be given a new heart, sensitive, docile, flexible and eminently responsive to the grace of Yahweh: "Behold the days are coming, says the Lord, when I will make a new covenant with the house of Israel...,not like the covenant which I made with their fathers when I took them by the hand to bring them out of the land of Egypt, my covenant which they broke, though I was their husband, says the Lord" (Jer 31,31-32). The new covenant here promised will alter Israel radically, for the grace of Yahweh is not an ineffectual attitude of benevolence, but rather a potent, powerful commiseration that will turn man into a new creature by giving him a new heart: "I will sprinkle clean water upon you, and you shall be clean from all your uncleannesses... A new heart I will give you, and a new spirit I will put within you; and I will take out of your flesh the heart of stone and give you a heart of flesh" (Ez 36,25-26). The grace of Yahweh has finally conquered Israel, his faithful love has overpowered her traditional lightheadedness and innate tendency to drift away.

But the ultimate and most powerful testimony of this transforming power of God's grace, however, is to be found in the book of Wisdom at the threshold of the New Testament period. Now it is not only the radical change in man that is brought about through the agency of a created gift, but divine Wisdom herself penetrates man: "In every generation she *passes into holy souls* and makes them friends of God" (Wis 7,27). "By Wisdom, God gives his creatures a reflection of his beauty. He communicates himself in a more intimate way, a way which supposes a welcoming response from the free creature.... Wisdom enters into the soul that opens up to it and renders it lovable to God".[2]

Yahweh's gracious love for his People is the heart of Israel's religion, the incessant object of its prayer, as manifested especially in the Psalms: "How precious is your steadfast love (*hesed*), O God. The children of God take refuge in the shadow of your wings, they feast on the abundance of your house, and you give them drink from the river of your delights" (Ps 36,6-8). "Your steadfast love (*hesed*) is better than life, my life will praise you" (Ps 63,3). In short, the God of the Psalms is a God of kindness and fidelity, of love and grace, the God who bends over man and gently draws him unto himself. For an Israelite, therefore, it is not man primarily but rather God himself who is "full of grace".

2) The Father's Unmerited Benevolence

When it first appeared, Christianity was a reality without precedent, but it was only gradually that the apostolic Church broke away from the moorings of Judaism. In order to express the heart of the new Christian movement, which is God's love and grace manifested in Christ, the biblical writers had at their disposal a number of religious terms, already utilized in the Old Testament and well-known to them. However, it is remarkable that they discarded all of them as unsuitable, and selected instead a Greek, non-biblical word entirely alien to the Jewish tradition: *charis* or grace. The newness of the

2 J. Guillet, *Themes of the Bible* (Notre Dame 1961), p. 35.

Christian experience, they felt, had to be conveyed by an entirely new term which they borrowed from profane usage.

Originally, *charis* was used to designate something that glitters or sparkles and therefore delights the eye. A softly burning light has *charis*, and so does a precious stone. By a transposition, however, the term came to designate not only the brightness of a material object, but also the favour bestowed on a person, the radiance of a generous heart. Its immediate Old Testament background is to be sought in *hen*, but "while the Greek retains primarily the objective value of the attractive object or of the gift granted, the Hebrew is primarily attracted to the personal gesture of the giver".[3] In other words, whereas the Greek looks at the gift, the Hebrew rather regards the giver. The word *charis* was obviously never used by Jesus (his mother tongue was Aramaic, not Greek!). Apparently it was Paul who introduced it for the first time into our Christian vocabulary.

He uses the term primarily in the sense of God's loving benevolence, which is at the root of man's salvation in Christ. He simply voices the overwhelming experience of the early Christian community, "of being submerged in a sudden overflowing of God's infinite generosity".[4] *Charis* is a golden link that unites giver and receiver, for it embraces simultaneously both the generosity of the former and the thankfulness of the latter. The giver, prompted by his grace, bestows a gift, and the receiver, equally under the influence of grace, responds with a deep sense of gratitude.[5] In either case grace designates a strictly personal attitude, a certain mutual, joyful openness between two persons. When applied to the relationship between God and man, it means at once both the gift of salvation granted by God and the grateful response offered by man. *Charis*, therefore, is nothing but a personal relationship to another in loving solicitude.

The fundamental meaning of the word in Paul is that of something which is freely given and unmerited, though this

3 J. Guillet, *Themes of the Bible*, p. 21.

4 J. Guillet, *Themes of the Bible*, p. 23.

5 So, for instance, the word *eu-charis-tia* contains a core of gratitude as its most fundamental meaning. The heart of the Christian Eucharist is precisely *charis*, simultaneously gift and thanksgiving.

general sense acquires a variety of different shades of meaning according to the context. In keeping with the Old Testament background, it usually designates the loving attitude of God with regard to men, manifested in concrete historical events as embodiments and externaly visible signs of God's grace. For instance, Paul will say that the Incarnation itself was an act of grace on the part of God, for "you know the *charis* of our Lord Jesus Christ, that though he was rich, yet for your sake he become poor" (2 Cor 8,9). Very appropriately the Church makes use of a similar passage in the Christmas liturgy: "The *charis* of God has dawned upon the world" (Tit 2,11), for Bethlehem is for humankind the beginning of salvation. But if Bethlehem is due to the Father's *charis*, so is Golgotha at the end: "We see Jesus...so that by the *charis* of God he might taste death for everyone" (Heb 2,9). So the entire life of Christ, from birth to death, is nothing but a tangible proof of the magnanimous *charis* of the Father.

But it is especially the risen, glorified Christ that is the incarnation of divine grace. Paul never seems to make use of *charis* in connection with the earthly Jesus, but always in reference to the glorified Lord. It almost looks as if the original meaning of the term, which referred to a shining or glittering object, were also applicable to the Easter Christ, radiant with paschal splendours. When trying to justify his Gentile mission to the Jerusalem authorities, and in obvious reference to his Damascus experience, when the glorified Jesus suddenly appeared to him in a flash of light, Paul says that "they (James, Peter and John) perceived the *charis* that was given to me" (Gal 2,9). It was a glittering grace imparted to Paul by the shining Christ in an atmosphere of brightness.

Behind the glorified Christ, however, and at a deeper level, lies the root of man's salvation in Christ: the *charis* of the Father. Paul writes in glowing terms to the Ephesians: "But God (the Father) who is rich is mercy, out of the great love with which he loved us...that...he might show the immeasurable riches of his *charis* in kindness towards us in Christ Jesus..." (Eph 2,4-7). Kindness, mercy, love, *charis*. By piling up synonyms Paul hopes somehow to convey to his readers the gratuitous goodness of the Father rendered visible in Christ Jesus. In fact, the entire economy of salvation in

Christ Jesus is for Paul nothing but an eloquent proof of the Father's grace: "Where sin increased *charis* abounded all the more, so that as sin reigned in death, *charis* might also reign through righteousness to eternal life through Jesus Christ our Lord" (Rom 5,21).

"From all these shades of meaning it is clear that the word *charis* is always used to emphasize that the gift is absolutely free".[6] In the last analysis, *charis* is *the Father's unmerited benevolence* towards sinful man.

And it is this divine benevolence that is forcefully expressed in Romans 3,23-24, a remarkable model of conciseness. Paul is expounding to his readers in Rome the fundamental Christian belief that for all, Jews and Gentiles, salvation rests on Jesus Christ alone. "Since all men have sinned and fall short of the splendour of God, they are justified (sanctified) by his *charis* as a gift, through...Jesus Christ, whom God put forward as an expiation by his blood". A typical Pauline mouthful, if there ever was one.

We have already seen in the first chapter, in connection with this very text, that Paul is here thinking of the crucifixion. The real expiatory (rather than "expiation") put forward by the Father is not the lid of the Ark kept in the Jerusalem Temple and sprinkled with blood by the high priest on the Day of Atonement, but rather the very person of Jesus hanging on the cross and covered with his own blood. This is the real expiatory through which God forgives man's sins. And this merciful forgiveness is the effect of his *charis*. Hence, what we see on Calvary is the Father's *charis*, lavish and gratuitous, embodied and rendered visible in the dying Christ nailed to the cross. For Paul *charis* is not only an invisible, internal attitude or subjective disposition, it is the bleeding Christ on the cross — this is the graphic, tangible representation of the Father's *charis*. For Paul hardly ever refers to Golgotha without bringing in also the person of the Father. Without the Father Calvary is incomplete, for it is he who accepted the salvific self-surrender of the dying Jesus, it is the Father who stood invisibly behind the cross offering to humankind the

6 S. Lyonnet, "Pauline Soteriology", in A. Robert - A. Feuillet, *Introduction to the New Testament* (New York 1965), p. 835.

broken body of his Son: this is the Father's *charis*, his grace, through which we are saved. Hence, for Paul grace, on the line of the Old Testament which he echoes, is an attitude of God towards men which is emphatically portrayed as *personal, gratuitous and markedly christological.*

The above is undoubtedly a very telling manifestation of the Father's grace which poured out on humankind through the vehicle of Christ's blood, but it is not the only one. In another passage, really marvelous in its briefness, Paul considers God's *charis* as effulgent or luminous, as a source of light. Writing to the Ephesians in the midst of a comprehensive, breathtaking overview of the entire landscape of man's salvation, he speaks quite spontaneously of "the effulgence of his *charis*, his free gift to us in the Beloved.... Such is the richness of the *charis* which he has showered on us" (Eph 1,6-7).

The Father's benevolence radiates outwardly and envelops men in its brilliance. It almost looks as if, when writing this, Paul had that passage of Exodus in mind which describes the splendour of Yahweh manifested to Moses on top of the mountain: "The effulgence of the Lord settled on Mount Sinai, and the cloud covered it six days....Now the appearance of the effulgence of the Lord was like a devouring fire..." (Ex 24,16-17). Similarly now it is the Father's grace that shines forth, as the deepest source of God's gifts and blessings received by men. God's *charis* glows and glitters — and bathes man in its light. A Christian has entered an almost luminous atmosphere, he is surrounded by light because he is enveloped by grace. The *charis* of the Father is shown to us "in the Beloved", that is, in Christ: "Anything exposed to the light will be illumined and everything illuminated turns into light. That is why he said... Christ will shine on you" (Eph 5,14). The radiant Christ of Easter, steeped in the splendour of God, is a manifestation of the Father's grace.

The blood of Christ and the light of Christ: two streams originating from the very same source, namely, the grace of the Father; two outward, visible signs of his invisible *charis*, which in Christ becomes almost tangible. Yet the grace of God is even richer than this. As we have seen above, it is deeply christological, but not only christological. In its ultimate expression, the Father's *charis* is profoundly trinitarian, as expressed in a beautifully comprehensive passage of the Pastorals: "When the kindness and love of God our Saviour for mankind were revealed...,it was for no reason except his own compassion that he saved us, by means of the cleansing water of rebirth and by renewing us in the Holy Spirit which he has so generously poured over us through Jesus Christ our Saviour. He did this so that we should be justified by his *charis*..." (Tit 3,4-7). It is almost the straight line pattern we encountered above when dealing with the rich eastern tradition of the indwelling: we receive the outpouring of the Holy Spirit from the Father through Christ, and are thereby sanctified, the deepest root of this sanctifying outpouring of the Spirit being precisely the Father's *charis*, his bountiful, lavish generosity and benevolence.

The initiative of the entire process of justification, sanctification and salvation lies hidden in the heart of the Father, it is rooted in his goodness. And the end and purpose of it all is "eternal life" (v. 7). Hence, here we have both the deepest root and the final fruit of man's baptismal transformation, respectively the Father's *charis* and eternal life, which is nothing but a sinking back into the Father, into the very *charis* from which the entire process started. The Father emerges, therefore, as the person who, out of sheer grace, both initiates and grounds the whole process of man's salvation. We owe it all to the unmerited grace of the Father.

In conclusion, this grace of God has been historically manifested through at least three different signs: the blood of Christ, the light of Christ, the waters of baptism. Blood, light, water: three visible, familiar elements that have, in the course of salvation history, become the privileged channels of transmission of God's unmerited grace.[7]

7 On the basis of Lk 1,28 Catholics have traditionally considered Mary to be "full of grace". Biblical mistranslations, however, can only offer an unreliable foundation for any subsequent theological construct. To build on such a foundation is to build on sand. Luke never said that Mary was full of grace; hence, to see in this passage the necessary biblical basis of the doctrine of Mary's Immaculate Conception is nothing but fanciful exegesis. Most modern translators have already abandoned St Jerome's Vulgate — responsible for the *gratia plena* — and rendered the passage correctly as "highly favoured" or its equivalent, all reference to grace having disappeared. The 1980 Catholic

3) God's life shared with men

The Bible has rightly been called "the word of God in the words of men", which goes to show that the same divine word can be transmitted differently according to the different mentality, cultural background and local conditions of the various biblical writers. Nobody will doubt that Paul is a deep thinker, possibly the deepest of the earliest Christian period, but if there is one that can match him in depth and originality it is John, writing almost half a century after Paul. While reflecting on the fundamental problem of man's salvation, Paul will trace it all back — as we have seen above — to the Father's grace, to which is ultimately due the beginning and the end, the initiative and the crowning of our salvation. John would agree wholeheartedly, no doubt, but he looks at the entire process of salvation from his own peculiar angle, and makes use of his own peculiar style. For John salvation is nothing but the process of sharing in God's own life, his own eternal life. Divine grace is the ultimate reality for Paul, divine life is the supreme gift for John. Both throw light on the relationship between God and man, but from two different perspectives which are mutually complementary.

Life. Divine life, man's life: a most fundamental reality which in John is as rich and suggestive as it is elusive and difficult to describe. And yet he himself has given us a kind of descriptive definition which he puts in the mouth of Jesus when praying to the Father shortly before his passion: "This is eternal life, that they know you, the only true God, and Jesus Christ whom you have sent" (Jn 17,3). In other words, life for John consists in "knowing" the Father and Jesus. Not theoretically but experientially, not academically but personally, not intellectually but intimately, not with the mind only but also with the heart. It is a knowledge soaked in affectivity and love. Hence, to put it more clearly and understandably for our contemporary mentality, *life is a warm, intimate, interpersonal communion with God pervaded by love.* It is a twofold relationship linking up the believer with Christ and the Father, a real participation in the very life of both.

edition of RSV has fortunately corrected the mistake of previous editions and rendered the text as "favoured one".

Surely John has the knack of conveying sublime realities through symbols that are simple, familiar, easy to grasp. Water, light, bread. Jesus promised the Samaritan woman a share in the divine gift of God under the deceptively simple imagery of water. Jesus speaks of "living water" (Jn 4, 10), of water of life; and she is promised "a spring of water welling up to eternal life" (Jn 4,14). It is the mystery of divine life communicated through the symbol of water. Jesus obviously implies, if I may pursue the imagery further, that this water given by him is to be drunk, and by being drunk it is to be assimilated and interiorized. The life of God is to become the life of man, God's supreme gift of his own life is to be taken in by man, he is to make it his own. Life starts flowing from God but it eventually reaches man. Its origin is in God, but here and now it is offered to and accepted by man. Now it is mine, not by creation but by reception.[8]

The immediate source of this torrent of life is Christ himself, the glorified Christ. He is the "bread of life" (Jn 6, 48), both because he has life and because he imparts that life to men: "Truly, truly I say to you, unless you eat the flesh of the Son of man and drink his blood, you have no life in you" (Jn 6,54). To receive the Eucharist is to live; it is from the eucharistic flesh of the transfigured Christ that life flows down to and floods the communicant. But besides the Eucharist, there is a second channel of transmission of divine life, even more fundamental, and that is living faith: "He who believes in me has eternal life" (Jn 6, 47). Believe and you will live. For it is through the personal opening of faith that divine life pours into the Christian. To believe in Jesus is to come to him, to adhere to him, to cling to him, and by clinging to him we drink from him, for he is the source of life: "If somebody is thirsty let him come to me and drink" (Jn 7,37). Life gushes forth from the risen Christ and is drunk in by the believer in plentiful draughts. Jesus does not have life, he is life.

8 Divine life is interiorized by man, but to press the matter further so as to try and detect in the Johannine life an explicit reference to sanctifying grace seems to be an anachronism. John's imagery is certainly suggestive, it is appealing — but it is also vague and unspecified, and it is better to keep it that way. To make it sharper and more concrete would be to go beyond John's own intention.

Jesus, however, is only the mediator, the intermediary *par excellence.* The life he so lavishly imparts to the believer is ultimately not his own, it is his Father's. Before becoming a source of life he is a recipient of that life, before being a giver he has become a receiver. Before that life starts flowing from him, it has flowed to him from above, from his Father. On Tabor, Jesus was the intermediary of that light which, originating from the Father, who "lives in unapproachable light" (1 Tim 6,16), radiated outwardly, enveloped Jesus, and from him extended to the three disciples. As a consequence, all shared God's own splendour, all were drawn into the brightness of God.

It is much the same with regard to life, the life that springs from the Father, flows down to and saturates Christ, and from him continues cascading down to the believer. Therefore it is not Christ's own life that we receive, it is the Father's, the ultimate source of life: "For as the Father has life in himself, so he has granted the Son also to have life in himself" (Jn 5, 26). This life, given to him in Christ, was for John a matter of personal experience, for the entire mystery of Christ is reduced to a mystery of life: "That which was from the beginning, which we have heard...seen... and touched with our hands concerning the word of life — the life that was made manifest, and we...proclaim to you the eternal life which was with the Father and was made manifest to us" (1 Jn 1,1-2) in Christ Jesus. Consequently, the possession of this life by the believer creates a communion of life with the Father and the Son.

The water of life issues from the Father, passes through Christ and from him it plunges down to man. Now the process is complete and man is finally in possession of divine life. And here lies the substantial difference between the *charis* of Paul and the life of John, for, whereas in Paul grace designates a loving attitude in God, namely, his unmerited benevolence, something that is intrinsic to God and cannot possibly be imparted to man, life in John is a reality that originally sprouted in God, but here and now is also shared by man. The Christian can feel in himself the effect of God's grace or benevolence, but properly speaking *charis* is a subjective attitude that is born in God and stays within God; it does not flow down to the believer, even if the believer is affected by it. John's life is very different, for ultimately, no matter how high its origin, it is ultimately received within man. Paul's *charis* was only God's; John's life is both God's and man's, once the divine gift has been imparted to man.

Now there is something new in man, a new principle of activity, a new type of life which is not human but divine. The seed of eternal life has already been implanted in the heart of man. Now — if we are allowed to use a Pauline expression to convey John's thought — man has become like a "new creature" (2 Cor 5,17). In spite of John's insistence on "having" and "receiving" it, this life can best be expressed by "the category of *personal relation*".[9] It is a new communion that has sprung up within man, a communion of personal intimacy with Jesus and his Father, for now man shares in the life of both, he has been drawn into the very life of God.

A few miles from Jerusalem, on the modern highway to Jericho, lies the sleepy village of Eliazarim, the biblical Bethany. There a typically Jewish tomb is shown to tourists, the very tomb — it is claimed — from which Jesus called his friend Lazarus back to life. Answering Martha's querulous remonstrances, Jesus gives us in a short sentence the very heart of the entire episode: "I am the resurrection, *I am life;* he who believes in me, though he die, yet shall he live" (Jn 11,25). Jesus' reply is transparent, crystal clear — and very misleading. His use of the future ("he shall live") in the context of the resurrection in which the promise is made might lead one to believe that Jesus is referring to a future occurrence, that he will be the source of life to the believer in the distant future, at the time of the resurrection.

Nothing could be further from the truth. The bestowal of Jesus' own life on the believer is a present reality that takes place here and now, not only in the future. The waterfall of divine life is rushing down already now. For according to John this life pours into us through two main channels, and both are operative now in our present pilgrim condition: faith and the Eucharist. "He who believes *has* eternal life" (Jn 6, 47) — in the present. Faith brings down God's life to

9 R. Schnackenburg, *The Gospel according to St John*, II (New York 1982), p. 356.

the believer, he lives because he believes. And similarly, in a dense eucharistic context, Jesus says: "As I . . . draw life from the Father, so whoever eats me will draw life from me" (Jn 6,57). The eating of his body and drinking of his blood are sacramental realities that take place in the present, and so is the communication of the life they impart to the disciple. The Christian believes now and he eats Christ's body now, and therefore he is soaked in divine life also now, not only later.

Yet this life received now through faith and the Eucharist thrusts the Christian forward, towards the future, for the immensely rich potentialities of this trinitarian life are not exhausted in the present. The participation in this life propels man necessarily towards the future. Jesus had already promised to the woman of Samaria: "The water that I shall give him will become in him a spring of water welling up to eternal life" (Jn 4,14). The disciple does have this water of life already now — but he does not yet have it in its fullness. The spring is already within him, for this is the life of Jesus and his Father, and Jesus is immanent in him and the Father dwells in him as in a temple. The disciple has both of them and therefore the water of life gushes forth from within him, it bubbles up inside his own person, and yet his thirst is not entirely slaked. The more he drinks the more he thirsts for the satiating fullness of Jesus' promise. The seer of the Apocalypse discloses the final reality, the only reality that will quench the disciple's thirst once and for all: "Then he showed me the river of the water of life, bright as crystal, flowing down from the throne of God (the Father) and of the Lamb" (Apoc 22,1). Then, and only then, will the disciple drink in the very fullness of God's own life.

John conveys much the same reality when he speaks in such glowing terms of the Christian as born of God, begotten by God. This is but another way of saying that he has in himself the very life of God. "We are called children of God and so we are" (1 Jn 3,2), because, John says forcefully, we are "born of God" (1 Jn 3,9), we are "begotten by him" (1 Jn 2,29). In a process similar to that of human generation the Father has transmitted his own life to us. To be "from God" (1 Jn 4,4) must be taken not only as a designation of our divine origin, but specifically as a true communication of divine life to men. God's life is our life.

4) The spirit of grace

Paul and John may have favoured different approaches to the reality of grace, but on the other hand one should not overlook their points of convergence: grace is rendered visible in Christ (Paul) and divine, trinitarian life pours down through Christ (John). Paul as well as John consider Christ as the absolutely indispensable mediator of man's sanctifying transformation. Neither grace nor life are operative except in Christ. Similarly, neither of them ever considers respectively grace and life as separated from their fountainhead, the Father. In other words, the two greatest thinkers of the New Testament period look upon grace and life as two strictly personal realities that certainly affect man deeply, but always in close conjunction with Christ and the Father. Never will they isolate grace and life from the strictly personal context in which they remain embedded.

Unfortunately, later post-biblical trends did not always adhere strictly to these wise perspectives. And here one notices a substantial difference of approach between East and West, between the "eastern lung" and the "western lung". Both keep breathing, certainly, but the air they inhale seems to be slightly different. The two sisters in the large family of the Catholic Church begin gradually to drift apart, and as a consequence, their conceptions of grace no longer tally. Their approaches and emphases are markedly different, and it would be simply too naive to claim arbitrarily that the two perspectives, eastern and western, are in fact mutually complementary, that each one of them lays stress on a particular aspect of the total comprehensive reality of God's grace operative in man.

a) *Eastern perspectives*

Originally, grace was not so much reflected upon in learned treatises as it was lived. The first generation of Christians was conscious of living an entirely new life, but there was no conscious effort at explicitating this inner experience. It was only three or four centuries later that the necessary theological reflection on grace began, and when it did it crystallized and clustered around two important centres, or rather, two gigantic figures that left an indelible mark on subsequent generations in the East as well as in the West: Cyril of Alexandria, whom we have already encountered above, and Augustine, both of them living on the northern shores of Africa, in regions that today we would designate as third world countries — Egypt and Algeria — but which at that time were outstanding theological centres respectively of the eastern and western churches. The East, led by Cyril, Bishop of Alexandria, heavily under the influence of the Johannine school, will emphasize strongly the divinizing aspect of transforming grace. In a generally calm atmosphere, free of disturbing polemics and futile controversies, the Orientals develop a theology of grace which is definitely more serene, more interior, more spiritual and mystical, less dramatic than that of the Latin West.

The theological attention of the East is focussed on the person of the Holy Spirit dwelling in the Christian, but by developing further John's approach, who exercised such an extraordinary influence on the see of Alexandria, the eastern writers will also mention explicitly the reality of grace, certainly present in man as an important element in the entire process of his divinization, but essentially distinct from the person of the indwelling Spirit. Man is sanctified by both the Holy Spirit *and* grace, by the very person of God living within man *and* by grace, a distinct, created reality which should not be confused with the person of the Spirit. The stress by far is on the Spirit, but the concomitant reality of grace is not neglected. The biblical insights of John, who spoke so eloquently of God's life present in man, begin now to lose their vagueness and gain in precision. The suggestive character of the Johannine notion of life continues, but its contours become sharper and more defined, with particular stress on the fact, that, though originally descending from God, that life is now man's own personal possession. It is God's gift, to be sure, but it is now a gift possessed by man.

For precision and clarity of expression Cyril is second to none. Commenting on Jn 1,13 within a baptismal context, he says: "The Spirit will be from God and God himself according to his nature; once we are given to share in him through our faith in Christ, we become sharers in the divine nature and are said to be born of God and are called gods; and this not only because *we are raised by grace* to this supernatural glory, but because we have God himself dwelling and abiding in us".[10] That grace, principle of man's divinization, is *not* the Holy Spirit, but a reality different, though inseparable, from him.

The divinity of the Holy Spirit is something that all of us know and readily take for granted without batting an eye, but in those early centuries things were not that simple. Cyril and other eastern doctors had to fight battles royal with their opponents in order to defend the Spirit's divinity. That polemical context has certainly grown obsolete for us now, for this point of doctrine has long since been settled and is no longer controversial. It is not therefore the historical and polemical context that matters for us now, but rather the concrete doctrine expressed within that theological framework. The text of Gen 1,26, on man being created to God's image and similitude, offers Cyril a convenient platform to expose his doctrine of the Spirit of grace: "If the essence of the Spirit were dissociated from the grace given through him, why did Moses say that the Creator of all, after shaping a creature, *breathed into him grace* through the Spirit of grace?".[11]

Should God's grace operative in man be graphically compared to a garb worn by him? This traditional comparison which goes back to Cyril and even further back than Cyril, will claim our attention later. Let it suffice for the moment, however, to quote the Alexandrian doctor once again: "Those who through faith in Christ are called to be children of God, have given up the lowliness of their own nature and, *shining with the grace of God... as with a resplendent garb*, are raised to supernatural dignity".[12]

Hence, for Cyril — and in this he simply echoes the common eastern tradition — the sanctification of the Christian is brought about, not just by one, but rather by two distinct principles: primarily by the personal Spirit dwelling in man,

10 *In Joannem* I, 9: PG 73, 157.
11 *Dialogi de Trinitate* 7: PG 75, 1088.
12 *In Joannem* I, 9: PG 73, 153.

and also by the accompanying grace which is inseparable from the Spirit. The lion's share, in Cyril's conception, goes to the Spirit, no doubt, for both these principles, though present, are of unequal importance and should therefore not be placed on the same footing. For ultimately it is the Spirit, namely, God himself that matters, even more than grace. Thus a perfect balance is kept between the two realities that, together, effect the internal divinization of the Christian: the Holy Spirit and grace, the Spirit being above grace. He is simply "the Spirit of grace" (Hebr 10,29).

b) *A western deviation?*

If we were to look at a map of the western Mediterranean in the early 5th century we might well have to use a magnifying glass to find the insignificant see of Hippo in western Africa (present-day port of Bone, in Algeria). And yet, it is from that small, unprepossessing see that a bright beacon of light shone forth to illumine the entire western Church. It was its bishop, Augustine, that would render the name of his see immortal. It is highly likely that at that time neither Augustine himself nor any of his contemporaries, whether faithful disciples or bitter adversaries — he had both in plenty — ever dreamed of the enormous influence he would exercise in subsequent centuries throughout the western world. The Bishop of Hippo shone brightly, and his light has not yet been extinguished. It is really amazing to see how one single bishop could influence Catholic thought so deeply for so long.

But Hippo was certainly not Alexandria, and Augustine was not Cyril. For these two African doctors, living approximately at the same time at opposite ends of the Mediterranean basin, are the two classical representatives, the two spokesmen, one could almost say, of respectively the western and eastern halves of Christianity. The calm, relatively peaceful atmosphere in which Cyril developed his conception of grace was poles apart from the thick, dark clouds of controversy that frequently swirled around the diocese of Hippo, engulfing its bishop and dragging him into bitter polemical encounters.

Augustine was a passionate character and a real genius in the ways of the intellect, towering head and shoulders above all his western contemporaries, whether African or Roman. But his passion and zest show even in his theology of grace, which is deeply marked by his youthful experience of lust and sin. His dark, gloomy conception of the sinfulness of man is to a large extent the theological reflection of his sinful youth, for one should not forget that at the age of 17 he had already fathered a child from one of his numerous mistresses. Many years later, when reminiscing over his youth, the old bishop could not possibly forget his early debaucheries. Man—all men, specially a man called Augustine — is by nature sinful, prone to evil from his birth, inclined always to yield to the enticing allurements of the flesh. He will often find himself caught up in the morass of sin, sunk in the mire and fouled by filth. In this condition he can only clamour for help from above, for he himself is part of a *massa damnata*, the mass of sinful humanity heading for destruction. Only a merciful intervention of the Almighty can save man. If he is eventually saved, it will be undoubtedly the result of God's unmerited grace, not the effect of man's personal merit. In his theology of grace, Augustine keeps his gaze turned continuously upward, to God, from whom alone salvation can come.

This being Augustine's experiential and intellectual background, it is but natural that he should insist, in season and out of season, on the absolute preeminence of God's saving grace. St John would have felt quite at home in the theological atmosphere of Hippo, for Augustine concurred wholeheartedly with John's contention that man's filiation as well as the totality of his salvation are not the result of natural birth but of supernatural faith. The echoes of John's theology still reverberate in western Africa four centuries later....

Augustine's doctrine is surely deep, it is profound and satisfying, but for a contemporary reader his somewhat abstract terminology leaves much to be desired. He is a child of his age, naturally, but the theological terms used by him, no matter how unappealing to us now, cover and convey a vision, a system that transcends the narrow geographical and historical boundaries of his time. The following excerpts from his numerous writings become instantly clear if we only keep in mind that for him the term "justice" is, for all practical purposes, almost equivalent to what today we would call "sanctifying grace", affecting man deeply and transforming him radically.

Some of his opponents — did you ever hear of a pious, ascetical British monk called Pelagius? —would contend that man is absolutely self-sufficient, that he can very well prescind from God and manage his own personal affairs even if unaided by grace. This is simply the proud glorification of man's self-sufficiency, his autonomy vis-à-vis God carried to heretical extremes. When confronted with this dangerous distortion of the Christian message, Augustine reacts sharply: "For what else is justice (grace) when it is in us, but the beauty of the interior man?".[13] "For it is God's justice that becomes our own when it is given to us. That is why it is called justice *of God*, lest man should think that he has it by himself".[14] In keeping with this divine origin of grace, he holds man's divinization to be strictly a supernatural gift which man himself cannot possibly attain: "It is clear therefore that he has called men gods as *deified by his grace*, not born by nature. For he deifies who is God, not through somebody else's participation but by himself...Those who become gods do so by his grace, they are not gods by nature".[15]

The great doctor is not lost in the high clouds of sterile speculation, however. Augustine is certainly a born thinker and an ardent pastor who tries hard (but does not always succeed) in bringing that exalted theology down to the level of his lay flock. So, for instance, he makes use of a popular imagery in a sermon which must have amused his listeners: "Let it be justice, but let it be from grace, let it be from God, let it not be yours. And 'let your priests put on justice' (Ps 131,16). But a vestment is received, it does not grow with one's hair".[16]

He has made his point: grace is an *additional* gift of God which cannot in any way be reduced to man's birth or to his merely human accomplishments. The origin of the gift lies in heaven, not on earth, but there and now, and in spite of its gratuitous origin, the gift is possessed by man. Augustine's adversaries contended arbitrarily that saving grace is nothing

13 *Epistola* 120, 19: *Patrologia Latina* (PL) 33, 463.
14 *Enarratio in Psalmos*, 30, 6: PL 36, 233.
15 *Ibid.*, p. 563-4.
16 *Sermo* 149: PL 38, 922.

but man's efforts to imitate the goodness of God, that this grace is reduced to the aspect of external imitation, that deep down man remains untouched by it. Augustine will not buy this, for he detects immediately its dreadful superficiality. The concrete case of baptized children offers him an excellent opportunity to explain the internal aspect of grace, which goes far deeper than any superficial, external imitation: "Over and above this imitation his grace effects our illumination and justification also internally.... For by means of this grace it incorporates into his Body baptized children who are yet unable to imitate anyone.... For his Spirit gives to the faithful a *very secret grace, which he noiselessly infuses into children*".[17]

And now Augustine's view grows larger. It is not only children, not only single men and women who are thus affected by God's grace working in them; it is the entire Church that is resplendent, beautified by God's grace. The passage is self-explanatory:

> And you, O Church, have beauty, for it is said of you in the Canticles: 'O beautiful among women'. It is said of you: 'Who is that coming up so white?' (Cant 8,5). What does it mean, white? Illumined: not white in the sense of painted, like some ladies who paint themselves wishing to appear what they are not; not white like a whitewashed wall.... A whitewashed wall is plastered on the outside, but inside it is mud. This is not the way she is white, but whitened, illumined, because she is not white by herself.... First you were black, but now you have become white through his grace.... Who is this, that is coming up so white? She is marvellous, one can hardly gaze on her...so beautiful, so resplendent, so immaculate and pure.[18]

It does not take a great intellectual acumen to see the substantial difference between the eastern and the western conceptions of grace, those, namely, developed by Cyril and Augustine. Both accept that grace is an objective reality in man distinct from the person of the indwelling Spirit. But whereas the Bishop of Alexandria will never separate the two

17 *De peccatorum meritis* 1,9-10; PL 44, 144, with emphasis added.
18 *Enarratio in Psalmos,* 103, 6: PL 37, 1340.

and — more important — will always grant pride of place to the Holy Spirit, attributing to grace only a subsidiary role, his episcopal counterpart at Hippo will almost reverse the stress, laying heavy emphasis on grace (or justice, as he calls it), and unduly relegating the person of the indwelling Spirit to the shadows. The trend, which some will not hesitate to brand openly as an unfortunate western deviation, has already set in, and subsequent centuries will only serve to accentuate it.

In fact, centuries roll by and the extraordinary prestige of Augustine in the Latin Church continues undimmed. He is universally acknowledged as an intellectual giant, deep and penetrating, subtle and versatile. By and large Augustine reigns supreme, but as far as his theology of the Spirit's indwelling is concerned his conception is certainly not up to the mark. Just as his riotous youth left an indelible mark on his spirit and even on his theology of sin and grace, so also the concrete historical circumstances in which he lived, often marked by bitter polemics and intellectual battles, influenced deeply his way of thinking. It has been said that probably he found it easier and more appealing to engage in theological jousts than to attend to the effective administration of his diocese. Be that as it may, his partial neglect of the Spirit as dwelling and active in man is hardly commendable. The misguided concentration on grace to the relative detriment of the Spirit will continue after his death virtually unchallenged, right into the golden period of the Middle Ages.

And then we encounter another intellectual luminary of the first magnitude: St Thomas, glorified and exalted both during his life and after his death. But Thomas experienced sustained opposition too. He was under a cloud for a time, called to task by the Bishop of Paris for being dangerously modern and imprudently flexible and accommodating. Pagan Aristotle was the big attraction of the period, and Thomas was of the opinion that the Christian message could and should be conveyed in Aristotelian thought-patterns and categories. This daring enterprise might have appeared temporarily useful and appealing, but in the long run it was to prove rather detrimental, an obstacle, in fact, rather than a help for a deeper understanding of the Gospel message. Working under the spell of Aristotle, Thomas will carry the

Augustinian trend still further: sanctifying grace (the expression is coined now for the first time) "in the sense of a quality is said to act on the soul, not in the manner of an efficient cause, but in the manner of a formal cause".[19] Grace is an "entitative habit",[20] "the originating principle of meritorious action by the intermediary action of the virtues".[21] "Grace, formally speaking, is in the essence of the soul prior to its powers".[22]

All this is exceedingly accurate and precise, no doubt, but also dreadfully dry. It is cold, it is academic, it is abstract, it is absolutely unappealing. We are already poles apart from the warm scriptural conception of grace as God's unmerited benevolence (Paul), or of life as a personal, intimate communion with God (John). Instead of that, we have but an "entitative habit" — whatever that is. This medieval conception should be deplored for what it is: a regrettable deviation from the rich biblical perspectives — which goes to show that not every adaptation to the mentality and spirit of the times is praiseworthy. If Thomas had firmly resisted the allurement of Aristotle and had stood firm against the fashion of the time; if he had expressed the message and doctrine of grace in traditional biblical categories, and made more room for the person of the indwelling Spirit, he would still enjoy today a reputation he no longer has. Hasty adaptations can prove ephemeral.

5) Sanctifying grace, a personal relationship

At this juncture and after all the different approaches to the mystery of grace given above, the reader may be a trifle confused or puzzled. When everything is said and done, what precisely is grace, and in the concrete, sanctifying grace? This mysterious reality which, according to its own name, transforms and sanctifies man so deeply, is often compared in popular spirituality to a white, resplendent garment that covers man and makes him respectable in the eyes of God. One of Jesus' parables comes to mind as an apparent biblical justification of this pastoral approach: a king gives a marriage

19 *Summa*, I-II, q. 110, a. 4.
20 *De Veritate*, 27, 2 ad 7.
21 *Summa*, I-II, q. 110, a. 4.
22 *Ibid.*

feast, but to his amazement, he finds in the banquet hall a guest without the "wedding garment" (Mt 22,11). The man is unceremoniously thrown out into the outer darkness. In the light of Is 61,10, which speaks of "the robe of righteousness", the wedding garment necessary to enter the royal feast has been authoritatively interpreted as "forgiveness and imputed righteousness",[23] namely, the state of friendship with God. In view of this biblical background it would seem that the tiny white tunic placed on a baby at the baptismal ceremony as a symbol of grace is more than justified. After all, whiteness means holiness.

This baptismal practice may be justified, but one has to acknowledge that it is also misleading, for it seems to suggest that the sanctifying grace which takes possession of the baptized child is an impersonal something rendering him agreeable in the eyes of God, a sort of a new quality that clings to him and makes him holy. The symbol may be graphic and clear, but it should be transcended, for deep down sanctifying grace is not a new quality adhering to man, but rather a new subjective disposition, a new attitude with regard to God that can best be described as an intimately personal relationship with him, an essential element in the affective and effective dialogue between the indwelling God and the believer who is indwelt.[24]

23 J. Jeremias, *Rediscovering the Parables* (London 1966), p. 150.

24 This new approach to be developed below obviously does not go counter to the official teaching of the Church crystallized in the decrees of the Council of Trent in the 16th century as the Catholic reaction against the attacks of early Protestants. The gist of Trent's doctrine can be reduced to the following: when man is justified (that is, sanctified) he becomes a *new* man, for sanctifying grace adheres to him, clings to him, rendering him internally and really acceptable to God; and man is also *free*, for this deep transformation in him does not take away, but rather leaves intact, his ineradicable freedom. Trent demands nothing else. Cf J. Neuner - J. Dupuis, *The Christian Faith*, 4th ed., (Bangalore 1982), nn. 1929-1933. On the other hand, a mechanical repetition of the conciliar formulas would be clearly insufficient, for, in the authoritative opinion of Pope John XXIII at the opening session of Vatican II, "The authentic doctrine should be studied and expounded in the methods of research and through the literary forms of modern thought" (Opening address of Pope John XXIII to the Council: W. Abbott, *The Documents of Vatican II,* New York 1966, p. 715). What follows in the text is but a modest attempt in this direction.

a) *God and man as persons*

In the very constitution of man there seems to be a twofold characteristic, a kind of tension between two sides of his human nature: he is an open spirit but he is also finite, limited. As spirit he is essentially open to the infinite, and this fundamental openness will be entirely satiated only when it is filled with the person of God himself. Man is open primarily to persons, and nothing short of God himself will ever satisfy this ineradicable openness to another person. This aspiration of man, this orientation towards another person, which need not always be conscious, constitutes the most profound characteristic of man, it is this that sets him off from other, nonrational creatures. The Lord said, "Let us make man in our image, after our likeness" (Gen 1,26). It is precisely this natural, inbuilt openness of his human spirit that makes man mirror in himself the very nature of God; it is this that constitutes him as the image and similitude of God.

Yet, at the same time, man is also finite, intrinsically limited. He is thrust outside himself, he aspires to another, but is unable to fulfil this fundamental aspiration by himself. He can and does tend towards God, but he cannot reach God without God. His unlimited capacity for God is crippled by his intrinsic powerlessness to reach the person to whom he tends. He is always a pilgrim, marching towards God, thirsting for God, longing for God, and yet incapable of ever reaching God by himself. God essentially transcends man.

This is man's intrinsic paradox: he is at once unlimited in his inner aspiration, but limited in his power to attain the person who would satisfy this inescapable longing. It is an unlimited aspiration constricted by a limited power of achievement. Therefore, since by his very nature man can only tend to, but never reach, the satiating possession of God, God's self-donation to man remains a gratuitous gift, an unmerited grace to which man has no right and to which he can lay no claim. Man, left to himself, can only stretch out his arms towards God in a gesture of longing, but he can never reach God. It is God himself who, in the touching imagery of Osee, has to stoop down, pick up the eager child, bring him to his cheek and offer him food (cf Os 11,1-4). The child can clamour for food, but it is only daddy that can give him that food. In reality man is confronted here with a double gift: on the one hand he is drawn to God, he thirsts for God "as the deer longs for flowing streams" (Ps 42,1). This longing for God is already a gift, for it is God himself who instilled it in the heart of man, it is God who has made the heart of man thirsty. By planting in man this unavoidable tendency towards himself, God was already gently drawing man towards him. But this pull towards God, though already a precious gift in itself, is clamouring for a complement; for a tendency without the possibility of satiation is not a gracious gift but a cruel punishment. The natural longing of man for God is not matched by a corresponding withdrawal of God from man. God is not teasing man, making him hungry, beckoning him forward, and then withdrawing the only food that can quench his hunger, which is God himself. If God made man instinctively hungry, it is because he wants to satiate that hunger. And he will.

When this finally happens, man will be confronted with yet another gratuitous gift: the possession of the self-giving God. If man's tendency towards God is itself a gift, so is also—and specially—the satiation of that hunger. Since man left to himself can only tend to, but never reach the fulfilling possession of God, God's self-donation to man remains necessarily a free gift flowing down from his munificence. We are already witnessing the relationship between two persons, God and man. For it is a personal "I-Thou" relationship that will eventually slake man's thirst for the infinite. Man is not interested in abstract, impersonal objects, but in living and loving persons. Man, as a finite person, can only be satiated by another, infinite person. This thirst, this opening of man to God coincides precisely with his capacity for grace, and man is open to grace only in as far as he is a person, marked in his very constitution both by the unlimited character of his tendency and by the limited nature of his capacity for fulfilment. It is only the free, personal self-gift of God inspired by love that can satisfy man's inner aspiration as person: man will find his fulfilment only in his interpersonal relationship with God.

But a personal relationship is necessarily a two-way traffic, for the self-gift of God is to be matched by a corresponding receptivity on the part of man, an intrinsic openness to receive freely the divine gift. This openness of man as person, this essential receptivity to the inflow of God's self-donation constitutes the very core of his personality. This is what St John of the Cross called "the bottom of the soul", the very centre, the very heart of man as person. It is here, in this intimately personal and sacred holy of holies that the person of man is open to God. It is here, in this inner sanctuary, that is found man's radical freedom, his profound, conscious and free acceptance of God's self-gift to him. For God never thrusts his free gifts upon man. He invites, persuades, coaxes man to accept the divine gift, but he will never force him to accept it. God has an almost scrupulous respect for the inner sanctuary of man, the sanctuary of his freedom, where God himself does not dare to tread. God outstretches his hand towards man in a loving gesture, requesting his response and expecting his acquiescence, but now it is up to man to grasp the outstretched hand and begin a personal dialogue with God.

Furthermore, this personal structure of openness and receptivity affects not only man, but also God himself. God, as person, is nothing but perfect self-possession and luminous transparency. Just like man, God is also open to Another in so far as each of the three divine Persons is essentially open to another Person within the trinitarian family of God. Hence, God finds his self-fulfilment within himself, and yet in Another. As person, therefore, God has the same structure as man, for he too is open and tends to another Person, but, unlike man, he finds the full satiation of his natural tendency within himself. The aspect of openness is common to both God and man, for this is but an essential dimension of personality itself whether human or divine. Within God himself the opening of each person is both filled and fulfilled by the self-gift of another divine Person. There is openness and self-gift in man, and there is openness and self-gift in God himself. Namely, whereas man is open to the grace flowing from above, God is simultaneously opening and self-satiation.

But enough of abstractions. This tendency, this thirst of the person for another person, which affects both God and man, is something that we see with absolute clarity in the case of Jesus himself. We all admire his unwavering fidelity towards his Father. The compass necessarily points north, and so also Jesus points towards his Father: "I always do whatever pleases him" (Jn 8,29). And it is the same John that gives us in two short sentences the profound mystery, the real reason that explains this admirable fidelity of Jesus to his *Abba:*

"The Son is turned towards his Father's breast" (Jn 1,18). This sentence probably does not refer to the Son's eternal dependence on the Father even prior to the Incarnation, but rather to the fidelity of the man Jesus, who is always attuned to his Father, turned towards his Father's "breast", viz., towards his heart. Jesus is always faithful. Yet this is not deep enough. With regard to his Father Jesus is luminous transparency, the Father simply shines through him. What Jesus says and does in his life of fidelity is but a reflection of what he is. His activity is but an echo of his personality.

The real reason, the only reason that explains this fidelity is the opening statement in John's gospel: "The Word is turned towards the Father" (Jn 1,1). Jesus is constantly turned towards his Father *because* in him the eternal Word is turned towards the Father. The fidelity of the man Jesus has deep trinitarian roots. John has just opened a window through which we can gain a glimpse into the eternal, unfathomable mystery of God, into his inner trinitarian life. The Son is turned towards the Father — and vice versa. The Son does not have that tendency, he *is* that tendency, for there is nothing in him except a personalized opening to, an inner thrust towards the Father, a thirst for the Father, a thirst that is reciprocated by the Father. Father and Son long for each other, if we are allowed to use our clumsy human terms; they tend to each other and give themselves to one another, each finding in the other his own self-fulfilment and perfect satiation. There is an irresistible torrent of life that links up in an eternal embrace Father and Son, who are really "meant for each other". This is the trinitarian undercurrent that explains the fidelity of the man Jesus towards his Father. In Jesus we see the outer surface, deep down we glimpse the inner mystery of the Son.

It is precisely this mystery of openness and self-gift, both within himself and outside himself, towards man, that makes of God sheer grace. *Man as person is open to grace, God as person is grace.*

b) *Grace as dialogue*

Within this personalistic framework, sanctifying grace can be viewed as a dialogue between the indwelling God and man who is indwelt. Prior to the indwelling, man as a creature was open to his Creator; now in the indwelling man as son is open to his Father dwelling within him. Man's natural openness to God has been raised and transformed by the presence of the indwelling and the inflow of divine grace, which render him capable of establishing a dialogue with God. "Deep down in our being, the ways of God's creative love awaken a gentle hunger, a nostalgic longing, a tender yearning for God. The icy crust of selfishness begins to thaw under the warmth of God's breath".[25]

God, dwelling in man, quietly lures and draws him towards his own interior, to the deeper layers, to the core of his own personality where the embrace of mutual opening and self-gift between the Holy Spirit and man takes place. The Spirit is present in man in a loving surrender, and this demands a similar surrender on the part of man. The Spirit, by being present, enables man to respond, to enter into dialogue with God: *this response of man to the indwelling God*, effected by God's presence and accepted by man's freedom, *is sanctifying grace*. For the Spirit dwells in free persons and solicits from man a response which is conscious and free, intimate and personal, and this active response is precisely sanctifying, transforming grace. Robots cannot receive the Spirit because they cannot freely respond to him, they cannot consciously open up to him.

It should be clear, therefore, that the indwelling of the Spirit and sanctifying grace constitute an unbreakable unity, they simply cannot be dissociated, or man's dialogue with God would be ruptured. The indwelling requires the active response of sanctifying grace and, contrariwise sanctifying grace presupposes the indwelling. The Holy Spirit stands at the door and knocks, requesting admission. He offers himself to man in the personal presence of the indwelling, and man

25 P. Fransen, *The New Life of Grace* (London 1969), p. 241.

responds to the divine initiative by accepting the invitation, opening himself to him, letting in the Spirit and drawing him down to the very core of his person. Now the personal dialogue has been established, with man hungry for God and athirst for his presence: this is sanctifying grace. Hence, this grace should not be conceived as a means of union with God, as a sort of bridge of union between the indwelling Spirit and man. No, sanctifying grace is rather man's impetus towards God present to him. By being present inside man, the Spirit awakens his hunger for God, makes his initial response sharper and his surrender more complete.

Sanctifying grace is not so much an immediate preparation disposing man for the indwelling, as the result, the effect of the indwelling. The sun and its rays are inseparable, and so when man has the sun within himself he cannot but be bathed in the soft glow of its rays. The entire landscape which is man is brightly illumined because he has the sun within himself — the indwelling Spirit. The union between the Spirit and man is direct and immediate, without any intermediate reality, even of the supernatural order. It is the Spirit himself that soaks man, gripping him from within, engulfing him, totally enveloping him. It is in this process itself of interpenetration between the Spirit and man that sanctifying grace is produced. It simply cannot exist apart from the indwelling, it is effected by the indwelling and sustained by it. In that admirable conciseness of the Latin language, medieval authors expressed this pithily: sanctifying grace is "*ex unione, in unione, ad unionem*": it arises from the union of the indwelling, thrives in the midst of this union, and urges man to deepen the same union. The indwelling and sanctifying grace are as inseparable as the two persons engaged in dialogue, God and man. The Spirit does not produce sanctifying grace in man as a preparatory step eventually conducive to his personal presence in him; he rather pours grace into man by being present within him.

This response of man to the indwelling God, or sanctifying grace, is no capital given to man by God once and for all; it is rather a grace which is *continuously being given* by the indwelling God. Man needs God's presence continuously in order to be able to respond to him, and this is probably the deepest reason why sanctifying grace cannot be conceived apart from the indwelling which sustains it uninterruptedly. Man cannot respond to God without God. He is totally enveloped in a mystery of an utterly gratuitous, unmerited grace. "Grace remains the living stream ceaselessly coming to me from God, permeating me and drawing me to God".[26] Just as in the internal, trinitarian life of God, the mutual giving and receiving constitute each of the divine Persons, so also in the mystery of grace man's maximum gift of self coincides with the reception of God within him. In the words of Protestant theologian D. Baillie, "There is no other way of giving ourselves to Him except by receiving Him, and there is no other way of receiving Him except by giving ourselves to Him".

c) *The three theological virtues*

The three virtues of faith, hope and love are nothing but the flowering of the indwelling and sanctifying grace. The indwelling and grace lie buried deep down within man, they are like the invisible roots of a tree, with the virtues rather like the bright flowers or the golden fruit externally visible. Cut the supply of sap, uproot the tree, and the flowers will soon wilt, fade and die, or the fruit will rot away — without indwelling and sanctifying grace the theological virtues cannot possibly survive.

Divine revelation is the personal act of God manifesting himself freely to man who, in response, gives himself over to God in an act of living *faith*. Both God's revelation and man's response in faith are entirely personal acts. Man believes in God whom he possesses but does not yet see, in order to see and be possessed by God in whom he now believes. It is through faith that man enters into personal communion with God, in a person-to-person relationship. Man's initial surrender to God in the act of faith brings about the intimate, mutual embrace of the indwelling and sanctifying grace. All three, faith, the indwelling and sanctifying grace are marked by a deeply personalistic dimension.

So also the deepest root and foundation of the virtue of

26 P. Fransen, *The New Life of Grace*, p. 243.

hope is God's personal attitude manifested in his promise, which is but an invitation to trust and confidence. God does not promise anything outside himself, he rather promises to man the total gift of his own person, to be given to man. Yet this promise does not remain outside man. He interiorizes the promise by placing his own destiny, in a movement of trustful love, into the hands of the promising God now dwelling in him. Now man's free response to the indwelling God (sanctifying grace) acquires the special colouring of trust and confidence in the promising God. Man, who through faith leaned on God's promise made in the past, is now through hope thrust forward towards the accomplishment of the same promise in the future. The possession of the indwelling and sanctifying grace are already a partial fulfilment of the promise, and at the same time the best guarantee that the plenitude of the promise will be fulfilled in the future. It is not for nothing that man has received within himself "the Spirit of the promise" (Eph 1,14) and has committed himself into the hands of the promising God: man hopes in God dwelling in him.

The strictly personal character of *love* is self-evident. Man's personal opening to God in the indwelling is necessarily prompted and pervaded by the mutual love of God and man, who give themselves to each other in the reciprocated intimacy of the indwelling. Man's personal self-gift to God, his free response to the divine request to dwell within man, is prompted by love as the only possible response to God's love for him. God, out of love, comes to dwell in man in a personal act of self-commitment; and similarly man, in an equally free, personal response suffused with love, gives himself to the indwelling God. Man's initial response, which is nothing but sanctifying grace, springs from and is coloured by a movement of selfless love for God. Hence, sanctifying grace and love are so closely connected as to be practically identifiable. For this love, if it be genuine, has to imply man's acceptance of God's presence, and this is grace; on the other hand, man's response to the presence of the Spirit is nothing but a self-gift to God, and this is effective love.

Hence, all three theological virtues bear a deeply personalistic stamp, since all three tend to establish a mutual relationship of openness and receptivity, on the one hand, and of self-gift on the other, between the indwelling God and man. Love is the most exalted of the three precisely because the personal element of self-giving reaches in it its culmination, and the lower status of faith and hope can be explained precisely because in them the personal element is lessintense. In the heavenly vision of God face to face faith and hope will vanish, for they were but temporary manifestations of this interpersonal relationship, whereas love will remain forever as the most perfect expression of the same relationship. Only love will stand the effulgence of the vision, whereas faith and hope will disintegrate like mist before the warmth of the rising sun.

Heaven will therefore be the perfect consummation of the personal communion which started with the indwelling, a communion which is destined to last forever. There, in the facial vision of God, we have a mystery of mutual indwelling and mutual presence, a mutual giving and receiving between Person and person, between God and man. Viewed from the angle of man's final destiny, the entire economy of salvation is a mystery of mutual personal presence between God and man. Man's unlimited aspiration towards self-fulfillment can be satisfied only by God's personal presence in him: man becomes fully a man when, through the indwelling Spirit, he becomes the son of God.

d) *The peculiar case of baptized children*

One can reasonably conceive sanctifying grace as a personal dialogue between the indwelling God and man, but when applied to the concrete case of baptized children this conception seems to break down completely. If there is something that is deeply rooted in Catholic tradition, it is the custom of infant baptism, which the Church is at present in no mood to alter. And probably she never will, for the first, faint traces of the practice are already discernible in the New Testament.

The personalistic approach explained above can be applied only with some difficulty to the case of baptized children, who are obviously incapable as yet of any conscious and deliberate act of self-surrender into the hands of the indwelling God. If sanctifying grace is but a free, conscious dialogue with God, and if those baptized children are incapable of such a dialogue, it would seem that they are deprived of grace. Since, on the other hand, it has been shown above that sanctifying grace and the indwelling are inseparable, the privation of grace seems to entail a similar privation of the indwelling. Therefore, it would seem that in spite of baptism, the child is only the child of his parents, not the child of God.

However, the case can be explained satisfactorily with the help of a familiar parable. In a family circle the mother is present to the child from the very start, but there is as yet no conscious response on the part of the child. Yet it is precisely this continuous maternal presence to the child that is preparing him for an eventual response. This response is still dormant and undeveloped, but it will eventually blossom forth, elicited by the continual loving presence of the mother.

Similarly, in the case of the baptized child the Holy Spirit is himself present to and dwelling in the child as the result of baptism, disposing him for an eventual response, conscious, deliberate and free, and this response will be his belated acceptance of the indwelling Spirit. The Spirit's presence in the child makes his future response possible, like the presence of the mother will eventually bring about the child's loving surrender to her person. At this early stage the child's personality is still dormant, and therefore its free response is also dormant, but the foundation of a future personal encounter with the Spirit has already been laid. This is *sanctifying grace in a dormant, undeveloped state*. Infant baptism is a clear sign of the Spirit's impatience to possess the child; he will not wait until the child becomes an adult capable of a personal decision. The Spirit enters the child already now, in spite of the lack of personal response, which will come only later. This early, unilateral activity of the Spirit in the child is a striking proof that in the process of man's salvation the initiative always belongs exclusively to God. The Spirit begins the process now; the child will react later to this loving initiative taken by the Spirit. When the child receives the Spirit unknowingly, there is as yet only monologue, not dialogue. It is a unilateral activity on the part of God by which he shows openly that he wants the child for himself. The full dialogue and the personal surrender on the part of the child turned adult will come only later. Child baptism is only a postponement, in no way a negation, of the dialogue.

But just as, in order to grasp fully all the potentialities hidden in Christian baptism, one should not take infant baptism as the ideal exemplar, so also the personalistic character of sanctifying grace should not be explained from the viewpoint of the child, but rather from that of a full-grown person. Theologically speaking, both infant baptism and infant indwelling are, despite their frequency, exceptions to the rule rather than the rule itself, and the personalistic nature of grace can never be fully understood from exceptions.

BIBLIOGRAPHY

Guillet, J.: *Themes of the Bible* (Notre Dame 1961), pp. 2-32.

Gleason, R.: *Grace* (New York 1962).

Rondet, H.: "Grace in St John and St Paul", in E. Fortman, ed., *The Theology of Man and Grace* (Milwaukee 1966), pp. 34-81.

Alfaro, J.: "Person and grace", *Theology Digest* 14 (1966), 3-7.

Rahner, K., *al.*: "Grace", in *Sacramentum Mundi* 2 (1968), 409-427.

Fransen, P.: *The New Life of Grace* (London 1969), pp. 87-106; 231-245.

Colborn, F.: "The theology of grace: present trends and future directions", *Theological Studies* 31 (1970), 692-712.

Conzelmann, H.: "Charis", in *Theological Dictionary of the New Testament* 9 (1974), 54-78.

Yarnold, E.: *The Second Gift. A Study of Grace* (Slough 1974), pp. 1-24.

Haight, R.: *The Experience and Language of Grace* (New York 1979), pp. 54-78.

Chapter Six

DOCILITY TO THE PROMPTINGS OF THE HOLY SPIRIT

At this juncture one cannot but be overwhelmed by the immensity of God's gift to the baptized Christian. Prompted by his unmerited benevolence towards man, the Father has made him his own son, immanent in Christ, temple of the Holy Spirit, and endowed with sanctifying grace. Man is simply caught up in a plethora of divine gifts streaming down to him from God's munificence. The result of it all is that man, after the reception of such an inflow of endowments, is profoundly transformed, thoroughly altered. He is simply a new man, a new creature.

But such a transformation cannot remain hidden within man, for fundamentally he has been given a new life, and life being necessarily dynamic, it has to burst forth and be seen exteriorly. The seed planted within man has to sprout and bear fruit. In other words, the new son of God is expected now to live accordingly, to show exteriorly the treasure he has within himself. Paul put it succinctly: "If we *live* by the Spirit, let us also *walk* by the Spirit" (Gal 5,25). The preceeding chapters have attempted to show to what a remarkable degree we live by the indwelling Spirit, present within us; it now remains to be shown that, consequently, we ought also to walk prompted, guided by the Spirit.

St John of the Cross says in one of his mystical writings that "the Holy Spirit rests at the bottom of the soul". Undoubtedly he has made the person of man his dwelling place, his temple, but he certainly does not "rest" there.

For he is the Spirit of life and to say life is to say dynamism, movement and growth. In a way, far from resting in the inner sanctuary of man, the Spirit shows himself "rest-less", for he prompts, illumines, inspires, suggests, cajoles, rebukes, strengthens, entices, allures, comforts man. Is he resting in man? Now a new world opens up before us, a world of frequent — to call it ceaseless would be an exaggeration — touches of the Spirit acting from within man, from the very centre of his person outwardly, as it were, towards his spiritual faculties, mind and will. Or rather, the possession of man by the Holy Spirit is so complete, so thorough, that there is absolutely no area, no nook or corner in man that does not come under the direct and immediate influence of the Spirit. Man's intellect and will, his heart and effectivity, his feelings and emotions, his spirit and even his body — nothing escapes the all-encompassing activity of the Spirit. He touches all the spheres of man's life; the entire landscape which is man is bathed in his light and watered by his vivifying stream. "Let the Holy Spirit fill you" (Eph 5,18), says a remarkably felicitous rendering of Paul's thought. The spring of the Spirit is bubbling up within man, spreading its refreshing influence to the most recondite areas of his person.

It is within this general context of the Spirit's activity inside man that one should view the comforting reality of his promptings or inspirations. Man is guided by the impulses of the Holy Spirit, who acts in him with gentle pressure through the power of his light. He grips man from within, bathing him in the glow of his light and supporting him with the comfort of his might.

1) The promptings of the Holy Spirit

And yet, this interior activity of the Spirit, moving man from within, is not the only way in which he can act on him. For the Spirit's activity and all-pervading influence reach the heart of man even prior to the indwelling. Here is a Christian who through his or her shameful behaviour has forfeited the gift of the indwelling Spirit. Even such a person is not beyond the reach of the Spirit's influence. The Holy Spirit has unfortunately been expelled from the sanctuary of man, but he persistently keeps knocking and requesting re-entry, through his persistent promptings. In this case obviously the promptings come from a source that is somewhat external to man, for the Spirit no longer dwells within him. Yet even then the insistent perseverance of the Holy Spirit does not cease, he continues to act on man.

It is this concrete instance, theologically important and pastorally relevant, that the Council of Trent had in mind when it stated with great precision, in the context of the sacrament of reconciliation, that attrition for one's sins "is a gift of God and a prompting of the Spirit, not indeed as already dwelling in the penitent but only moving him".[1] The indwelling of the Spirit is *a* source, the main source from which the promptings proceed, but it is certainly not the only source. To speak of the Spirit acting from within and from without man may look somewhat crude and inappropriate, since God pervades continuously the entirety of man, but on the other hand we have already established above that the interior source of the promptings, the indwelling presence of the Spirit, differs from God's general, all-pervading presence in the universe. Both types of presence can be a source of inspirations or motions of the Spirit, for even after having been ousted from the inner sanctuary of man, the Spirit does not abandon him, leaving him to his own devices. Even in this case, the promptings show that the Spirit persues unremittingly the person of the sinner, that God will never give him up.

The Spirit of light. When in trouble and darkness, some Christians turn to the Spirit asking him for light, that the blessed rays of the Spirit may pierce and eventually dispel the oppressive darkness. It is precisely this that Paul does almost spontaneously when praying for his congregation at Ephesus: "May...the Father of glory (effulgence) give you a spirit of wisdom and perception...to bring you to full knowledge of him. May he enlighten the eyes of your mind..." (Eph 1,17-18).[2] Wisdom, perception, knowledge, light: four different ways of saying much the same thing,

1 J. Neuner - J. Dupuis, *The Christian Faith,* n. 1624.

2 The French *Traduction Oecuménique de la Bible* gives a very suggestive alternative translation: "may God open your hearts to his light".

namely, that God, through his Spirit, sheds light abundantly on man's mind, that man is illumined from within, that he has within himself the intimate source of light.

Following St John Christian tradition has always designated the Holy Spirit as the "Spirit of truth" (Jn 14,17). "When the Spirit of truth comes he will guide you into all the truth" (Jn 16,13). The disciple will be led internally by the Spirit to grasp, interiorize and assimilate the teaching of Christ. The Spirit will not be a new source of strange, esoteric truths, but rather a source of new depth and penetration. The old truths proceeding for Christ will shine out with a new splendour, maybe a new internal coherence, a new compulsion, gentle and pursuasive — thanks to the Spirit of truth acting in the heart of the believer. It is simply the irresistible attraction of truth, of whatever is genuine and real, as opposed to the enticing mirage of untruth, which lacks reality, solidity, consistency. The Spirit is himself truth and — more important for us now — he is the blessed source of truth for man, the bright lamp shining in the heart of man.

The Holy Spirit is like an intermediary of light that fathoms the secrets lying buried deep down in the heart of the Father and passes them on to man. He scrutinizes the depths of God and communicates that knowledge to man. He is a luminous bridge between the Father and man, moving from the heart of God to the mind of man. It is this striking conception that, almost casually, dropped from the pen of Paul writing to the Corinthians: "The Spirit reaches the depths of everything, even the depths of God (the Father)....The depths of God can only be known by the Spirit of God....Now we have received the Spirit that comes from God, *to teach us to understand* the gifts that he has given us" (1 Cor 2,10-12). "The depths", repeated three times by Paul in two short verses. There is something deep down in the heart and mind of God that only the Spirit can scrutinize.

The BBC of London reported yesterday evening that a team of experts dropped to a depth of two and a half miles in the North Atlantic to gain a better knowledge of the wreck of the famous *Titanic*, which sank to its watery grave there way back in 1912. By means of a tiny but highly sophisticated, unmanned submersible — a robot, really — the experts succeeded to a remarkable degree in scrutinizing the two fractured sections of the ill-fated ship lying on the ocean floor. In two days the mechanical robot snapped 60,000 stunningly accurate, clear photographs, and transmitted them up to the surface. The experts were both astonished and thrilled by the incredible knowledge acquired. The depths of the ocean were no longer a mystery, for they had been suddenly illumined and captured in still photographs and video tapes. The light that had penetrated the dark secrets of the ocean was now their own light, for the submersible had acted as an intermediary of light, it had shed light both on the ocean floor where the ship's wreck lay, and on the mind of the researchers.

This is precisely the function performed by the luminous Spirit of God according to Paul: he too searches the depths of the Father's heart where the destiny of man is written, and drops down to the depths of man, flooding him with divine light and transmitting to him the knowledge he has gained at the bottom of God's heart. His function is that of an intermediary who transmits knowledge, not from the bottom to the surface, but rather — and here the comparison of the *Titanic* breaks down, as most comparisons eventually do when pressed too far — from bottom ot bottom, from the depth of the Father to the depth of man. The Spirit is the Spirit of light, and his path is always marked by a trail of brightness, by the gentle glow of his own radiance.

The Spirit of power. Light is certainly precious, but even more so is the gift of power and inner strength. In our own life, lack of light may lead us to make a mistake, but lack of strength often leads us to sin, and nobody in his senses would fail to realize that sin is more serious a reality and a simple mistake. We surely need light, but what we most often lack is inner strength, power and courage to act according to the lights we have.

From the biblical viewpoint the Spirit is often associated with light, but he is also — and primarily — the Spirit of power and might, of vigour and strength. The mighty power of God. Already in Old Testament times the "Spirit of Yahweh" was very closely associated with power and strength, whether physical (Samson tore a lion to pieces with his bare hands after "the Spirit of the Lord came mightily upon him:

(Judg 14,6) or moral (the future Messiah will receive "the Spirit of might:" Is 11,2). And so in keeping with this biblical tradition it is said of Mary, the mother of Jesus: "The Holy Spirit will come upon you, and the power of the most High will overshadow you" (Lk 1,35), where "Holy Spirit" and "power of the Most High" are perfectly synonymous. The conception of Jesus is the result of the Spirit's power acting on the gentle woman from Nazareth. Little wonder that Mark should narrate how, three decades later, the Spirit "drove him (Jesus) into the wilderness" (Mk 1,12) after his baptism. Subsequent biblical tradition viewed the baptism of Jesus and the manifestation of the Spirit in the waters of the Jordan as the moment when "God anointed Jesus of Nazareth with the Holy Spirit and with power" (Ac 10,38). After his forty-day retreat in the imposing wilderness, not far from the Jordan and Jericho, Jesus returned to his own hometown of Nazareth "in the power of the Spirit" (Lk 4,14). Incarnation, baptism, desert experience, return to Nazareth: all four acts were accomplished in the power of the Spirit.

So far Jesus of Nazareth. If the Holy Spirit manifested his power on Jesus so ostensively at the key moments of his life, he cannot be expected to act otherwise on the Christian, who is continuously subject to the power of the Spirit dwelling in him. The Christian breathes in the illumining might of the Holy Spirit, for he should "let the Spirit fill him" (Eph 5,18).

This seems to be self-evident for Paul. There is in his letter to the Ephesians an exceedingly beautiful passage, both rich and highly spiritual, where Paul voices his conviction that the Christian should draw strength from his own personal depths, namely, from the person of the Spirit dwelling within him: "For this reason I bow my knees before the Father... that according to the riches of his own effulgence, he may grant you *to be strengthened with might through his Spirit* in the inner man...that you may have the power to comprehend...and to know the love of Christ...that you may be filled with all the fullness of God" (Eph 3, 14-19). "To be strengthened with might": how else can we be strengthened if not with the personalized might of God which is the Holy Spirit? Paul, on his knees, is so overwhelmed by this divine power that he seems to have slipped up: we usually grasp and understand something by means of light, but Paul speaks rather of "the power to comprehend", in a felicitous mixture of light and power, the two arms of the Holy Spirit. For the Spirit simultaneously enlightens and strengthens, illumines and fortifies, and this double stream proceeding from him is directed "*into* the inner man", like an explosion of light and an infusion of strength, both sinking down into the inner spiritual recesses of man. This prayer of Paul for his Christians could hardly be more trinitarian: he is beseeching the Father to strengthen men with the strength of his Spirit and to fill them with the fullness of Christ. Paul's prayer seems to flower spontaneously into a trinitarian plenitude.

We begin now to get a glimpse of Paul's petitionary prayer. Ephesus or Rome, it makes no difference; whether he knows his addressees personally or not, it does not matter, for his petition is the same. Now he writes to far away Rome and prays to God for the unknown Christians there, "that by the power of the Holy Spirit you may abound in hope" (Rom 15,13). Similarly he is convinced that his successful preaching in Corinth was done, not on the flimsy basis of rhetorical eloquence and human wisdom, but "in demonstration of the Spirit and power" (1 Cor 2,5). Paul's prayer turns to the power of the Spirit, and his apostolate similarly rests on the strength of the Spirit, which goes to show that prayer and apostolate, the two lungs through which he breathes, are both entirely filled with the might of the Spirit acting in him, the reason being that "God's gift was not a spirit of timidity but the Spirit of power" (2 Tim 1,7).

And it is obvious that this should be so, as is evident from one of the last moments of the earthly life of Jesus. On the Mount of Olives, on the outskirts of Jerusalem, Jesus is about to depart to his Father, but just before doing so he turns to his disciples gathered for the last time around him, and makes them a final promise: "You shall receive the power when the Holy Spirit has come upon you" (Ac 1,8). After Pentecost, they will bear witness to him in Judea and Samaria and to the ends of the earth, but this act of witnessing will be done in the power of the Spirit.[3]

3 The same Luke makes use of a slightly different expression when describing the same scene at the end of the Gospel: "And behold, I send the promise of my

When viewed against this biblical backdrop, it is difficult to understand how and why the Holy Spirit has been constantly associated in Catholic tradition with love rather than with power. For it has become almost a theological and spiritual platitude, thoughtlessly repeated by so many, that the Holy Spirit is the Spirit of love. Nothing of consequence can be objected against this, but on the other hand one must confess that this is an abstract — and typically Latin, western— theological construct, rather than explicit biblical teaching. It is true that in a few places — which can be counted on the fingers of one hand — the Holy Spirit makes his appearances in the New Testament accompanied by love or charity, but it is not here that the emphasis lies, not by a long shot. And a few scattered references, probably to be found exclusively in the letters of Paul, hardly justify our constant linking of the Holy Spirit with love. The scriptural trend, explicit and insistent, both in the Old and in the New Testament, connects the Spirit with power and strength, very rarely with love. One must confess that in this respect our Catholic liturgy, too, could certainly be improved.

The Spirit of comfort and joy. It will be remembered that in the Johannine school the Holy Spirit was known as the Paraclete, namely, the Spirit of *paraklesis* or comfort. The comforting function of the Spirit seems to be encrusted into his very name. We all know what comfort is, yet we find it difficult to define it. The Oxford Dictionary derives it from the Latin "cum-fortis" — the idea of vigour and strength once again. Hence, its original meaning is "to strengthen, to encourage, to support, to invigorate"; but the current sense is rather "to soothe in grief or trouble, to console".[4] All these different shades of meaning are rightly attributed to the Holy Spirit acting in the Christian. It is therefore a pardonable mistake to oversimplify the role and function of the Spirit by

Father (viz. the Spirit of the promise) upon you; but stay in the city until you are *clothed with power* from on high" (Lk 24,49). In a way this is a bit of an anticlimax, for Paul strongly emphasizes that the Spirit is not like an external piece of clothing one puts on and off; he rather acts and strengthens the disciple from within. But the connection between power and the Spirit, which was Luke's only contention here, is clearly made.

4 *The Shorter Oxford Dictionary*, Vol. I, 3rd ed., (Oxford 1950), p. 347.

referring to him as "comforter" or "consoler", for in reality he is both. The Spirit is this, certainly, and much more. He is, in the words of the Church's liturgy for the feast of Pentecost, "the father of the poor"; in our labour he is rest and solace; in the heat of passion, coolness and refreshment; in pain and bereavement, soothing comfort and consolation. He removes the stain of sin, waters what is bleak and dry, heals what is sick and wounded, bends what is stiff and rigid, warms up and melts the icy coldness of our heart. He is the consoler who, like the Father, "wipes away every tear from our eyes" (Apoc 7,17).

Though immediately imparted to the Christian by the soothing presence of the Holy Spirit, this comfort proceeds ultimately from the source of all consolation — the Father. Paul almost bursts into song: "Blessed be the Father of mercies and God of all comfort (*paraklesis*), who comforts us in all our affliction, so that we may be able to comfort those who are in pain and affliction, with the comfort with which we ourselves are comforted by God" (2 Cor 1,3-4). As many as five times in one single sentence does Paul refer here to the function which is typical of the Spirit: to comfort, to soothe, to console.

But perhaps even more clearly and repeatedly the Holy Spirit is spoken of in the New Testament as the source of joy. Already at the Last Supper, according to John's narrative, on hearing that Jesus was about to depart, the disciples had been saddened; and yet, after his actual departure to his Father they "returned to Jerusalem in great joy", for moments before he had made them the final promise, "I send to you the promise of my Father" (Lk 24,49.52) in a clear reference to Pentecost. The announcement of Jesus' departure saddens them, but the promise of the imminent outpouring of the pentecostal Spirit is enough to set their hearts aglow with joy.

This is precisely Paul's wish to the Roman Christians, and they needed it badly, for a few years later an attrocious, bloody persecution would break out in the capital of the Empire, sending thousands of them to their deaths: "Be aglow with the Spirit...rejoice in your hope" (Rom 12,12); "for the kingdom of God...means...peace and joy in the Holy Spirit" (Rom 14,17). And finally that absolutely marvelous prayer of Paul, so dense and so rich, and yet so very touching: "May the God of hope fill you with all joy and peace in believing, so that by the power of the Holy Spirit you may abound in hope" (Rom 15,13). Hope, joy, peace, power: this is the spiritual climate created by the Holy Spirit. When a person is converted to Christianity and for the first time believes in the Lord Jesus, he enters a new, joyful atmosphere because he is penetrated by the Holy Spirit: "And the disciples (converts of Paul and Barnabas) were filled with joy and with the Holy Spirit" (Ac 13,52).

This is the language of the Holy Spirit. His activity in the Christian is both variegated and consistent, for as he acted in New Testament times, so he acts now. Quietly, silently, unobtrusively, he instills in the believer light, strength, joy, comfort. It requires a certain spiritual finesse and sensitivity to detect his touches and discern his voice, that is for sure. But let us, for the time being, restrict our consideration to the fact that his comforting presence is always there, that he is noiselessly active and anonymously efficient, touching, whispering, suggesting, instructing, always active and yet elusive, persistent and yet difficult to grasp, real and effective, yet diaphanous. Have you ever tried to catch and retain with your bare hands water or air? You may feel refreshed by the cooling stream and caressed by the soothing breeze, you do feel their effects, but how are you to grasp them? Such is the Spirit of God acting within the Christian through his promptings and inspirations.

2) Promptings and providence

The Spirit can and does act in a variety of ways. He can illumine the believer from within, brightening his mind and warming his will; but he can also act on him from without, through providential historical circumstances and especially through the instrumentality of other persons who become, when employed by the Spirit, genuine channels of supernatural grace.

St Cyril, Bishop of Jerusalem in the 4th century, undoubtedly had the enviable knack of putting across to his congregation — often enough made up of neophytes preparing for baptism — the deepest mysteries of the faith in the simplest of terms, transparently clear both to the learned and to the unlettered. As remarked in an earlier chapter, his famous catechetical instructions are a perfect model of the pastoral approach. Others may be deeper, more profound than Cyril; but few will be his equals when it comes to concreteness of language and persuasiveness of expression. His way of preaching on the Holy Spirit, so direct, simple and personal, remains appealing even to a modern reader. The two following long quotes are worth pondering:

> The Holy Spirit is not like this....For his arrival is calm and smooth, his perception mild and sweetscented, his yoke extremely light. Glittering rays of light and knowledge forestall his arrival. He is endowed with the heart of a real protector, for he comes to save, heal, teach, advise, strengthen, console, illumine the mind.... And just as if somebody is in darkness and then, seeing suddenly the sun, he receives light in his eyes and sees clearly what before the could not make out; so also he who is given the gift of the Holy Spirit is illumined in his mind and raised above his human condition, he sees what before he did not understand.[5]

> If sometime, just as you are idly sitting, a thought of chastity or virginity occurs to you, it is his (the Spirit's) doctrine. Does it not often happen that a girl about to get married leaves everything after having been instructed by him about virginity? ....Does it not happen that a youngster, seeing a beautifully shaped woman, closes his eyes and refuses to look and thus avoids defilement? Where does this come from? It is the Holy Spirit that illumined the youngster's mind.... What a precious thing, really, this Holy Spirit, so good....[6]

Cyril seems to have been particularly fond of the metaphor of the light. The illumining action of the Spirit is not, however, restricted to those in whom he dwells, for is extends far and wide to all men and women of good will, whether Christians or non-Christians. The Spirit's encompassing activity goes beyond the narrow confines of the Church:

> I would like you to think, after receiving his light, of all the Christians of this parish, of all the Christians in

5 *Catechesis* 16: *On the Holy Spirit* 1, 16: PG 33, 939.
6 *Ibid.*, 19: PG 33, 943-4.

Palestine. Furthermore, extend your gaze to the entire Roman Empire, and from there to the whole world: Persians, Indians, Goths, French and Spaniards, Africans and Ethiopians and others of whom we don't even know the name.... See how he (the Spirit) rules, governs and gives them gifts; how he grants...to this chastity, to that perpetual virginity, to the other a desire for poverty...; and just as the light, by one single burst of rays, illumines everything, so also the Holy Spirit enlightens the minds of all who have eyes to see.[7]

A few decades after Cyril and hundreds of miles away from Jerusalem, the cathedral of insignificant Hippo, in North Africa, resounded with a similar teaching from the great St Augustine. The Spirit, says the African doctor, seems to have a kind of natural inclination towards self-effacement. His action is often clearly detectable, but his face is not; he seems to intervene and act, and then withdraw behind a cloud, as it were, leaving the person concerned in uncertainty as to the real origin of such an action. The Spirit seems to delight in acting through historical channels, through providential circumstances that no one will probably ever think of connecting with him. It is precisely this important insight that Augustine will quite naturally convey to his flock. He rhetorically fancies God addressing a non-Christian thus:

> You did not become an adulterer....It is I who governed you for myself, who kept you for myself. You had no adviser for your adultery; I arranged it that you should have no adviser. There was neither time nor place (for your adultery); it is my work that there should be none. There was an adviser, time was not lacking, place was not lacking: I frightened you not to consent. Acknowledge therefore the grace of him to whom you owe not to have consented.[8]

7 *Ibid.*, 22: PG 33, 947.

8 *Sermo* 99, 6: PL 38, 598. But Augustine the preacher knows only too well that his proverbial eloquence will leave his listeners cold unless the Spirit touches them directly through his grace: "The Holy Spirit works internally....For even if God, by making use of the preacher subject to him, speaks to his external senses in a human manner, *unless he rules and acts in the mind through his internal grace*, allthe preaching of the truth is useless to man" (*De Civitate Dei* XV, 6: PL 41 442).

The communication of grace by the Spirit follows oftentimes the very same pattern as the Incarnation. The Word of God appeared in and through the man Jesus, was enfleshed in the son of Mary within a concrete historical and geographical framework. Jesus was "full of grace and truth" (Jn 1,14), that is, he was nothing but the loving kindness and fidelity of his Father rendered visible, tangible. God poured his grace in and through him, and this fundamental event has left a deep imprint on the whole of the Christian economy of salvation.

So also now the Spirit's promptings come to us enfleshed, incarnated in concrete historical circumstances that consequently become channels of grace. The trivialities of our daily life, the unglamorous events of our daily existence, can be turned into mysterious, yet real instruments of grace. The Spirit often acts, not only directly and immediately from within man, but also by means of these providential channels of grace. The modality of the bestowal is of little consequence, what really matters is that, whether directly from within or indirectly from without, the promptings of the Spirit do reach the believer, and they probably reach him oftener than he or she imagines. Grace comes to us always enveloped in time and space, never disincarnate. The Spirit seems to have a strange penchant to hide behind the gray monotony of our daily occupations, behind the daily dullness of our regular, unobtrusive lives, behind the humdrum of trivial "coincidences" and uninspiring routine. Nature and grace remain distinct, but they are closely interlocked, nature conveying grace, and grace pouring in through nature, for both of them are supple instruments in the hands of the Spirit.

A particular modality of this historical aspect of grace, of this external tangibility of the Spirit's promptings, is the fact that these inspirations often reach man not only encased within the framework of time and space, but specifically through the living instrumentality of other men and women. Now it is not only concrete historical circumstances, but also the living community of other persons that becomes for me the channel of grace. The believer always and necessarily finds himself caught up in the midst of interpersonal relationships, in a web of social contacts and mutual exchanges. It stands to reason, therefore, that the Holy Spirit should not modify but rather utilize this concrete historical setup to impart his promptings to the Christian.

The teaching of the New Testament is in this regard quite explicit: "How are men to believe in him (Christ) of whom they have never heard? And how are they to hear without a preacher?" (Rom 10,14). On the day of Pentecost "those who received his (Peter's) word were baptized, and they were added that day three thousand souls" (Ac 2,41): here the grace of baptism comes to the new converts through Peter's speech. Similarly years later Lydia, a rich woman and disciple of Paul, listened to him and "the Lord opened her heart to give heed to what was said by Paul", and she was baptized (Ac 16,14).

This pattern has not changed. In fact, modern and even contemporary history shows that, just as in the days of old, now also the Spirit makes use of the surrounding community of men and women as human instruments of supernatural grace. The fact that, due to man's dullness and insensitivity, these promptings go often unheeded is no reason to doubt their origin. We are subjected to a fairly intense "bombardment" of God's whispers, inspirations and warnings which we tend to neglect only to our own detriment. As concrete examples of the manner in which the Spirit's promptings reach and affect persons of heightened spiritual sensitivity, we can give two well known cases: the inspiration received by Pope John XXIII to convoke a council and the reform of the Carmelites through St Teresa of Avila in the 16th century.

We are all more or less familiar with that extraordinary event which has gone down in history as Vatican II. We have not yet tapped all the enormous resources for revival and renewal which lie hidden, and to some extent dormant, within the sixteen conciliar documents. But just now we are interested in knowing how that puzzling, plumpy figure, Pope John, conceived the unusual, totally unexpected idea of calling a council. Conflicting views among modern biographers and confidants of the Pope do not make the task of the historian precisely easy. Where did Pope John get that strange idea from? Was it possibly suggested to him by one of his aides? Had the foundations for the future council perhaps been laid by his immediate predecessor?

It would seem that Pope Pius XII had already considered seriously the possibility of convoking an ecumenical council, but finally decided against it. In any case these tentative plans and early probings had apparently been shrouded in secrecy, and absolutely nothing transpired to the world outside the Vatican. And so Roncalli, the patriarch of Venice and future Pope John the XXIII, seems to have been blissfully unaware of them. At the end of 1962, already as Bishop of Rome, he wrote down in his spiritual diary and *exclusively for his own personal use,*[9] the following incredible statement: "Without any forethought, I put forward, in one of my first talks with my Secretary of State, on 20 January 1959, the idea of an ecumenical council, a diocesan synod and the revision of the Code of Canon Law, all this being *quite contrary to any previous supposition or idea of my own on this subject.* I was the first to be surprised at my proposal, *which was entirely my own idea*".[10]

9 I italize this sentence because critical voices have been heard which almost contemptuously sneer at the assertion that the first idea of convoking the council was given to Pope John directly by God. If this is found unacceptable as being too naive, it would seem that the only viable alternative is to accuse the Pope of lying when he recorded in his journal that, in fact, nobody had suggested the idea to him. Spiritual diaries always record confidences of the author, written exclusively for his own personal use, not for the benefit of the gallery. And the amusing — or shall I say, exasperating? — thing is that these "enlightened" critics dismiss the Pope's explicit statement as incredible without having even read his diary.

10 Pope John XXIII, *Journal of a Soul* (London 1965), p. 326. P. Hebblethwaite, in his recent, widely acclaimed biography of the Pope (*John XXIII, Pope of the Council*, London 1984), entitles chapter 14 very appropriately, 'The inspiration of the Council'. "What Pope John most wanted to know was whether the idea was not some wild fantasy or spectacular improvisation; but an inspiration that bound him, as ever, to submit to the Lord...Pope John habitually used the word 'inspiration' to explain how the idea of the Council came to him... The idea of the Council was an 'inspiration' in the sense defined above. *That much was certainly true*" (*Ibid.*, pp. 308 and 318). Two months after his election he confided to G. Rossi: "The H. Spirit doesn't help the Pope. I'm simply his helper. He did everything. *The Council is his idea*" (*Ibid.*, p. 312). In fact, Pope John mentioned his plan of calling a council to his confidant L. Capovilla already on 30 October, 1958, just two days after his election. (cf. P. Hebblethwaite, *Pope John*, p. 306). Subsequently the Pope found in the Vatican archives Pius XII's plan to convoke a council, dating back to 1948. Hence it can be said that Pius XII strengthened and confirmed an idea that was already planted in Pope John's mind independently of his predecessors.

It was as simple as that. A new idea, a fresh thought that came suddenly to the Pope's mind apparently from nowhere and — this is to be strongly remarked — when he least expected it. But was it, as he put it four years later, "entirely my own idea"? Who shaped that idea for the first time in the Pope's mind? Was it his own personal creation or rather the unexpected prompting from "somebody" dwelling within that bulky frame? Was Pope John the creator or rather the receiver, the beneficiary of the new idea?

Subsequent events have proved beyond all doubt that Pope John's "crazy idea" — for so it looked to several of the assembled cardinals when he broke the news to them on 25 January 1959 — bore all the marks of the Spirit's action. No, it was not his own idea, it was not he who conceived the idea first, but the Spirit who whispered it to him a few months after his election to the papacy. The extreme simplicity of it all makes the whole thing almost unbelievable, and yet it is true: the Spirit, wishing to bring about a deep transformation in the Church, chooses an old man to be the Pope, and almost immediately suggests to him the idea of calling a council for the purpose of the Church's renewal. Reacting firmly against mounting opposition to his plan, the Pope convokes the council, inaugurates it, turns the Church upside down and dies of cancer at the age of 81. His task is accomplished. Is it credible that an event of such a magnitude and lasting significance as Vatican II should hang on the tiny thread of an inspiration given to the Pope? That is what the chronicles say....

A second, and to some extent even a more remarkable case is that of the reform of the Carmel in the sixteenth century, accomplished primarily by St Teresa of Avila. Outside the ancient walls of the city of Avila there still stands today the imposing convent of the Incarnation where, in the month of September 1560, a nun called Teresa, spiritually mediocre but psychologically exceptionally gifted, conceived the idea of reforming the Carmel. The spiritual climate within the enclosure was at that time plainly deplorable: "The convent was more like a main street or a fair in the market-place. The number of nuns, to which must be added that of secular persons in the convent, was always excessive, and those who troubled to observe the Constitutions were in the minority".[11] The deadly cancer of religious laxity had spread to other convents of the Order already much before Teresa. In fact, in moments of religious daydreaming Teresa, no paragon of virtue herself, sucked in as she was by the general tide of soft living, used to ponder over what the Order had been like "before Pope Eugene IV...mitigated the rigours of the primitive Rule, thus turning Carmels, which were formerly strongholds of penance and prayer, into sanctimonious houses of refuge for lonely bachelors and spinsters".[12]

A few years ago, in the course of the work of restoration of part of the same convent, two rooms built one upon the other were accidentally discovered, which were probably those used by Teresa herself. She slept on the first floor and it was there that she used to receive many visitors for their mutual entertainment. It all happened there, sometime in the course of 1560. Sitting on a cushion on the floor as was the Moorish custom at that time, six women were merrily chatting away with Teresa working at her embroidery, whilst "from the patio used for recreation rose the sound of flutes and tambourines through which could be heard someone singing one of the latest songs".[13] Not a particularly religious atmosphere, on the whole. And then, out of the blue, a young lay boarder, a 17-year old niece of Teresa, who was one of the group, suddenly burst out: "Let us go away then, all of us here! And let us organize a solitary life for ourselves, like the hermits of old".[14]

This homely scene was the origin of the Carmelite reform. It would seem that, even before this incident, Teresa had already thought of reforming the Carmel, but acutely conscious that she should start by reforming herself, and especially daunted by the enormous difficulties involved, she had persued the idea no further. It seems to have been a kind of vague desire, a hazy conception, a dreamer's wish with blurred contours and no consistency. But after hearing her own niece's crazy proposal said almost in jest, the familiar

11 M. Auclair, *Teresa of Avila* (New York 1961), p. 118.
12 *Ibid.*, p. 120.
13 *Ibid.*, p. 121.
14 *Ibid.* The girl's name was Maria de Ocampo.

but vague idea begins to crystallize and take sharp, concrete form in Teresa's mind. The girl's unexpected and impractical suggestion acts as a catalyst within Teresa. Later on the Lord was to confirm to her directly and repeatedly that the reform of the Carmel was no wild wish, but his own desire which he had entrusted to her. The rest we know: Painfully — and very shrewdly — Teresa breaks away from the convent of the Incarnation and, in Avila itself, opens the first convent of the reform. Other convents would soon mushroom throughout Spain and beyond. The idea of reforming the Carmel had finally taken shape; in fact, it was now an accomplished reality.[15a]

The final, definitive impulse, therefore, did not come to Teresa directly, but only through the intermediary agency of her niece, a plain, ordinary girl who was not even a postulant. God has strange ways to accomplish his plans. The Spirit suggested the convocation of the council directly to Pope John, and the reform of the Carmel indirectly to Teresa. Both the enterprises were beset with staggering difficulties that would have broken weaker spirits. Was the final impetus to reform the Carmel any less precious because the Spirit chose to reach Teresa only indirectly, through

15 Other biographers of the saint differ slightly from M. Auclair, whom I have followed in the text. The exhaustive work of Efrén de la Madre de Dios and O. Steggink (*Tiempo y Vida de Sta. Teresa,* Madrid 1968) seems to attribute to Teresa's niece, not only a strengthening or confirmation of the idea of the reform in Teresa's mind, but the very origin of the idea.

15a New York, early 1958. A few months before Pope John XXIII was elected to the papacy the Holy Spirit was active thousands of miles away west of Rome. This time the Spirit's instrument was David Wilkerson, a married Protestant pastor. Let him narrate his own extraordinary experience: "I was dumbfounded by a thought that sprung suddenly into my mind — full-blown, as though it had come into me from somewhere else: 'Go to New York and help these boys' ". He laughs out loud, for the idea is simply preposterous. Yet "the thought was still there, vivid as ever, apparently completely independent of my own feelings and ideas". He tries gain to surpress the crazy idea. "It was no use. The idea would not go away. I was to go to New York and furthermore I was to go at once" His wife is informed, but she remains skeptical: " 'You really feel this is the Holy Spirit leading you?', Gwen asked. 'Yes, I do, honey'....I knew I could not bring this about...perhaps I could act as a channel through which the Spirit could reach those boys" (D. Wilkerson, *The Cross and the Switchblade,* New York 1962, pp. 7, 8, 13, 14, 55). This was the unobtrusive beginning of an unbelievably successful apostolate somebody else, at a moment when she was working, chatting and listening to music, rather than absorbed in prayer? In both the cases God acted on Pope John and Teresa when they least expected to receive an influx of grace from above. It was the Spirit who, once again, stepped into the world half-hidden behind the cloud of trivial historical circumstances. But it was he, whispering to the man at the Vatican and goading the nun at Avila. If John and Teresa had refused to yield — as they were perfectly free to do — the Church at large would be all the poorer, for today we would have neither a reformed Carmel nor Vatican II.

3) Man's response drenched in grace

The promptings of the Spirit are certainly precious, and so is the reality of sanctifying grace. These two types of grace are distinct and yet they are intimately connected. In fact, one can almost say that they are one single current of grace in two different stages of evolution or growth. Initially the Holy Spirit gives himself to the Christian in the intimate union of the indwelling, and this personal self-communication of God is accepted by man, who freely responds to the indwelling Spirit by giving himself over to him: this response on the part of man — we saw it above — is sanctifying grace. The mutual self-gift and acceptance of the Spirit and man constitute an unbreakable unity, the indwelling and sanctifying grace being like the two faces of the same coin, two sides of the total reality which is the radical transformation of man.

But that probably happened long ago in the life of the Christian, perhaps as far back as the time of his baptism. That original reality, that mutual encounter in the life of the believer is to be rendered actual and concrete here and now in particular historical situations. That early surrender of man has to find an echo in his concrete daily existence. The Spirit gave himself over to man and that self-offer continues

among the murderous gangs of teenager boys in the slums of New York. Pope John, Teresa or Rev. Wilkerson, men or women, Catholics or Protestants, people in the centre or in the periphery, in the 16th or in the 20th century: the ways of the Holy Spirit are always the same. Wilkerson's account reads like a contemporary version of the book of Acts, with the Holy Spirit acting in New York now as he acted in Palestine in the first century.

now, for the Spirit, rather than given once and for all, is in reality being given; and similarly, man also gives himself continuously to the indwelling Spirit. It is the indwelling rendered actual and man's corresponding surrender to the Spirit rendered tangible.

It happens also in marriage. The initial mutual surrender of husband and wife took place years ago, on the wedding day itself, and that mutual consent, which constitutes the core of marriage, far from being subsequently revoked is rather rendered tangible and concrete in smaller daily surrenders which are but a distant echo of the solemn consent of the wedding day. So also, the Spirit graciously consented to dwell in man, man gratefully accepted the indwelling and now, years after the original embrace of the indwelling, that mutual union still reverberates within man, he still feels in himself ripples of that original impact, of that moment when the Spirit was accepted within man's inner sanctuary.

Now the Spirit, residing in the deepest core of the believer, extends his sanctifying influence to all of man's faculties, like the rising sun which bathes in its light the entire landscape. The sun shines within man, and therefore he cannot but feel in all his faculties the caress of the sun's rays. Man, who is already permanently oriented towards the Spirit (and this is sanctifying grace), now feels within himself the promptings that proceed from his own interior where the Spirit dwells, promptings which are clamouring for acceptance, for submission and surrender. Man accepted the indwelling then and should therefore accept the promptings of the same Spirit now. An original surrender that is not carried over and manifested in daily surrenders to the promptings shwould be somewhat incongruous.

Hence the promptings issue forth from the indwelling like rivulets from a common spring, soaking up the entire landscape which is man. Tiny trickles or mighty torrents — depending on the strength and intensity of the inspirations that issue from the centre — these rivulets will eventually reach far and wide and affect the entirety of man. We see, therefore, that sanctifying grace and the divine promptings originate from a common source internal to man: the indwelling Spirit.

This may be the right time to warn the reader of a very

common misconception. The promptings, once their origin has been detected with sufficient clarity, ought to be accepted, man should respond to them favourably. In other words, it is usually said that man must cooperate with grace. Yet this common expression, endlessly repeated, is liable to be misunderstood. Many seem to imagine that God offers man a particular inspiration, man discerns it, accepts it with his own free will and eventually puts it into practice. An extremely neat process, a very clear solution — as clear and neat as it is wrong. In fact it is plainly heretical. It is only ignorance that saves most Christians from heresy — even those who claim to be well instructed, but whose knowledge in reality leaves much to be desired.

We should not overlook the fact that already the New Testament stresses forcefully the absolute primacy of God's electing grace. Rebecca, Isaac's wife, had conceived Esau and Jacob, and before they were born and, therefore, prior to any possibility of human cooperation, God intervened. Commenting on this, Paul states: "Though they were not yet born and had done nothing either good or bad, in order that God's purpose of election might continue...she was told, 'The elder will serve the younger'" (Rom 9,11-12). How could two unborn babies "cooperate" with God's electing grace? Similarly Paul exhorts the Philippians: "Work out your own salvation with fear and trembling; for God is at work in you, both to will and to work for his own pleasure" (Phil 2,12-13). "God is at work *to will*...." The Philippians might have fondly imagined that their salvation was primarily a matter of will power, and Paul dispels their illusion: God is secretly working even in the sacred sanctuary of your will; your desires and aspirations are certainly yours, no doubt, but the fact is that God's grace has secretly penetrated even there. Man cannot even will his own salvation without the help of God's grace.

This should be enough to shatter man's cherished illusion that besides being free to cooperate with grace — this much is correct—this cooperation is entirely and exclusively his own. He seems to have dreamed up a scheme that looks exceedingly simple and reasonable: God offers me a handshake, I accept it, and that is the end of the story. How blind we can be! We seem to forget that man's free cooperation with grace, his response to the offer of grace, *is itself drenched in grace*. Without God's help man is unable to accept his offer, unable to respond, and to hold the opposite is plain heresy. This profound truth means, therefore, that when God offers man his saving grace in any form — for instance, in the form of a particular prompting from the Spirit — his action is actually twofold: he extends to man the offer of his grace *and* secretly disposes, helps man to accept the offer. After the offer is made, the Spirit does not leave man to the vagaries of his own free will, he rather coaxes man to gratefully surrender to the inspiration. It is as if God were working simultaneously with two hands: with one he offers his grace, with the other he gently — ever so gently — draws man to the offered gift, in such a way that the acceptance is entirely man's — but also God's. Our acceptance of grace is totally penetrated, soaked in grace. If God were to limit his action to the mere offer of grace, naked grace, man would never be able to accept it.

This is clearly exemplified in the case of our thanksgiving to God for whatever gifts we have received from him. It would be wrong to imagine that, overwhelmed by the divine liberality, we at last have a chance to turn to God with a big "thank you". For the reality is that we cannot thank God without God. Our act of thanksgiving, if it is genuine, is the result of his secret grace working in us. The Church's liturgy expresses this beautifully: "You have no need of our praise, yet our desire to thank you is itself your gift".[16]

Yet, one should also emphasize strongly that this profound truth, this all-pervading action of grace, does not in any way turn man into a robot. No matter how intense and all-encompassing the influence of grace, man always retains his freedom untouched, as one of his most cherished possessions. No matter how ardently the Spirit desires man's cooperation to the offer of his grace, he will never, *never* curtail his freedom in the least. If there is an area in man where even God dreads to tread it is the sanctuary of his freedom, one of the greatest gifts man has received from God. God has an almost

16 Preface IV for Weekdays.

excessive reverence for man's freedom, for it is precisely through this freedom that man primarily mirrors the nature of God. It would obviously be absurd on the part of God to interfere with and dim, no matter how slightly, his own reflection on the surface of man. At the end we realize that God's grace reigns supreme — and so does man's freedom. The reconciliation of these two realities will always remain an unfathomable mystery locked away in the profundity of God's heart.

4) DOCILITY TO THE SPIRIT

The Spirit does not rest, he acts, and he acts probably much oftener than we imagine. To this activity on the part of the Spirit there corresponds an attitude of docility on the part of man. The promptings of the Spirit, whatever concrete shape they take, whether they come as a flash of light to the mind or as an impulse to the will or a burst of devotion or a touch of soothing comfort to the effectivity or a remembrance to the memory — all of them, once their supernatural origin has been ascertained with sufficient clarity, should always be received with the acquiescence of a docile heart. Man can never be too docile to the Spirit, too submissive to his voice. In this domain the only rule is that of the maximum. It is true that in the past certain spiritual sects have gone off the bend for claiming total docility to the demands and suggestions of the indwelling Spirit. But this happened because of their fundamental lack of fidelity, in spite of loud protestations to the contrary, for in reality they narrowed down the vast field of the Spirit's promptings to only those allegedly perceived in their own heart, neglecting the external, but equally precious sources of concrete historical circumstances and the surrounding community of men and women.[17]

The ideal of docility to the voice of the Spirit is much older than Christianity itself, for it already pervaded the

17 Vatican II, probably for the first time in the history of magisterial documents, explicitly exhorts priests to this docility in the hands of the Spirit: "In the very act of preaching his word they will be... led by the Spirit .... They will attain to that liberty which... will make them docile to the divine voice which makes itself heard in everyday life" (*Presbyterorum Ordinis*, nn. 13, 17: W. Abbott, *The Documents of Vatican II*, p. 535).

entire religious life of the Israelites: "I will put my Spirit within you and cause you to walk in my statutes and be careful to observe my ordinances" (Ez 36,27). The ideal was transparently clear: it is the presence of the Spirit within man that will gradually bend his will and soften up his heart "to walk in my statutes", namely, to be docile to the Spirit's voice.

However, ideals may be clear and have a compelling force of their own, but they are not always easy to realize. In fact, the sin of infidelity was a national plague in Israel for long stretches of its tortuous history. Prophets came along, thundering from the housetops and either threatening divine punishment or enticing the people back into the right path of fidelity. No use, the national plague continued, rendering many of the prophets' efforts futile, sterile: "They rebelled and grieved the Holy Spirit" (Is 63,10). Even gigantic spiritual leaders like Moses were infected by the national sickness of indocility: "They angered him (Yahweh) at the waters of Meribah, and it went ill with Moses on their account; for they made his spirit bitter (*marah:* they rendered his spirit indocile)..." (Ps 106,33).

This widespread lack of docility to Yahweh, this national rebelliousness, is colourfully described with a variety of graphic metaphors: "They did not obey or incline their ear, but walked in...the stubborness of their evil hearts, and went backward and not forward...; they did not listen to me or incline their ear, but stiffened their neck" (Jer 7,24-26). Yahweh, through Isaiah, complains bitterly that "the heart of these people (is) gross and their ears heavy", their eyes are as good as shut (Is 6,10). This lack of docility and innate rebelliousness enkindle God's anger: "And the Lord said to Moses, 'I have seen these people, and behold it is a stiff-necked people; now therefore let me alone, that my wrath may burn hot against them...'" (Ex 32,9-10).

A momentary conversion is soon followed by a widespread relapse into the old sin of infidelity, and Yahweh's reaction is already predictable: "Behold, their ears are closed, they cannot listen; behold the word of the Lord is to them like an object of scorn, they take no pleasure in it. Therefore I am full of the wrath of the Lord; I am weary of holding it in"

(Jer 6,10-11). The deepest root of this constant indocility to Yahweh's persistent request and pressing commands is the extreme hardness of their hearts, which apparently nothing can pierce or penetrate. They simply have "a heart of stone", dry, hard, obtuse, impenetratable; the much desired docility can be achieved only by implanting in them "a heart of flesh" (Ez 11,19) which is soft, open, flexible, docile, sensitive to the inner touches of God. Nothing short of a heart transplant will improve their condition and endow them with the gift of docility.

And yet, the pious Israelite longs to be ruled by the Spirit of Yahweh, as exemplified in the prayer of the psalmist: "I have fled to you for shelter, teach me to do your will, for you are my God! *Let your good Spirit lead me*" (Ps 143,10). This ought to be also the ideal of all the disciples of Jesus: to be constantly guided by his Spirit, the Holy Spirit, just as the Israelites of old in their weary, endless journey through the desert were always guided by Yahweh; they had only to follow him and they would be safe: "And the Lord went before them by day in a pillar of cloud to lead them along the way, and by night in a pillar of fire to give them light, that they might travel by day and by night" (Ex 13,21). The Holy Spirit always marches ahead of the Christian, guiding him along the way. We have only "to follow him". "Therefore, as the Holy Spirit says, 'today, when you hear his voice, do not harden your hearts' " (Hebr 3,7-8). Listen, submit and you will live.

To hear his voice is to hear the voice of the Shepherd. In the agricultural setting of Palestine, both before and during Jesus' lifetime, flocks and shepherds were a common sight (and to some extent they are still even today). So the image of the shepherd came spontaneously to the mind of the Jewish biblical writers. After the rigours of the Exile, Yahweh will lead his people back to Palestine. "They had left in tears, I will comfort them as I lead them back; I will lead them to streams of water" (Jer 31,9). He will lead them, not through a cloud and a pillar of fire this time, but directly by himself. The psalmist relishes this imagery, which he aptly interiorizes through prayer: "He guides me by paths of virtue....Though I pass through a gloomy valley I fear no harm; you are beside me..." (Ps 23,4). Proximity, guidance, protection, security, comfort and confidence: all this and much more is the shepherd to the flock. It is all so very simple, really; all the sheep have to do is faithfully follow the directions of the shepherd.

Jesus knew it well, for not far from Nazareth lies the exceedingly beautiful valley of Jezreel, where flocks of white sheep graze freely to their hearts' content. Green pastures, streams of living water, shepherds and flocks — and not very far, the northern tip of the sea of Tiberias. "I am the good shepherd...the sheep hear his voice, and he calls his own sheep by name and leads them out...; the sheep follow him, for they know his voice...they do not know the voice of strangers..." (Jn 10,2-5.18). The Christian seems to be endowed with a fundamental power, a remarkable instinct of discernment to distinguish between the voice of the shepherd and that of strangers. Jesus calls his sheep by name, one by one, for he knows them all singly. To him the flock is not an amorphous mass of similar sheep, faceless and anonymous, but rather a series of individuals with distinctive features and proper names, all equally precious in his eyes, but all of them endowed with the same quality, the same instinctive reaction: they all naturally tend to follow him, they are happy and contented with his leadership. Docile and confident they just follow him...

This pastoral imagery caught on well even in important urban centres like pagan Rome. Modern visitors to the catacumbs may be surprised to see that the cross, the traditional symbol of Christianity, is hardly found in those subterranean, cavernous burial chambers. Instead of the cross one sees in plentiful profusion the image of the Good Shepherd crudely scratched on the ancient walls. Apparently the early Christians, many of them earmarked for an eventual martyrdom at the Colosseum, were apparently impressed, not by the dying Jesus on Golgotha, but rather by his continuous role of shepherding the flock. And they certainly followed him all the way to the very end: they were ready to be thrown to the beasts and give up their earthly life rather than betray their newly acquired Christian faith. Once again it is all so disarmingly simple: all they had to do — and did — was to show docility to the Shepherd who went always ahead of them. It is docility to his voice, even when the voice leads them to the dreadful amphitheatre....This is simply evangelical docility, stubborn to the point of martyrdom.

Twenty centuries later the Roman Colosseum lies almost in ruins, an object of curiosity or admiration to the casual tourist. The historical circumstances have obviously changed, Nero is long dead and hungry lions do not roar anymore, eager to snatch their victims away and tear them to shreds. But that marvelous docility that led the Roman Christians to martyrdom still lives on. The absolute demand for docility will never fail. Only that this historical, Roman imagery, must now be interiorized. Docility to the Shepherd takes now the shape of an incessant, demanding docility to the Spirit of Jesus dwelling in the Christian, whispering to him to be faithful, to obey and submit, to be docile and responsive to the voice of God precisely because the Holy Spirit has made of him the son of God: "For all who are moved by the Spirit of God are sons of God" (Rom 8,14). And their *Abba* wants sons and daughters who are docile, not rebellious. A docility to the Spirit which is firm, constant, unremitting — this is the flowering of sonship and the indwelling. To possess so intimately the Holy Spirit and not to be docile to him would be almost contradictory. We possess the Spirit so that he, in turn, may possess us. To hold is to be held. One should almost pray to the Spirit with the words of the psalmist: "Into your hands I commend my spirit" (Ps 30,6). For total docility may well amount to unbloody martyrdom.

Let me conclude this section with a beautiful passage of St Augustine which sounds almost like a prayer:

> But let them rather understand, that if they are sons of God, they are led forth by the Spirit, so that they may do what is to be done, and once they have acted, let them thank Him by whom they act. For they are acted upon so that they may act, not that they may not act...so that, when they act as they should, that is, with love and delight of justice, they may joyfully receive that sweetness which the Lord gives.[18]

18 *De correptione et gratia* 2, 918.

5) ON DISCERNING THE VOICE OF THE SPIRIT

Docility to the Spirit necessarily presupposes a previous discernment of his voice, whether this voice comes to man from within or from without. Before submitting to the Spirit, the reasonable Christian has to be morally certain that it is precisely the Spirit and not an alien voice he is submitting to. For the fact is that the Spirit's activity is so very subtle, so fused and intermingled with man's own psychological activity, that oftentimes a clear separation, a discerning judgment as regards the origin of the voice or prompting is extremely difficult. The genuine voice of the Spirit may at first sight look like a merely human suggestion, for he seems to delight in self-effacement, in acting and then leaving behind hardly any trace of his action. But the opposite is also true, namely, at other times apparent signs of genuineness may be nothing but a deceptive mirage, a shadow without consistency; the allegedly divine voice may come in reality from man's own faculties in a purely natural process which has absolutely nothing to do with the Holy Spirit.

Discernment is difficult, and yet it is a must. A famed Superior general stated emphatically in Rome a few years ago that what the Church needs most of all today, in the prevalent doctrinal confusion, is precisely the faculty of discernment of spirits, the uncanny sixth sense to detect what comes from above and what is merely the product of man's human reasoning. It is true that Paul considers the ability to discern as a precious charismatic gift not granted to all: "To each is given the manifestation of the Spirit for the common good...to another the ability to distinguish between spirits" (1 Cor 12,10). A heightened sensitivity able to discern the Spirit may be an uncommon charismatic gift, but a certain elementary facility to handle the more plain, ordinary cases seems to be the common patrimony of all Christians, "who have their faculties trained *by practice* to distinguish good from evil" (Hebr 5,14).

John is equally insistent that this quality of discernment is to be exercised by all, if they are to avoid the pitfall of believing any spirit that claims to be from God: "Beloved, do not believe every spirit, but *test the spirits*, to see whether they are from God, for many false prophets have gone out into the world" (1 Jn 4,1). Similarly Paul, who himself exercised such a fine discernment in his apostolic life, never tires of exhorting his Christians to do the same, for all are expected to have the ability "of knowing the will of God and discerning the best" (Rom 2,18). "Now you are the light in the Lord; walk as children of light...discern what is agreeable to the Lord" (Eph 5,8-10). Paul not only exhorts, he prays for the gift of discernment: "My prayer is that your love may abound more and more, with knowledge and all discernment, so that you may approve what is best" (Phil 1,9-10).

It is obvious from what has already preceded that a coldly intellectual approach to the problem of discernment would be totally insufficient, for the Spirit often acts in the realm of feelings and affectivity. Often enough the good pleasure of the Spirit is to be sensed or felt rather than theoretically understood. Man's feelings can be the privileged channels through which God's voice resounds in the sanctuary of man's heart. In order to detect his voice, however, a minimum of experience may be highly desirable, if not absolutely indispensable. A calm, introspective attitude is the only way to listen to the Spirit's voice. Vatican II explicitly recommends "the intimate understanding of the spiritual things they experience".[19] This obviously implies the exercise of a fine sensitivity constantly awake as a sign of spiritual maturity. The Christian is expected to hear the voice of the Spirit and submit to it in the calm secrecy of his heart, momentarily withdrawn from the bustle of the world and often unnoticed by others.

The Spirit's variegated activity in the Christian is a real marvel. He is many-faceted, he is like a single ray of light that impinges on a prism and breaks up into a multiplicity of colours. What are all the colours of the rainbow but the result of the refraction of one single ray of light? This multifarious activity of the Spirit surely cannot be controlled, it can even hardly be classified, for it often breaks the most elaborate moulds.

On occasion the Spirit can act within the heart and mind of the believer with devastating force, brushing aside all

19 *Dei Verbum* n. 9: W. Abbott *The Documents of Vatican II*, p. 116.

obstacles and knocking down all obstructing barriers. He can act like a mighty flood, frightening and irresistible, laying waste everything in its path. At other times his action, whether in history or in man — the two privileged platforms of his activity — resembles rather a conflagration, a mighty blaze of roaring flames and crackling fire, reducing everything to ashes. Frightful, but real. Yet the destructive force of a conflagration can be matched by the fury of a hurricane that cuts a swath of devastation, leaving in its wake uprooted trees and telephone poles twisted into grotesque shapes, a heap of ruins and desolation. But what are a flood, a blaze, a hurricane if not water, fire and wind, the three biblical symbols of the Holy Spirit's action? A peaceful, cooling stream may turn into a flood, as much as the gentle caress of a warming fire may become a blaze, and a soothing breeze may develop into a storm. There are two sides to each of these natural symbols, reflecting respectively the two faces of the Spirit, gentle and forceful, soothing and powerful, delicate and vigorous.

But in the activity of the Spirit usually gentleness prevails over force, and persuasion over compulsion. He often speaks in whispers that go undetected. He delights in an atmosphere of delicacy, and finds us too rough; he likes hearts that are sensitive and pliable, and finds us too hard; he has a penchant for calmness and tranquility, and finds us too noisy. The net result is the widespread illusion that all this talk about the whispers and promptings of the Holy Spirit is nothing but the result of a heated imagination, a fairy tale, a hazy dream. We claim it never happens when in reality it is probably happening all the time. Oftener than not we do sense the movement, the stirring of the waters, but fail to detect the source or — worse still — attribute it to ourselves, to merely natural causes. Then the Spirit quietly withdraws — temporarily — until a more opportune time.

There is a little passage tucked away in the book of Wisdom which in one single stroke describes the qualities that, according to the author's mind, apply to divine wisdom, but they happen to fit extremely well the nature and the activity of the Holy Spirit as well. It is Wisdom 7,22-23.

The Spirit — or rather his activity in man — is *subtle.*

The original word is used of garments that are sheer, transparent, diaphanous. It would apply to those Indian sarees which are so incredibly fine and delicate that one of them, six yards long, can be folded into a matchbox. The same word is also used of a gentle breeze which can be felt but not seen, that is difficult to detect. The Spirit is subtle and delicate, impossible to seize, hold and control, all-pervasive and evasive, unpredictable, whose arrival cannot be foreseen and whose activity cannot be planned.

Besides being subtle and extremely delicate, the Holy Spirit's action is also *keen*, *irresistible*. It is keen and sharp like a sword that cuts through. It penetrates man deeply, down to his deepest layers. This irresistible nature of the Spirit's activity is well exemplified in the case of the Old Testament prophets: the Spirit "fell" on the prophet, "lifted" the prophet, the Spirit "enveloped" the prophet; "the Spirit entered" the prophet etc....Simply put, the Spirit is and remains in command, because he is primarily the Spirit of power and strength.

And yet, he is also *kindly*, *humane*. Properly speaking the Spirit is *philanthropon*, good and loving, fond of man. His strength and his kindness are but two sides of the same coin; it is simply his power and might at the service of this loving kindness. Two qualities that, far from being contradictory, bespeak the richness of his character and the plenitude of his activity, man being the beneficiary of both.

Finally, the Spirit is *tranquil*, calm and peaceful, free from anxiety. In keeping with his nature he inspires peace and instills tranquility. He pacifies, avoids tumult and delights in serenity. Like Jesus when he stilled the storm, the Spirit also calms and pacifies, he is the Spirit of profound quiet and noiseless repose. He is peace personified, and consequently his arrival is immediately detectable by the deep atmosphere of quietude which envelops him and radiates from him.[20]

When confronted with such a rich, dynamic personality, the attitude of the Christian should be that of King Solomon in his beautiful prayer to Yahweh: "Give your servant

20 Cf. G. Montague, *The Holy Spirit: Growth of a Biblical Tradition* (New York 1976), pp. 107-109.

therefore an understanding mind...*that I may discern* between good and evil....It pleased the Lord that Solomon had asked for this..." (1 Kings 3,9-10).

a) *Criteria of discernment: Christ and the Church*

The expression "discernment of spirits", in the plural, seems to have acquired right of citizenship in Christian literature, but it may be advisable to drop it in favour of "discernment of the Spirit", in the singular. For the former expression implies what seems to have become somewhat problematic, viz. the existence of a personal, evil spirit attempting to seduce man. Hence, according to traditional doctrine, a given inspiration, motion or prompting could, theoretically, proceed from a triple source: it could come from the Spirit of God, from man's own psychological faculties or from the devil. The very existence of the devil as a person, however, has of late become debatable and uncertain. Pope Paul VI expressed firmly his conviction that a personal devil, as the immediate source of much of the evil that plagues the world today, is a frightful reality to be reckoned with. Other reputable Catholic voices, however, beg to differ, claiming that what traditionally was attributed to the evil spirit can be now explained satisfactorily with the available techniques of modern psychology and pathology. The source of the "temptation" would be simply the interplay of psychological or even biological forces within man, not necessarily a personal, evil spirit enticing him along the path of sin.

Let the controversy rage, for it does not affect us directly now. For our purpose it is enough to reach a state of reasonable, moral certainty regarding the origin of a given inspiration: does it come from the Holy Spirit or from some other source distinct from the Spirit? This should suffice as an objective basis of judgment, for it would be hazardous to build the entire edifice of discernment on the shaky foundation of a personal evil spirit whose very existence has become uncertain.

If a particular prompting, an impulse or idea proceeds from the Holy Spirit, it has necessarily to bear a christological stamp, for the Spirit cannot possibly act if not in full conformity with Christ and his teachings. The New Testament is explicit: "No one speaking by the Spirit of God ever says 'Jesus be cursed.', and no one can say 'Jesus is Lord' except by the Holy Spirit" (1 Cor 12,3). "By this you know the Spirit of God...every spirit that does not confess Jesus is not of God" (1 Jn 4,2-3).

Since the Holy Spirit is not a spirit of self-advertisement but of self-effacement, his action in the Christian has necessarily to point to Christ rather than to himself. He acts like John the Baptist, who pointed to Christ. It is simply inconceivable that the Spirit should lead the believer away from Christ; the Spirit will rather draw him deeper into Christ, increasing in him his personal attachment to Christ. Consequently, a Christian who acts or teaches in a manner contrary to the word of Jesus' Gospel, contrary to Scripture may be deceived by his own sick mind or be led by the spirit of darkness, but he is certainly not led by the Spirit of Jesus.

The theological reason for this assertion is twofold: the immediate source of the outpouring of the Spirit in the Church is the glorified humanity of Jesus, for it is from him that the Christian is "made to drink of one Spirit" (1 Cor 12,13). Not in vain had Jesus promised: "If somebody is thirsty let him come to me and drink....Now this he said about the Spirit" (Jn 7,37-39). The Holy Spirit is the supreme gift of Jesus, and therefore the personal gift cannot possibly act unless in conformity with the giver. An idea, proposal or attitude not in keeping with the ideals or mentality of Christ can safely be discarded as spurious and false.

Secondly, and at a deeper level, the Spirit gushes out from the man Jesus because eternally the Spirit proceeds from the Son. Even prior to the Incarnation, in the inaccessible heights of God's eternal trinitarian life, in the internal silence and undisturbed serenity of God's own life, the Spirit proceeds from the Father, ultimate source of all life, through the Son. The Spirit draws his own life directly and immediately from the Son and, therefore, after the Incarnation, when immersed in the ceaseless flow of history, he cannot but act entirely in conformity with the immediate origin of his own life: the Son, now incarnate and visible. Hence, the christological stamp of any inspiration or impulse coming from the Spirit is nothing but an echo of the incessant flow of life that takes place within the trinitarian family of God.

All this is certainly clear and compelling — but also excessively general and consequently not always very useful when one is confronted with the eminently practical task of discernment. For no Christian worthy of the name will ever act or teach if not in explicit conformity with Christ's Gospel, for an open rejection of such Gospel would be self-condemnatory. If an alleged prophet, for instance, preaches a doctrine that clashes with that of Christ, he is obviously putting paid to his mission, he is committing spiritual suicide. Even false prophets know this much and proceed accordingly. No, their activity is not so crude and confrontational. A direct, frontal attack on the Christian bastions stands no chance of succeeding, a more subtle approach is likely to be used, and so, in order to unmask this subtlety we need a second criterion of discernment which is certainly more refined and delicate, more difficult to handle.

Christ is active within the boundaries of his Church, hence the alleged inspiration and origin we are trying to detect is bound to bear, not only a christological character, but also an ecclesial imprint. For the Holy Spirit was given by the glorified Christ primarily "to his beloved spouse, the Church", to use the authoritative expression of the Council of Trent. It is the Church at large that is the prime beneficiary of the pentecostal outpouring, and the individual Christian only in as far as he or she is a member of the Church. Genuine gifts of the Spirit always "build up the Church" (1 Cor 12,12), they are constructive, not destructive of the Church. Hence, if a particular prompting allegedly coming from the Spirit disregards or — worse still — opposes the Church of Christ, it should be considered as highly suspicious, to say the least.

This ecclesial character implies in practice the acceptance of the Church's doctrine. John taught this long ago: "Whoever knows God listens to us (the authentic teachers), and he who is not from God does not listen to us. By this we know the Spirit of truth and the spirit of error" (1 Jn 4,6). But here John is speaking of the apostolic doctrine, which is obviously normative for all at all times. Surely the official magisterium of the Church, pope and bishops, does teach authoritatively, but their teaching is not restricted to doctrines explicitly revealed by God; they often teach what is not directly contained in the New Testament. In other words, a doctrine of faith is obviously to be accepted always and at all times, and this doctrine of faith can safely be used as a viable criterion for discernment. Just as an inspiration, if genuine, cannot go counter to the teaching of Jesus, so also it cannot contradict an article of faith proposed by the Church's official magisterium. This is plain and without dispute.

Yet, this does not necessarily imply blind and uncritical acceptance of each and everyone of the Church's doctrines if they are not of faith. Legitimate reaction and even critical dissent from a given doctrine — even if it is official — can still bear the signature of the Spirit. The Old Testament prophets were known for their sustained opposition to accepted institutions and traditional practices (which usually implied doctrine), and yet they were led by the Spirit of God. The fact that the magisterium upholds strongly and insistently a particular doctrine is not in itself an absolute guarantee that the doctrine in question is correct and sanctioned by the Spirit; just as opposition to such a doctrine from the periphery of the Church is not a sure sign that such an opposition is condemned by the Spirit. For history shows both that official doctrines once loudly proclaimed have later been retracted as inaccurate or even erroneous, and that what often looks dangerously *avant-garde* and unorthodox today may be accepted as genuine Catholic doctrine tomorrow. Change is the price of progress and change is usually brought about by reaction and critical opposition, not by blind and uncritical acceptance. Hence, a temporary opposition to the Church's official doctrine need not always be branded as inimical to the Spirit of God. History teaches that often enough this is not the case, for the Spirit at times hides behind, but actively supports, critical reactions to official positions. To condemn all such reactions as illegitimate and opposed to the Spirit of God would be far too simplistic and naive, not to say downright false. We should always learn from history.[21]

21 In his pastoral visit to the U.S. in 1979, John Paul II touched in his numerous speeches on some extremely sensitive doctrinal issues like premarital sex, abortion, contraception, homosexuality, divorce, intercommunion with Protestants and the priesthood of women. The unhesitating pontifical answer to all these issues was a categorical repudiation as being contrary to the spirit

But a stubborn opposition of the self-styled "prophet" which eventually leads him to break with the visible Church is an unmistakable sign that he was deceived. He might have been led by the Spirit initially, but his eventual departure from the Church cannot possibly have been sanctioned by the Spirit, who remains emphatically the Spirit *of the Church*, given to her and to the individual through her. K. Rahner's drastic opinion commands respect: "That is not true Spirit of Christ which leads us outside the Church". I could not agree more. The Spirit may impel a committed Christian to take a critical stand and firmly voice his responsible opposition to a widespread, even official doctrine or practice, as long as he remains within the Churh; but the same Spirit will never prompt him to take the dreadful step of leaving the Church. The fatal step, if taken, is exclusively due to him, not to the Spirit. In any case this ecclesial criterion may offer an objective basis of judgment, but the Christian should refrain from passing judgment on the subjective responsibility and possible guilt of the defector from the Church. "For it is none of my business to judge outsiders" (1 Cor 5,12), said Paul long ago.

Hence, this ecclesial criterion of discernment should be used with cautious flexibility, for man's self-deception and the Spirit's guidance may be hopelessly intermingled. It remains a valid, but delicate criterion which can be easily misused both by the traditionalists who tend to apply it indiscriminately in too rigid a manner; and by the liberals who at times show an unacceptable disregard for whatever is official and comes from the centre. This criterion is not easy to handle correctly, and yet it remains absolutely indispensable in order to discern the voice of the Spirit both within man and in history.

of Christ. Obviously this kind of blanket condemnation was far too sweeping to be credible. A little more discriminatory judgment and a higher sensitivity to the situation of the local American church would have had the effect of making the papal stand less drastic — and more acceptable. Which goes to show that we ought to use the criteria for discernment even with regard to authoritative voices coming from the centre of the Church.

b) *Criteria of discernment: peace, joy, certitude*

Though obviously valid in themselves, the two external criteria so far examined are clearly insufficient, for the Holy Spirit, besides being the Spirit of Christ and of the Church, dwells in the individual, and therefore his activity should also be detected within the individual himself. It is in this subjective or internal area that the detection of the Spirit's voice is more delicate and the practical application of the criteria of discernment more hazardous.

Joy and peace, taken either singly or together, are often the sign of the Spirit's presence, "for God is not a God of confusion but of peace" (1 Cor 14,33). By this criterion Paul distinguishes the desires of the flesh from those of the Spirit: "To set the mind on the Spirit is life and peace" (Rom 8,6). This joyful peace, proceeding from the Spirit, spreads throughout the community: "For the kingdom of God does not mean food and drink but...joy and peace in the Holy Spirit" (Rom 14,17). The Holy Spirit simply radiates peace and joy: "The fruit of the Spirit is love, joy, peace..." (Gal 5,22).

This joyful peace, illumined by the rays of the Spirit, implies on the psychological level the complete harmonizing of man's inner tendencies. It is from harmony rediscovered, from the harmonious equilibrium of man's conflicting tendencies, that peace comes. When acted upon by the Spirit it is as if man were experiencing within himself an anticipated echo of his final destiny: "Enter into the joy of your master" (Mt 25,21). The disciple experiences now the reality of Jesus' parting gift, just before his passion: "I give you my peace" (Jn 14,27). This promise was fulfilled on Easter Sunday, when Jesus suddenly appeared to his terrified disciples behind closed doors: "*Peace* be with you....The disciples were filled with *joy*" (Jn 20,19). But, not satisfied with imparting to them this precious double gift, Jesus immediately proceeds to give them the very root from which joy and peace proceed: "Receive the Holy Spirit" (Jn 20,22). This is Jesus' supreme Easter gift, the bestowal of the Holy Spirit who, once received by the disciples, envelops them in a dense atmosphere of joy and peace, as a clear, tangible sign that the Spirit is within them. The Easter message is interiorized by the Spirit, rendered personal and concrete, discernible and tangible.

And as the Spirit of Jesus acted then, so he acts now. It is a matter of personal experience, so many times perceived in the course of spiritual retreats. The retreatant is trying hard to disclose to the director the nature of his or her prayer experience. He falters and stumbles, unable to put in words what he felt in prayer. The director, taught by long experience, knows the signs of the Spirit's presence only too well, but purposely does not prompt the answer, only encourages the retreatant to express it in his own words. And, sure enough, the two words that come out time and again are precisely "joy" and "peace" or their equivalents. The Spirit has not changed his ways, his activity is detectable today by the very same signs that accompanied his presence at the time of Jesus. The Spirit has quietly held the retreatant in his two arms, joy and peace, and consequently the person cannot but experience this twofold feeling intensely.

Not in vain had the departing Jesus promised his disciples in his valedictory discourse that they would "know him" (the Spirit) (Jn 14,17). Intense prayer is the privileged moment when this promise becomes real, for it is primarily in prayer that the disciple is overwhelmed by that deep sense of quiet joy and joyful peace which is more intimately felt that can be adequately described. The Spirit, acting from within the prayerful retreatant, draws him unto himself, flooding him with ineffable serenity and overwhelming him with happiness, not a boisterous happiness, but a quiet, silent, profound, all-pervading joy that seems to sink down and penetrate the innermost recesses of his person. The disciple feels now tightly pressed by the two arms of the Spirit, he feels an intimate peace that can only be matched by his intense, quiet joy: the Spirit is certainly at work, his traces can surely be detected in the experience the retreatant has undergone.

Man's conflict and disquiet usually arise from his self-centredness and egoistic tendencies, but when the Spirit acts man is withdrawn — at least momentarily — from his own self into the person of the Spirit, and then necessarily peace and joy ensue. The Spirit himself does not have peace and joy, he *is* peace and joy, and therefore when he draws man into himself, man begins to sink into an all-pervading atmosphere of joyful peace and peaceful joy. This is the language of the Spirit, at the same time muffled and eloquent. A disciple attuned to the harmonies of this language will listen and act accordingly.

But the Holy Spirit, who is the source of the gift of tongues, seems to delight in speaking to the Christian in other languages besides that of peace and joy. He is the Spirit of truth, namely— —we saw it above —the Spirit of light and intellectual penetration, certainly, but also the Spirit of genuineness, firmness and stability the, Spirit that dispels all doubts. He is the Spirit of certainty, and this characteristic of his becomes in the present context another criterion of discernment to detect his action.

It is remarkable that most of the Old Testament prophets had no other means to authenticate their mission except the appeal to their own subjective experience implied in their personal call to prophecy. They felt called by Yahweh, they were absolutely certain that the call was genuine, and apart from this subjective certitude they had no other credentials to produce. "The word of Yahweh was addressed to me" (Jer 1,4). How does Jeremiah know it is the word of the Lord and not his own overheated imagination? He only appeals to his personal experience and subjective certitude, and he is right. It was much the same with Amos: "It was Yahweh who took me from herding the flock, and Yahweh who said, 'Go, prophesy to my people Israel'" (Am 7,15). It was Yahweh....Amos had no means to prove it except by appealing to his own personal, unshakable conviction. He felt it within himself, he was sure it was Yahweh. Paul himself never had the least doubt that on the way to Damascus he had had a genuine, in fact, a shattering experience. He was so utterly convinced of the genuineness of the vision, that he almost boasted of it: the Father "was pleased to reveal his Son to me" (Gal 1,16). The light of the risen Christ had penetrated his mind and created in him an unshakable conviction. He could do nothing but appeal to the inner certitude left in him by that memorable encounter. And the pillars of the Jerusalem church, James, Peter and John, authoritatively accepted Paul's testimony as genuine beyond all doubt, in spite of resting on such an apparently flimsy basis.

And yet this criterion of one's own subjective certitude remains essentially ambivalent, for in this delicate area the danger of self-deception is great: a firm, unwavering conviction regarding the authenticity of a spiritual experience is not an infallible sign of its genuineness. However, despite its hazardous use, the criterion remains valid, for in some cases this absolute conviction that grips the person cannot be explained by appealing to natural causes. It may well be an inner, authentic experience that defies rationalization: the Christian has felt the Spirit acting within himself and he is absolutely sure of it. The Spirit of truth has momentarily gripped the person, communicating to him at the same time a share in his divine firmness and certitude. The disciple is now certain that it was the Spirit who touched him, and he is certain with the shared certainty of God himself.

The corroborative testimony of genuine mystical experience may be pertinent and to the point. Not only Amos and Paul, but Teresa of Avila, too, has recourse to the very same criterion of interior certainty in order to discern the action of God: "God implants himself in the interior of that soul in such a way that...*it cannot possibly doubt* that God has been in her and she has been in God; so firmly does this truth remain within her that...it can never forget *nor doubt* that she has received it...; because of a *certainty* which remains in the soul, which can be put there only by God".[22]

The original certainty of this experience can be further strengthened when the effects of the Spirit's action are scrutinized. The Bible attests that the word of God is eminently powerful, "sharper than any two-edged sword" (Hebr 4,12), that besides conveying light to the mind, it is also endowed with an inbuilt power of its own that can affect the will. There are times when the Spirit makes use of this very power of the spoken word to increase the certainty that God has been at work. A sudden, totally unexpected and complete change in the psychological state of the person concerned may be a pointer to the divine origin of the

22 *Interior Castle*, mansion 5, ch. 1 (English translation by Allison Peers, London 1979, p. 51). I have modified slightly the translation so as to bring it closer to the original Spanish. Teresa returns to the same criterion in the more difficult case envisaged in the 6th mansion, ch.3.

experience. An internal storm that is suddenly, almost inexplicably stilled, or a very deep hurt that is entirely eradicated, wiped out without a trace as the result of a personal word or touch of the Spirit, can be a sure testimony of his action. The person has only to look within himself and notice with amazement the sudden change that has taken place in his own psychological disposition: a clear sign that the Spirit has been active.

Once again St Teresa confirms this in her usual transparent style: "In this tempest there is no help for it but to wait upon the mercy of God, who suddenly, at the most unlooked-for hour, with a single word, or on some chance occasion, lifts the whole of this burden from the soul, so that it seems as if it had never been clouded over, but is full of sunshine and far happier than it was before".[23]

From all that has preceded two important conclusions can be drawn:

In order to discern the Spirit of light from the spirit of darkness a *comprehensive criterion* should always be used. At the end, the more we utilize this global criterion of discernment the greater the certainty that we have detected correctly the voice of the Spirit. The use of one single criterion may not be sufficient to dispel the doubt, whereas the use of all the main criteria may well provide the desired moral certainty. This is precisely the most marked characteristic of John's teaching, for whom this all-embracing criterion includes the following: doctrinal confession, authority of the Church, concrete fidelity to God manifested in fraternal love, necessity of interior experience, and communion with the indwelling persons. All these criteria stand together or fall together, and the clear absence of anyone of them would be a sure sign that the Spirit is not at work.

Secondly, the capacity of discernment is *subject to growth:* initial gropings and unavoidable blunders will gradually yield to a certain connaturality in discerning the Spirit's voice, and this is surely the sign of maturity, for maturity implies a capacity to differentiate in a practical manner interior experiences and operations. A mature Christian who not only believes in, but lives the doctrine of the indwelling,

23 *Interior Caste,* mansion 6, ch. 1: English ed., p. 73.

is a person who has passed from structure to stricture: he is less concerned about external structures for their own sake and more attuned to the discerned demands of the indwelling Spirit, and therefore more accountable to the Spirit and his strictures in case of wilful negligence of his voice. This gradual growth in the ability to discern the Spirit's action necessarily implies the following elements: inner experience; repeated reflection on this experience; enlightened discrimination between the different experiences by applying the various criteria for discernment; evaluation of past experiences and decisions reached; and especially a lived openness and increased sensitivity to the activity of the Spirit in him.

6) The sevenfold gift of the spirit

The Middle Ages made much of a spiritual reality that seems to be largely forgotten nowadays: the sevenfold gift of the Holy Spirit. This multifaceted gift is something peculiar and distinct, closely associated with, but different from, the promptings of the Spirit, on the one hand, and from the three theological virtues on the other. Christian tradition has always based this doctrine of the seven gifts of the Spirit on the classical passage of Isaiah 11,2, which joyfully announces a profusion of spiritual gifts to be poured out on the future Messiah: "And the Spirit of the Lord shall rest upon him, the spirit of wisdom and insight, the spirit of counsel and power, the spirit of knowledge and the fear of the Lord". The traditional number seven is of course rather fanciful, for Isaiah's original Hebrew mentions only six, not seven gifts. But the exact number is immaterial, for the intention of the author is to convey the fullness, the plenitude of spiritual motions, promptings or inspirations, rather than to specify their precise number.

The scriptural foundation of this doctrine of the gifts, however, goes far beyond this isolated passage of Isaiah. For the New Testament repeatedly mentions the activity of the Spirit in the life of the Christian, and it is this that should be considered as the true scriptural foundation: the Spirit is said to rule the just, to lead and help them when they have to face civil courts, to teach them to pray to the Father, to lead them into the fullness of truth. In a word, the entire life of the Christian should be guided by the Holy Spirit. The disciple of Jesus is frequently being acted upon by the Spirit: "All those who are moved by the Spirit of God are sons of God" (Rom 8,14).

Far more important than the exact number of the gifts coming from the Spirit is the purpose for which these gifts are given. Many centuries ago St Thomas stated succintly: "The gifts are perceptions of man whereby he becomes amenable to the promptings of the Holy Spirit".[24] A firm grasp of this doctrine is of the utmost spiritual importance. Briefly put, one could say that the gifts of the Spirit are simultaneously principles of docility and principles of action.

As *principles of docility* the gifts shape, prepare and predispose man for the future promptings of the Spirit, for, whereas human virtues are ruled by reason, the regulating principle of the gifts is higher: the indwelling Spirit himself moving the believer through his inspirations. The gifts render the Christian docile, supple, flexible, responsive to the promptings of the Spirit, ever ready to comply with his wishes. They are like a receiving station always attuned to catch the waves proceeding from the centre, from the indwelling Spirit.

Anybody acquainted with the Indian countryside will understand the following simile. No farmer in his senses will sow the seed in the month of April, when a fierce sun beats down mercilessly on the entire landscape, turning plots of arable land into a patched, bleak, thirsty ground. If the seed were to be sown in those conditions it would soon dry up and die, deprived of the necessary moisture. But let the first monsoon showers come, and the very same land, as if by a miracle, will be no longer dry, hard and cracked, but moist, soft and receptive, ready to receive and suck in the seed. The farmer knows it: the time of sowing has arrived. The seed should be scattered now, for the torrential monsoon rains have turned the earth into highly receptive ground. Now the seed will sprout and produce the desired harvest.

It is much the same with regard to the ground which is man. The seed of the promptings will not fructify unless the ground has been rendered soft and amenable, sensitive and

24 *Summa*, I-II, 1. 68, a. 3.

docile through the sevenfold gifts of the Spirit. It is therefore the Spirit himself, that, through his gifts, quietly disposes man for the eventual reception of his own inspirations. The spirit of man is to be rendered receptive first, and that is precisely the function of the gifts. The Holy Spirit not only dwells within the Christian, he also acts within him; not only acts in him, but before acting predisposes him for his future action — through his gifts. The Spirit seems to be more active in us that we are ourselves. Rather than possess the Spirit we are possessed by him; once again, to hold is to be held. Or better still, it is a mutual, reciprocal possession, the perfect fusion of man's free spontaneity and docile submission, of his liberty and his docility. If the seed of the prompting falls on receptive ground, it will certainly sprout, and according to Jesus' parable, bear rich fruit, thirtyfold, sixtyfold, or hundredfold, depending on each one's docility to the seed of the word of God.

Over and above this, the gifts of the Spirit are also *principles of action*, not only of reception. Once the prompting is received within the spirit of man rendered docile by the gifts, it is the gifts themselves that will urge man to action. But it is to be noted that often enough this activity inspired by the gifts does not tend outwardly, but rather inwardly; it is a peculiar activity which is directed towards the interior of man, to his innermost sanctuary where the Holy Spirit resides. This is the reason why at times even a heroic submission to the voice of the Spirit can pass totally undetected by the outside world. A dogged, protracted fidelity to the inner voice of the Spirit, or a sensitive reaction to his touch is something that is usually performed noiselessly, without fanfare, something that nearly always remains hidden within the secrecy of one's heart.

The gifts are ruled directly by the Spirit, not by human reason; and although his inspirations cannot contradict the sound demands of reason, they keep a certain independence from them, for ultimately it is the Spirit that governs the son of God, and the Spirit "blows where he wills". A saint, ruled by the Spirit and his gifts, can be the most unpredictable person. For, in the words of St Thomas, "the spiritual man is inclined to act, not by the promptings of his own will, but by the instinct of the Holy Spirit".[25]

At other times, however, the gifts are principles of external, visible apostolic activity. It would be a serious mistake — but a mistake that is fairly widespread nowadays — to imagine that this attention to the interior, this inner disposition of being attuned to the voice and touch of the Spirit dwelling within man is something exclusively meant for contemplatives, whose only task in life is to pray, listen to the whispers of the Spirit and submit to them in the noiseless atmosphere of the cloister. This, of course, is totally false. For the history of Christianity shows abundantly that oftentimes it is the Spirit that impels men and women to ceaseless apostolic action. This action, when not impregnated by the Spirit, can be nothing but an exercise in futility, a stage performance for the amusement of the gallery, "a noisy gong or a clanging cymbal" (1 Cor 13,1). But it can also be genuine, the fruit of an intense life lived in the Spirit, the result of the sevenfold gift of the Spirit impelling the Christian, not inwardly but outwardly, thrusting him into the bustle of the world and the noisy community of men.

Hence, the gifts can be principles of both receptivity and activity, of internal docility and apostolic action, urging the Christian either to quiet contemplation or to dynamic apostolic action. God knows that both are badly needed in the Church of God, and since the Holy Spirit is primarily the Spirit of the Church, he acts within her shaping and disposing men and women for both these tasks, for quiet withdrawal from the world and for apostolic immersion in the world. In a word, "man is acted upon by the Spirit that he may act".[26]

Doctrine, however clear, runs the risk of remaining theoretical unless it is visibly exemplified in historical figures, in men and women who were habitually guided by the Spirit, attentive to his promptings and sensitive to his touches. One such a person seems to be, not only Teresa of Avila, but our contemporary Mother Teresa of Calcutta. After having

25 *In Rom* 8, 14.
26 St Thomas, *Summa*, I-II, q. 68, a. 3.

spent fifteen of her thirty-six years as a teaching Loretto nun, she began to see, according to Fr. Julien Henry, her confidant, "the dire poverty of many people in and around Calcutta. *She felt an inner prompting* to do something to relieve the hardships of the very poor, and to lead them to God.... *She obeys his* (God's) promptings, his direction, without question".[27]

Yet this is too vague and general. The Spirit is gradually preparing Teresa, and once he is satisfied that the ground is already soft and receptive, he drops the seed, as often happens, in the most unexpected circumstances. Teresa of Avila had received the call to reform the Carmel — it will be remembered — when she was surrounded by women, merrily chatting away and listening to music — certainly not a propitious atmosphere for the Spirit to act, according to human wisdom. Now it is another Teresa who, unexpectedly, feels within her the divine command — when travelling by train. "Then came God's call. 'It was, Mother Teresa told me' — her confidant Fr. Henry continues — 'on the 10th of September, 1946, in the train that took me to Darjeeling that I heard the call of God'. In quiet, intimate prayer with her Lord, she heard distinctly what she says was for her 'a call within a call'. 'The message' she explains, 'was quite clear: I was to leave the convent and help the poor whilst living among them. It was an order' ".[28]

In keeping with her spiritual principle of submitting to the Spirit's promptings — even when they happen to come, not in the solitude of the chapel, but in the rattle of a speeding train — she bows. And so two years later, "in response to God's call, on the 16th of August, 1948 (she) walked out of the (Loretto) convent, closed the door behind her and found herself on a Calcutta street, alone, in the dark...with no shelter, no company, no helper, no money, no employment, no promise, no guarantee, no security".[29] She had nothing to go by except the dim light of the past prompting from God. The Spirit had plucked her out of her religious house where she had lived a comparatively comfortable life, and thrust

27 E. Le Joly, *We do it for Jesus. Mother Teresa and the Missionaries of Charity* (Delhi 1977), pp. 14, 17.

28 *Ibid.*, p. 17.

29 *Ibid.*, pp. 21, 22.

her into the appalling filth and squalor of the Calcutta slums.

All this is past history, but her astounding apostolic achievements are present, not past. In her case, the Spirit's promptings have driven her into ceaseless apostolic action, just like her namesake from Avila four centuries earlier. Mother Teresa's Missionaries of Charity soon fan out of Calcutta, their convents mushroom in and outside India, and today their houses, in the service of the poorest of the poor, girdle the globe. It all goes back to the "queer" idea — it was so labeled at that time — she received one day when travelling by train. . . . All this shows that the Spirit continues to be active in his saints, and active in the most unpredictable manner. When we least expect he intervenes, shattering human plans and upsetting human predictions. By his activity he reminds us periodically that he remains the Lord of the Church and the supreme master of history.

It should be noted, finally, that with regard to the gifts of the Spirit there is no golden mean, as it happens in the case of the moral virtues, which should always keep to the middle path, without sliding into either defect or excess. This rule does not apply to the three theological virtues, nor to the gifts: one can never believe in God too much, or hope in his promises too much, or love him too much. Similarly, it is just not possible to be excessively docile to his promptings. Here the only regulating principle is that of the maximum, which certainly does not set aside the virtue of prudence, but rather subjects it to a higher principle: the person of the Holy Spirit himself.

It is the Spirit who, abiding in man, brings about in him a reconciliation of opposites, a harmony between apparently contradictory tendencies: "Only he who is a member of the Church and independent, humble and daring, obedient and conscious of his own responsibility; a person who prays and acts, adhering to the Church in her past and in her future — only such a man as this makes room for the Spirit of God".[30] But it is not in the glamour and glow of pagentry that man surrenders to the inner voice of the Spirit and attains thereby this reconciliation of opposites, this harmonious balance

30 K. Rahner, "Do not stifle the Spirit", *Theological Investigations* 7 (London 1971), p. 84.

between daring activity and humble receptivity. Rather, it is in the drabness and dullness of everyday life, in the unobtrusive, yet tenacious fulfillment of one's duty and in the midst of wearisome struggles, "in quiet and recollection that the living God fills the hearts of the believers with the Holy Spirit who is eternal life".[31]

Bibliography

Bardy, G. and others: "Dons du Saint Esprit", *Dictionnaire de Spiritualité* 3 (1957) 1579-1641.

Lecuyer, J.: "Docilité au Saint Esprit", *Dictionnaire de Spiritualité* 3 (1957) 1471-1497.

Philipon, M.: *Les Dons du Saint Esprit* (Paris 1964) 113-154.

Schmaus, M.: "Gifts of the Spirit", *Sacramentum Mundi* 3 (1969) 59-61.

Guillet, J.: *Discernment of Spirits* (Collegeville 1970).

Sheets, J.: "Profile of the Spirit: a theology of the discernment of spirits", *Review for Religious* 30 (1971) 363-376.

Therrien, V.: *Le Discernment dans les Ecrits Pauliniens* (Paris 1973)

"Discernment of the Spirit and of spirits", *Concilium*, Nov. 1978.

Rulla, L.: "The discernment of spirits and Christian anthropology", *Gregorianum*, 59 (1978) 537-569.

Albrecht, B.: "Discernment of spirits", *Review for Religious* 38 (1979) 382-398.

Sieben, H.: "Paix interieure", *Dictionnaire de Spiritualité* 12 (1983) 56-73.

31 K. Rahner, *Ibid.*, p. 86.

Chapter Seven

EXPERIENCE OF THE SPIRIT'S PRESENCE

The promptings of the Spirit as well as the habitual attitude of docility they presuppose in the Christian are both based ultimately on the astonishing reality of the Holy Spirit's personal presence within man, and, more pointedly yet, within the materiality of his body. The Spirit dwells there permanently as in a temple, but this presence is apprehended in dark, impenetrable faith. We all believe that the Spirit lives in the sanctuary of man's body, but is everything left to faith? Is faith not helped by a minimum of personal experience? And if the answer to this question is in the affirmative, is this precious experience limited to the delicate operations of the Spirit within man, or can it be extended deeper still to the very root from which they proceed, namely, the person of the Spirit himself?

Given the intimate interlocking, the near fusion of man's psychological faculties and the action of the Holy Spirit, it would certainly be strange if the Spirit's presence were limited exclusively to the obscure realm of faith, if he did not make his presence somehow felt in man's affectivity. Even at this stage and before examining the question more in detail, in seems to be hardly credible that the Spirit, who grips man so forcefully from within, should leave absolutely no traces of his presence in man's heart; hardly possible that man should not, sooner or later, perceive his presence and feel his touch. For man's spiritual faculties, intellect and will, do not exhaust his personality; there is still the very vast area of his affectivity and feelings to be reckoned with, and it is precisely in this area that one can often detect traces of the Spirit's activity. The Holy Spirit is not only intellectually apprehended, he is also sensibly felt.

Faith and experience. The much vaunted role and importance of experience should not be exaggerated, for within the body of Christian belief experience performs a role that is subsidiary to that of faith. We hope to be saved one day, not primarily because we experienced God in our earthly pilgrimage, but rather because we firmly held on to him in the dark, because we believed in him. Yet, once the primary and absolutely indispensable function of faith is clearly and unambiguously established, there is no denying that experience, too, plays an important role in man's relationship with God. In the long run it is very hard to cling only to dark faith, unsupported by experience. Faith should always stand, firm and unwavering, but it is advisable and desirable to offer it the prop of personal experience. There are buildings that were once firmly and securely constructed, but with the passage of time they tend to decay, they may be able to stand only if supported by additional props. Obviously there is no opposition, no quarrel of any kind between faith and experience, for ideally both should be blended into a harmonious whole, but on the other hand, to openly acknowledge the importance of experience does not imply a diminution of the higher importance of faith. Experience should be built on faith, but faith cannot be built on experience, for in this case faith would rest on man, not on God, and a faith that rests on man is no genuine Christian faith at all, but a pale surrogate that will collapse at the slightest pressure.

Experience of the Spirit's presence does not follow automatically from his presence within man. For the Spirit may be present, and yet man may well be opaque to his light and closed to his inspirations, in which case he cannot be said to live by the Spirit or walk by the Spirit. And much less can he then claim to be conscious of the Spirit's presence. Whereas it should be "a normal thing for a Christian to experience the Spirit".[1] He possesses the Holy Spirit and

1 J. Mouroux, *The Christian Experience* (London 1954), p. 128.

he knows it, both from faith and from his own personal experience: this is the perfect Christian.

1) The spirit's presence experientially perceived

Almost certainly the reader was baptized in childhood. Infant baptism, as remarked above, is a very ancient and traditional practice, probably with roots in the New Testament itself, a practice to which many Christian Churches are still strongly attached. This custom is certainly a remarkable testimony of the Spirit's impatience to enter and possess the child, no doubt. But the practice is also beset by difficulties and obscurities. Most of the Christians of the first generation were baptized in an adult, mature age, not in childhood, and as such were open not only to the inflow of the Spirit who entered them through the waters of baptism, but also to the personal experience of his presence. Apparently that first baptismal effusion of the Spirit was accompanied by a vivid consciousness of his possession. Those early Christians not only believed that after baptism they had the Spirit, they also experienced his presence.

Paul's Christians in Galatia were still very raw. Sometime after being baptized they happened to fall under the spell of their former Jewish practices and traditions. They were not entirely uprooted from the soil of Judaism. After all, they had lived for long years as faithful followers of Yahweh and his Law, before this man Paul showed them convincingly the inadequacy of it all when compared with a life-giving surrender into the hands of the glorified Christ through faith. And now their former religious spirit, thoroughly Jewish, begins to entice them again, to beckon them back to the practices they had already abandoned. And this return to the past implies necessarily a corresponding devaluation of their faith in Christ. They seem to be wavering in their Christian convictions, they are still fettered by their Jewish past, and therefore unable to commit themselves fully to Christ through faith. It is this pitiful situation that makes Paul react sharply with a typical blast: "Are you people in Galatia really mad? Who has bewitched you, before whose eyes Jesus Christ was publicly portrayed as crucified? Let me ask you only this: Did you *receive the Spirit* by works of the Law or by hearing with faith?....Having begun with the Spirit, are you now ending with the flesh? Did you *experience* so many things in vain?" (Gal 3,1-4).

They were certainly adults, those unsteady Galatians who had permitted their faith in Christ to be weakened, and as adults at the time of their initial conversion to Christianity they had experienced the Spirit working in them. It is more than likely that here Paul has in mind not only the personal presence of the Spirit in them as the result of their baptism, but also the profussion of charismatic gifts that, at that time, often accompanied the indwelling of the Spirit. In any case Paul takes it for granted — and that is one of his main arguments to convince the Galatians of the foolishness of their behaviour — that at the time of their baptism they had, in fact, *experienced the Spirit*. It is remarkable that Paul does not so much appeal to their Christian faith as to their personal experience, which renders their present wavering all the more ununderstandable. And the almost casual way in which Paul refers to this experience seems to show that for him it was something perfectly normal and not at all extraordinary. For Paul is not writing to a hand-picked batch of mystics endowed with special graces, but rather to plain, ordinary Christians, laymen and laywomen of Galatia. The mature Christian can and should experience the Spirit.

It would be wrong to imagine that this experience of the Holy Spirit's presence was limited to the moments of initial fervour accompanying their first conversion. In a subsequent passage that is so often quoted in connection with the doctrine of the discernment of spirits, Paul portrays graphically a twofold experience that takes place within the baptized Christian. Two conflicting forces within him clash violently, both demanding his allegiance: his sinful self-centredness and the person of the Holy Spirit dwelling in him. And the mutual opposition of those two forces obviously takes place within man's conscious faculties, he has a personal experience of both: "Self-indulgence is the opposite of the Spirit, the Spirit is totally against such a thing....When self-indulgence is at work, the results are obvious: fornication, gross indecency and sexual irresponsibility; idolatry and sorcery; feuds and wrangling, jealousy, bad temper and quarrels, disagreements, factions, envy, drunkenness, orgies and similar things.... What the Spirit brings is very different: love, joy, peace, patience, goodness, truthfulness, gentleness and self-control" (Gal 5,17-23).

The two ruling forces within man speak contradictory language to his consciousness. Man experiences both within himself, and through a protracted process of reflection, he can detect their origin, namely, either his own self-indulgence or the personal Spirit. Love, peace, joy, gentleness....Nearly all of them defy accurate definition, but they are all the object of experience, an experience which is produced within man by the Holy Spirit abiding in him. The touch of the Spirit is felt deep down within man's affectivity, as an incontrovertible testimony of his presence. The Spirit's presence is not only believed in the darkness of faith, it is also grasped, however faintly, in the realm of one's personal experience.

Yet, there is nothing in all this that is peculiar or exclusive to the Galatians whom Paul knew well. He is so utterly convinced of the importance of this experience of the Spirit's presence that he returns to it when sending a despatch to the Christians in Rome, largely unknown to him. They too, whether Jewish Christians or Gentile Christians, are possessed by the same Spirit, whose presence they should normally perceive within themselves, particularly in their prayer life. Romans 7 is a pathetic description of the inner psychological struggle in the Christian-to-be, prior to his baptism. He feels torn asunder between the rectitude of his conscience, on the one hand, which tells him clearly what to do, and the sinful inclination of his self-indulgence on the other, which drags him down into the path of sin. He suffers from excess of light and lack of strength, for his conscience is crystal clear, but his will is weak and irresolute. He experiences simultaneously light and darkness, the call to freedom and the slavery of the power of sin, an experience of defeat and a secret longing for help. His condition is simply pathetic.

And now, it is into this fearsome psychological struggle that the Holy Spirit bursts, shedding on man further light, but specially instilling into his wavering will the strength he so badly needed but did not have. Now — in Romans 8, that is — the Spirt of Christ takes over and claims the Christian to himself, making him the son of the Father. It is at this juncture that Paul adds something very remarkable: "When we cry 'Abba, (my) Father!' it is the Spirit himself bearing witness with our spirit that we are children of God" (Rom 8,16-17).

Both the Holy Spirit and our own human spirit are fused into one single act of Christian prayer. Notice that, in a certain way, the action of the Spirit is twofold, he is present in man, and over and above this presence he testifies together with our spirit[2] that we are the sons of God. He gives us our sonship and wants us to be aware of the gift. Man has a new status and, thanks to the Spirit, he is conscious of it. His prayer to the Father, full of childlike confidence and trust, proceeds from his own spirit transformed by the Holy Spirit. The Christian who prays this way is consciously aware that the Spirit is manifesting his presence to him. It is as if Paul were telling the Christians in Rome: "Whenever you cry *Abba*... God assures you that you can be absolutely certain that you really are his children".[3] This prayerful cry is an unmistakable sign of the Spirit's presence within man. Prayer, therefore, the prayer of the son of God, emerges now as the privileged moment when he becomes conscious of this status, gifted to him by the Holy Spirit.

Hence, Paul leaves no room for doubt: the Christian, in prayer and outside prayer, should normally have an initial experience of the Spirit's presence. This is nothing so very extraordinary, this can be expected of all "who have tasted the heavenly gift and have become partakers of the Holy Spirit" (Hebr 6,5). The experience of the Spirit is not an esoteric gift granted to a chosen few, but rather the common patrimony of all Christians.

2) Limitations of this experience

The Christian ought to experience the Spirit, but the fact remains that Paul "knows of no pure and unveiled experience of the Spirit here on earth".[4] For, to begin with,

2 The could text also be translated as "testifies *to* our spirit", in which case the direct action of the Spirit in man's consciousness would be still clearer.

3 J. Jeremias, *The Prayers of Jesus*, p. 65.

4 J. Mouroux, *The Christian Experience*, p. 150.

this experience, though undoubtedly genuine, is both partial and indirect, enveloped as it is in the obscurity of faith. It is a luminous and experiential, but at the same time dark apprehension of the Spirit. It is an experience steeped in the dark light of faith, if one may use such a paradoxical expression. The Christian has been radically transformed by the indwelling of the Spirit, but the Spirit's activity within him is apprehended only through the necessary medium of signs. The Spirit, in spite of acting so powerfully and distinctly, seems to elude the grasp of man. The believer who has the Spirit can feel that he is "strengthened with might with the Spirit in the inner man" (Eph 3,16); he can experience his mind flooded with the light proceeding from "the Spirit of truth" (Jn 14,17); he can taste an intense, ineffable "joy inspired by the Holy Spirit" (1 Thess 1,6); he can be "aglow with the Spirit" (Rom 12,11), turned into a focus of light to others around him; he can be drenched in deep peace, experiencing within himself the truth of Jesus' promised gift, "My peace I give you" (Jn 14,27); he can find delight in the comfort or *paraklesis* of the Paraclete as he would in a soothing balm.

He can feel, taste and relish all this and much more still, but even this cumulative experience will give him only access to the operations of the Spirit, not to the very person of the Spirit from whom they proceed. He perceives clearly the rivulets, but he cannot get to the spring from which they flow. Even in the intimacies of the indwelling the person of the Spirit seems to elude the grasp of man, he seems to withdraw behind a cloud of incense which renders his features blurred and hazy. His presence can be indirectly deduced, rather than directly apprehended. His traditional self-effacement seems to render the task of inquisitive man particularly difficult. He touches man and then withdraws into his inner sanctuary, leaving him puzzled as to who has touched him. He seems to take delight in acting behind the screen of anonymity, hidden and almost disguised, as it were, behind man's natural activity. He seems to be a voice without a speaker, able to touch and caress without hands, to speak without words. He makes his presence intimately felt, yet he remains eminently elusive, enigmatic, mysterious.

But this is only the general rule. For there are rare occasions when the intermediary signs grow thinner and thinner, when they become increasingly transparent, almost diaphanous, until *the very person of the indwelling Spirit is grasped directly* and immediately, with a burning, searing consciousness of his presence. But even then in an atmosphere of transfigured faith: this is genuine mysticism. In extreme cases the mystic sees/feels the Spirit present within him, when not only the operations, but the very person of the Spirit bursts into man's consciousness with a vividness that defies description: this is the authentic, precious experience of the indwelling Spirit and a close foreshadowing of the final vision of God. Momentarily man has been allowed to drink, not only from the rivulets, but from the very spring. Yet this intense, ineffable experience remains extremely rare, certainly beyond the grasp of the vast majority of Christians.

Barring therefore this exceptional case, the apprehension of the Spirit is, as a rule, only indirect, and as a consequence, the certainty we may have of possessing the Spirit here and now is also indirect, based as it is on faith and our limited personal experience of the indwelling. For this certainly rests on the firmness of God's fidelity, but it concerns a man still immersed in the uncertainties of his pilgrim state. Its luminous origin is in God, but its possession is subject to the fickleness of man. We can never be absolutely certain, with a certainty that dispels all doubt, that we are indwelt by the Spirit. Paul confirms this repeatedly: "I am not aware of anything against myself, but I am not thereby acquitted. It is the Lord who judges me" (1 Cor 4,4). "Therefore let anyone who thinks that he stands take heed lest he fall" (1 Cor 10,12). "Work out your salvation with fear and trembling" (Phil 2,12).

The relative certainty we may have of our state of friendship with God (or our state of grace, to use the traditional expression) certainly rests on faith, but it is not the object of faith. In other words, the highest possible degree of certainty we can have about anything at all is the certainty of faith, which is restricted to what God has explicitly revealed to us. So, for instance, we firmly believe that Christ died for our sins, because this is explicitly stated in the New

Testament. When accepting this salvific truth in faith no mistake of any kind is possible, for we rely exclusively on the testimony of God himself.

But the certainty regarding our possession of the Spirit is quite a different matter. Here we can have only a lower degree of certainty, not the certainty of faith. The fact of the indwelling of the Spirit in general is clearly New Testament doctrine, explicitly revealed by God, but the indwelling presence of the Spirit in this concrete person here and now has never been revealed by God anywhere, and hence, properly speaking, it cannot be the object of faith, it cannot be believed. Here there is no room for faith, for my Christian faith does not demand that I believe this unhesitatingly.

The possession of the Spirit may be, on the whole, certain, but it is also clouded in partial uncertainty on account of the unpredictable creature in whom the Spirit dwells: it is simply the certainty of hope, not of faith. We are confident of the fact of the indwelling, we have the guarantee of certain signs which are pointers to its reality, but we can have no indisputable evidence of it. Absolutely speaking, a mistake of judgment could be possible. In other words, we do have *a strong moral certainty* of possessing the Spirit here and now, and that is enough. For the certainty of this possession depends on man's continuous fidelity to the Spirit, and this fidelity is to be sustained, kept up every day, it is not given to man once and for all. The indirect certainty of having the Spirit is shrouded in the uncertainty of man's response. Man's past betrayals cannot but cast a pall of doubt on his present response. "It is the certainty of faith (viz. based on faith), not of sight; of hope, not of possession; stronger than all doubt and fear, but founded paradoxically on a God who is invisible; held fast not from below but from above; thrown up like an anchor into the mystery of God".[5]

5 J. Mouroux, *The Christian Experience*, p. 156. This question was discussed explicitly and for a long time in the course of the Council of Trent, and at the end, following the Council's wise policy of *not* settling issues which were freely debated among Catholic theologians, the conciliar Fathers left the question open. After endless discussions, the final formula agreed on by all was: "No one can know with the certainty of faith which cannot be sbuject to error, that he has obtained God's grace" (Neuner-Dupuis, *The Christian Faith*, n. 1936).

3) The touch of the Spirit in prayer

It is perfectly true, on the one hand, that the Holy Spirit is most unpredictable, that he seems to delight in springing surprises and acting from within the sanctified Christian when least expected. The historical cases of the two Teresas, of Avila and Calcutta, who both felt the Spirit at "the wrong time", as it were, significantly show a certain tendency on the part of the Spirit to act in an unforeseeable manner. On the other hand, however, despite this unpredictability, he seems to be most "at home" in an atmosphere of prayer, as if withdrawal, silence and recollection were the right climate for him to act.

This is noticeable already in the New Testament. Jesus' baptism is described by Luke thus: "When Jesus had also been baptized *and was praying*, the heaven was opened and the Holy Spirit descended upon him" (Lk 3,21-22). It is the same Luke, so sensitive always to the dimension of prayer, who recounts later on the remarkable episode of the conversion of Cornelius, the Roman centurion, through the instrumentality oj Peter. "The next day...Peter went up to the housetop *to pray*, about the sixth hour....And while Peter was pondering the vision, the Spirit said to him..." (Act 10,9.19). Similarly soon after Jesus' final departure to his Father, it is narrated how the Eleven "*devoted themselves to prayer*, together with the women and Mary the mother of Jesus....When the day of Pentecost had come...they were all filled with the Holy Sporit" (Ac 1,14; 2,1-4). Jesus, Peter, the disciples: the Spirii comes mightily upon all of them precisely as they were pratying. There seems to be something in prayer that brings the Spirit down, that induces him to act.

This scriptural insight is abundantly corroborated by numerous testimonies of contemplatives that haltingly describe their prayer experiences. The exper ienced, felt, piesence of God in them is by no means restricted to the summit of mystical life, for it also extends — though, admittedly, in a lesser degree — to the lower stages of contemplation. I am about to quote some remarkable cases, but it would be a

That is to say, nobody can be infallibly certain that he or she possesses the indwelling. This is the official and definite Catholic stand.

serious mistake on the part of the reader to believe that these cases are the exclusive privilege of a chosen few. I have myself come across numerous cases of genuine personal experience of God in prayer in various degrees of intensity. One certainly need not be Teresa of Avila or John of the Cross to have an experiential knowledge of God in prayer. God is far more generous with his prayer gifts than we usually imagine.

The man of prayer not only knows about the Spirit in an abstract, academic manner, he "knows" the Spirit in the Semitic, biblical sense, he feels, tastes and relishes the Spirit's presence. Intellectual knowledge has become for him a matter of personal experience. When in prayer he turns inwardly towards his heart, he detects there with affective, loving knowledge the presence of the Spirit. This experiential perception of the indwelling grows from the obscure, vague feeling characteristic of the initial stages, to the extremely vivid, searing experience of the Spirit at the summit, when the Spirit grips man from within with a directness and immediacy that dispel all doubts regarding his presence. The Spirit is inside him, and he knows it; not only does he believe it, he feels, senses, grasps it. In this kind of prayer not only is man certain with a certainty of hope or moral certainty, he is also certain with a *certainty of personal experience*. Now there is no intellectual deduction, but experiential feeling; no laborious reasoning, but immediate contact; no abstract process, but instinctual apprehension. Peace and joy, which were already present before, grow now considerably in intensity, for man is touching their very source: the indwelling Spirit. This is but a dim foretaste of the future, heavenly bliss.

All this, I am afraid, may sound highly theoretical unless it is backed up by those who have actually experienced in themselves the incredible proximity of God. Their testimonies are so abundant that a very strict selection will be necessary. We open up the series with a beautiful, lengthy prayer of St Symeon, a remarkable Oriental mystic of the tenth century. He describes in glowing terms his experience of the glorified Jesus thus:

> You were close to me, you washed me....I saw the

> lightning shining around me and the rays of your face mixed with the water, and I was stupified, finding myself sprinkled with luminous water....Then...you deigned to show me your face, like a sun without a shape.... After having shown yourself again and again, and concealed yourself again and again...I saw the lightning flashes of your face and its brilliance....You showed yourself to me in this way after you had purified my understanding in clarity by the light of the Holy Spirit.
>
> One day...suddenly a divine light shone down from on high on him (Symeon) in great profusion, and completely filled the place where he was standing....All he could see everywhere was light....He was entirely present to this immaterial light and it seemed to him that he had himself become light...He was overwhelmed with tears and with inexplicable joy and happiness.[6]

This extraordinary testimony of the immanence of the transfigured Christ in St Symeon is matched by similar experiences of the indwelling, the inwardness of God's presence within the Christian. As far as clarity of expression is concerned St Teresa of Avila is second to none: "I used unexpectedly to experience a feeling of the presence of God, of such a kind that I could not possibly doubt that *he was inside me* or that I was wholly engulfed in him".[7] And again: "God visits the soul in a manner which prevents it doubting...that *he was within it* (the soul) and that it dwells in him. So firmly is it convinced of this truth...that it can never doubt the fact".[8]

Teresa's partner in the arduous task of reforming the Carmel, St John of the Cross, was also blessed with similar experiences:

> Moreover, a soul is conscious that in that vigour of the bridegroom's delightful communication, the Holy Spirit rouses and invites it by the immense glory he marvelously and with gentle affection places before its eyes, telling it what He told the bride in the Canticles: 'Show me your face, let your voice sound in my ears, because

6 As quoted by Y. Congar, *I Believe in the Holy Spirit,* I (London 1983), pp. 93-94.

7 *Life*, X, 1: A. Peers, *The Complete Works of St Teresa of Jesus*, I (London 1946), p. 58. I have slightly retouched the translation.

8 *Interior Castle*, 5th mansion, ch. 1, n. 8.

your voice is sweet and your face is beautiful' (Cant 2,14). The soul, in a sublime experience of glory, feels and understands most distinctly all these things which the Holy Spirit, desiring to introuduce it into that glory, shows it in this gentle and tender blaze.[9]

Other, even if less well known, spiritual masters describe much the same experience: "It is a very precious gift by which God manifests himself *in the depths and innermost centre of the soul* with a very strong light".[10] The effects of serenity and peace experienced in prayer "proceed from the gift of wisdom (in Latin *sapientia*, from *sapere*, to taste) which brings the soul near to God, making him present in his light, so that not only does she believe in his presence, but *she actually feels it* with a very sweet spiritual sensation".[11] This is a typical description of the feeling characteristic of the prayer of quiet.

Such a distinct spiritual sensation refers to the so-called spiritual senses, by which the intimate divine presence is sometimes expressed. It is an eminently spiritual perception which bears some resemblance to the activity of the bodily senses, particularly to the *sense of touch*. When a person comes towards me from a distance, first I see him, then as he approaches I hear his voice, and finally we shake hands: seeing, hearing, touching. But surprisingly, in the prayer of quiet and union — the threshold of mystical life — the very first sense to be activated is that of touch, followed in the subsequent stages by the senses of hearing and seeing.

In the initial stages of the prayer of quiet or union the person experiences a vague, but at the same time clearly noticeable sensation of immersion or saturation, by which God makes his presence known. It is a sensation similar to that experienced by a man who, motionless and with his eyes closed, perceives the presence of his own body. It is a gentle, yet poweful pull to the interior where the Spirit dwells, that almost instinctively forces him to close his eyes. He

9 *The Living Flame of Love*, I, 28: K. Kavanaugh - O. Rodrigues, *The Collected Works of St John of the Cross* (Washington 1973), pp. 590-591.

10 Alvarez de Paz, *De inquisitione pacis*, V, 3,4, as quoted by A. Poulain, *The Graces of Interior Prayer* (St Louis 1950), p. 76.

11 Scaramelli, *Directorium mysticum*, treatise 3, n. 26. as quoted by A. Poulain *op. cit.*, p. 78.

experiences a reaction similar to that of the touch-me-not, the strange plant that shrivels and curls up as soon as it is touched, as if in a gesture of self-protection. So also, acting from the depths of the person, the Spirit touches him gently, attracts him to himself, invites him to momentarily experience God within himself and find repose and tranquility in the indwelling God. Or again, it is like the encompassing sensation of entering a new atmosphere, warm, intimate, delightful, as if a man coming from the outer cold were to step into a warm, cozy room. The feeling is difficult to put into words, yet we have all experienced it. These inadequate, clumsy comparisons may give an idea of this experience of the indwelling Spirit in prayer.

"The first prayer of which I was conscious", says Teresa, "is a certain interior recollection...; the soul seems to have other senses within itself, which bear some likeness to the exterior senses it possesses".[12] The great Franciscan doctor St Boneventure had said much the same thing three centuries before Teresa: "The word 'wisdom', taken in its most exact sense, indicates an experiential knowledge of God; it is one of the seven gifts of the Holy Spirit which comes into operation when we taste the divine sweetness".[13]

Here is another remarkable testimony of St John of the Cross, combining in one the two senses of taste and touch. The union "consists in a certain touch of the divinity produced in the soul, and thus it is *God himself who is experienced and tasted* there. Although the touch of knowledge and delight that penetrates the substance of the soul is not manifest and clear, as in glory, it is so sublime and lofty that the devil is unable to meddle;...nor infuse a savor and delight like it".[14]

12 St Teresa, *Relation* 3. The strong impression of being touched and tenderly caressed by God comes forcefully in the following passage of the same Teresa: "When this most wealthy spouse is pleased...to caress souls...the soul seems to herself to be suspended in those divine arms and to rest on that divine side...and she does nothing but enjoy....She sees herself...caressed by Him...; she does not know what to compare it to, except the caressing of a mother who, tenderly loving her infant, thus nurses and fondles him" (*Conceptions of the love of God*, Ch. 4)

13 *Sententiarum*, book III, d. 35, a. 1, q. 1, as quoted by Poulain, *op. cit.*, p. 96.

14 *The Ascent of Mount Carmel*, book II, ch. 25, n. 5: Kavanaugh - Rodrigues, *The Collected Works of St John of the Cross*, p. 195.

It is comparatively rare that the person should experience the intimate presence and touch of the Word, the Son, as distinct from the humanity of Jesus: "O you, then, delicate touch, the Word, the Son of God, through the delicacy of your divine being you subtly penetrate the substance of my soul and *lightly touching it all*, absorb it entirely in yourself in divine modes of delight and sweetnesses.... O, then, very delicate, exceedingly delicate, touch of the Word...".[15]

Let a touching prayer of St Augustine be the last of this string of telling testimonies: "I love a certain light, and a certain voice, and a certain fragrancy...and a certain embrace when I love my God, the light, the voice, the fragrancy... and the embrace of my inward man".[16]

Some of these remarkable manifestations of the indwelling in the psychological sphere of man's consciousness are reserved to a few, no doubt, endowed with special graces of of mystical prayer; but, on the other hand, this exclusiveness should not be exaggerated. Among persons seriously devoted to prayer it is not at all rare — in fact, it is rather common — to find people who have experienced in their own lives, and experienced it repeatedly, that God dwells permanently within them. This is something they not only believe as a fundamental tenet of the Christian faith, but something they feel and sense, particularly in prayer. For the initial stages of this experiential knowledge are typical of the prayer of quiet and union, and this type of prayer is given to many of those who practice prayer assiduously. In any case, whether this precious experience of the indwelling is given to many or just a few, the incontrovertible fact remains that the indwelling itself is offered to absolutely all, and in the last analysis it is the possession of the indwelling God rather than its conscious apprehension that matters.

4) Affective and bodily repercussions

It can never be sufficiently emphasized that the Spirit takes firm hold of the entire man, spirit, body, superior and inferior faculties, intellect, will, memory, imagination, heart

15 St John of the Cross, *The Living Flame of Love:* Kavanaugh-Rodrigues, *The Collected Works of St John of the Cross*, p. 601.

16 *Confessions*, b. X, ch. 6.

and affectivity: there is absolutely no psychological area in man which can escape the hold of the indwelling Spirit. Consequently the entire realm of feelings, pleasure and sensible delectation is also drawn into the sanctifying touch and all-embracing influence of the Holy Spirit acting from within man. This being the case, it would certainly be surprising if the intimate experience of his action did not leave any trace in man's affectivity, even in his body.

We should not forget that the doctrine of the Spirit's indwelling, as expressed by St John, is enveloped in a very dense atmosphere of intimacy and love. Affective repercussions of the indwelling are simply unavoidable. For before the time of Jesus the indwelling had already been promised with a strong affective colouring: "And you will know that I am the Lord. . .when I will put my Spirit within you" (Ez 37, 13-14). The Spirit is promised so that, once given, he may be felt and tasted, relished and savoured. In biblical language this is experienced in the "heart" of man, namely, in the inwardness of man, in that area of himself which he holds most intimate and personal.

Now man's affectivity is not destroyed but transformed. An adherence to the Spirit which does not include a minimum of affectivity will not last, for man is a composite being, not a pure spirit, and the affectivity is an integral part of his personhood. As a consequence of the indwelling, new forces are awakened in man; there is a new affectivity grafted upon the previous natural affectivity, which springs up under the influence of the Holy Spirit. A new world of desires, forces, joys and repugnances, longings and inclinations invades man, drawing him powerfully towards the very core of his person where the Spirit abides. This new affectivity tends to grow and develop gradually, imperceptibly. It is primarily spiritual, but also psychosomatic, for, according to Paul, it is emphatically man's body that is the temple of the Spirit.

But this affectivity as much as the freedom that purifies it, is essentially ambivalent, for when it is subsumed by the Spirit and integrated into a genuine Christian life led by the Spirit, it can become a sign of the perfection of the indwelling, a testimony of its strength and all-pervasive force. At the same time, however, the affectivity is a constant threat to the indwelling, for the flesh often works via the affectivity. Man has simply to put up with this unavoidable ambivalence which can never be completely eradicated, for the affectivity is the region of man which lives simultaneously in two conflicting worlds, it is a frontier between the divine and the human. Man is the son of God, and yet a potential betrayer of God; beckoned to the summits, and yet constantly dragged down to the depths; with his mind and heart bathed in the light of God, and his affectivity and body often sucked up by the morass of sin; genuinely longing for God, and secretly thirsting for the flesh; outstretching one arm to God and the other to the sinful world around him. Such is the complexity of man. Since his affectivity is at once the abode of God and the fifth columnist of the flesh, an attitude of cautious optimism seems to be called for.

I have briefly commented above on Galatians 5,16-22, where Paul speaks of the fruits of the Spirit and the fruits of the flesh, the two conflicting forces within man. For Paul "flesh" in a generic sense simply means man's earthbound tendencies, the longings, desires and inclinations that keep him fettered to his own egotism. But language keeps evolving, and so for us now the very same term "flesh" has acquired a certain sexual connotation, and if taken in this restricted sense, the astonishing fact is that the indweling Spirit seems to be closely associated with sex.

These two forces are like two conflicting armies facing each other in the battlefield, with a few miles of no man's land in between. This sort of buffer zone can be successively occupied by both the armies, with one of them invading the zone and then, for strategic or tactical reasons, pulling back and leaving it free for the other army to fill the gap and occupy the land. We witness successive waves of advance and withdrawal, of temporary occupation and subsequent retreat. May be this military comparison has now been rendered somewhat obsolete by modern technological advances and the fast mobility of armies, but at least it is apt to convey the central idea, namely, the alternative occupation of the very same territory by opposing forces.

It is much the same with the Spirit and the affectivity of man in general, or with his fleshly, sexual tendencies in particular. To be strongly sexed, far from being a shameful imperfection, a deplorable weakness in the Christian, is rather a God-given gift, for which he or she ought to be grateful to God. Doctor Alexis Carrel in his book *Man the Unknown* remarks pointedly that great Christian saints are usually persons very strongly sexed (and the names of lustful Augustine and worldly Ignatius come immediately to mind). For them sex was not an obstacle but rather a positive help to reach God; not a slippery platform but a ladder to climb to God. It was a roaring waterfall endowed with a devastating force which, if properly channeled, could be put to extremely useful purposes: it could, if firmly controlled, lead men and women not away from, but rather deeper into, the sphere of the divine.

There are people who wonder in amazement what the indwelling of the Spirit has to do with man's sinful flesh and specifically with his innate sexual tendencies. The Spirit and sex seem to be poles apart, at opposite ends of the spectrum, and yet, the fact is that there is a strange proximity, a puzzling connection between the two. Like the two opposing armies, the Holy Spirit and sex seem to lay claim successively on the no man's land which is the affectivity. It is not so rare to find cases, not only in reliable, reputable biographies of genuine mystics of the past,[17] but also among our own contemporaries, both men and women who experience in quick succession the vivid presence of the indwelling God, his unbelievable proximity, and then the sudden and sobering pull of their sexual instincts. At times the vehemence of the latter is such as to cast doubts on the genuineness of the former.

17 St Alphonsus Rodrigues, a Jesuit brother of the late 16th century, is a case in point. He joined the band of Ignatius after his wife's death, and even as an old man he still had extremely vivid and disturbing memories of the intimacies of his married life. Yet, despite this strong sexual drive, nobody doubts today the genuineness of the mystical graces he received in prayer. An even clearer case is that of Blessed Angela de Foligno, an obscure Italian mystic of the 13th century. The incredible intesity of her sexual impulse at times prompted her to undertake certain absurd practices against her own body, in the false belief that such practices would quench the fire she felt within her. Fortunately her director ordered her to stop them and she obeyed. These and many other cases offer clear evidence that the Spirit and sex can take possession of a person's affectivity and bodily faculties, not only successively but also simultaneously.

If the person is not well instructed, he or she is likely to come to the erroneous conclusion that the caresses of God he thought he had experienced shortly before were nothing but an illusion. The sexual pull can be so strong that the conclusion seems to be almost unavoidable: the alleged experience of God which has preceded could not possibly have been genuine. The sexual drive is certainly real and tangible, the rest was simply daydreaming, a trick of one's overheated imagination.

This hasty — and yet rather common! — conclusion is of course totally wrong. The experience of the indwelling in prayer, no matter how genuine and real, does not in any way alter man's psychological and biological make-up. One should start off by deepening his own conviction that the innate, powerful sexual drives are a perfectly natural element in man or woman. Sexual frigidity is no virtue of any kind, it is rather a deficiency, an imperfection. If the sexual instinct — the strongest in human beings after that of self-preservation, according to psychologists — is implanted by God at conception, as it is, there is no earthly reason why one should feel ashamed of it. To reject it as embarrassing or humiliating would be as absurd as to feel ashamed of being hungry and thirsty after a day's fast. If the sexual drive is in itself natural and normal, an indication of a perfectly healthy personality, why should the genuine experience of God in prayer supress it? Cannot God co-exist with his own creation? If God is not ashamed of what he himself has made, why should we? The conclusion of these brief reflections is that the experience of the Spirit and sex in quick succession is something entirely normal and should therefore not, by itself, cast any doubt on the authenticity of any spiritual experience.

But there is more to it yet. That the Holy Spirit and man's sexual instincts should occupy and deeply affect man's affectivity in quick succession is perhaps understandable. But is it possible that both these forces — the two conflicting armies in our example — should claim possession of man's affectivity *simultaneously*? Is it credible that man should experience at the same time the caress of God and the drag of the flesh? Not only is this possible, it is a fact. One does come across repeatedly eloquent testimonies of such strange coexistence, so bewildering at first and yet so very real.

In reality, however, there is nothing puzzling here. At a given moment the indwelling Spirit makes his presence felt vividly, man experiences a gripping, burning perception of God that reaches down to his lower faculties; even his sexual powers, before calm and dormant, are now awakened by the intensity of the prayer experience, and they obviously tend to react in their own way, namely, sexually. A sexual bodily reaction, strong and localized, sets in, and the individual, unless he or she be balanced and well instructed, is likely to be disturbed by the scruples which are likely to ensue. He may consider the sudden sexual awakening and especially the clearly noticeable bodily reaction unmistakable signs of the false character of his alleged spiritual experience. He will react almost instinctively and come once again to the wrong conclusion that, since a genuine intervention of the Spirit cannot possibly provoke a sexual reaction, the so-called prayer experience was totally and clearly false. For the Spirit delights in purity, not in sex. Proceeding along the same lines, he is likely to conclude that the devil is responsible for it all. Mediocre spiritual directors, endowed with greater zeal than prudence, and crippled by their rudimentary knowledge of the higher stages of prayer, are likely to increase the individual's scruples and confirm him in his conviction that the devil is clearly trying to deceive him. Therefore — he will conclude — the only prudent, reasonable course of action is to ignore totally such deceitful spiritual experiences which could lead him into an extremely dangerous path.

The verdict is exceedingly clear — as clear as it is wrong. For in reality, despite the intensity and vehemence of the sexual reaction, the spiritual experience could have been and *probably was genuine*. If such prayer experience is to be proved wrong, one needs stronger and much more convincing arguments than a merely sexual bodily reaction, no matter how strong and disturbing. A simple comparison will clarify this. Here is a lake with clean, clear, crystal-like waters. The surface of the lake is placid and undisturbed, like the surface of a looking glass. If you drop a stone in the centre of the lake, a series of ripples will be formed, which, in gradually widening concentric circles, will expand further and further away, right out to the very shore of the lake. Properly speaking, the stone has caused only the first ripple, the one closest to the impact; but the first ripple expands outwardly and creates a second; the second makes the third and so on, in an endless chain reaction.

Similarly the Holy Spirit at a given moment, usually in prayer, grips man forcefully from within, drawing him towards his own depths where the Spirit resides. When the pull of the Spirit is strong, all of man's faculties, superior and inferior, spiritual and bodily, react like successive ripples. Even the body, so closely connected with the sexual instinct, tends to react according to its own nature, namely, sexually. But properly speaking the Spirit has produced only the first ripple, not the rest. All the others are but the natural, normal reaction of the totality of man's faculties. The Spirit momentarily touches man and, after causing a chain reaction in his interior, withdraws again. After his withdrawal, the ripples continue expanding almost mechanically, and one of them happens to be the sexual bodily reaction. The Spirit is *not* immediately responsible for the bodily repercussion, which is rather the result of an entirely normal psychosomatic activity set in motion by the Spirit's intervention, an activity for which he cannot be held directly responsible.

Neglect of this fundamental distinction may lead the upset individual to reject a spiritual experience which is absolutely genuine in itself, and in so doing he will be acting against the Holy Spirit. One should rather calmly scrutinize the entire process, resolutely put aside all short-sighted notions that the sexual reaction is necessarily evil, and in perfect calm and serenity discern the genuine action of the Spirit. Once this action has been singled out, one should, with complete peace of mind, appreciate and cherish the legitimate spiritual experience, thank God for it and simply ignore as totally unimportant the rest of the process, particularly the sexual ripple. The Spirit had nothing to do with it, but he had no reason to intervene and prevent it either, for in itself — let us repeat it again — it is no more sinful or humiliating than the experience of acute thirst after a long trek in the hot sun.[18]

18 A married brother of Teresa of Avila, a pious man who had made a fortune in the recently discovered Americas, was greatly troubled by his sexual instincts in prayer. His Carmelite sister apparently could not enlighten him,

The bodily repercussion of the experience of the Spirit's presence, however, is by no means limited to the sexual area. There are many other bodily effects which are likely to cause far less anxiety to the individual. It might be useful to remind the reader at this juncture that the Holy Spirit, according to scriptural doctrine, dwells in the human body, and is therefore natural that in moments when the Spirit's presence is strongly felt, there should also be some bodily repercussions. The first of the higher stages of prayer, viz. the prayer of quiet, when the Spirit's activity begins to extend to the body also, is characterized by the instinctive tendency to close one's eyes or, if they are kept open, the vision is likely to be somewhat impaired, with the objects around perceived as if enveloped by a thin mist. Other physical reactions are typical, like the general impression of light, either as an explosion of brightness or as a soft, all-encompassing glow; a noticeable oppression of the chest, with accompanying breathing difficulties; a physical, very marked feeling of sweetness in the throat; a certain heaviness in the head; a sort of electric current or tremor running throughout the body; a perceptible chill in the limbs, accompanied sometimes by an ardour in the face or chest; a fullness or saturation in the chest; silent tears rolling down the cheeks; etc....

These effects are fairly common and their presence or absence is not a sure guide to assess the intensity of one's prayer, for a very intense experience of the Spirit's touch may not be accompanied by any perceptible bodily reaction. All these effects tend first to intensify in the higher stages of prayer, and then, at the very summit, they either diminish considerably or disappear altogether, almost as if the affective and bodily faculties had grown accustomed to the indwelling God.

but she had the good sense of referring him to John of the Cross who, with characteristic delicacy and lucidity, laid his scruples to rest. The apostolate of retreats teaches that the more intense the touch of the Spirit, the stronger will at times be (but by no means always) the intensity of the individual's sexual reaction, including an erection in men and a discharge in women. Once instructed, the retreatant usually reacts well and tends calmly to disregard such sexual experiences in prayer as unimportant. This is the right attitude to take.

Possibly the most typical of these sensitive repercussions is the phenomenon known as ligature. This word "indicates that the soul is in the condition of the man whose limbs are bound more or less tightly with bands, and who can therefore move with difficulty".[19] The individual has already experienced a gentle pull to the interior where the Spirit resides, which commonly compels him to close his eyes. In addition to that, his will is absorbed in God, tasting his intimate presence, and now he begins to experience, to his own amazement, the impossibility of reciting vocal prayers, as if his tongue were suddenly heavy and unable to pronounce distinct words. The usual recitation of the rosary or of the breviary, for instance, may take much longer than usual, or, in extreme cases, it may have to be given up altogether. It is as if a gradually expanding wave were affecting not only his spiritual faculties but even his body, which is progressively paralyzed, gripped from within and rendered momentarily inactive.

The Spirit has come out of his inner sanctuary, as it were, and made his presence felt in the body. These bodily effects cannot and should not be resisted. To oppose them would be tantamount to opposing the Holy Spirit himself, who with muted eloquence is showing that he delights in dwelling in the human body as in a temple. Before, the Christian knew this only through faith, but now he knows it also with the certainty of his personal experience.

Bibliography

Mouroux, J.: *The Christian Experience* (London 1954), pp. 121-159; 234-273.

Fransen, P.: "Towards a psychology of divine grace," *Cross Currents* 8 (1958) 211-232.

Rahner, K.: *The Dynamic Element in the Church* (New York 1964), pp. 84-170.

Rahner, K.: "Reflections on the experience of grace", *Theological Investigations* 3 (1967) 86-91.

19 A. Poulain, *The Graces of Interior Prayer*, p. 178.

Fransen, P.: *The New Life of Grace* (London 1969), pp. 273-324.

Bertrand, G.: "Expérience mystique de l'inhabitation", *Dictionnaire de Spiritualité* 7(1971) 1757-1767.

Mollat, D.: "The role of experience in the N. Testament teaching on baptism and the coming of the Spirit", *One in Christ* 10 (1974) 129-147.

Le Guillou, M.: *Les Temoins sont parmis nous.* L'*Expérience de Dieu dans l'Esprit Saint* (Paris 1976), pp. 8-31.

Ditmanson, H.: *Grace and Experience in Theology* (Minneapolis 1977).

Haight, R.: *The Experience and Language of Grace* (New York 1979), pp. 6-31.

Gogan, B.: "Is there direct experience of God?", *The Way* 22 (1982) 122-132.

Chapter Eight

GROWTH IN THE LIFE OF THE SPIRIT

The Christian, rendered God's son at baptism, is endowed with the "Spirit of life" (Rom 8,2), and life by its very nature implies necessarily dynamism and growth. A living organism that becomes stunted is as good as dead, and the same applies to the trinitarian divine life infused in man by the Holy Spirit living in him. His faith is a principle of life, but on the other hand, this living faith should normally flow over into works. Faith cannot possibly be constrained within man, locked up in his inner sanctuary. Sooner or later it will burst forth and give birth to works of eternal life. Faith is like a mother, and the deeds or works performed by the Christian are like her daughters. Both of them, faith as well as the works that issue forth from faith, are necessarily imbued with life. Endowed with living faith, the Christian now produces works of eternal life. Ultimately both of them, faith and works, are traceable to the very same origin, the person of the indwelling Spirit. It was the Spirit that instilled faith in man's heart, and now it is the same Spirit that makes that faith overflow into externally manifest works. The initial personal surrender to God which is faith would remain somewhat vague and abstract if it were not to explode, as it were, into tangible works.

And so these works of life are in reality the fruits of the Spirit. The seed of life planted in the believer at the moment of his or her baptism should normally grow, and this dynamic development usually takes place in two different ways, both of them equally biblical and therefore equally legitimate. One line of approach — extremely popular in Catholic spirituality — is to consider the good deeds of the sanctified Christian as deserving a recompense, as productive of an eternal reward. In other words, they are viewed as meritorious works, for these works are endowed with an intrinsic dignity of their own, they are enlivened by the Holy Spirit and, therefore, on the basis of these deeds, man can lay claim to an eternal recompense.

This is theologically quite correct, though dangerously oversimplified, but there is a second and even better way to view the same reality of growth. Man possesses the Spirit, and the waters of the Spirit, bubbling up from within him, well up into eternal life. Now it is not so much an external reward that is meted out to man, as an internal principle of life that dynamically grows from within him. He is progressively being filled with the pure waters of the Spirit, the seed of life is bound to grow because it is being ceaselessly watered. As a consequence of this internal growth the divine life imparted by the Holy Spirit penetrates man ever more deeply, possesses him ever more thoroughly. He is slowly but unremittingly being soaked in trinitarian life. The external reward or recompense has been interiorized and rendered more dynamic. The Christian life grows from within, not from without; it develops by its own intrinsic dynamism, not merely by periodic additions coming from an external source.

The two principles that make the original living seed grow are the reception of the sacraments (particularly of the Eucharist, which is the bread of life) and the plethora of good works the Christian performs in the course of the day. Each one of these works which spring from his living faith makes the seed grow and divine life develop. Viewed from this angle of dynamic growth, docility to the promptings of the Spirit, which induces man to act and perform good deeds, emerges as a vital principle of development and growth. We listen to the Spirit and perform good works, and thereby the seed of life keeps growing, the plant keeps soaring higher and higher, impelled from within by an irrepressible force that thrusts it heavenward.

1) God's generosity and man's claim

We should always keep in mind the general, fundamental principle that the initiative in man's salvation is not his, but exclusively God's. The deepest root of man's eventual salvation lies hidden in God's heart, for it was God's unmerited, gratuitous love that first promised to save man, and now it is God's own unshakable fidelity to that original promise that will bring about man's salvation.

A few days after God's enfleshment in Mary's womb in Nazareth she, in the presence of her cousin Elizabeth, burst into song: "My soul magnifies the Lord...(for) he has helped his servant Israel in remembrance of his mercies, as he spoke to our fathers..." (Lk 1,54-56). In other words, the Incarnation is the result of God's promise that he would send a Saviour. A few weeks later the child Jesus was brought to the Temple, and taking him in his arms, the good old man Simeon exclaimed: "My eyes have seen your salvation, which you have prepared in the presence of all peoples" (Lk 2,30-31). Man's salvation is traceable to a promise, and that promise was made freely and unexpectedly by God himself. It is he who spontaneously began the entire process of man's salvation. Hence, if later we speak—as we necessarily must—of man's indispensable cooperation, we should never lose sight of the fact that this cooperation is only the second step in the process, not the first. Man can only react to God's initial action. Man's cooperation is deeply imbued in an atmosphere of complete gratuitousness and unmerited grace.

And so, by promising, God begins the process alone, but he does not finish it alone, for God's Spirit necessarily evokes in man a reaction of grateful response. God promises salvation and, in addition to it, promises also a reward to man's indispensable cooperation. The reward may be steeped in grace, no doubt, but it is a real reward nevertheless, a deserved recompense to man's sincere efforts.

We are constantly forced to use the inadequate tools of human language in order to express divine, transcendent realities, and this happens also with the peculiar biblical notion of reward or recompense. The just man who tries his best and performs his task according to his capabilities deserves a reward for his performance. In order to express this idea the New Testament does not hesitate to borrow a term from the non-biblical, commercial world: *misthos*, meaning wages, the payment that is due to the labourer after he has accomplished his task. One comes across this expression often enough in the gospels: "The labourer deserves his *misthos* (wages)" (Lk 10,7); "call the workers and pay them their *misthon*" (Mt 20,8); those engaged by the father of the prodigal son are called *misthioi* (Lk 15,17). Hence, the term itself seems to imply a certain necessity of payment.

However, all the above are only parables. More directly and pointedly Jesus presents eternal life as a reward promised to man. In the mist of the Sermon on the Mount Jesus says: "Rejoice and be glad, for your reward is great in heaven" (Mt 5,12). Those who show brotherly concern towards the poor and needy will hear from Christ: "Come, O blessed of my Father, inherit the kingdom prepared for you" (Mt 25,34). Jesus, in answer to Peter's anxious question regarding his future, replies: "In the new world...you who have followed me will also sit on twelve thrones..." (Mt 19,28). Just before his passion the departing Jesus tries to lift the flagging spirits of his disciples by means of a promise: "There are many mansions in my Father's house" (Jn 14,2). Jesus explicitly speaks of "the reward from your Father in heaven" (Mt 6,1); and "anyone who does them (the commandments)...shall be called great in the kingdom of heaven" (Mt 5,19).

In view of this insistence on the part of Jesus, who emphatically and repeatedly speaks of heaven as a reward, it is difficult to understand the extreme reluctance of some Christians to even make the slightest reference to our future abode in heaven. They pretend to live a very disinterested life, in devoted service to the poor and marginalized members of society, and according to them any idea of a final reward smacks of sentimentality, as suitable only for old women and children. They seem to be shy and embarrassed to lift their eyes and fix their gaze, however briefly, in the world to come. Their vision is remarkably narrow, short-sighted, and their so-called selfless behaviour is not particularly biblical, for the Jesus of the gospels — we have seen above — so many times held aloft before his troubled disciples their final, heavenly destiny. And this destiny is presented time and again as something almost due to them, as a reward or recompense for their upright behaviour.

Yet, God does not bestow his final reward as a magistrate who judges justly, but as a father who gives generously. His justice is surely kept, but it is subsumed into his generous bounty. Even when man's diligence is demanded, God's reward is said to be beyond all proportion, as measured not so much by the intrinsic dignity of man's work as by his own innate generosity. It thus emerges that the final reward depends on God's bounty even more than on man's deserts. When everything is said and done, is man's final destiny a reward due to him or rather God's gratuitous gift? Does it make any sense to speak in this context of a claim on the part of man? Two parables in Matthew's gospel, if taken jointly, give us a total, comprehensive view of this complex reality.

Matthew 20,1-16 is the well-known parable of the labourers who are hired to work in the vineyard. They toil all day and "when evening came the owner of the vineyard said to the steward, 'Call the labourers and pay them their *misthon* (wages), beginning from the last, up to the first' " (Mt 20,8). Since, contrary to their expectations, the wages received are the same for all, the unavoidable grumbling ensues. Pat comes the owner's answer: "Do you begrudge my generosity?" (v. 15). The final payment, therefore, seems to be less the just retribution of something due than the manifestation of God's gratuitous promise. What stands out at the moment of payment is the master's fidelity to his word as well as his munificence, rather than the amount of work performed by the labourers. The spotlight is trained on the employer rather than on the employees. The thrust of the parable — in fact, the only point that should be stressed — is *God's bounty*, rather than man's work. God will reward man justly according to his work, but the stress of the parable is rather on God's bountiful generosity which bestows a reward far beyond the deserts of man.

This passage is possibly the Matthean counterpart of the popular parable of the prodigal son in Luke, for at the end both express the same greatness of God's generous love. It is not God's strict justice that stands out in either of them, but rather his bountiful generosity. "God's love lavishes itself prodigally in a unique way, which is possible only for

God, upon children whose intentions, though imperfect, are good".[1] Jesus seems to retain the term *misthos* in order to express man's obligation with regard to God, rather than God's obligation with regard to man.

The above parable offers us only one side of the total picture, the other face being supplied by *Matthew 25,31-46*, the famous passage of the sheep and the goats, which deals with the conferral of man's final reward for the deeds performed. When compared to the previous parable, it will be noticed that now the emphasis falls *on man* rather than on God. Now it is not God's bounty that is stressed, but rather the intrinsic value of the work performed by man. Attention is now focussed on man's accomplishments, rather than on God's generosity. It is man that has the centre stage, rather than God. And within this general framework, one should notice the remarkable connection between the work performed by man and the reward bestowed by God: "Come, blessed of my Father. . . *for* I was hungry and you gave me food, I was thirsty and you gave me drink" (v. 35). Not only does Christ impart the final recompense (identified with the heavenly kingdom), but furthermore he brings out with extreme force the reason for this bestowal of the reward: *because* I was hungry and you gave me food. The good action accomplished by man finds an echo in the final kingdom, his performance on earth reverberates in the heavenly world to come. Not only will the final reward be given, it will be given as a recompense to man's concern for the poor manifested in deeds. Man simply deserves a reward and he will receive it.

One can easily see that these two parables in Matthew's gospel, far from being contradictory, are rather mutually complementary. For, if God's bountiful largesse remains absolutely essential (Mt 20), man's work is also indispensable (Mt 25). A total, comprehensive picture emerges from the harmonious combination of both the aspects, God's generous love and man's faithful work. Both are absolutely needed in order to have a complete view of the whole.

Jesus' doctrine of man's final reward, therefore, seems to include the following elements: (i) Man's salvation can be

1 H. Preisker, "Misthos", *Theological Dictionary of the New Testament*, 4 (Grand Rapids 1967), p. 717.

accomplished only by God himself; (ii) the final reward proceeds from God's generosity more than from the intrinsic worth of man's work; (iii) yet, man's work is absolutely indispensable and deserves a reward, a recompense. Jesus seems to have accepted a concept of reward current in Judaism at that time, and to have transcended it by steeping it in the surrounding atmosphere of God's loving generosity. "There is reward only in so far as God is sheer love, which is unintelligible to merc justice".[2]

2) The growing fruitfulness of Christian life

When confronted with a particular reality that is in itself rich and complex, the temptation to oversimplify the whole is almost unavoidable. All of us seem to have a natural tendency to avoid unnecessary complexities and instead to be attracted by what is simple and uncomplicated. It is precisely this that one notices fairly clearly when considering, for instance, the way the two Christian families, Catholic and Protestant, look at the biblical doctrine of man's eternal reward. Catholics will always emphasize the dimension of man's responsibility and man's accomplishments, which undoubtedly deserve an eternal reward from God. Protestants, on the contrary, will tend to look askance at these human endeavours and, whilst most certainly accepting them, they will keep repeating in season and out of season that, when all is said and done, eternal life is essentially a gratuitous, unmerited gift from God's benevolence to sinful man.

Both are partly right and partly wrong. Right in what they affirm and wrong in what they instinctively tend, not to deny openly, but certainly to soft-pedal, to disregard. For Catholics man's achievements are surely real, and so is therefore his claim to an increase in life now and an eternal heavenly reward later, but they should always remember that these achievements are based on sheer, gratuitous grace. Deep down, my accomplishments are in reality God's gifts to me. Similarly Protestants would be well advised to keep in mind that everything cannot be simplistically reduced to God's grace, that man's works are to be reckoned with, as

2 H. Preisker, "Misthos", p. 719.

endowed with an intrinsic worth of their own, for they proceed from a person indwelt by the Spirit who has made him the son of God. If Catholics tend perhaps to overinsist on man's achievements, Protestants seem forever inclined to lay excessive stress on God's role in the complex process of man's salvation, forgetting the absolute necessity of human cooperation with God's grace.

a) *Saul and Paul*

It may well be that both these attitudes are to some extent traceable to the New Testament itself, which Catholics as well as Protestants cherish as indisputably normative for their Christian life. The New Testament is certainly a complex book, not half as simple as some people seem fondly to imagine. According to biblical teaching, are the growth in our present Christian life and the attainment of our future heavenly life the result of man's personal accomplishments or are they rather God's unmerited grace to him?

Probably Paul was not much of an athlete himself, but he was surely acquainted with the Olympic games that took place in Greece every four years. If the way he writes and the comparisons he uses are an indication of his personal experience, he must have seen more than once the athletes competing in the field, especially the runners on the track, straining every muscle and dashing forward to grab the coveted prize. A perfect imagery of Christian life: "Do you not know that in a race all the runners compete but only one receives the prize? So run that you may obtain it. . . . They do it to receive a perishable wreath, but we an imperishable" (1 Cor 9,24-25). Paul compares his own life to two races: one when Christ ran after him and caught up with him, and that was his Damascus experience; and the other when, after Damascus, he started running after Christ: "Straining forward to what lies ahead, I press on towards the goal for the prize. . ." (Phil 3,13-14). At the end of his life, when his eternal crown is already within reach, he comes back to the same simile: "I have finished the race. . ." (2 Tim 4,7). A Christian runs towards the attainment of his crown, which will be his final reward, the recompense to a life spent in the service of God.

At other times Paul drops all imagery and
uncompromisingly the naked truth: "He (God) will
to every man according to his works, to those who by pa
and well-doing seek for glory and honour and immort...ty,
he will give eternal life" (Rom 2,6-7). Not only man's works in general, but specifically his sufferings are deserving of a crown of glory: "We suffer with him (Christ) in order that we may also be glorified with him" (Rom 8,17).

All this is perfectly clear, is surely convincing. But there is nothing typically Christian in all this. Paul did not need his shattering Damascus experience to know this, for even Saul the Pharisee knew in practice this fundamental doctrine. As a pious Jew well versed in the faith of his ancestors, Paul obviously knew that man's works will have a harvest of eternal life, that God, the just judge, will reward him with an everlasting inheritance.

If this were all there is to it, the general picture would be simple enough: man tries his best, he exerts himself to the utmost, and God will see to it that at the end he receives an adequate recompense. However, matters are a little more complicated than that, for there is in Paul a second line of thought that seems to contradict the first. A Christian, after running the race, may certainly claim his reward, he may produce before the judge all his remarkable achievements, his "love, joy, peace, patience, kindness, goodness, faithfulness, gentleness, self control" (Gal 5,22-23). This colourful rainbow of Christian virtues may constitute his passport into heaven, but on the other hand he should always remember that all this is "the fruit of the Spirit" (Gal 5,22). The Christian did perform all these remarkable good deeds, but in reality it is the Holy Spirit who helped him from within to put up such a remarkable display of upright Christian living. Without the Spirit's help he would have been unable to do it, and the bestowal of the Spirit is nothing but sheer grace springing from God's gratuitous, unmerited love: "God's love has been poured into our hearts through the Holy Spirit who has been given to us" (Rom 5,5).

Further down, and so as to dispel all doubt, Paul states categorically: "The free gift of God is eternal life in Christ Jesus our Lord" (Rom 6,23). Heaven is a gift, and gifts are not grasped or merited or claimed, they are only received with gratitude on one's knees; and this gift on the part of God is utterly free, for when bestowing it God was not compelled or even persuaded by man's upright life and remarkable performance, but simply by his own free love, and love cannot be compelled, it can only be reciprocated. For, in the last analysis, the life and work of the Christian is not a matter of his own ability to seize the prize, but rather a question of being filled, controlled and impelled by the Spirit of God, who has been given to him gratuitously, as a seal of ownership, (2 Cor 1,22) to signify that he belongs to God.

Even at a deeper level than that of the Holy Spirit's indwelling, we encounter the Christian's living faith, for it is faith that brings down on man the unspeakable gift of the Holy Spirit, it is by believing in Christ and committing oneself unreservedly to him that the gates of man's heart are thrown open to the invasion of the Holy Spirit. The Christian possesses now the Holy Spirit because he is a believer, because he has faith. And this faith is a gift: "By grace you have been saved through faith; and this is not your own doing, it is a gift of God" (Eph 2,8).

And so Paul has proved himself a traditionalist and an innovator at the same time. He has received from his Jewish past the idea that God will reward his work, but he has placed this very traditional axis of Jewish morality on an entirely new basis, a new foundation: faith and the Holy Spirit. Now the entire structure of man's achievements and eventual reward is made to rest on a new, exclusively Christian foundation which Paul did not inherit from the past. The edifice of man's reward is not new, but Paul has supplied the old building with an entirely new foundation. At the end, if man's personal accomplishments are made to rest on a gratuitous basis, it would seem that the whole construction is, in a way, a gift. Remove the unmerited foundation and the whole structure of man's proud achievements will come down with a mighty crash. Man's achievements that do not solidly rest upon God's double free gift of faith and the Holy Spirit are not even worth considering. Even at the peak of his glory and when basking in the glow of his own accomplishments, man depends entirely on God.

Ultimately it is not a question of the Christian avidly counting the number of good works performed, with his gaze intently fixed on an eventual reward (as popular Catholic piety has tended to do for a long time). For Paul the radical question is whether man lives by the Spirit, produces fruits of the Spirit and is subject to the Spirit, not to the all-pervading influence of sin. The old Jewish concept of man's reward has been maintained, but also entirely transformed and christianized by being immersed in an enveloping atmosphere which is deeply gratuitous.

In the light of the above, the traditional discrepancy between the two Christian families, Catholic and Protestant, should cease, and a harmonious — because it is ultimately biblical — reconciliation of opposites could and should be worked out. The traditional Catholic insistence on "meritorious works" (the terminology is certainly jarring, but I shall return to this later) could be kept as substantially correct, provided it is subsumed into the larger and deeper context of the gift of faith as proceeding from the gratuitous grace of the Father. And this grace is far too high for man, he cannot possibly scale to such heights, which remain inaccessible to him, beyond his "meritorious" grasp. At such a high altitude we encounter only sheer grace. But on the other hand, our Protestant brothers should not forget that *both* the trends explained above are equally biblical, and therefore we cannot speak of the perfectly legitimate dimension of man's reward as having a "disruptive and confusing influence on the doctrine of justification".[3] The deliberate exclusion of one of these two biblical trends amounts to an arbitrary, irresponsible distortion of the biblical datum. The danger of facile oversimplification does not seem to affect only the Catholic side.

b) *Internal growth of sanctification*

But probably more important than this traditional discrepancy of the two great Christian Churches in their respective understandings of Paul's complex doctrine is the firm grasp of the fruitfulness of our Christian life. Not only

3 H. Preisker, "Mysthos", p. 721.

is man entitled to claim from God an eternal reward after he has finished the race — provided this be properly understood — but, even now, during his pilgrim state, he experiences a growth in the divine, trinitarian life he received in baptism. Reward implies an external action whereby the judge metes out to man the recompense for his achievement. But over and above that, man experiences within himself an internal growth, a dynamic development of the seed planted in him at his baptism. Life keeps developing, keeps growing. The sanctification of man is not a dead capital given to him once and for all; it is rather something endowed with all the potentialities of life, and life means expansion and growth.

It is this inner fruitfulness of Christian life that Paul develops, briefly but forcefully, in *Romans 6,20-23.* An exceedingly dense passage, once again, which is consistently weakened by English translators.[4] The text reads: "When you were slaves of sin, you were free as regards justification. What fruit did you gather then from actions that make you blush today? For their result (or goal) was death. But now, free from sin and turned into slaves of God, you have fruits that lead into sanctification, and their goal is eternal life. For the wages of sin is death, but the gratuitous gift of God is eternal life in Christ Jesus our Lord."

Paul is an Oriental to the core, and as such, seems to be particularly fond of metaphors and contrasts. To speak of fruitfulness of Christian life probably would have sounded to him far too abstract and unappealing. Instead, he has recourse to a comparison only too well known to his Roman readers, many of whom — perhaps most — came from Jewish stock. For if there is something that runs through the Old Testament it is that sin leads to death. Already the narrative of the garden of Eden in the book of Genesis had shown with forceful clarity that sin is the cause of death, and now Paul makes use of that popular teaching as a dark, somber backdrop

4 I have consulted RSV, the English Jerusalem Bible, the New English Bible, the New English version and the New American Bible: all five translations unduly dilute Paul's thought. On the contrary, the original French Jerusalem Bible and the *Traduction Oecuménique de la Bible* keep the strength and vigour of the original Greek. The translation of the passage given in the text is my own.

against which his positive doctrine on the dynamism of Christian life will stand out brightly.

Paul is satisfied with a passing, but forceful reference to this internal link that connects sin and death. The terms he uses are highly significant, for much of the strength of the passage lies precisely in the choice and deliberate repetition of the same expressions. Death — total death, that is, physical, spiritual and final death or damnation — is brought about by the power of sin that constantly drags man down. It is a power originally foreign to man, but which has now come to dwell in him, enticing him on the slippery road to sin, a power that often sprouts into actual, personal sins. This dreadful power as well as the actual sins man commits under its influence will, if uncontrolled, eventually lead man to damnation, to his final death. In this somber scenario sin is the aggressor, endowed with an enormous force of its own that eventually may destroy man totally. Sin is a killer and man runs the risk of perishing at its hands. In other words, and so as to come closer to Paul's own terminology, death is the goal of sin. It is as if sin had deliberately marshalled its forces to bring about the total ruin of man. Man's death is not imposed on him from without, it rather grows from within him, internally, effected by the power of sin. Simply put, the death of man is the goal of sin. If man dies and is finally destroyed, sin has accomplished its task.

This conception is certainly powerful, it is compelling, but it is not here that Paul's main interest lies. The connection between sin and death is nothing but the dark, dismal backdrop that is introduced for the sake of contrast. For Paul is primarily interested in positive doctrine, not in negative statements. And so, after this preparatory step, after this transitional passage through darkness, he comes now to the fullness of light in the very heart of the passage. On the positive side Paul sees a most attractive connection, almost an unbroken chain of enticing realities: baptismal justification grows into sanctification and, on its part, sanctification develops into eternal life as its final and definite goal. Paul's thought is so compact that it requires some explanation.

It is an agricultural comparison Paul has in mind. Baptismal justification, namely, the radical transformation man undergoes at the moment of his baptism, is in itself an astonishing reality which has poured on man, through the opening gates of faith, a torrent of gifts: he has become the son of God, has received the personal presence of the Holy Spirit, is endowed with sanctifying grace, flooded with divine life and grafted on to the risen Christ. All this wealth of endowments man already has in his own possession, but the reality is still richer. The totality of these divine gifts has been planted in man like a seed, and any seed is bound to grow, sprout and fructify. Impelled by its own internal potentialities the seed tends necessarily to produce fruit.

Similarly, Paul says, our baptismal transformation (which technically he calls justification) is bursting with life, it is like the seed that is unable to keep within itself all the vitality that is packed within it. Eventually, just like any other seed, it will also burst out, it will grow and expand, it will dynamically tend to produce the fruit of sanctification. Justification grows into sanctification as a sign that the original seed has already achieved the first stage of development.

The first, but not the last. For life is restless and the movement forward continues. Now the agricultural imagery drops out, but the development goes on, unstoppable. If baptismal justification has grown into sanctification, sanctification itself thrusts forward to the final goal of eternal life. As man's total death is the goal of sin, so now, positively, Christian sanctification tends to the goal of eternal life. Now the process of growth is over: the tiny baptismal seed has expanded and developed into life eternal. This is the final goal of the entire process. Now, and only now, is the end really achieved, when sanctification finally flowers into eternal life.

At the end Paul closes the entire process with a lapidary sentence of the utmost significance. Man could feel quite satisfied, almost boastful of his double achievement of having developed the original baptismal endownment into sanctification, and sanctification into life eternal. To a large extent it is his own work, his own performance. However, Paul wants it clearly understood that this remarkable achievement of man pales into significance when compared with the role played by God. And so Paul concludes, "The *gratuitous gift* of God is eternal life in Christ Jesus our Lord". All temptation of boastfulness is thereby shattered. Despite the growth and fruitfulness of his Christian life, when all is said and done, eternal life is a gift proceeding from the Father's munificence. This limpid statement at the end seems to be a deliberate attempt on the part of Paul to forestall any mercenary interpretation of his doctrine of reward. If man is bound to produce in earnest, he is also bound to receive in gratitude.

And yet, despite this strong insistence on the utter gratuitousness of the final reward, Paul keeps exhorting his Christians to ever greater efforts, almost as if everything depended on them. Paul's theological pendulum is constantly swaying from one pole of Christian existence to the other. In one passage he speaks — we have just seen — as if everything depended on God and his unmerited grace, and in the next he lays heavy emphasis on man's necessary effort and unavoidable responsibility. Obviously sanctification is a gift of God unmerited and unmeritable, and yet the Corinthians are exhorted to "make holiness perfect in the fear of God" (2 Cor 7,1). Of course Paul "planted, Apollos watered, but God gave the growth" (1 Cor 3,6); yet, Christians in Thessalonika are encouraged to "make even greater progress" (1 Thess 4,1).

Man's growth in sanctification is God's work, but it is also man's. The attainment of the final goal of eternal life depends on man — but it is primarily God's gift. It is man's achievement, but it is also a reception, a gift. This complementary coexistence of divine and human activities is nowhere better expressed than in this programmatic, paradoxical statement of Paul's: "Work out your own salvation with fear and trembling, for God is at work in you...to will" (Phil 2,12-13). Earnest exhortation to man's effort and sobering realization of God's work, this is, shortly put, the complexity of Christian life. Human activity is absolutely indispensable for the growth and development of trinitarian life, but this human activity is the result of God's grace. Man, apart from God, cannot cooperate with him.

In order to increase our trinitarian life we need fidelity to Christ and docility to the Holy Spirit, but this docility is itself a gift of God. One could perhaps say that man's activity in the realm of grace is a divine-human action issuing both from the Spirit that indwells and from man who is indwelt.

The Spirit increases that life because of an activity that is both the Spirit's and man's. In this growth, the increase of trinitarian life in man is in proportion to the Spirit's activity in him: a maximum of activity on the part of the Spirit (if man lets him act freely) brings forth a maximum increase in man's divine life. "Let the Holy Spirit fill you" (Eph 5,18). There is a delightful touch of passivity here which is extremely significant: don't try to fill yourselves, let the Spirit do it.... Man has within himself the very spring of this new blessed life that progressively fills him, the Holy Spirit. "The water that I shall give him will turn into a spring inside him, welling up to eternal life" (Jn 4,14).

Impelled by the Spirit, man acts, and these actions, imbued as they are with the vitality of the Spirit himself, and proceeding as they do from the divinized spirit of man, are not only externally visible manifestations of man's robust spiritual health, they are also causes of a further increase in sanctity. Man's apparently trivial daily actions have a vitality of their own, for they rebound, as it were, backwards, to the very root from which they proceed. In an ordinary family, the child is surely the manifestation and visible sign of the mutual love of husband and wife, he is the fruit of their love. But the child is more than that, for besides proceeding from that mutual love, he makes that love grow, he unconsciously, to be sure, but nevertheless powerfully, binds both the parents more tightly, as it were, with yet stronger bonds of love. The child is simultaneously the fruit of love and the cause of a deeper love.

It is much the same with regard to man's daily actions. They proceed from the divinized spirit of man, they are posited under the direct influence of the Holy Spirit, even if man is not consciously aware of such an influence every time. Those actions are pointers to the interior of man from where they proceed, they indicate that man has been raised to a higher level, that he is a member of the trinitarian family and a priviledged sharer in their very life. But besides doing all this, such actions of man make this trinitarian life grow further still.

It would be a serious error to believe that the trinitarian life that floods the son of God can grow only through the reception of the sacraments. The sacraments — particularly that of the Eucharist — are special moments of grace that signal a fresh infusion of divine life in man. But the sacraments are only one, maybe the best, means to make God's life grow in man, they are definitely not the only means. For, besides his sacramental activity, man is also immersed in all the innumerable actions of his daily life, no matter how dull, obscure and unpretentious. Not only the sacraments, but even these trivial actions proceed from the Spirit, and as such, they are also channels through which trinitarian life pours into man. These actions, therefore, are endowed with a worth and a dignity of their own, they constitute the rungs of the ladder that helps man attain the heights of eternal life.[5]

Among these actions that fill the Christian's life, there is one of common occurrence which deserves special attention: suffering. To encourage the sufferer to put up with adversity by simply keeping his gaze fixed on the eternal reward that will be the crown of his suffering is often decried by some as nothing but a piece of cheap, sentimental spirituality unworthy of a truly committed Christian. One should obviously try and alleviate the neighbour's suffering or eliminate it altogether if possible, for suffering in any form is evil, and as such it should be surpressed. An immediate reference to heaven as a palliative for suffering may be too facile or simplistic a solution, which is certainly open to abuse and even ridicule. Yet in itself this way of acting is perfectly legitimate because it is entirely biblical, and therefore thoroughly Christian. Sneers and ironical smiles, dismissive gestures and impatient

5 The historical background to this point of doctrine is of no interest to the average Catholic reader. Opposing firmly certain mistaken notions of the early Reformers, the Council of Trent stated with its proverbial clarity that "the justified...go from strength to strength, renewed...everyday....When faith is active along with works (Jas 2,22), *they increase in the very justice* they have received through the grace of Christ, and are *further justified*, as it is written: 'Let the holy still be holy' (Apoc 22,11)...and again, 'You see that the man is justified by works and not by faith alone' (Jas 2,24). It is this increase in faith that the holy Church asks for" (Neuner-Dupuis, *The Christian Faith*, n. 1937). The Council's language is somewhat technical, as could be expected, but the doctrine couched in such terminology is, from the spiritual and pastoral viewpoint, exceedingly practical. What I have given in the text above is in reality nothing but a paraphrase of Trent.

shrugging of shoulders will not change that — unless of course we are ready to dismiss both Jesus and Paul as cheap sentimentalists.

Writing to the Romans, Paul has waxed eloquent on the reality of the Spirit's indwelling and the Christian's divine filiation; then suddenly, and for no apparent reason, he turns to the reality of suffering:"...We are children of God, and if children then heirs, heirs of God and fellow heirs of Christ, provided we suffer with him *in order that we may also be glorified with him*" (Rom 8,16-17). Paul is holding aloft the torch of the eternal heavenly reward as an encouragement to help them pull through their sufferings. The personal possession of the Spirit and the reality of suffering can be simultaneous. And if suffering deserves an eternal reward, it is because it is rooted in the Spirit. Suffering without the Spirit has little value, but suffering that is enlivened by the indwelling Spirit can be precious. Yet, here Paul is not encouraging the Roman Christians to embrace suffering for the sake of an eventual reward; he is rather explaining why, in spite of the indwelling, they suffer. It is not easy-goingness that Paul fears, but doctrinal doubts against the faith. Paul is not trying to toughen up Christians who had grown soft and slack, he is rather concerned about strengthening their faith in the presence of the Spirit: suffering is no argument against the reality of their divine sonship. The Christian suffers now "in order to be glorified" later, but this suffering is less the subjective choice of the individual than the objective disposition of God. It expersses divine finality, not human election.

We see at the end that the scriptural doctrine of reward is both complex and immensely rich. God's life in man has to expand and grow, and at the end he may certainly claim his recompense and reward for a life well spent in the faithful service of his God. Yet it is also true that the deepest foundation of man's divinized activity and God's bestowal of a generous reward is the Father's faithful love which prompts him to promise and grant his own life to sinful man.

3) Merited reward or unmerited grace?

Merit. Meritorious works. Merited reward. Probably many a Catholic reader will feel quite at home with such expressions, which will certainly strike a chord in his heart.

For the notion of merit seems to have gone into the very bloodstream of Catholic spirituality and life. He is moving in familiar territory now, for this way of speaking resonates with what he considers to be genuinely Catholic faith. Hasn't God, after all, put our final destiny into our own hands, so that by our own efforts we may scale the heights of heaven? Doesn't the choice between salvation and damnation depend on man? Is he not endowed with the frightening but precious gift of freedom? If he works at his salvation "with fear and trembling" (Phil 2,12) is he not entitled to a reward that, in strict justice, God owes to him? Will not the final reward be strictly in proportion to his own performance here below?

Endless questions that convey a typically Catholic frame of mind. The usual Catholic answer to these questions is certainly correct, but in most cases also badly one-sided. It is extremely difficult to keep a balanced view that reconciles into a harmonious whole the two essential roles played by God's grace and man's freedom. Both are to be upheld with equal firmness, or we begin to slide dangerously along the slippery path of heresy. This is acknowledged by all in theory, but in practice, and due to a variety of reasons, Catholics seem to have made a clear choice: my responsibility, my liberty, my reward, my recompense, *my merit.* Is there not too much of "I trouble" involved here? What has happened to the essential role to be played by God's grace? We claim to be responsible Christians, standing on our own two feet, without perhaps realizing that God has been supporting us all the time lest we fall. Have we perhaps dangerously forgotten — though acknowledging it in theory — that man's boastful merits are preceded by God's merciful grace? Who has started the entire process of salvation, man or God?

We Catholics should openly recognize that "merit" is an ugly word that is not found anywhere in the Bible, is apt to blur the correct perspectives of man's relationship with God, and is likely to create considerable ecumenical difficulties with our Protestant brothers. Why stick so stubbornly to a term which is beset with so many difficulties? And it is certainly surprising that, given the widespread anti-juridicial trend that is sweeping throughout the Church today, we still cling to this unappealing notion of merit, which both in its origin and in its meaning has clearly juridical connotations and a markedly juridical background.

It all goes back to a certain African lawyer of the third century, called Tertullian. Surely a profound thinker in many respects, but also a thoroughly legalistic mind if ever there was one. For him the relation between God and man is like the relation between a master and his servants. His overriding principle is that everything should be weighed on the scales of the law. Man should submit to God's will, but at the end he can face the master with an outstretched hand, demanding the reward that is due to him, for "a good deed has God as his debtor".[6] Scriptural passages which have nothing to do with merit are unscrupulously twisted and made to fit that legalistic framework: "How can there be many mansions in the Father's house (Jn 14,2) if not on account of the diversity of merits? How can a star differ from another in splendour (1 Cor 15,39) unless by the diversity of rays?"[7] He posits the dubious principle that works are meritorious in proportion to the difficulty with which they are performed: the harder the work the greater the merit.

The deviation has already set in, and it will continue unabated and uncorrected for many centuries to come, in fact, right down to the present time, even if in a less crude, somewhat milder form. Catholic catechisms and Catholic spirituality will faithfully echo the same distorted conception. It is simply amazing that an African lawyer of the early centuries should have left such a deep impring on our Catholic system.

Fortunately, however, Africa could also boast of another voice, much more reliable and far deeper than that of the fiery lawyer: Augustine, the eloquent bishop we have already encountered before. If Tertullian marks a deviation of the biblical perspectives, Augustine represents a rightful development of the same perspectives. By the time of Augustine the term "merit" had come to stay, and so he makes use of it liberally, but there is no trace whatever in him of any juridical, legalistic approach. His favourite, fundamental principle to which he will return constantly in his letters and sermons

6 Tertullian, *De Poenitentia*, 2.
7 Tertullian, *Ibid.*

as well as in learned theological treatises, is that man does have merit, no doubt, but this merit is preceded by and imbued with, God's unmerited grace. "Therefore the merits of the just are nil? They exist, most certainly, for they are just. But they had no merits in order to become just".[8]

May be there is a faint echo of his sinful youth in Augustine's conception. He would never extol unduly the achievements of sinful man who, left to himself, can only slip up and fall. If he is to stand at all, it is because of the support liberally offered him by God's grace. Let God take that grace away and man will collapse and disintegrate. Man is certainly endowed with freedom, but this freedom is being constantly harassed and assaulted by man's sinful drives and evil tendencies. He is in desperate need of God's grace. The root of man's merit is his freedom, certainly, but neither merit nor freedom can stand without God's grace. It is grace that explains merit, not the other way around. Human merit would be nothing but a shadow without consistency if God were to withdraw his grace. Man's dependence on God is complete, total.

I have always had my doubts if Augustine's listeners who packed his cathedral at Hippo were able to follow the flowing eloquence of their famed bishop. On more than one occasion, I am afraid, they must have been left wondering as to what precisely their shepherd meant, for the penetrating insights of his thought must have gone right over their heads. A modern reader is often compelled to read some of his passages a second time in order to grasp their depth and understand them fully. Here is a couple of examples of typically Augustinian thought, profound and convincing. The bishop is preaching: "I have received because I have merited. Do not think that you have received by meriting, for you would have not merited anything unless you had received. *It is grace that precedes your merit;* not grace from merit, but merit from grace".[9] His technical treatises also show the same density of thought: "Assuredly, once grace is given, our good merits begin, but through that grace. For if grace is with-

8 *Epistolae*, 194, 6.
9 *Sermo* 169, 3.

drawn, man simply falls, he does not stand, but is knocked down by his own free will".[10]

This grace man needs is absolutely gratuitous, it is a sheer gift on the part of God, as clearly seen in the case of Christ's death: "And no merits of ours preceeded for which the Son of God should die; rather his mercy was great because we had no merits".[11] And again: "Why grace? Because it is gratuitously given. Why is it gratuitously given? Because your merits did not precede it, but God's benefits overtook you".[12]

Hence, grace is the root and the foundation of merit, for it is from grace that merit grows, and without grace merit would be non-existent. The following passage, taken again from one of his sermons, is a real masterpiece of rhetoric, depth and clarity, which was later to be quoted by the Council of Trent and thereby be fixed in Catholic memory. Augustine is addressing Paul rhetorically: "Excuse me, Paul, but I have not known anything of you except bad deeds. . . . Hence, when God crowns your own merits, he is actually crowning his own gifts. . ;a crown is given to your merits, but they are God's merits, these merits of yours. . .".[13]

All this is certainly profound, it is most satisfying. But Augustine's mind is restless, it probes deeper still and will not cease in its quest until it has reached rock bottom. Here we find Augustine at his best. It would seem that once we have traced the reality of man's merit to the grace that feeds and supports it, there is nothing else to look for. Yet there is a still deeper layer that lies beneath God's grace: God's gratuitous *promise*. If grace explains merit, it is the promise that explains grace. God gives grace and thereby brings about human merit because he has promised it, and he is always faithful to his own promise. God is certainly bound to give man a reward if he dies crowned with merits, but the ultimate, the deepest reason for this divine obligation is to be found, not in man, but in God; not in man's merit, not even in God's grace, but rather in God's promise to give grace.

10 *De gratia et libero arbitrio* VI, 13.
11 *Enarratio in Psalmos* 85, 2.
12 *Enarratio in Psalmos* 30, 1.
13 *Sermo* 333, 5.

Ultimately it is God's fidelity to his promise that will save man: "God has become a debtor, not by receiving something from us, but *by promising* what pleases him".[14] "In this way we can exact from our Lord, so as to say: Give us what you have promised, because we have done what you commanded us to do".[15]

Following Augustine, we have finally touched rock bottom, we can proceed no further, for we have reached the very heart of God where it all started, his faithful love that prompted him to make and keep his promise, to bestow grace on man bountifully, so as to enable him to produce his tiny merit and be satisfied with it. These merits are real, they do exist, but in order to be real they are to be steeped in the profound atmosphere of God's unmerited grace.

And so in the last analysis Augustine simply confirms Paul's thought and even takes it one step deeper: there is no contradiction in viewing man's eternal glory simultaneously as a reward due to man, and as a gratuitous gift not due to him. Heaven is the final reward to man's merits, but these merits have been preceded and sustained all along by God's grace. If grace precedes merit it is because God transcends man.

4) Ecumenical perspectives

The juridical deviation of Tertullian we observed above has left a deep imprint in Catholic ethos and spirituality. Many centuries ago he took a wrong turn on the road and we are still suffering from that mistake. It was the beginning of a regrettable deviation in Catholic theology that was further accentuated in subsequent centuries. It would of course be a dreadful oversimplification to lay all the blame at the doorstep of the African lawyer, but he must surely accept a large share of responsibility. Oddly enough, and despite the enormous influence Augustine has always exercised on Catholic thought, in the area of merit and reward we are now considering, his views — perhaps one-sided here and there because of his polemical attitude — did not always prevail. In fact, some of them were rejected outright.

14 *Sermo* 158, 2.
15 *Ibid.*

Be that as it may, the terminology of merit and reward has come to stay, it has become so deeply imbedded in Catholic consciousness that any attempt to modify it seems to be doomed to failure from the start. The Catholic faithful believe, cherish and practice to a large extent the form of spirituality that rests on this notion of merit. It is uncritically transmitted from one generation to the next, faithfully received and faithfully handed on unaltered. And yet all is not well with this strange notion of merit. It is certainly a matter of amazement to see how easily the average Catholic faithful exemplify in their daily lives mental and religious attitudes that sometimes seem to be tainted by heretical doctrines. The very word "heresy" comes from the Greek root *haireo*, which means to select, to choose. When, in the fairly complex doctrine of man's relations with God, we select and stress one particular aspect, we run the serious risk of losing a comprehensive view of the entire landscape. Selectivity is often arbitrary and always dangerous, for imperceptibly it may put us on the wrong track and lead us astray. A slight deviation that is not promptly corrected, a partial view that is not integrated into the whole may, in the long run, have fatal consequences, not only theoretical but spiritual and practical as well. For concrete spiritual attitudes are usually based, consciously or not, on doctrine. A slight doctrinal twist may soon bring on a similar twisted, unbalanced and unhealthy spiritual attitude.

But enough of generalities. Something of the above seems to have happened in our traditional understanding of merit and final reward. There is absolutely nothing objectionable in the *official* Catholic doctrine in this area, as embodied particularly in the decrees of the Council of Trent. But popular spirituality and practical attitudes do not always follow the Church's official doctrine, and often enough such attitudes and practices turn around a single catchword — like the word "merit". Despite the long Catholic tradition behind it, one has to acknowledge that this is an unfortunate word that is not to be found in the New Testament. For these and other reasons it might perhaps be advisable to impose a moratorium on its use or even to discard it altogether from our spiritual vocabulary, for the limited advantages which accrue to its use seem to be far outweighed by the disadvantages inherent in it. Its uncontrolled usage, so common still in Catholic spirituality, carries with it the danger of an unconscious, subtle relapse into a Pelagian mentality[16] which would reduce the function of God to that of confirming what the scales of man have measured. Excessive and unguarded talk about man's merits and man's rightful claim to his reward may imply the tacit assumption of man's equal partnership with God where his salvation is concerned, and this is nothing but a practical distortion of the biblical notion of the covenant. For the covenant is based on the saving initiative taken by God, who cannot surrender his sovereignty in favour of man.

Even if this frequent reference to man's merits did not cover a spirituality of doubtful value, it would still be wise to drop the term and convey the same reality with other expressions, at least for ecumenical reasons. Frankly, Protestants are still allergic to the word "merit". Maybe in their eyes the term is still charged with excessively emotional overtones, remnants of the polemical attitudes of the past. Maybe that this almost instinctive rejection of the term and all it implies is not always entirely justified. Maybe. But on the other hand, we should not forget the explicit recommendation of Vatican II to use terms that "our separated brethren too can really understand".[17] In fact, "merit" is a term they can easily *mis*understand. For them it is simply a loaded word evocative of attitudes that in their estimation come dangerously close to heresy, and elementary courtesy as well as fundamental ecumenical concern demand that we be sensitive to their misgivings.[18]

16 Pelagianism was a deadly heresy that erupted at the time of St Augustine, in the early fifth century. Its main tenet was the excessive glorification of man's autonomy before God and the consequent denial of the absolute necessity of grace.

17 *Unitatis Redintegratio* n. 11: W. Abbott, *The Documents of Vatican II*, p. 354.

18 One can understand, for instance, Calvin's bitter complaint against the indiscriminate use of the term "merit" in his time: "I wish that this sobriety should have been kept by Christians; that they should not. . .have taken up terms that are foreign to Scripture which can create great difficulties and bear little fruit" (*Institutes of the Christian Religion* VI, p. 305).

The stubborn Catholic attachment to "merit" and the almost instinctive Protestant rejection of the same term have created unnecessary difficulties in the past, which should be avoided in the present. Yet, neither of the two Christian families is entirely free from blame in this regard. For if Catholic theology and specially popular Catholic piety have often conceived and expressed the doctrine almost along Pelagian lines by overstressing man's achievements, thereby provoking a partially justified Protestant reaction; Protestant theology, on its part, seems to have unduly minimized the profound transformation effected in man by God's grace, which divinizes him not only nominally but really, making him a true heir to eternal life.

If Catholics have not always avoided the pitfall of practical Palagianism, neither have Protestants kept always clear of superficial nominalism. The fundamental reality is God's gratuitous promise and grace, as correctly stressed by Protestants; but this promise is made to man and transforming grace is given to man, to make of him a new creature, as rightly emphasized by Catholics. The root of the doctrine of reward and merit lies in God, but its reality is in man. Since both sides emphasize an aspect that is pefectly legitimate in itself, a comprehensive, harmonious view of the whole should lay equal stress on both the dimensions. If a proper balance is kept between the two perspectives, which respectively stress the roles played by God's grace and man's freedom, Catholics and Protestants can safely bury their differences.

As a matter of fact, this is precisely what has happened recently. The U.S. ecumenical team, made up of representatives of the Lutheran and Catholic Churches, published in 1983 an official document which shows to what a remarkable extent the polemical attitudes of the past have finally yielded to concord and agreement. Not only has the bitter polemical climate of the past entirely vanished, but even more importantly, formerly devisive issues in the area of grace and sanctification show now an extraordinary degree of convergence, not to say agreement. Not all outstanding differences have been satisfactorily ironed out; but at least as regards the nature of our eternal reward American Lutherans and Catholics seem to be perfectly agreed: "The eternal reward promised to the just is a gift, for it rests entirely on the grace of God in Christ, only mediator between God and fallen mankind. The good works of the justified, performed in grace, will be rewarded by God, the just judge who, faithful to his promises, 'will render to every man according to his works' (Rom 2,6)".[19] Catholics as well as Protestants have every reason to thank God for this remarkable achievement which augurs well for the future.

5) The spirit, our reward

The term "reward" or "recompense" may be a suitable substitute for the obnoxious "merit", as being more biblical, more ecumenical, and less charged with emotional overtones. But this suggested substitution does not solve the problem entirely, for reward and recompense usually refer to the heavenly kingdom, and one should try and find a suitable way to explain satisfactorily not only the reception of the final crown at the end, but also the growth of divine life here and now.

"You shall be my people and I will be your God" (Ez 36,28) is the sum total of the personal, warm, intimate relationship binding Yahweh and Israel. This was their Covenant, cherished by all, priests, prophets and people, as the axis of their entire moral and spiritual system. On the other hand, Christianity has not cancelled, it has rather interiorized this covenantal relationship. Now we have, not a remote Yahweh linked with his People from afar, as it were, but the Spirit abiding himself in the Christian, in a close bond of intimacy beyond description. It is within the context of this relationship, rendered even warmer and more intimate by the indwelling Spirit, that we should place the consideration of man's reward.

It is not only the intrinsic dignity of the person performing the good work that should constantly be kept in mind, but also God's attitude with regard to him. The indwelling Spirit and man who is indwelt are closely bound together, almost fused into one. The Spirit gives himself together with the

19 US Lutheran/Catholic ecumenical commission, "La justification par la foi" n. 156: *Docum. Cathol.* 82 (1985) p. 15.

reward, or rather he himself is the reward. Hence, man's recompense is not like a capital or bank account which lies passive and grows progressively larger; it is rather *the person of the Holy Spirit himself* that is our riches. Properly speaking man's reward is not a gift, even a gratuitous, unmerited gift, but the Giver himself, and therefore, when man receives his reward, he does not receive something outside God and distinct from him, but the very person of God, both here on earth in the indwelling and later in the consummation of the heavenly kingdom. Merit, reward, recompense: all three equally abstract and therefore unsatisfactory notions. It is not an abstraction, however refined, that will quench man's thirst, but rather the very person of God. Similarly, God's innate proclivity to give will not be entirely satiated unless he gives himself to man. Man craves for God and God craves for man, and this mutual longing will be satisfied partially with the indwelling and totally in the heavenly consummation.

Hence, the son of God should long, not for the gifts but for the person of the Giver; not for eternal glory but for the eternally Glorified; not for everlasting life but for him who is our everlasting Life; not for eternal rest but for him who is our eternal Rest; not for the resurrection but for the Resurrected; not for the transfiguration but for the Transfigured; not for the spirit of God but for the Holy Spirit — he is our personal reward.

Theologically, the reality of man's reward rests on a double basis: the intrinsic worth of the work performed by a person who is immanent in the risen Christ, indwelt by the Holy Spirit, endowed with sanctifying grace, turned into a son of God and divinized in his very being by receiving his share in the life of God. The works produced by such a person cannot but have a very high worth of their own. If the source is so rich, how will the rivulets be? If waters gush forth from a gold mine, it is impossible that the stream should not carry particles, however tiny, of the precious metal.

But besides this inner value and intrinsic worth of the actions performed by the Christian, and even more important than they, is God's fidelity to the promise he made, out of a gracious, entirely unmerited love. "I shall put my Spirit within you" (Ez 36,27). That is the promise, the rest follows.

It was certainly not man who prompted God to make this astonishing commitment; the promise was not wrested forcefully by man, for, to begin with, he would have never dreamt of asking for such an assurance. The original blueprint of the promise was conceived, not in the mind of man, but in the heart of God. It is there that the secret lay buried for centuries and millennia until it began to take concrete shape in Christ.

Man's work and God's grace. Out of this kind of "mystical marriage" the child we call reward or recompense is born. Both the parents are obviously essential for the birth of the child but, unlike in a human marriage, the parents are not of equal worth. Man's work, left to itself, would never be able to produce such a reward. His work is certainly worth a reward, but the root of this dignity inherent in man does not lie in himself, it lies in God, for our deserts are strictly dependent on his promise and grace, which lie out of the meriting grasp of man. Augustine's expression can hardly be improved: "In crowning our merits God is crowning his own gifts". Man's reward is God's gift, because both reward and merit are identified, fused into the very person of God himself.

Hence, we should resolutely dispel the false and dangerous notion — apparently still lurking in some people's minds — that the doctrine of man's reward can be explained satisfactorily by simply applying the principles of commutative justice, as if God were bound in justice to repay man for his behaviour, almost as if man had, during his earthly pilgrimage, accumulated cheques which he can cash on arrival at the pearly gates of heaven. To consider the doctrine of reward from this mercenary angle would obviously be a serious distortion, a real travesty of the truth. For the plane on which we are now moving is not that of a sordid bargain struck out in spirit of strict justice, but that of a personal relation of faith and love. It is not law but love that governs the doctrine of man's reward.

This being the nature of our reward, which is not a thing but a living and loving Person, its dynamic growth should be explained accordingly. Many of the Catholic faithful are quite used to the expression "increase in sanctifying grace", which is rather unfortunate, for it seems to reduce the strictly personal reality of grace to a sort of dead capital which would yield an ever richer interest. The indwelling of the Spirit and sanctifying grace are the two indispensable sides of an intimate, interpersonal relationship between the Holy Spirit and man in an act of mutual self-surrender. The Spirit gives himself over to man in the indwelling, and man reciprocates by giving himself to the Spirit in sanctifying grace. And this personal relationship, just as it happens in our purely human relationships, can always grow stronger and more intimate, in proportion as the initial mutual self-surrender is deepened and perfected. The embrace between the indwelling God and man becomes tighter, the union fuller. And so this growth in trinitarian life consists in being more intensely acted upon by the Holy Spirit, in being more receptive to his wishes and more sensitive to his touches, in acting more after one has been acted upon.

An increase in docility to the Spirit implies necessarily a corresponding growth in divine, trinitarian life on the part of man. In other words, growth in the indwelling is nothing but *man's deeper penetration into the person of the Holy Spirit*. In the words of K. Rahner: "This means nothing other than man is more and more, ever more deeply, ever more existentially, seized by God's life, and that this life claims him more and more in all the dimensions of his existence.... It is simply the presence of God's love growing more intense, more radical and the transforming union becoming greater".[20]

This internal growth of the indwelling is effected very specially by the reception of eucharistic communion. Most people's understanding of communion is narrowly reduced to the firm realization that the glorified Jesus has come into their hearts, and this incredible reality seems to blind them to any other dimension of the eucharistic mystery. The rich and extraordinarily satisfying Oriental tradition is almost entirely lost sight of, a tradition that considers the transfigured Christ as a privileged channel of transmission through which the person of the Holy Spirit is poured again into the communicant. The Spirit, already dwelling in the communicant—for when approaching the eucharistic table he has obviously

20 K. Rahner, "The comfort of time", *Theological Investigations* 3 (London 1967), p. 143.

to be in a state of grace, to use the traditional, but unsatisfactory expression — intensifies his presence within him as a result of communion. The reception of the Eucharist makes the indwelling grow in depth and intensity.[21]

But, apart from this sacramental growth, and restricting now our attention exlusively to the field of man's daily actions, we can say that this intensification of the indwelling follows a twofold pattern: on the one hand, the indwelling Spirit impels man outwardly, as it were, to perform good deeds in the surrounding community of men and women. If so performed, under the influence of the Spirit, these works or fruits of the Spirit make the indwelling grow in intensity, they make it sink deeper roots into the heart of the son of God. Exterior apostolic activity, for instance, if properly performed, results in a deepening of the indwelling and intensification of sanctifying grace. One becomes holier by acting; man's external acts are the channels through which God's own life keeps flowing into the heart of man.

Over and above these exterior works, the Spirit impels man also inwardly, towards the Spirit himself, in the silent, unassuming docility of a dedicated life ever attuned to the inner voice of the Spirit coming from within — these "works", too, make the indwelling grow. It is the same Spirit acting in man on two different levels, and just as an exclusive insistence on the interior or contemplative dimension would result in a narrow individualism and dangerous subjectivism (man being excessively wrapped up within himself); so also an exaggerated, one-sided insistence on external works would eventually issue into a form of hollow, superficial activism. Growth in divine life implies a balanced development of both the tendencies, outward and inward.

Not only the indwelling, but the entire supernatural structure of the Christian keeps growing: the interior presence of the Spirit certainly becomes more intense, but along with it his immanence in the glorified Christ grows deeper, his sanctifying grace develops further, the trinitarian life claims him more and more. These four realities present in man are like four branches of the same tree that either become stunted

21 For the close connection between eucharistic communion and the Holy Spirit see my previous book, *Body Broken and Blood Shed* (Anand 1986), pp. 287-293.

together or grow and develop together. The sap flows freely from the roots into the four branches of the tree, causing new shoots to appear on all four of them, and eventually making the shoots burst into flowers and fruits. There is an irresistible vitality growing through a healthy tree that simply cannot be quenched, cannot be contained. Life is irrepressible.

The rule governing the growth of the indwelling is a kind of mutual cooperation between the Spirit and man. On our part, the required cooperation consists in an ever greater opening to the influence of the Spirit, letting ourselves be ruled by him more and more. And on his part, he cooperates in our growth in as ar fas he measures the bestowal of his gifts in proportion to our openness to him. The more man opens to the Spirit, the more will the Spirit give himself to man; and the more the Spirit gives himself to man, the more will man's capacity of reception increase. The more man drinks from the Spirit, the thirstier he will become, longing for a greater and greater outpouring of the same Spirit. This is a kind of "vicious circle" which should never be broken.

The Holy Spirit adapts himself to our receptivity and to our wilful surrender to his influence. Ultimately, the terse expression of the Council of Trent proves absolutely correct: The Christian receives a share of trinitarian life "according to the measure which 'the Holy Spirit apportions to each one individually as he wills' (1 Cor 12,11) and according to each one's personal disposition and cooperation".[22] In the final stages of this growth and transformation man becomes utterly docile to the Holy Spirit and lives by the Spirit's own life: "A saint is a man completely transparent to the activity of the Spirit" (T. Torrance).

Bibliography

Journnet, C.: *The Meaning of Grace* (London 1960), pp. 67-89.

Emery, P.: *Christ, Notre Récompense* (Neuchatel 1962).

Gleason, R.: *Grace* (New York 1962), pp. 173-185.

Montague, G.: "Misthos", *Theological Dictionary of the New Testament* 4 (1967), pp. 695-723.

22 Neuner-Dupuis, *The Christian Faith*, n. 1932.

Rahner, K.: "The comfort of time", *Theological Investigations* 3 (1967), pp. 141-161.

Fransen, P.: *The New Life of Grace* (London 1969), pp. 201-230.

Molinski, W.: "Merit", *Sacramentum Mundi* 4 (1969), pp. 11-14.

Solignac, A.: "Mérite et vie spirituelle", *Dictionnaire de Spiritualité* 10 (1980), pp. 1040-1051.

Chapter Nine

THE SPIRIT OF FREEDOM

"Brethren, you are called to freedom....Where the Spirit of the Lord is, there is freedom". Ever since these words of Paul resounded like a clarion call, the theme of Christian liberty or freedom has always been a delicious, heady wine to drink. Who does not like to be free from all constrictions, external or internal? One has only to look at the political map of the the world and see how the bug of freedom, liberation and independence has progressively bitten every nation on the planet, both in the East and in the West. There seems to be some secret impulse in man that prompts him to be free, to attain a mature level of independence in every sphere, religious, political, economic and spiritual. Man is born unto freedom, and any form of slavery seems to go counter to his innermost longings and most cherished ideals. Why this universal clamour for freedom, this restlessness before it is achieved and this sense of satisfaction and pride when it is accomplished?

This is a perfectly natural, human phenomenon that has nothing to do with being or not being a Christian. Man's thirst for freedom is prior to his baptism, for it is simply branded in his very constitution as man. Take away his liberty and he ceases to be a man. Man has not created this longing for freedom, he has only received it as a gratuitous gift from God. And it is in this ground, so naturally predisposed to freedom, that man receives the person of the Spirit. The Christian is profoundly transformed when the Holy Spirit invades him and takes full possession of him; he becomes a new creature, he acquires something he did not have before. And yet, in a certain way, man is *not* changed. Before the penetration of the Holy Spirit he was endowed with a passionate longing, an ineradicable desire for freedom, and after the Spirit's arrival this longing, far from being assuaged, is further intensified. The Holy Spirit does not suppress or diminish the longing, he rather enhances it. Despite the new reality in his life which is the Holy Spirit, man retains all his essential characteristic features. He was free and he remains free, for the Holy Spirit and man's freedom seem to enjoy each other's company, they seem to have been made "for each other". The enormous reality of the indwelling is given to man as a free and responsible person, free in his responsibility and conscious of his own freedom. Man's freedom and God's Spirit are intimately interlocked, whether man denies the Spirit access to the inner sanctuary of his freedom, or he opens up freely to the person of the Spirit, gaining thereby a more exalted form of freedom.

Liberty seems to run in the very bloodstream of the People of God. Our own spiritual ancestors, the Israelites of old, were for many centuries nothing but a pitiable batch of slaves living in abject conditions under the heel of their Egyptian masters. But in the midst of that enveloping darkness, a tiny light flickered, a light that had been lit centuries before in the form of a vague, indistinct promise that one day they would regain their freedom. And regain it they did. With characteristic unpredictability God intervenes at the darkest hour and sends them an old man to lead them out of slavery and help them obtain their cherished freedom. After some initial hesitation and even reluctance, Moses complies and achieves the impossible: he breaks the fetters that kept the Israelites chained to their taskmasters and joyfully leads them into freedom.

It is now, and only now, after they have attained their freedom, that the scattered mass of individuals is forged together into unity to constitute the People of God. As long as they were not free they could not be the People of God, but as soon as they form a free nation the People of God is born. This simple but remarkable historical fact shows clearly how absolutely essential freedom is to the People of

God. The birth of God's People and the attainment of freedom simply coincide. Freedom is deeply rooted in the very being of the People of God. A people without freedom may be somebody's else people, but surely not God's own People. God wants his People to be free.

Yet this freedom seems to be a precious gift, difficult to retain and difficult to regain if it is lost. Centuries roll by and the Israelites lose their precious freedom again, it simply slips off their fingers. The People are savagely uprooted from their Promised Land and thrown into slavery once more, with their freedom shattered to pieces. They languish in pagan Babylon, but God seems to be endowed with a very retentive memory — he will not forget his People, he promises them a *goel*, a liberator, a leader who will eventually lead them back into freedom. In fact, Yahweh himself will be their liberator: "Thus says the Lord, your liberator.... For your sake, I will...break down all the bars" (Is 43,14). In Hebrew law the *goel* is a close relative who is bound to defend his clan, to free his brother when the latter has fallen into slavery, and to protect widows. The consistent use of the term in Isaiah's prophecy implies the persistence of a close family bond between Yahweh and his People. If their freedom is threatened or temporarily lost, Yahweh himself, their *goel*, will intervene, for freedom must be restored. And so the last centuries before the arrival of the Messiah are filled with an anxious expectation of Israel's final liberation. Official Jewish prayers request the *goel* of Israel to hurry and not delay. It is an impatient expectation of freedom: "O Israel, hope in the Lord....He will free Israel from all its iniquities" (Ps 130,8). The very term "redemption", to which we are so used, means in reality liberation unto freedom, a victorious liberation accomplished by Yahweh.

1) The luminous liberty of the children of God

There is little doubt that the great champion of Christian freedom is Paul. It is true that much before Paul appeared on the scene, it had already been taught quite explicitly that man is endowed with the liberty of free choice, that God has put his destiny into his own hands, that he stands before God as a responsible person, accountable for his actions. The very core of the Jewish religious system was the Sinaitic Covenant made between Yahweh and his People, and this Covenant implied an explicit injunction from Yahweh to keep its terms. The People pledged themselves to observe its ordinances: "All that the Lord has spoken we will do, and we will be obedient" (Ex 24,7) — and such a pledge necessarily implies freedom so to act. Despite such resounding promise on the part of the People, however, very soon the Covenant was in a shambles, and the entire life and action of the prophets can be reduced to a repeated entreaty to the People to repent and be faithful to Yahweh — and repentance and fidelity are meaningless unless they rest on the exercise of personal freedom.

Probably nowhere is man's responsibility for his own actions more vividly expressed than in this passage from Sirach 11,16: "To act faithfully is a matter of your choice. He has placed before you fire and water: stretch out your hand for whatever you need". Man is responsible for his own actions, for which he will eventually be either rewarded or punished — and again responsibility is necessarily built upon freedom. To pursue the same point further would be labouring the obvious, so clear and undisputed is this biblical teaching on the freedom of man.

But when Paul proclaims so loudly and emphatically the reality of Christian freedom he means something quite different. Obviously man is endowed with a freedom of choice, we need neither Christianity nor Paul to know this. But Paul's insistence points in a different direction altogether. When he announces so solemnly to the churches he has founded and to those he has not founded, to Corinth and Galatia as well as to Rome, the message of the Christian's fundamental freedom, he has in mind a type of freedom whose meaning is not at all obvious; a peculiar freedom, in fact, which is typically Christian, for it is closely connected with Jesus and the Spirit of Jesus.

Paul seems to delight in speaking in glowing terms of "the luminous liberty of the children of God" (Rom 8,21)[1],

1 This is certainly not a fanciful, poetic translation of Rom 8,21, but rather its exact rendering. To speak of "the glorious liberty of the children of God" (RSV) is rather flat and unappealing. For Paul seems to conceive Christian

which is but the result of the Holy Spirit dwelling within them. "The Son makes you free" (Jn 8,36). Perfectly true, but John did not bother to tell us how. Even before John, Paul had said much the same thing, perhaps more emphatically and certainly more elaborately, in clear reference to the Spirit of Jesus. In a typically concise manner, Paul writes to the Romans a bold programmatic statement which in a way is the sum total of his doctrine of freedom: "For the law of the Spirit of life in Christ Jesus has set me free from the law of sin and death" (Rom 8,2). A terse, limpid expression if there ever was one, but an expression which, if left unexplained, would mean next to nothing to a modern reader. Its setting is markedly Jewish, but its implications are definitely universal.

Before man falls under the spell and influence of Christ, Paul conceives him as essentially unfree. In fact, he is constrained by three shackles which are to be broken if he is to be set free, the shackles being the Law, Sin, and Death. As long as he is fettered by all three, man is nothing but a slave, not a free man. All three are personifications of evil powers that hinder man's freedom. Reader, beware, for Paul's thought is not half as obvious as it looks. When we hear or read about sin, we think we understand its meaning, for all of us can appeal to our personal experience as sinners before God. If there is something profoundly human, something that absolutely all men and women are familiar with, it is the reality of sin, the blemish of our personal sins. This is precisely what Paul does *not* mean. His mental framework is totally different from ours; for him Sin (with capital S) is rather the personification of the power of sin, the power that keeps man in bondage and deprives him of his freedom. It is an evil force unleashed into a world at the dawn of humankind, "a personified, malovolent power, hostile to God and alienating man from him, which strode upon the stage of

freedom as endowed with a certain splendour or effulgence of its own, almost as if it were a focus of light that spreads its glow and illumines the surrounding area. I find this extremely suggestive and exegetically correct. In fact, a slavishly literal translation of Rom 8,21 should read: "...the liberty of the splendour of the children of God".

human history at the time of Adam's transgression".[2] It is both this power of Sin and man's personal sins begotten by it that keep man under constraint and prevent the flowering of his freedom.

St Augustine seems to have had a perfect grasp of Paul's thought when he stated that the sinner retains his free will but has lost his freedom. For only the latter is an exclusive privilege of the children of God, not the former. Man's free will, through which he partly mirrors God, is so deeply embedded in human nature that sin cannot possibly destroy it, at least not usually. It is precisely because the sinner retains his free will that there is hope for his conversion; it is by exercising that free will of his that he can eventually turn to God. But as long as he remains sunk in sin he does not have the luminous freedom which only the Spirit of Jesus can give. If he is in sin he is in darkness, he cannot have a share in the effulgence that radiates from the inner source of the Spirit. In Paul's conception he is simply not free, he is rather the slave of sin. When man's natural capacity for choosing between good and evil — namely, his free will — is subsumed and penetrated by the Holy Spirit, then man becomes free, basking once again in the glow that envelopes him from within. Now he is in the Spirit, he is in the light, he is in freedom. In addition to his free will which he never lost, he has acquired the luminous freedom of God's children. When this happens, it means that the tyrannical power of Sin has finally been ousted, has been expelled, and its place taken by the person of the Holy Spirit that illumines man internally. The Spirit has made him free. It is true that even after this freedom has been bestowed on him his flesh, that is, his earthbound tendencies and sinful inclinations, remain in him and will always remain as long as he lives, for this constant allurement of sin, this downward pull can and does coexist side by side with the indwelling Spirit. But the main thing is that, once baptized and sanctified, he is no longer under the malovelent influence of the power of Sin — the first of the

2 J. Fitzmyer, "The letter to the Romans", in *The Jerome Biblical Commentary* (Bangalore 1972), p. 307.

three shackles has been broken and the journey towards freedom has begun.[3]

a) *Freedom from the Law*

Paul's fight for Christian freedom continues: the individual, baptized and united to Christ, is not only free from the clutches of the power of Sin, he is also free from the Law. The Christian, ruled by the Spirit and in the measure in which he is ruled by the Spirit, is free from any law that constrains him from without, for he is governed by the Spirit from within.

I realize that this is a delicate matter and that the chances of being misunderstood are great. But the doctrine is of the utmost importance, and therefore it should be carefully handled. Our aim should be to throw light on the situation of the contemporary Christian and the freedom he enjoys in Jesus Christ, but in order to reach this goal we should, once again, start with Paul. The very term "law" is likely to raise quite a few eyebrows of surprise and even displeasure among the readers, so allergic most of us feel today to anything at all that smacks of legalism, laws and regulations.

Yet, this was not at all the mentality of the Jews, and even of the first generation Christians coming from a Jewish background. We may frown on the law, but the Israelites worshipped it as a manifestation of Yahweh's holy will. For them the Law (in the singular and capitalized) does not spell constriction but salvation; it is not something to be avoided but something to be embraced; it is not an obstacle but a help. The Jew cherishes the Law and reveres it, for in his estimation it is not a bundle of lifeless prescriptions and dry, dead regulations, but rather a spring of life, the enfleshment in tangible form of God's saving designs for his People. The Law is the word of life, it is the bread of life, it is refreshing waters — almost exactly the very metaphors which the New Testament applies to Jesus. The Jew worships the Law as we

3 The shackle of Death snapped, properly speaking, on Golgotha, when Jesus died so that man may not die. For a Christian physical death is nothing but a transition, a passage into the splendours of the transfigured Christ. A further explanation of this would take us too far afield; for a detailed treatment see my previous book *Life Beyond Death* (Anand 1985), pp. 17-41.

Christians worship Christ, the Son of God, for both of them, the Law and Christ, are but the embodiment of God's saving designs for his People.

Paul's stand with regard to the Law was almost revolutionary. Some of his churches in Greece had their crop of Christian Judaizers, namely, those Christians of Jewish origin who believed in Christ, certainly, but were unable to break free from their Jewish past, specifically from the reverence and awe they felt towards the Law. Hence, the allurement of compromise was great, they would commit themselves to Christ in living faith, but at the same time they would feel in conscience constrained to be faithful to their Jewish heritage. Why not worship both the old Law and the new Christ? Was there any contradiction between the two? Couldn't a person be faithful to both Christ and the Law? Could he not be saved by believing in both Christ and the Law?

All these assumptions might have looked very reasonable to them, a balanced midway between submission to the past and opening to the present, between obedience to Moses and obedience to Christ. But such a way of reasoning makes fiery Paul flare up and react sharply, almost angrily: "You, stupid Galatians!" (Gal 3,1). For Paul such an attitude was nothing but a shameful compromise that puts in jeopardy the uniqueness of faith in Christ as the only way to salvation. The Law — Paul argues — had a useful role to peform in the past, but no longer now.

After the arrival of Christ on the scene, after his death and resurrection, man is saved exclusively by faith in Christ, no longer by observing an obsolete Law. No compromise of any kind is possible here, for any lingering reverence and respect paid to the Law, no matter how minimal, would be derogatory to the unicity of Christ. One has to choose either for Christ or for the Law, not for both. And for the Christian the choice is obvious, he should firmly cling to Christ and drop the Law. After believing in Christ he is simply *free from the Law*, the old Law does not bind him in any way — the second fetter has snapped. This newly acquired freedom should be maintained intact at all costs. Any subservience to the Law of their ancestors would be equivalent to a corresponding curtailment of Christian freedom, and for

Paul this is simply intolerable, for freedom is a gift we have received from Christ, and the gift must be kept and cherished, not sacrificed on the altar of a compromise solution. Christian freedom has to be luminous, it has to shine out, and the reappearance of the Law would have the unavoidable effect of dimming its brightness.

We have somehow penetrated into Paul's mind, but we have not yet grasped fully his mentality. In his uncompromising rejection of the Law and his spirited defense of Christian liberty, what exactly does Paul mean by Law? Does he have in mind the Mosaic Law and nothing else? Does he mean to say that the minute prescriptions of the old Jewish Law are no longer binding on Christians, that male children are not bound to be circumcized anymore, that women need not go to the Jerusalem Temple for their purification after childbirth, that the annual Passover celebration is no longer binding, that nobody is forced to attend the synagogue services, that the Law of the Sabbath can be broken with impunity? Does Paul mean all that and nothing more? Frankly, if all Paul had in mind was to declare that the innumerable legalistic prescriptions that in the course of time had crystallized around the central core of the Mosaic Law had lost their binding power, that the Christian was no longer bound to observe them; if he meant that and nothing else, then there was no need to react as sharply as he did. For in that case the newly acquired Christian freedom would be nothing but a platitude, something hardly worth fighting for. Paul would be simply overreacting, putting up a fight and taking up an uncompromising attitude that were simply uncalled for. In this case Paul would be making much ado about nothing or next to nothing.

No, Paul knows only too well what exactly he is upholding. He is definitely not overreacting, for the principle of Christian freedom he is defending is of the utmost importance. And it is precisely at this point that Paul's doctrine begins to resonate for a modern reader with echoes that sound strangely familiar. There is something in the strong stand taken by Paul that transcends his own concrete historical situation, something that goes far beyond the restricted boundaries of first century Greece or Rome. Paul is fighting a battle of lasting significance, he is not engaged in local skirmishes of limited value. When Paul rejects the Law as being of no use at all for a Christian he is not only rejecting the Mosaic Law, but something much broader than that. Paul is keeping his distance from the Jewish Law, certainly, but in doing so he has a dig at the law in general, any law whatsoever. The concrete, historical circumstances which prompted him to react the way he did were only an occasion, a platform from which he launched out his attack on the law in general. When upholding Christian liberty Paul was not concerned with the rejection of the Mosaic Law only, but with the rejection of the law, period. In the considered opinion of Catholic exegete S. Lyonnet, one of the greatest authorities on St Paul, the concept of law in Paul "applies to whatever verifies in itself the notion of law, it applies to *any norm imposed on the human conscience from without*".[4]

I am fully aware — and so is the reader, I hope — that now we are treading dangerous ground. This is definitely slippery terrain and we must be careful to keep our balance lest we fall. The Christian is free from any law and all laws. Is this possible? Is this not tantamount to proclaiming, loud and clear, the principle of complete lawlessness? Is this really Christian freedom or rather a parody of freedom? This may be dangerous doctrine, easily twisted and misunderstood, but in itself it is perfectly correct. We have seen above that Sin, one of the three typically Pauline actors on the stage of human history, does not mean for Paul any concrete, specified sin, but rather the power of sin in general that drags man down all the time. It is a personified power of sin. Similarly and in keeping with the same mentality, the Law — another actor — is not restricted to this or that concrete law, it simply means the law in general, for the concept is applicable to any law whatsoever. It clicks. Sin and Law have in Paul the same wide range and universal connotation, neither of them is restricted, both are equally broad and general. And it is from the law understood in this broad, general sense that the

4 S. Lyonnet, "St Paul: liberty and law", *The Bridge* 4 (1961), p. 237. In substantial agreement with Lyonnet, J. Huby is also of the opinion that Paul takes the law "not in its ritual and ceremonial aspects, but in its moral, permanent content" (*St Paul, Epitre aux Romains*, Paris 1957, p. 234).

Christian is declared to be free.

The Christian has attained freedom from the law.

b) *Freedom for the Spirit*

No, there is no danger of lawlessness, the Holy Spirit will take care of that. Now that the Christian has been rendered free from the law — any law imposed on his conscience from outside — he is directly under the "the law of the Spirit" (Rom 8,2). Only that now the principle controlling him is no longer a law acting on him from outside, but a person operating from within him. This new "law" is, according to St Thomas, "identified either with the person of the Spirit or with his activity in us".[5] The new law the Christian is bound to obey is not a new legal code given by the Spirit, it is rather the Spirit himself as a dynamic, internal principle of action. The old Law has faded away, powerless to transform the Christian, and the person of the Holy Spirit has taken over. In a way Christian freedom amounts to a change of masters, for now the Christian does not act out of external compulsion restrained by the law, but rather out of internal conviction, constrained by the Spirit.

The Christian, therefore, does not become an amoral man, free from the restriction of the law so that he may sin; he is an individual ruled by the Spirit from within: "If you are led by the Spirit you are not under the law" (Gal 5,19). Consequently, total freedom from the law does not lead to lawlessness and amorality, but rather to perfect docility to the Spirit, a docility that will eventually produce the fruits of the Spirit. Before, the Christian lived under the structures of the law, now he lives under the strictures of the Spirit. God's will is not overthrown, it is rather spiritualized and interiorized by the indwelling Spirit. The Holy Spirit has absorbed the law unto himself, as it were, and therefore in submitting to the Spirit the Christian submits to the law. His new concern is to submit to the Spirit, not to the law, but in submitting to the Spirit in reality he is keeping the law in a new, interiorized form. In other words, he still keeps the law, but the motive of its observance is now changed. He no

5 *In Rom* 8,2.

longer submits to the external law out of fear, but to the internal Spirit out of love. Law has been replaced by love. This is the nature of Christian freedom. The believer in Jesus should not be primarily concerned about the external law, but about the internal Spirit. He is free from the law, free for the Spirit.

All of us remember that memorable 20 July, 1969, when for the first time in history man conquered the moon. American astronauts N. Armstrong and E. Aldvin landed safely on the surface of the earth's satellite, and after a cursory inspection of the lunar wilderness, left the moon to come home. Their mission accomplished, the lunar module lifted off the ground and rejoined the mother ship which had been circling the moon. And then, with a powerful boost, they escaped the gravitational pull of the moon and quietly headed for home. Gradually they came within range of the earth's gravitational field and eventually landed safely on the Pacific Ocean.

Something similar happens to the Christian. As he acquires his new freedom in Christ he is boosted up out of the force of gravity of the law, to be gradually sucked in by the internal pull of the Spirit acting from within him. The journey may be difficult and arduous, but the general direction is clear: a gradually increasing influence of the Holy Spirit in his life will measure the extent of his real freedom. It is rather unfortunate that so many Christians seem to be still blissfully unaware of the interior pull they experience from within. They seem to be mesmerized by the firmness of the lunar surface, in reality so cold and desolate, so lifeless and forbidding.... Can't they feel the exhilaration of gradually losing sight of the receding law to fall into the embrace of the beckoning Spirit, who looms progressively larger and larger, so warm and welcoming, so cordial and hospitable?

It happens all the time that Christians who ought to be preeminently free men and women still act as if they were slaves of the law, unspiritual and unfree. A few years ago it was reported that the French Episcopal Conference had authoritatively decided that the traditional Sunday Mass obligation would no longer bind French Catholics under pain of mortal sin. They were definitely encouraged to keep up the practice, but there could no longer be a question of committing a grievous sin in case of neglect. The first noticeable result of the announcement was that Sunday Mass attendance, which was already very low, especially in urban centres, dropped further still by another 15 percent. As soon as the obligation under sin ceased, attendance dropped. The corelation is unmistakable: thousands of French Catholics had apparently kept the precept of Sunday Mass out of a false respect for the law, out of fear of committing a grievous sin. Merely fear of breaking the law is an attitude unworthy of a Christian who claims to be free from the law. If those thousands of Catholics had always attended Sunday Mass out of internal conviction rather than out of external compulsion, out of fear of breaking the law and thereby lapsing into sin, that significant drop in Mass attendance would not have taken place. Which goes to show that unfortunately fear of the law is still present in many Christians. They are simply not yet acting as free men and women.[6]

And yet, even for the son of God indwelt and ruled by the Spirit, to some extent the precepts of the law remain and they are still useful, they have a function to perform. For, imbued as he is with a profound sense of Christian frealism, the Christian will soberly acknowledge that as long as he lives, and due to the possible misuse of his freedom and the frequent harassment of his own flesh, he can always fall. His innate sinful inclinations often tend to obscure his vision, clouding his mind and preventing a clear perception of the voice of the Spirit. To discern the Spirit's wishes is not easy, and the

6 Certain religious houses of both the sexes do not seem to display a mentality very different from that of those French Catholics mentioned above; for instance, as soon as the external props of laws and regulations concerning daily prayer are dropped, the practice of daily prayer also drops. It is all very nice to appeal eloquently to trust and the sense of responsibility, but experience seems to show that in some religious communities both are in short supply. If certain constricting regulations regarding time and place for daily prayer are lifted on the ground that religious are supposed to be mature and responsible adults who do not need such a fixed, oppressive framework, daily prayer may experience a sudden slump. So much for the much vaunted sense of responsibility and maturity of some religious. Obviously the remedy does not lie in multiplying external rules and regulations, but in strengthening the individual's sense of interior, genuine Christian freedom.

Christian knows it. In this state of weakness and imperfection the external precepts of the law, already interiorized, can be a valuable help for him to detect the voice of the Spirit, to discriminate between the Spirit's directives and his own illusory suggestions. The precept of the law remains a useful help for the discernment of spirits which must necessarily precede his subjection to the Spirit. The precept can help docility to the Spirit. The principal element by far is the person of the Holy Spirit, with the precept as a secondary, subsidiary help. To reverse the order and grant to the precept a supremacy it does not have would be tantamount to surrendering man's liberty, returning to sheer external legalism. But to neglect the precept under the pretext of an enlightened conscience and a higher submission to the Spirit would spell dangerous subjectivism. The external precept should never constitute an ideal to be realized, but rather a limit not to be transgressed. The Spirit draws the precept into himself, but he does not destroy it. The Christian has attained his cherished freedom, he is now free from the law and free for the Spirit.

The life and bustle of a modern airport supply us with a useful simile. If the airport is well provided with all the necessary technological instruments, night landing is a matter of routine, not at all hazardous. The pilot, after touching down, and as he puts the brakes on, has only to follow the central lane which is clearly demarcated on both sides by a long stream of red lights. As long as he keeps within the lane, with red lights to his right and to his left, he is perfectly safe. In some international airports, after the plane has landed and so as to facilitate the pilot's task of parking his huge aircraft in the place assigned to it, they have a tiny yellow car moving in front of the plane with the inscription 'Follow me' clearly written on the back of the car in bold letters. The pilot has only to follow the car and he will reach a convenient parking lot.

For the son of God ruled by the Holy Spirit, the precepts of the law perform the same function as the red lights marking the edge of the runway. Just as the pilot would almost certainly meet with disaster if, relying on his own counsel and experience, he were to disregard the red lights and cut across them, trying to find a new way to the parking lot; so also the Christian who, claiming to be entirely free from the law, ignores the red lights of the precepts that keep flickering in the distance as a warning signal, is surely courting disaster. Although he can easily detect the red lights with his peripheral vision, his attention should obviously be riveted on the Spirit who, just like the small yellow car, is guiding him forward with one single message — 'Follow me'. The red lights of the precepts are nothing but an outer limit not to be transgressed, but an important limit which the Christian can ignore only at his own risk.

2) Authority and freedom, gifts of the spirit

A comprehensive view of the freedom from the law the Christian has gained requires that now we take one step further and reflect for a while on the very source from which the law proceeds — authority. For the law — any law — is necessarily a creature of authority, which often claims, rightly or wrongly, to be guided by the Spirit of God, an authority whose utterances are often portrayed as the sacred will of God which the son of God ought always to humbly accept and faithfully execute. Disobedience to authority — it is claimed — could be an unmistakable sign of a rebellious spirit which is foreign to the Spirit of God. This current contention is partly correct, but it also covers a dreadful oversimplification that seems to neglect almost entirely one of the two sources utilized by the Spirit to instruct the individual.

For the liberty of the children of God moves constantly between two opposing poles: external authority and submission to conscience. Authority is certainly a source of the law, but to claim that freedom from the law necessarily implies a corresponding freedom from authority would be a highly dangerous conclusion which is totally unwarranted. The conflicts that often arise between authority and the inalienable freedom of the individual arise oftener than not from a basic misunderstanding of both. It is not only freedom, but authority as well that has its ultimate source in the Spirit of God. In the last analysis authority and freedom are both the gift of the Spirit to the individual Christian.

a) *The scriptural viewpoint*

Authority is certainly not a prominent theme in the New Testament, and if it was overdeveloped later on in Christian tradition it was due largely to special historical circumstances. Much of the New Testament teaching on authority is there as a warning, rather than as a model of imitation. Jesus seems to have been less concerned with describing the contents and nature of authority than with rejecting certain false presumptions in its exercise. The angle from which the biblical concept of authority should be viewed is that of the Covenant which was a creation of the Spirit. The relation existing between the rulers and the ruled is that of an interpersonal relationship governed by the Spirit, a relationship in which the holder of authority will trust and await the response of the same Spirit in his fellow Christian.

The New Testament avoids or very rarely uses terms that would signify authority in the sense of power. Jesus undoubtedly has an authority which he derives from his Father and transmits to his disciples, an authority that in biblical terminology is called *exousia*, a word of difficult description, for its contents are rather imprecise. It does not seem to mean primarily the legal power of jurisdiction, yet there are clear cases in the New Testament when the exercise of such a power comes very close to it.

The Syrian community where Matthew's gospel originated seems to have been troubled by the problem of authority. In the general context of fraternal correction, Jesus, proceeding by progressively widening circles, recommends that the erring brother be corrected privately; if that fails, that he be reprimanded in the presence of two witnesses or even of the entire congregation. But in case even that proves fruitless, then "let him be to you as a Gentile and a tax-collector" (Mt 18, 17), which comes rather close to what today we call in juridical terms excommunication. Even more clearly than Matthew, Paul states firmly and uncompromisingly that the Christian who is having sexual relations with his stepmother should be "removed from among you" (1 Cor 5,2), namely, thrown out of the local church, excommunicated. These are probably extreme cases of rare occurrence, but they serve to show that Christians of the first generation were conscious of possessing an authority which on occasion could and should be exercised juridically. *Exousia* may not be in itself a juridical concept, but on the other hand it cannot be watered down to mere persuasion and exhortation. It is certainly much more than that.

And yet, it remains true that Paul, who is certainly conscious of his own authority given to him directly by the Lord, does not usually pull rank. He has other means to obtain the submission and compliance of those under him. For instance, he authenticates his authority by appealing to his own spiritual gifts, in a manner that sounds somewhat demure and almost diffident: "And I think I have the Spirit of God" (1 Cor 7,40) At times he is almost apologetic and clearly on the defensive when exercising his legitimate authority: "For even if I boast a little too much of our authority, which the Lord gave for building you up...I shall not be put to shame" (2 Cor 10.8). The real seal of his authority is the way the Spirit of the Lord has blessed his apostolic labours in Corinth: "Are we beginning to command ourselves again?....You yourselves are our letter of recommendation... written...with the Spirit of the living God" (2 Cor 3,1-3)

He seems to have a preference for exhortation and persuasion rather than naked commands and peremptory orders, and this in spite of the clearly discernible authoritarian streak in his temperament and his fiercely independent spirit. He seems to be convinced that in the long run pursuasion will be more effective than injunction: "But we were gentle among you, like a nurse taking care of his children, so being affectionately desirous of you....You are witnesses, and God also, how holy and righteous and blameless was our behaviour to you believers, for you know how...we exhorted each one of you" (1 Thess 2, 7-12). And surprisingly, with disarming sincerity he will appeal even to his own weakness in which God himself is rendered present and manifest (2 Cor 11, 30). In sum, despite his indisputable authority, Paul persuades, exhorts, encourages or reproves — but he seldom commands. For, in spite of superficial appearances to the contrary, he is not at all a boastful man, his only glory and pride lie in the grace and mercy of God who has gratuitously called him both to Christianity and to the apostolate.

A particular reality is best known by the consideration of the goal or purpose to which it tends, and the exclusive purpose of authority is *diakonia* or service. There is no other reason for the very existence of authority except to serve those under authority. The Twelve are called in the Synoptics *douloi*, that is, servants, slaves of the faithful over whom they preside. Shortly before his death, when his earthly life is about to be snuffed out, Jesus gives a parting advice to the close circle of the Twelve to whom he has transmitted a share in the authority he himself received from his Father: "Those in authority over them (the Gentiles) are called benefactors. But not so with you....rather let...the leader (become) as one who serves....I am among you as one who serves" (Lk 22,25-27). Paul has imbibed this Christian spirit thoroughly: "For though I am free from all men, I have made myself a slave of all" (1 Cor 9,19).

Shortly, it is *exousia* for the sake of *diakonia*, authority for the sake of service. The nature and extension of Christian authority are determined by their goal and purpose, which is not to dominate but to serve. Service should always remain the controlling factor of authority. Any form of authority that oversteps the boundaries of service to the community is already questionable because it is no longer Christian.

This rather peculiar nature of Christian authority is counterbalanced by a profound respect for the dignity of the individual. When reading the Bible at times one has the impression that God has almost put aside the usual channels of authority so as to deal directly with the individual. There are a number of biblical passages that unfortunately have been played down in the Catholic tradition, so very conscious always of the God-given authority possessed by office-holders. As God's spokesman Jeremiah is announcing the new Covenant in which God will deal directly with his People: "I will put my law within them and I will write it upon their hearts; and I will be their God and they shall be my people. *And no longer shall each man teach his neighbour*...For all shall know me, from the least of them to the greatest" (Jer 31,33-34). In later times this prophecy is combined with a similar announcment by Isaiah: "All your sons shall be taught by the Lord"

(Is 54,13). God will intervene directly with each and everyone of the chosen People: "I will put my Spirit within you" (Ez 36,27). Does the Christian still need the person in authority above him when he has the Holy Spirit within him?

This tradition of God's direct dealings with each individual is carried over into the New Testament and emphasized even further: "You have no need that anyone should write to you, *for you yourselves have been taught by God* to love one another" (1 Thess 4,9). John is of the same opinion: "The anointing... abides in you, *and you have no need that anyone should teach you*" (1 Jn 2,27).

These texts are explicit, they are embarrassing and, if taken in isolation, they could be dangerous. But they should be quoted at some length, for they lay stress on a dimension that has perhaps been overlooked in the Catholic tradition. They certainly do not give a global, comprehensive picture of the dealings of God with men, but they constitute one aspect — and an exceedingly important aspect — of the whole. A proper biblical synthesis must take this trend into account, absolutely.

Not only is the Christian directly taught by God, he is also endowed with the rather disturbing gift of *parresia*, boldness, freedom of speech, sincerity, outspokenness. This refers to the dealings with God and man, and comprehensively it could be defined as "the unhampered and joyful word both in prayer and in dealings with men".[7] Boldness with God is the freedom of a heart which is always open to God, free to say anything to him in prayer; and similarly boldness with men is the candour of free speech, of open sincerity towards men and women. Both these forms of boldness are to be found in the heart that is indwelt by the Spirit, who is the Spirit of transparency, sincerity, truth and freedom.

Biblical writers seem to consider *parresia* as a very precious gift bestowed by the Spirit on the Christian, a gift which should be the object of intense petitionary prayer, as is clearly shown in a remarkable, if seldom quoted, passage from Acts. Peter and John have just been released from jail, after being told by the Jerusalem religious authorities "to refrain from

7 H. Schlier, "Parresia", *Theological Dictionary of the New Testament*, V (Grand Rapids 1967), p. 883.

all public speaking" (Ac 4,18). Once relaesed, the two Apostles decide, quietly but firmly, to make use of their God-given freedom and disregard totally the injunction of the authorities. They return to their Christian friends and immediately all of them drift into prayer, a most peculiar, astonishing prayer: "'And now, O Lord, mark their threats and enable thy servants to speak thy word *with boldness* (*parresia*)'....The building rocked and all were filled with the Holy Spirit and spoke out the word of God *with boldness*" (Ac 4,29-31).

A truly extraordinary passage. The Jerusalem religious authorities, supposedly holding the place of God and conveying his holy will to the people, command Peter and John to keep their mouths shut and refrain from public speaking. But once released, the very first thing they do is break the command: in fact, they do exactly the opposite of what they have been commanded. And in this open conflict between the authorities and the two Apostles, the Holy Spirit clearly takes the side of Peter and John, who break the precept with divine approval. The only object of their ensuing prayer is contradictorily opposed to the injunction of the authorities: they will not keep quiet, they will not be silenced, they will proclaim the meassage of Jesus with *parresia*. The Holy Spirit descends on the entire group of the disciples in a kind of mini-Pentecost and makes the whole building rock. Boldness of speech and action bears clearly the seal of the Spirit.[8]

b) *An unavoidable, healthy tension*

And so the New Testament has sown the seeds of an unavoidable tension between the *exousia* of authority and the *parresia* of the individual. As often happens with the New

8 This is not the only passage where *parresia* or boldness is extolled as a gift of the Holy Spirit. In fact, Luke mentions it repeatedly in other places as well, especially in connection with the Church's missionary expansion as narrated in Acts. In view of this explicit and repeated scriptural backing, it is hard to understand that short-sighted form of spirituality found in so many religious houses of women who wrongly decry boldness as a dangerous defect in religious life to be corrected, usually in the younger members. Have these people ever read and pondered over the book of Acts, I wonder? Boldness, if well understood, is not only not a defect to be suppressed, it is rather a precious gift to be sought in prayer.

Testament, there is not the slightest attempt at a synthesis, both the sides run parallel, legitimate authority and bold, irrepressible freedom. The conflict seems to be simply unavoidable, and yet in reality there should be no conflict, no clash of any sort, for both sides hold briefs from the Holy Spirit, both are his precious gifts to the Christian community. For if it is true that the ultimate source of legitimate authority is God, it is not less true that the ultimate foundation of Christian freedom is also the Spirit of God. Hence, the tension can only be transcended when both those in authority and those under authority are governed by the same Holy Spirit.

But should we really transcend this tension or rather live with it? For tension is often a sign of life, and since the Church is a living organism, it is unavoidable and not necessarily a defect to be deplored, that a certain tension should exist within her between the two poles of authority and freedom. Perfect peace and complete lack of tension could mean either that a harmonious balance between the two sides has been reached, or that one of the two poles has prevailed over the other. Tensions are not only unavoidable, they can be definitely healthy — provided they are the right kind of tensions.

A healthy tension should start off by recognizing that freedom is not a concession by authority, for freedom exists in the Christian prior to the exercise of authority. Those in authority can only restrain and control that freedom, but they cannot grant it, for it is granted directly by God himself. Similarly authority is not man-made but God-given. The supreme origin of both the poles of this tension lies in the Spirit. On the other hand, and in spite of their exalted origin, neither authority nor freedom can be unlimited, for unlimited authority would spell dictatorial authoritarianism, just as unlimited freedom would result in abselute anarchy, and both these extremes are obviously to be avoided, as being entirely foreign to the Spirit.[9]

9 I have seen in some religious communities a subtle form of authoritarianism that hides behind the mask of concern and solicitude. The deplorable practice of certain religious Superiors of referring often to their charges as "the little ones",

Freedom is to be restrained by authority and authority by freedom. It is only this mutual check and restraint, based on mutual respect, that will produce a healthy tension. Where the point of restraint is to be placed is a matter of experience and mutual agreement, for a unilateral decision in this matter would inevitably tilt the balance unduly in favour of authority or of freedom, and this would in turn mean the replacement of mutual respect by mutual suspicion. A healthy tension demands strength on both sides. "Weak persons in authority and strong persons under authority would almost automatically mean that internecine strife exists. Yet it is also true that strong persons in authority and weak persons under authority leads to the corruption of freedom and responsibility and the relaxation even of a healthy tension".[10] A rope can be kept taut only when both sides pull strongly in opposite directions; if the rope begins to dangle it is an unmistakable sign that one of the two sides has been overpowered by the other.

A concrete means to produce and keep up this salutary tension is the free exercise of public opinion, whereby authority is confronted with freedom. The introduction of this principle into the life of the Church has been decried by some as a surrender on the part of the Church to the spirit of the world. For what has the spirit of the world — and of worldly politics at that — to do with the Spirit of God? Plenty. For salvation is essentially social, communitarian, and therefore it stands to reason to consider the ecclesial community as one of the channels of transmission through which light pours into the Church. Why should the Spirit choose only single individuals as signs of his presence and transmitters of his light, rather than full Christian communities?

In any case the absolute necessity of public opinion in the Church was openly recognized already in 1950 by Pope Pius XII in a famous speech to an international gathering of Catholic writers: "Whenever there is no manifest expression of public opinion at all, and above all, whenever one must

no matter what their age, should be unmasked and denounced for what it is: an irresponsible abuse of authority, which willy-nilly fosters in those under authority a corresponding spirit of infantilism that is poles apart from true Christian maturity.

10 J. McKenzie, *Authority in the Church* (London 1966), p. 165.

admit that public opinion does not exist at all, this lack must be regarded as a fault, a weakness and a disease in the life of that society....There would be something lacking in her life if there were no public opinion in the Church—a lack for which the pastors as well as the faithful would be to blame".[11] More recently and in the same vein Vatican II also stated: "Every layman should reveal to them (the bishops) his needs and desires, with that freedom and confidence which befits the son of God....An individual layman...*is permitted and sometimes even obliged* to express his opinion on the things that concern the good of the Church".[12]

We should not be satisfied with positing the general principle, we should also examine its implications, even if they are somewhat unsettling for some. The expression of public opinion with regard to authority is necessarily ambivalent, for by its very nature it may imply approval as well as criticism. "Public opinion in the Church, if it is limited to enthusiastic approval of all hierarchical and pastoral decisions, has as much meaning as an election in Russia".[13] Just as authority can control freedom and keep it within bounds, so also can freedom exercise a necessary restraint on authority — through, among other means, the responsible use of public opinion. In the last analysis harmony and equilibrium between the two poles will be kept only if those in authority as well as those under authority humbly acknowledge that neither of the two sides has the monopoly of the Spirit. Authority should recognize, not only in theory, but also in practice, that the Spirit dwells and acts in the individual, just as the individual should also acknowledge that the person in authority too is the temple of the Spirit and the legitimate transmitter of his wishes. The only person who has no restraint is the Spirit himself, and he exercises his unlimited freedom by speaking to the individual through authority, and to authority through the voice of the individual.[14]

11 *Acta Apostolicae Sedis* 42 (1950), pp. 251, 256.

12 *Lumen Gentium*, 37: W. Abbott, *The Documents of Vatican* II, p. 64.

13 J. McKenzie, *Authority in the Church*, p. 171.

14 At the moment of writing (November 1986) we are all aware of the open conflict in the American church between moral theologian Charles E. Curran and the Roman Congregation for the Doctrine of the Faith. Even deeper

Authority and freedom may have to live always in a certain degree of tension, but this tension is bound to evolve because freedom is bound to grow. The Christian is not given this freedom as a treasure full and complete from the start. The plant of Christian freedom keeps growing. Freedom is less a gift than it is a task, a vocation, a call beckoning man forward into the future. Freedom is not a privilege to be enjoyed, but rather a task to be fulfilled. Man is condemned to freedom, he is bound in conscience to make it expand and grow, to develop it unto the fullness of maturity. The attainment of a fully developed freedom is an unmistakable sign that man has reached his Christian perfection.

3) The clear conscience of the Christian

On the other hand, a fully developed freedom results in a fully developed conscience. The exercise of Christian freedom requires the light of the Spirit, since freedom from the law can in no way be identified with lawlessness or licentiousness. The free man has a conscience to follow, a conscience illumined by the Spirit. In fact , light pours into the sacred sanctuary of man's conscience from two different sources: the voice of the Spirit dwelling in him, and the external voice of authority. The inner recesses of man's conscience are brightened with light streaming in from these two open windows, and he can keep either of them shut only to his own personal detriment. The Spirit reaches the conscience of the Christian through these two channels, either directly from within or indirectly from without, from external authority. Exclusive insistence on the internal voice of the Spirit to the neglect of external authority would obviously issue into dangerous

and more fundamental than the concrete moral issues involved, is the right and duty of the competent theologian to dissent from official teaching if there are sufficient grounds for it. Curran's license to teach has been withdrawn, and therefore Rome has won the first round, but the unequal match still continues. In the midst of all the dust raised by the controversy which is still raging in the U.S., it is not easy to discern the voice of the Spirit. In this case the assumption that the Spirit speaks more distinctly through the channels of central authority would be as gratuitous and arbitrary as the dangerous illusion that individual theologians are untouchable *prima donnas* beyond the reach of authority. Only time will show where the action of the Spirit lies.

subjectivism, for man would run the risk of mistaking his own wishes for the wishes of the Spirit or vice versa, just as an exclusive preoccupation with authority — on the plea of playing safe — to the neglect of the interior voice of the Spirit coming from man's own heart would lead to dead legalism,

Both these avenues of access to man's conscience should be kept open to the Holy Spirit, and the blocking of either of them would be a splendid means "to quench the Spirit" (1 Thess 5,19). "A Christian is a man who follows his conscience illuminated both by the teachings of the Church and by the inner light of faith, both of these sustained, guided and confirmed by the divine illumination of the Spirit".[15]

Conscience is the necessary means by which the promptings of the Spirit are manifested to the individual. Docility to the Spirit is nothing but submission to one's own conscience illumined by the Spirit, but on the other hand, the humble, sincere listening to the voice of authority is also absolutely essential for the right discernment of the voice of the Spirit prior to submission to his voice. For authrrity is a legitimate way set up by the Spirit in order to shape and form the conscience of the faithful: "In the formation of their conscience the Christian faithful ought carefully to attend to the sacred and certain doctrine of the Church", says Vatican II.[16] This is nothing but a faithful echo of the New Testament: "By the open statement of the truth we would commend ourselves to every man's conscience in the sight of God" (2 Cor 4,2).

Internal coherence and peaceful agreement between conscience and authority is of course the ideal, but it cannot be denied that often enough the reality of Christian life is a little more complicated than that. An open clash between these two possible voices of the Spirit, conscience and authority, should obviously be avoided as far as possible. The Spirit cannot possibly speak contradictory language to the individual, and therefore if these two voices do not convey the same message, if they do not speak in unison, it means that one of the two is obviously wrong and it may not be easy to dicide in practice which of the two is at fault.

15 P. Fransen, "Grace and freedom", *Homiletic and Pastoral Review* 65 (1964/65), p. 745.

16 *Dignitatis Humanae*, 14: W. Abbott, *The Documents of Vatican II*, p. 694.

In this case a priori assumptions in favour either of authority or of the individual conscience should find no place in the solution of the conflict. Authority should take with the utmost seriousness the opinion of the individual even when it happens to disagree with its own, for it could well be that the Spirit is thereby asking the person in authority to rectify his or her mistaken opinion which does not tally with the opinion of the Spirit. The office-holder should be open to the voice of the Spirit even when it comes from below, from the individual concerned who is, after all, indwelt and acted upon by the Holy Spirit. The gratuitous assumption that the Spirit communicates his wishes always and exclusively through the channels of authority would be perilous. For the function of authority is to humbly listen to and faithfully convey to the individual the good wishes of the Spirit, not to quench them by forcing them into fixed, stereotyped channels.

But, on the other hand, the individual should also be under no illusion. Appeals to one's own conscience against the decisions of legitimate authority may on occasion be justified, for the Christian may never — *never* — act against his or her conscience, even when this conscience is objectively mistaken and not properly formed. The individual Christian may be accutely conscious that the Spirit has made him his own privileged temple, that he ought always to listen and be sensitive to the good pleasure of the Spirit who has possessed him entirely and now dwells within him uniterruptedly. After all — he can rightly claim — the Holy Spirit is much closer to him than the external source of authority, and that seems to entitle him in cases of conflict to give preference to the interior voice of his conscience over that of authority. For he is keenly aware that to carry out the injunctions of authority blindly, on the ground that it is God's representative even when issuing a wrong order, would be too facile a solution and a splendid way to stifle the voice of the Spirit.

All this the individual knows and lives out in his daily life, but with true Christian realism he should also accept that in his area the danger of self-deception is great. He should sincerely acknowledge before God that it is easy to masquerade one's own selfish wishes as the wishes of the

Holy Spirit "who speaks to his conscience from within". Here particularly it is true that, as the British say, "the wish is father to the thought". We can always give our own selfish wishes a certain veneer of credibility by attributing them to the Holy Spirit. We have seen in chapter six above that the Spirit speaks to the Christian very often through the voice of others, and therefore a fortiori through the voice of authority. This avenue is also open to the Spirit, and this is something the Christian can ignore at his own risk.

Yet, after all is said and done, it should be clearly stated that if protracted dialogue, consultation and intense prayer have been unable to resolve the conflict between authority and conscience, *conscience should prevail over authority*. Authority would be seriously wrong in forcefully bending a reluctant conscience to itself. If, despite the undoubtedly good intention on both sides, the discrepancy of views persists, the holder of authority should give conscience the benefit of the doubt and yield to it. In this case imposition of raw, naked power from above would be both irresponsible and clearly un-Christian. The individual conscience has finally prevailed, but this should remain an exceptional solution of comparatively rare occurrence. Normally the conscience of the Christian should incorporate and assimilate the external norms of authority so as to become a truly enlightened Christian conscience. Conscientious objectors should be the exception, not the rule.[17]

4) Light and shadows

Stephen, the first Christian martyr, must have been as fiery a character as Saul who watched his martyrdom,

17 The conscientious objector constitutes a delicate case, difficult to handle. The principle is applicable to political and military life (the Vietnam war had its share of conscientious objectors among the American servicemen) as well as to the sphere of obedience in religious life. To appeal to the testimony of one's conscience when confronted with an unpleasant order is undoubtedly a very easy and comfortable solution to bend the Superior's wishes to one's own. If prayer, dialogue and the mediation of a third party have failed to bring about a reconciliation of views, the Superior should yield, "but a man who time after time is unable to obey with a good conscience, should consider some other path of life in which he can serve God with greater tranquility" (*Documents of the 31st General Congregation of the Society of Jesus*, Anand 1967, p. 74). Such a man does not seem to be meant for religious life.

for according to the narrative of Luke in Acts, shortly before he surrendered his life to God he is supposed to have castigated severely his Jewish executioners: "You stiff-necked people... you always resist the Holy Spirit" (Ac 7,51). It would surely be exaggerated to say that the Christian always resists the Holy Spirit — and here we must make an allowance for Stephen's rhetorical language — but, on the other hand, who will deny that all of us occasionally oppose the Spirit's wishes and are opaque to his light?

The luminous liberty of the children of God is a splendid reality, no doubt, but it is only one side of the total picture. It is surely reasonable to emphasize the positive rather than the negative, to be attracted by the light, rather than by darkness. And yet one should, above all, be realistic: man is a strange creature, he is but a chiaroscuro, a perpetual blend of light and shadows. Human freedom is necessarily ambivalent, and its missuse by man remains always a distinct possibility. Our Lutheran brothers are fond of repeating that we Christians are simultaneously saints and sinners, and this paradoxical formula contains a huge grain of truth, for the son of God is a citizen of two worlds, enjoying the presence of the Spirit and feeling deep down within himself the constant allurement of sin; experiencing both the gentle touch of the Spirit and the caress of sin; longing for God with unquenchable thirst and coveting the transient pleasures of sin. In a word, he is at once bathed in the splendour of God and enveloped in the surrounding darkness of sin.

It is this inconsistency in man that is beautifully described in the following prayer of the Oriental mystic St Symeon the New Theologian:

> I thank you that you, even when I was sitting in darkness, revealed yourself to me, you enlightened me, you granted me to see the light of your countenance that is unbearable to all.
>
> I remained seated in the middle of the darkness, I know, but while I was there, surrounded by darkness, you appeared as light, illumining me completely from your total light.
>
> And I became light in the light, I who was found in the midst of darkness. Neither the darkness extiguished your

> light completely, nor did the light dissipate the invisible darkness, but they were together, yet completely separate, without confusion, far from each other, surely not at all mixed, except in the same spot where they filled everything. . . .
>
> So I am in the darkness, yet still I am in the middle of the light.
>
> How can darkness receive within itself a light and, without being dissipated by the light, it still remains in the middle of the light?.[18]

The possession of the Spirit by man is always subject to the uncertainties of his rebellious will and the vagaries of his heart, for "we have this treasure in earthen vessels" (2 Cor 4,7), fragile and breakable. The permanence of concupiscence in the Christian as long as he lives can be the source of continuous infidelities to the Spirit. Man's endowment of the Spirit is not yet final, it is rather subject to the fickleness and instability characteristic of human nature. For, although the life of the faithful unfolds in the power of the Spirit, we still "groan inwardly, as we wait for. . . the redemption of our bodies" (Rom 8,23). Our Christian life "is made up of absence as much as of presence, of promise not less than of possession, of fear as much as of confidence".[19] This is man's concrete existential situation. We are saved — but only in hope.

And precisely because we are saved only in hope, our life is deeply marked by the uncertainties characteristic of the pilgrim state. The Holy Spirit, despite his indwelling presence in man, does not transform him totally from the start; the Christian experiences gradual growth, painful struggles and occasional setbacks. His gaze is riveted on the final goal, but this goal is still beyond reach. The anchor of hope — a favourite symbol of the early Christians, visible still today in so many chambers of the impressive Roman catacumbs — gives man certain stability in the midst of stormy weather. It is curious to observe in Paul, on the one hand, the strong assertion that we possess a variety of gifts which come to us along with the Holy Spirit; and, on the

18 *Hymns of Divine Love*, hymn 24, as quoted by G. Maloney, *Invaded by God*, pp. 130-131.

19 J. Mouroux, *The Christian Experience*, p. 158.

other, the constantly repeated affirmation that we have these gifts only in hope. Contradiction? No way, for this reconciliation of opposites, of what we already have and of what we shall have; of present realities and future accomplishments, of present inception and future completion, is typical of the life of the Christian here and now. It is light and shadows once again, blended together....

So, for instance, Paul will say in a clear reference to baptism, "You were washed, you were sanctified, you were justified" (1 Cor 6,11): the Corinthians' sanctification is a thing of the past, attained at the moment of their baptism already; and yet, "through the Spirit, by faith, we wait for the hope of righteousness' (Gal 5,5). It is much the same with regard to sonship: "The proof that you are sons is that God has sent the Spirit of the Son into our hearts" (Gal 4,6); and yet this privilege of sonship seems to be still in the distant future, for "we ourselves who had the firstfruits of the same Spirit, groan inwardly as we wait for the adoption as sons" (Rom 8,23). Similarly, one would expect our glorification to be reserved exclusively for the future, but Paul seems to think differently, for on the one hand, "when Christ...appears, then you also will appear with him in glory" (Gal 3,4); you will appear at the time of his so-called second coming — in the future. But, on the other, "those whom he (God) justified, he also glorified" (Rom 8,30) — in the past. And again as regards our final resurrection, the Father "will give life to our mortal bodies also through his Spirit" (Rom 8,11); and yet, surprisingly, "God ...raised us up with him (Christ) and made us sit with him in the heavenly places" (Eph 2,6), as if our resurrection were already a thing of the past.

One couid possibly lengthen the list, but let the above examples suffice as an indication of Paul's mentality. Sanctification, sonship, resurrection, glorification: four realities intimately connected with the Holy Spirit which are at once the object of present possession and of future realization. They are present and yet they lie in the future. They are already possessed and not yet possessed, already enjoyed and still to be enjoyed, pointing simultaneously to an actual, real inception and to a future accomplishment. The profound reason for this state of affairs is that these four realities are but the flowering of the indwelling, its expansion in Christian life, and the indwelling is essentially marked by a certain incompleteness, a certain lack of fullness. For the Spirit is given us only as an *arrhabon*, a pledge, a down payment , not yet the full sum; as firstfruits, not yet as the full harvest. And this state of incompleteness we observe in the indwelling unavoidably colours also all the realities that spring from it. The root of the indwelling, though extremely precious in itself, has not yet reached the status of full maturity, it lacks perfection, it lacks fullness, and this state of underdevelopment, as it were, affects also the four branches that proceed from the same root. The indwelling of the Holy Spirit within the body of the Christian is an unbelievable, puzzling reality, and yet it is only a starting point, a beginning, and no more. This is the deep foundation of the Christian's peculiar status, of his essentially ambivalent position, at once glorious and fearful, dazzling and yet shadowy. For it all hinges on the indwelling, and the indwelling can be lost.

There are three fifth columnists living within the fortress of man that can play havoc to him: the incomplete nature of the indwelling, man's earthbound tendencies, and his ineradicable freedom of choice. If the three of them gang up and unleash a simultaneous attack on the citadel of the Christian he is sure to be in deep trouble.

That man is a continuous blend of light and shadows, that he is possessed by the Spirit and yet in the grip of the flesh, is nowhere better expressed than in Galatians 5,16-26, as we have already seen above. The Christian is a veritable battlefield where the Holy Spirit seems to be unable or unwilling to subjugate the flesh completely, for man's self-centredness and egotistic tendencies are too deeply rooted for that. The Spirit is, biblically speaking, the Spirit of power, and it is just as well, for the enemy he is confronting in man is not precisely weak. Since the indwelling has not yet blossomed out into full perfection, the Spirit's grip on man is somewhat precarious, and his sinful flesh is constantly urging him to break loose from the Spirit, "for the desires of the flesh are against the Spirit and the desires of the Spirit are against the flesh" (Gal 5,17).

Furthermore, to compound the difficulty we have to

reckon, not only with an imperfect indwelling and the constant drag of the flesh, but also with actual lapses into sin. The power of man's innate self-centredness is rendered visible when man is not only enticed by sin but actually succumbs to it. "If we say we have not sinned, we deceive ourselves, and the truth is not in us...If we say we have not sinned, we make him (Jesus) a liar..." (1 Jn 1,8-10). If the tendency to sin is universal, knowing of no exceptions, so are also the actual lapses into sin: "For we all make many mistakes..." (Jas 3,2). Jesus himself took all this for granted, for in repeating so often his own prayer we beg from God "forgive us our trespasses" (Mt 6,12). Notice that it is the faithful who are expected to pray this way, not only the sinner. And frequent request for divine forgiveness necessarily implies frequent sin.[20] How right was St Symeon when he said: "Neither the darkness extinguished your light completely, nor did the light dissipate the invisible darkness, *but they are together*...." As long as he lives, the Christian will be not only the son of God, but also the sinful son of God.

5) The possible loss of the indwelling

Man's liberty remains essentially unscathed by the ravages of original sin, but this liberty is the brittle carrier of the indwelling Spirit, constantly threatened by external allurements and internal propensities. The reality of sin, even of grievous personal sin, is too widespread to be denied; for all of us it is simply a matter of experience, either personal or pastoral. That the state of friendship with God can be destroyed by sin is a certain Catholic truth that hardly needs an explanation.[21]

It was Paul more than any other New Testament writer who waxed eloquent when writing in glowing terms about the reality of the indwelling of the Spirit, and yet, endowed

20 This scriptural teachig is echoed faithfully by the Council of Trent: "If any one says...that a man once justified can avoid all sins, even venial ones throughout his entire life...*anathema sit*" (Neuner-Dupuis, *The Christian Faith*, n. 1973).

21 The very same canon of the Council of Trent quoted above states also: "If anyone says that a man once justified cannot sin again and cannot lose grace...*anathema sit*" (Neuner-Duouis, *Ibid.*)

as he was with a profound sense of Christian sobriety and realism, Paul never failed to warn his readers not to be overconfident, for even treasures owned for a long time can be lost: "Let anyone who thinks that he stands take heed lest he fall" (1 Cor 10, 12). The famous passage from Galatians on the inner struggle between the Spirit and the flesh, repeatedly quoted above, ends with a salutary admonition: "I warn you, as I warned you before, that those who do such things shall not inherit the kingdom of God" (Gal 5,21) —which is tantamount as saying that they will be rejected by God as being deprived of his grace and his Spirit. Paul's message to the church of Rome comes back on the same fundamental principle: "If you live according to the flesh you will die" (Rom 8,13), and for Paul to die is not only to expire physically, but to reach the end of the pilgrimage in a state of enmity with God, not upheld by his Spirit from within.

It would be futile to continue labouring the obvious. The son of God remains free, the indwelling Spirit penetrates him deeply, to the very core of his being, but at the same time he leaves his freedom untouched, entirely unaffected. And precisely because his freedom is unaffected by the internal grip of the Spirit, man retains his dreadful privilege of turning against the Spirit and expelling him from his temple which is the heart of man. When a grievous sin is committed, it means that, momentarily at least, the Holy Spirit has been overpowered by man, that the Spirit no longer dwells in man.

Both scripturally and theologically the possibility of losing the indwelling is unambiguous, transparently clear, but it poses the pastoral difficulty of determining how and when this loss takes place. It is generally assumed that a single mortal sin is sufficient to make one lose the state of grace, bar him from the reception of the Eucharist, establish him in a state of enmity with God, and seriously endanger his eternal salvation. God's grace would be lost and, after due repentance, could be regained again. Man would be acquiring and losing sanctifying grace as he puts on and off a coat. Yet, this kind of quick and repeated transition from grace to sin and back, from light to darkness and back to light is clearly unsatisfactory, it is hardly believable. Man is endowed with far greater stability than this current explanation would make us believe. The real solution to the puzzle of these quick transitions lies elsewhere, in the psychological make-up of man.

a) *The multiple layers in man's freedom*

Man's freedom is an extremely complex reality. We are constantly making use of it and yet we hardly understand how it works, the forces that move it, its inner nature, its power and weakness, the internal contradictions that beset it. Man's freedom is like an ocean with an infinite number of layers, of currents and undercurrents that either move peacefully, making hardly a ripple on the outer surface, or churn forcefully the impenetrable depths of the ocean. There are innumerable levels of depth, but most of the activity takes place on the upper layers next to the surface, whilst the bottom of the ocean, which hardly ever stirs, usually remains dark, undisturbed, impenetrable.

Similarly, man's freedom is structured in a series of layers, outer, middle and inner, and it is deep down at the very bottom that he takes a radical decision, there that he makes a fundamental option for or against God. It is at this deep level that man constitutes himself as a lover of God or a selfish sinner. The centre of gravity in man's psychological structure is his *core freedom*, and it is by making use of this freedom, at the deepest possible level of his personality, that he takes his destiny into his own hands and decides for or against God. This fundamental option which springs from man's core freedom is a general orientation of his life, a sort of spiritual climate in which he lives and acts, a radical tendency that dominates and colours his entire life.

This is the bottom of the ocean which is man, and it is here, at the deepest possible layer, that man makes this radical, fundamental option. It is here, at these unfathomable depths that, through a deep, personal act of living faith and active love, he tends to God with his whole being, that he honestly and sincerely decides to cling to God. If so, he is clearly sanctified and transformed by the indwelling person of the Holy Spirit. It is this radical decision for God, taken at this particular level of depth, that brings about the presence of the Spirit. For the Spirit delights to dwell in the depths of man, not in the outer surface. Once man has cast his anchor into God, he has a "reborn dynamism of life that arises in the depth of his being thanks to the growing power of the divine indwelling".[22]

But man's freedom being essentially ambivalent, it is also here, at this deep level of his personality that he can turn against God, choosing self in preference to God. In this case his self-centredness has prevailed, for the Holy Spirit is totally absent from such unilateral self-destructive decision. Man is now in total darkness, as impenetrable as the bottom of the ocean which is never pierced by light.

In both these possibilities, for or against God, man's core freedom is involved. It is here, at the deepest layer of his personality that man has opened up to the irruption of God's transforming love, or blindly closed himself up in an act of self-destruction. But either way he remains free. His core freedom at such a deep level can be activated only by himself, for no outer force can penetrate him to such depths. It is a dreadful option he was faced with, and he has made his choice. It will not be easy to change it, for such depths are not easily reached, such a fundamental option in either direction, for or aganist God, cannot possibly be subject to quick changes. Here, at the bottom of the ocean, quickly repeated transitions from light to darkness and back to light are hardly possible. There is a certain stillness, a certain stability and permanence at such depths that cannot be easily altered. At this level quick and easy fluctuations are just not possible.

But such depths are forbidding, impenetrable; let us climb to the upper layers closer to the surface. For man can and does exercise his freedom also in more superficial a manner, without necessarily taking his eternal destiny into his hands each and every time he acts. In other words, he can also act with his *peripheral freedom*, which is the true, genuine form of freedom that his engaged in most of our daily actions. The waters of the ocean, after all, are churned and stirred usually close to the surface, where most of the activity takes place.

Man is such a complex creature thaı it is quite possible

22 P. Fransen, *The New Life of Grace*, p. 103.

for him to be honestly and sincerely oriented towards God with his core freedom, and at the same time to act against God at the more superficial level with his peripheral freedom. Once man is turned towards God and once this tendency has been sealed and strengthened by the indwelling Spirit, all his other actions should logically be subsumed by this general orientation that marks him so deeply, but at times man is not a particularly logical creature. On occasion he may act simultaneously for and against God at two different levels of his freedom: at the bottom, he is definitely for God, he has not consciously changed his positive, fundamental orientation; but at the same time the waters in the upper layers are moving temporarily in the opposite direction. Man can "affirm God from the centre of his person and reject him from a more peripheral dimension of his person".[23] This looks almost contradictory and should logically not happen, but it is happening all the time.

b) *Sinfulness and sin*

Both the core freedom as well as the more superficial peripheral freedom tend naturally to manifest themselves in external acts, but these acts retain their value only as symbols of man's deeper orientation for or against God. They are like the little bubbles that come up to the surface from the depths of the ocean. Hence, moral goodness does not consist in the sum total of these acts, for they are only the external manifestation, the visible expression of man's inner, deeper attitude which has been built gradually. Visible currents on the surface are but the effect of much deeper undercurrents down below.

In the case of a negative, sinful fundamental option, it is the attitude itself, the tendency that is sinful, rather than the single acts that radiate from it like the spokes of a wheel. Properly speaking man is not sinful because he commits sin, rather he commits sin because he is sinful in the depths of his core freedom. In this case, sin is not something man can

23 B. Schüler, *Gesetz und Freiheit* (Düsseldorf 1966), p. 102, as quoted by J. Glaser, "Transition between grace and sin: fresh perspectives", *Theological Studies* 29 (1968), p. 265.

commit instantly, for no one can change suddenly his fundamental option for God into a fundamental option for sin. It is not the rivulets issuing from the spring, but the spring itself that is poisoned.

This conception of sinfulness and sin is quite in keeping with the biblical notion of the Covenant. From the biblical viewpoint sin is the rupture of the covenanted relationship between God and his People. The sinner sets up another relationship with someone other than God, he enters into a "covenant" which is but a caricature of the real Covenant with God. He has wilfully withdrawn from the Covenant of love and given a new orientation to his life. In the New Testament the Covenant has been interiorized by the indwelling of the Spirit and hence, when man voluntarily breaks the Covenant, he forfeits the indwelling. Yet there are sins and sins, and not every sin destroys the indwelling. "There is sin that is mortal" (1 Jn 5,16), namely, mortal in the Johannine sense that it destroys man's radical orientation towards God. This is a really mortal sin, a sin that kills the indwelling and other concomittant realities, for a radical, negative attitude against God taken in the depths of man's core freedom cannot coexist with the indwelling. Light and darkness cannot live together, for they are contradictorily opposed, mutually destructive.

Man's fundamental option towards God cannot be reversed by just one sinful act taken in isolation and performed in the twinkling of an eye. Each single act lacks the power to turn round man's deep-seated orientation towards God, for this tendency is too deep for a sinful act to reverse it. This general inclination is like the waters of a river flowing peacefully towards the ocean. There are, however, times when in a particular spot and due to a violent, but temporary whirlwind, the waters begin to flow up stream, in the opposite direction. Yet this anomaly will not last long. After a few minutes the massive strength of the general current flowing down stream will overpower the rebellious whirlwind, and so the waters in that particular spot will eventually be subsumed into the normal, general flow towards the ocean.

Maybe family life offers an even better example, for in it we are dealing, not with lifeless water but with personal relationships. Here is a couple very much in love, leading a perfectly normal, healthy family life. Everything is going smoothly, there are no dark clouds on the horizon. And then, suddenly, out of the blue a violent marital storm breaks out, tempers are frayed, patience is in short supply and mutual recriminations are flung angrily by the spouses at each other. The quarrel is certainly violent but mercifully it is short-lived, and it will very soon be forgotten, there will be sunshine again in the domestic skies. One single moment of disagreement, no matter how sharp and violent, cannot possibly destroy the deep marital bond based on genuine, selfless love, between husband and wife. The quarrel is unusual, it is exceptional and by itself, if taken in isolation, it simply cannot destroy the sincere, mutual current of love which drives husband and wife towards each other. The sharp quarrel was only a passing phenomenon, a temporary occurrence.

So also, the covenanted relationship between God and man cannot be destroyed by a single "mortal sin". In a moment of weakness a Christian may yield to the downward pull of the flesh, but taken by itself, this single sinful act, usually performed with man's peripheral freedom, does not have sufficient power to change man's fundamental orientation towards God which engages his deeper core freedom. The whirlwind will pass off and the marital quarrel will cease, but the general orientation will continue. Just one sinful act does not seem to be capable of destroying the indwelling and turning man's general direction towards God into a general trend against him. This is, generally speaking, simply not possible.[24]

Yet, one should be cautious and realistic. Each sinful act may not, by itself, destroy the indwelling and the life of grace in the Christian, but it should be like a red light of danger flickering in the distance. The danger of losing the

24 I deliberately say "generally speaking", for there are may be exceptions to the general rule. In the early Church there were certain sins like apostasy, murder and adultery (the "big three") that had to be submitted to the power of the keys, usually in an act of public penance, due to the gravity of the fault and the particular malice involved. Other sins, even those that today we would consider mortal, but which spring from weakness rather than malice, were forgiven by the Church often enough in the course of an eucharistic service.

indwelling is still remote, but if the same sinful act is repeated over and over again, the remote danger may become proximate. For, after all, the mere repetition of acts creates a habit, and a sinful habit is already dangerously close to a negative orientation against God. The indwelling is in danger, and if the repeated warnings of the red light go unheeded, the Holy Spirit will, sooner or later, walk out of the temple. The Christian should not unnecessarily play with fire.

Hence, in order to judge the morality of a particular act, one should consider the personal disposition of the individual, the degree in which his freedom is engaged, more than the objective sinfulness of the act itself. This is no weakening of morals, but rather a realistic reassessment of the dreadful reality of sin. For this conception is like a two-edged sword: if man's fundamental option against God (and the indwelling which goes along with it) cannot easily be lost, the same holds good for the sinner who tries to reorient himself again towards God. If sin is a general attitude more than an act, repentance is also an attitude. Neither sin nor repentance from sin can be attained quickly, for both imply that man commits his core freedom either way and changes his orientation radically, and this, though possible, is not easy. A quick transition from darkness to light and back to darkness is not so difficult when only our peripheral freedom is involved (and only this type of freedom is engaged in most cases), but man's fundamental option has a certain stability which is not subject to sudden fluctuations.

The conclusion from all the above is that the indwelling of the Holy Spirit and all the other realities that go along with it, like sanctifying grace, immanence in the risen Christ, divine sonship etc. are lost by man only when his fundamental orientation towards God is changed radically in the opposite direction, when the goal of his endeavours is no longer God but someone or something other than God. The Holy Spirit will not lose his grip on man so easily, for a really mortal sin in the sense explained, namely, as destructive of the indwelling, is probably not such a common occurrence as some people imagine. God's love for man, manifested in the reality of the indwelling, is far greater than man's self-destructive capabilities.

BIBLIOGRAPHY

Henry, A.: *The Holy Spirit* (London 1960), pp. 118-138.

Lyonnet, S.: "St Paul: liberty and law", *The Bridge* 4 (1961) 229-252.

Spicq, C.: *St Paul and Christian Living* (Dublin 1964), pp. 56-84.

Fransen, P.: "Grace and Freedom", *Homiletic and Pastoral Review* 65 (1965) 731-754.

Fransen, P.: "Man and freedom", in J. Alfaro, others, *Man before God* (New York 1966), pp. 68-89.

McKenzie, J.: *Authority in the Church* (London 1966).

Küng, H.: *The Church* (London 1967), pp. 150-162.

Cerfaux, L.: *The Christian in the Theology of St Paul* (London 1967), pp. 452-460.

Murray, R.: "Authority and the Spirit in the New Testament" in J. Dalrymple, others, *Authority in a Changing Church* (London 1968), pp. 12-38.

O'Shea, K.: "The reality of sin: a theological and pastoral critique", *Theological Studies* 29 (1968) 241-259.

Glaser, J.: "Transition between grace and sin: fresh perspectives", *Theological Studies* 29 (1968) 260-274.

Fransen, P.: *The New Life of Grace* (London 1969), pp. 231-272.

Rahner, K.: "Justified and sinner at the same time", *Theological Investigations* 6 (1969) 218-230.

Maguire, D.: "The Spirit and Church Authority", in D. Callahan, ed., *God, Jesus, Spirit* (New York 1969), pp. 330-348.

Guillet, J., others: "Liberté", *Dictionnaire de Spiritualité* 6 (1976) 779-838.

Rahner, K.: *Meditations on Freedom and the Spirit* (London 1977), pp. 75-115.

Callahan, S.: "Conscience reconsidered", *America*, 1 November 1986, pp. 251-253.

Chapter Ten

THE CHARISMATIC SPIRIT

There are fashions in theology and spirituality, just as there are fashions in dress. Nowadays the "in thing", bandied about in season and out of season, is the charismatic dimension of the Church. This is something that had unfortunately been kept in the shadows for centuries and which, after Vatican II, seems to have burst upon the Church almost suddenly. It seems to give certain people a good deal of satisfaction to speak of the charismatic Church, of charismatic leaders, not only in the religious but even in the political sphere; of charism retreats in religious communities, of the need to take a "prophetic stand" in certain situations, of the Charismatic Renewal, of the gift of tongues, present now as much as in the early Church, of baptism in the Spirit, of charismatic retreats, of charismatic meetings....

Endless talk about charisms fills the air, but this loose and constant reference to charisms at every opportunity seems to have brought on a sort of "charismania", which in turn has led to "a kind of inflation in the theological sphere resulting in a devaluation of the currency".[1] The fairly general conspiracy of silence against charisms we have suffered for centuries is certainly to be deplored, but this widespread and uncritical use of alleged charisms seems to be in danger of becoming but a fashionable slogan. On the whole the present reawakening of this charismatic consciousness in the Church is surly to be welcome, but if we are to avoid turning

1 E. O'Connor, *The Pentecostal Movement* (Notre Dame 1971), p. 226.

it into a passing fad we should be far more critical and discriminating in the use of the term "charism". "All that glitters is not gold" said Shakespeare long ago, and the very same principle applies now to this sudden explosion of charismatic talk in the contemporary Church.

Possibly one of the reasons why this constant talk of charisms has caught on so well in our contemporary culture is the fact that this charismatic consciousness bears a marked affinity to the ideal of democracy, cherished today all the world over. Gone is the time when the Church was, for all practical purposes, identified exclusively with the hierarchy, the enormous mass of lay people being but "the children of holy mother the Church", whose only task was to obey the clear directions issued by an enlightened hierarchy. In a sharp, in certain quarters almost violent reaction against this false conception, the laity have become increasingly conscious of possessing charisms of their own which can by no means be reduced to passive compliance with the directives coming from above.

There is a widespread realization nowadays that the Church is not precisely a monarchy divinely ordained in a pyramidal structure from pope down to bishops to priests to lay people. The Church is the entire People of God, all are baptized, all are sons and daughters of God, all are indwelt by the same Holy Spirit, all are endowed with charisms. There is a certain air of equality and fraternity pervading the Church today; a spirit of democracy seems to have replaced the previous monarchical conception, and one of the elements that foster this democratic mentality is precisely the acute consciousness that charisms are not restricted to the hierarchy, that the charismatic effusion — and, according to some, profusion — of charisms affects not only the hierarchy, above, but the entire People of God. In past centuries and until comparatively recent times, the conception of the Church followed the political model of the then prevailing monarchies, and so also now we seem to be bending over backwards to follow the present political model of democracy. This may be an added reason why this unrestricted talk of charisms, with its inherent levelling power, is so very welcome in our contemporary Church.

In addition to this general spirit of democracy or power by the people, we seem to be today acutely conscious and highly appreciative of the social or communitarian dimension affecting any problem under consideration. Exclusively individualistic attitudes no longer carry the day, it is the community that prevails. Within this communal framework charisms seem to fulfil a felt need, for they have a strictly communitarian dimension or goal, as they are given by the Spirit primarily for the upbuilding of the community of the Church rather than for the sanctification of the individual. Charisms are communal gifts which, though possessed by an individual, in a certain way belong to the community. In other words, charisms have an essentially ecclesial function to perform.

1) A GRADUAL CHARISMATIC EXPANSION

Much of this recurrent talk of charisms seems to arise from lack of precision. We keep hearing that Pope John XXIII was a charismatic figure — which is almost certainly true, despite some rather obvious shadows both in his character and in his papal ministry — that John F. Kennedy was a charismatic president, that Indira Gandhi had a charisma of her own, that Martin Luther King exercised a charismatic role in the fight for human brotherhood and peace. Loose talk. And yet accepted by many, which goes to show that the contours of this particular gift called charism have become somewhat blurred and indistinct.

In an attempt at precision, and exclusively from the scriptural point of view, charism could be defined as God's call to individual persons with a view to a specific service within the community, including the ability to perform this service. The reception of a charism should be in reality a very sobering, humbling experience, for the recipient is but a channel of transmission through which the gift pours from the Spirit into the community. Charisms are not primarily given as a means to sanctify the individual, for in granting them God has rather the community in mind. God selects an individual and enriches him or her with one or more particular charisms in order to reach and influence the community — any community, religious or ecclesial — to which the charismatic belongs. When granting the charism God is not primarily interested in the single charismatic, but rather in the surrounding community. One may enjoy speaking of the liberating force of charisms, but the fact remains that, as we shall see further down, the reception of a charism can be an extremely painful experience.

The ability to perform the particular service to which the charismatic is called need not always be strictly supernatural, for a genuine charism can in itself be nothing but a natural capacity which is subsequently energized by the Holy Spirit for the purpose of building up the Church. Hence a natural talent — let us say, a rich character endowed with the innate qualities of a leader — is, strictly speaking, not yet a charism, but only the raw material which will turn into a charism proper when it is subsumed by the Holy Spirt for a supernatural purpose. Fiery tempers and strong characters like John the Baptist and specially Paul of Tarsus had a temperamental richness that was later utilized by the Spirit for the sake of the surrounding community. Natural talents and inborn dispositions are huge blocks of granite that may eventually be hewn by the Spirit for the building up of the Christian community.

But let us turn specifically to the Bible. The Holy Spirit is portrayed biblically as the Spirit of life and vitality and power — and yet he can be dreadfully slow in the accomplishment of this salvific designs. It is still an open, controversial question, whether the indwelling of the Holy Spirit is a strictly christological gift given at Easter for the first time, or rather an Old Testament reality that was only intensified rather than created on Easter Sunday. Probably we shall never know with certainty and it really does not matter too much. But when we turn from the indwelling to charisms, all doubt vanishes: there were truly charismatic figures in the Old Testament as well as in the New. Charisms of the Spirit are definitely not an exclusive privilege of the Christian era.

But the appearance and especially the expansion of these charisms was a painfully slow process. The Holy Spirit seems to have taken his own sweet time to make his charismatic presence felt in the world. By taking a bird's-eye view of the entire landscape of salvation history, one can clearly discern the lines of a gradual development, a slow but steady progress towards the final goal of a truly universal effusion of charisms on the entire community of humankind. The main stages in this expansion resemble the progressively widening ripples on the surface of a lake hit by a stone, ripples which will keep growing wider and wider until they reach the shore. For long centuries the charisms of the Spirit were reduced to the leaders of the community of Israel, whether religious or political; then the future Messiah was announced, to be endowed with the plenitude of charisms by the Spirit; the next ripple on the lake is the unfulfilled promise of a universal outpouring on the entire community of the People of God, not only on its leaders; then the promise is fulfilled and the pentecostal event takes place; and finally the Spirit's charismatic effusion reaches out even to those outside Christianity. Now the evolution is complete and the last ripple has reached the shore of the lake. But it has been an exasperatingly slow process of expansion which has taken centuries to complete. The Holy Spirit widens his activity gradually, securely, irresistibly, bursting through constrictions and juridical structures until the end of the evolution is reached, and what he had in mind from the beginning is finally accomplished.

First, the leaders. If there is a man in the history of the chosen People who towers head and shoulders above all the rest, it is surely Moses. Plucked out by an unexpected command of Yahweh from the bucolic surroundings of Median and sent in his old age to Egypt, he accomplishes the impossible, and under his leadership the People of God is born. Somewhere along the endless trek through the desert, with nothing to eat but manna, the rabble grumbles against Moses and Moses grumbles against God, for the task allotted to him seems to be beyond his strength, and poor Moses feels despondent, dispirited: "Where am I to get meat to give to all these people? For they weep before me and say, 'Give us meat that we may eat'. I am not able to carry all these people alone, the burden is too heavy for me'" (Num 11,13-14).

Yahweh listens to Moses' anguished complaint and answers his plea by supplying him with charismatic collaborators who will share the burden of leadership with him. Moses receives a divine command to meet the difficulty:

"Gather for me seventy men of the elders of Israel...and let them take their stand there with you...and I will take some of the spirit which is upon you and put it upon them; and they shall bear the burden of the people with you" (Num 11,16-17). Moses does as he is told and gathers the seventy elders around his tent. "Then the Lord came down from the cloud...and *took some of the spirit that was upon him and put it upon the seventy elders;* and when the spirit rested upon them, *they prophesied*" (Num 11,25). Subsequently pressure is brought to bear on Moses to stop two men from prophesying, on the ground that they did not belong to the group of seventy elders. But Moses will not yield to pressure: "Are you jealous for my sake? Would that all the Lord's people were prophets, that the Lord would put his Spirit upon them!" (Num 11,29).

A most remarkable episode, indeed. It is possibly the first clear manifestation of a charismatic outpouring on the recently constituted People of God. The Lord answers Moses's prayer through charisms, in the concrete with the particular and exceedingly precious gift of prophecy, understood in the classical biblical sense of oracle of Yahweh, rather than as a foreknowledge of the future. Moses is indirectly but clearly extolled as a mighty prophetic figure, for it is his spirit that overflows into the elders and makes them prophesy. Moses is no longer the only transmitter of the divine will, the only court of appeal, the only intermediary between the hungry, despondent people and Yahweh. Seventy other men share the same task under his leadership.

This first charismatic effusion was communitarian on two counts: it was given to a group of seventy men gathered together, almost as a sort of a distant rehearsal for the future pentecostal outpouring; and, specially, the charism of prophecy is given them for the sake of the people, to help Moses in his task of leading them to the Promised Land. The Spirit acts on the rulers for the sake of the ruled, to enable them to carry more easily the burden of government. Yet this charismatic effusion was not a permanent, but rather a transitory, intermittent gift: "When the Spirit came on them they prophesied, *but not again*" (Num 11,25). Apparently it was an *ad hoc* solution for a particularly difficult situation. Not all charisms are permanent, they are rather like the waters of the ocean that momentarily fill the caves on the seashore at high tide, and after a few hours, when the low tide sets in, withdraw again into the sea. It was meant to be but a temporary filling of the caves.

At unpredictable intervals, however, the waters return and fill the caves again. Now, the forty-year long desert experience of the People of God is about to come to an end and the Israelites reach the exceedingly beautiful valley of the Jordan and the oasis of Jericho, where they encamp. The people who had occupied the land for generations grow understandably wary when they see the Israelite refugees from Egypt descend on them like a swarm of locusts. They send for Balaam the prophet who does not belong to the chosen People, but God has no favourites: "And Balaam lifted up his eyes and saw Israel encamping tribe by tribe. And the Spirit of God came upon him" (Num 24,2). Both Jewish and non-Jewish leaders have received an outpouring of the Spirit of the Lord. Similarly a few years later, when the Israelites are under attack, God raises Gideon to rule and defend his People: "But the Spirit of the Lord took possession of Gideon..." (Judg 6,34).

Not only Israel's political leaders, but also and especially its prophets are endowed with the charismatic gift of the Spirit, who descends on them mightily. Ezechiel is a typical case,: "And the Spirit of the Lord fell upon me" (Ez 11,5); "and the Spirit lifted me up and took me away" (Ez 3,14). The vehemence of the Spirit's action is remarkable: "And the Spirit took me up...the Spirit also lifted me and brought me into Chaldea....The hand of the Lord was upon me and brought me forth in the Spirit of the lord....And the Spirit entered into me...and he set me upon my feet" (Ez 3,12; 8,3; 11,24). The Spirit fills the prophet to enable him to perform his task. It is, once again, a charism received by him for the sake of the people.

Something rather peculiar to this charismatic effusion on the leaders is that apparently it could be transmitted either by the laying-on of hands or by anointing. So, for instance, when Moses, 120 years old, dies on Mount Nebo, after gazing in front of him at the Promised Land across the Jordan, he is succeeded by Nun, who "was full of the spirit of wisdom, and Moses had laid his hands upon him" (Deut 34,9). And centuries later another mighty figure in Israelite history, king David, whose memory is cherished in Israel to this very day, was chosen by God and anointed king: "Then Samuel took the horn of oil and anointed him in the midst of his brothers; and the Spirit of the Lord came mightily upon David from that day forward" (1 Sam 16,13). The modality of transmission of the Spirit, whether by imposition of hands or by anointing, matters little, the important thing is to note that the Spirit is given only to the rulers, not yet to the community of the ruled. So far, the community is certainly the ultimate beneficiary for whose sake the charism is given, but not yet the direct recipient of the charism itself.

Among the leaders of Israel, however, none can compare with the future Messiah for profusion of charismatic gifts. Isaiah had already announced centuries before the coming of Jesus: "The Spirit of the Lord will rest upon him, the spirit of wisdom and understanding, the spirit of council and might, the spirit of knowledge and the fear of the Lord" (Is 11,2). The word used in the passage is *ruah*, spirit, breathing, inspiration, motion — in other words, charisms which will be poured profusely on the Messiah to enable him to perform his task. When the prophecy is fulfilled and Jesus, soon after his baptism in the Jordan, returns to his hometown of Nazareth and goes to the synagogue for the liturgical service of the sabbath, he picks up the roll of Isaiah's prophecy and applies the passage selected to himself: "The Spirit of the Lord is upon me, because it has anointed me to preach the good news to the poor... to proclaim relief to captives... to set at liberty those who are oppressed" (Lk 4,18). "To preach... to proclaim... to set at liberty": the objective and ultimate goal is always the community, the Messiah is endowed charismatically for the sake of the community. It would hardly be possible to express more forcefully that charisms are always given to a person for the sake of others.

Finally, after centuries of expectation, the Spirit reaches another stage in his charismatic expansion. Now it is not only the leaders that are the direct beneficiaries of the Spirit's effusion, but also the community itself. At first, this new stage is reached somewhat demurely, for it is not the outpouring itself that is accomplished, but rather the prophetic announcement of a future effusion that is made. Now the community makes its first timid appearance as the direct object of the Lord's charismatic largesse: "I shall pour out water on the thirsty land. . . . I shall pour out my Spirit on your descendants" (Is 44,3).

A very suggestive prophecy couched in poetical language, no doubt, but also somewhat vague, unspecified. However, once the community itself begins to hold the centre stage, subsequent prophecies regarding the outpouring of the Spirit become sharper, more precise. Joel is a case in point. In answer to the anguished cry of his People, God makes a promise of bountiful help: not only will their harvest be plentiful but, even more precious than corn and wine, the Spirit of the Lord will come down on the entire community, which will as a consequence become a community of prophets: "And it shall come to pass afterwards that I will pour out my Spirit on all flesh; your sons and your daughters will prophesy, your old men shall dream dreams, and your young men shall see visions. Even upon the menservants and maidservants in those days I will pour out my Spirit" (Jl 2,28-29).

Hereafter absolutely all will prophesy. The gift of prophecy, that is, the ability to read God's mind and interpret and announce it to the community, will no longer be restricted to a chosen few, it will rather be extended to the entire community regardless of sex, age and social status. All will have direct access to God thanks to the Spirit. The leaders have lost the monopoly of the Spirit which they had had for centuries, the gift of prophesy has now become a common and, in this sense, a very "democratic" gift that will be shared by the entire People of God.

The Old Testament makes no further progress, however. Even this bountiful outpouring of the Spirit is only announced, it is not yet realized. Four more centuries will roll by and the joyous announcement is still unfulfilled. Memories of the promise concerning this general charismatic effusion of prophecy begin to grow dim and, contrary to popular expectation, Israel has to do without prophets for centuries. In fact, for nearly half a millennium Israel goes dry and the waters of the Spirit no longer seem to run through her. The oasis has become a prophetic desert. Has Yahweh forgotten his promise? Whatever has happened to Joel's prophecy?

2) An explosion of charisms

In the prophetic field, a certain vagueness is very often a sign of genuineness. Prophecies that are exact and accurate as regards dates and historical circumstances are already suspect. It will be noticed that Joel's prophecy regarding the future outpouring of the Spirit had very blurred contours, it was vague and unspecified. No, God had not forgotten his promise, but he did not seem to be in a hurry to fulfil it, either. Sometime in the future the Spirit would come down mightily on the people, but not just yet. The New Testament tradition has interpreted Joel's prophecy as having been fulfilled on Pentecost day: "This is what was spoken by the prophet Joel.... I will pour out my Spirit upon all flesh" (Ac 2,16-17). Joel was a pointer to Pentecost, but we are already benefiting from hindsight.

Chronologically it would seem that the Christian Pentecost was the very first manifestation of the charismatic Spirit in New Testament times. Jesus had departed to his Father after enjoining the Eleven not to move from Jerusalem: "Stay in the city until you are clothed with power from on high" (Lk 24,49); "before many days you shall be baptized with the Holy Spirit" (Ac 1,5). Then came the sudden charismatic explosion of Pentecost, but in order to understand its import we need a brief flashback into the previous history of Israel, specifically into its desert experience.

Many of our Catholic faithful seem to imagine that Pentecost has been from the very beginning a typical, exclusively Christian feast. This is a grievous misconception, of course, for such a feast was already celebrated probably a full millennium before the Christian era. Passover and Pentecost were the two main liturgical feasts in the Jewish calendar, commemorating respectively two historical events: the deliverance from Egypt and the subsequent making of the Sinaitic Covenant. The Exodus, which blends together election, deliverance and Covenant, was the axis around which the entire history of Israel turned. Though extraordinarily important in themselves, neither the event of the

Exodus nor its liturgical celebration in the feast of the Passover will retain our attention now, for neither of them is directly related to the Spirit.

Moses had finally succeeded in breaking the shackles of the Israelites, Egyptian slavery. Under his leadership, "on the third new moon after the people of Israel had gone forth out of the land of Egypt, on that day they came into the wilderness of Sinai" (Ex 19,1). The vague expression "on the third new moon" was subsequently interpreted in Jewish tradition as 50 days after their deliverance from Egypt — hence the feast of *Pentekostê* (fifty, in Greek). Though the exact location of Sinai is still disputed, it is probably to be identified with the present Jebel Musa which rises majestically 7467 feet on the southern tip of the Sinai peninsula, between the two gulfs of Suez and Aqaba. It is there that the Sinaitic Covenant will be made between Yahweh and his chosen People, but prior to that, Exodus 19 records an extraordinary theophany or manifestation of Yahweh in the midst of a terrific mountain storm or perhaps even of a volcanic activity.[2]

The vivid description of the divine theophany resembles almost the account of an eyewitness: "On the morning of the third day there were thunders and lightenings, and a thick cloud upon the mountain, and a very loud trumpet blast, so that all the people who were in the camp trembled... And Mount Sinai was wrapped in smoke because the Lord descended upon it in fire;...and the whole mountain quaked greatly. And the sound of the trumpet grew louder and louder..." (Ex 19,16-19).[3]

2 The interpretation is uncertain, for in Exodus 19 there are traces of both. The opinion favouring the volcanic activity would seem to clash with the geographical location of southern Sinai, for there are no active volcanoes in that area. However, both the precise location where the theophany took place as well as the exact description of the historical occurrence are now for us of secondary importance, and need not detain us further. Cf. J. Huesman, "Exodus", in *The Jerome Biblical Commentary*, I, p. 56 and M. Noth, *Exodus* (London 1962), pp. 158-160.

3 Despite appearances to the contrary, however, the vividness of the description obviously does not come from an eyewitness; it is rather the result of an endless retelling of the story, trasmitted first orally from generation to generation. "Much of the description here, then, constitutes not a historical report, but

An awesome scenario, surely: lightening, smoke, clouds, *fire and wind*,as the suitable framework for the manifestation of Yahweh prior to the making of the Covenant. A purely natural phenomenon (mountain storm? volcanic eruption?) has been reflected upon and turned into a divine theophany. For our immediate purpose it is interesting to note that according to a popular interpretation of this passage among the rabbis, at the moment of the promulgation of the Law on Sinai the voice of Yahweh was heard by all the nations, dividing itself for this purpose into as many *languages* as peoples. Moreover, according to a Jewish tradition, on that occasion the voice came from the midst of *fire*, and was understood by all those present. The Jewish writer Philo states that "the voice of the Lord has appeared in *tongues of fire*".

Fire, wind, tongues. This interpretation of Exodus 19 had been common in the synagogue services for a very long time before the Christian era. Hence, the Lucan description of Pentecost will be nothing but a New Testament echo of the same tradition.

a) *The pentecostal effusion*

"Before many days you shall be baptized with the Holy Spirit" (Ac 1,5). How many days after the Ascension of Jesus did the descent of his Spirit take place? Fifty days — *pentekosté* — after Easter? We just do not know, but we would be well advised not to confuse liturgy and history. Liturgically we are all aware of the fifty-day gap between our two great feasts of Easter and Pentecost, but this is certainly artificial, no more than a convenient chronological framework for the Church to link both the solemnities. It really does not matter at all to know when exactly it all happened. The theological and spiritual content of Pentecost is far more important than the knowledge of the exact historical sequence of events.

rather a theological interpretation of the events as they were subsequently liturgically r-enacted for the people of Israel. . . .Some authors consider the trumpet blast (vv. 16, 19) to represent figuratively a mighty wind" (J. Huesman, "Exodus", p. 56).

"When the day of Pentecost had come, they were all together in one place. And suddenly a sound came from heaven like the rush of a mighty *wind*, and it filled all the house where they were sitting. And there appeared to them *tongues* as of *fire*, distributed and resting on each one of them. And they were all filled with the Holy Spirit and began to speak in other tongues, as the Spirit gave them utterance" (Ac 2, 1-4). Wind, tongues, fire again. Just like in the divine theophany on Sinai, only that now it is not the awesome presence of Yahweh that is announced, but the comforting outpouring of the Holy Spirit that is proclaimed. The recent promise made by the departing Jesus has been fulfilled, and the Church, filled with the Spirit, comes into existence.

It has often been remarked that Luke seems to establish a remarkable parallelism between the birth of Jesus and the birth of the Church, for in his conception both are characterized by the bountiful effusion of charismatic gifts. The persons that hover around the newly born Messiah are said to be under the influence of the Holy Spirit. For instance, May is told that the Holy Spirit "will come upon you" (Lk 1,35), her cousin Elizabeth "was filled with the Holy Spirit" (Lk 1,41), and similarly her husband Zechariah was also "filled with the Holy Spirit" (Lk 1,67). In the Jerusalem Temple the baby Jesus was lifted up by Simeon, the old man of whom it was said that "the Holy Spirit was upon him" (Lk 2,25). The Holy Spirit, so active at the time of Jesus' conception and birth, shows a similar activity at the moment of the Church's birth at Pentecost. He had acted charismatically then, and he acts charismatically now at Pentecost, though in a different manner.[4]

Pentecost was apparently the first instance, clearly attested, of a charismatic outpouring of the Spirit in the form of the

4 That the Church was born on the day of Pentecost is a common assumption. For instance, the preface for the feast of Pentecost reads: "Today we celebrate the great beginning of your Church"; and Vatican II indirectly affirms the same thing, cf *Ad Gentes* 4 (W. Abbott, *The Documents of Vatican II*, p. 588). However, this seems to be a reasonable theological construct rather than an historical occurrence. For it is the indwelling of the Spirit in the Church, not his charismatic action that should mark the beginning of the Church, and the indwelling started on Easter Sunday already, when the risen Jesus breathed on the gathered disciples and imparted to them the Holy Spirit.

gift of tongues. Christian literature, poetry and art have all waxed eloquent when referring to or graphically depicting this extraordinary phenomenon of the infant Church. We all celebrate joyfully the feast of Pentecost year after year, blissfully unaware of the serious difficulties involved in the understanding of the passage from Acts quoted above. For behind the cover of deceitfully simple language Luke conveys a rather complicated theology of his own.

Pious Jews and raw Christians that they were, the Eleven had gathered in Jerusalem for the celebration of the solemn Jewish feast of Pentecost, apparently "together with several women, including Mary the mother of Jesus and with his brothers" (Ac 1,14). Then the unpredictable Holy Spirit descends mightily on the entire group of Christians, men and women, when they least expected, filling them all and making them the first beneficiaries of the strange charismatic gift of tongues. From the Lucan narrative several things are clear, and some others are not. Luke describes a gift which is actually twofold, for it affects both the speakers as well as the listeners: "They began to speak in other tongues" (Ac 2,4), and on the other hand the multitude was "bewildered because each one heard them speaking in his own language" (Ac 2,6). Years later Paul will speak of the necessity of interpreting such a gift of tongues, so as to make it understandable to the audience, but no interpretation seems to have been necessary on Pentecost day, and here lies precisely the quasi-miraculous character of the event.

The gift of tongues. We too easily assume that this was fundamentally a missionary gift whose only purpose was to spread the Gospel, but this does not seem to have been the primary purpose of the charism. For the Apostles tell "the mighty works of God" (Ac 2,11), and this seems to be primarily an act of praise directed to God, not to men, an instance of prayer, rather than of preaching. But, on the other hand, there is also a proclamation to the people (Ac 2,14ff). Hence, the gift of tongues is presented as simultaneously a gift of prayer and of proclamation, directed both to God and to men. Later on the very same gift will be given also to Cornelius, the pious Roman centurion, as we shall see, and there only divine praise is mentioned, not preaching. In any case the fairly common assertion that this was a form of static speech seems to be but a gratuitous assumption unwarranted by the text.

Furthermore, the gift of tongues is remarkable for its universal character, which runs throughout the entire narrative. The Jerusalem audience must have been a motley cosmopolitan crowd, with foreigners coming from every corner of the Roman Empire: Parthians and Medes, residents of Mesopotamia, Judea and Cappadocia, Pontus and Asia... even visitors from far away Rome (Ac 2,9-10). All are supposed to have flocked to Jerusalem for the solemn feast of Pentecost with no inkling that a new religion had just been born. It has been estimated that the population of Jerusalem at the time of Jesus was no more than 30,000 and that for the feast of the Passover it swelled up to approximately 150,000. Even if the feast of Pentecost rated slightly below that of the Passover, the throng of people flocking to Jerusalem must undoubtedly have been considerable.

And yet there is a touch of artificiality and literary license in the Lucan description, which probably is not entirely historical. There is general agreement today to consider this long enumeration of nationalities as nothing but a literary device used by Luke to stress the aspect of universality. For the usage of foreign tongues was clearly unnecessary to proclaim the Gospel of Jesus, since all the diaspora Jews present in Jerusalem for the feast knew Greek, the *lingua franca* of the Empire, in addition to Aramaic, their own mother tongue. Hence, the outburst in foreign tongues would have been a totally unnecessary display of fireworks, uncalled for and redundant. The complete listing of foreigners in a broad geographical sweep from East to West aims at showing that "the apostolic utterance at Pentecost becomes the inauguration of a truly universal preaching that will transcend every boundary and nationality and speech".[5]

So far the narrative of Luke. Yet we should keep in mind that Luke is both a historian and a theologian, and it is precisely this double characteristic of his that renders the

5 J. Fitzmyer, "The Acts of the Apostles", in *The Jerome Biblical Commentary*, II, p. 172.

description of the pentecostal event so difficult to interpret. He was not an eyewitness to the events he narrates, he rather puts them down in writing about half a century later. And therefore today's reader can legitimately ask: what actually happened in Jerusalem the year 30 A.D.? What is the historical nucleus on which the Lucan narrative is built? Is Luke faithfully reporting as a conscientious historian or freely interpreting and reflecting on past events as a theologian? Is the narrative in Acts an historical account or rather a theological construct?

It is probably both, it is history and theology blended together in a measure and proportion that it is very difficult to determine. As it stands, the account is somewhat confusing, for if the reference to foreign tongues understood by the audience were historical, the subsequent cynical remark, "they are filled with new wine" (Ac 2,13) would be meaningless. It is probable "that a solid oral tradition attested the first public proclamation of Jesus' Gospel among circumstances of frenzied enthusiasm".[6] This first proclamation would have been interspersed with an outburst of *glossolalia* or gift of tongues, possibly in the sense of "speaking in tongues" rather than "foreign tongues": this seems to be a modification introduced by Luke to strengthen his mission theology of proclamation. In conclusion, all agree today that the account of Pentecost rests on a firm historical foundation which is difficult to determine accurately. There is a solid historical rock on which the narrative of the pentecostal outpouring rests, but the rock itself is difficult to detect, for so far it has proved somewhat elusive. It would seem that the detection of the precise historical event shares the twofold characteristic typical of the Holy Spirit's action: we sense that it is there, certainly, but at the same time it is difficult to grasp, it is evasive and slippery.

Probably of greater spiritual moment is to remark that this first manifestation of the charismatic Spirit in the infant Church took place after protracted prayer, for the biblical narrative says that just before Pentecost the Eleven and the group of women in Jerusalem "with one accord

6 J. Fitzmyer, "The Acts of the Apostles", p. 172.

devoted themselves to prayer" (Ac 1,14). Nothing new, for we have already remarked before — but the thing in itself is so important that it bears repetition — that the Spirit often acts in a prayerful atmosphere. Prayer, especially community prayer, seems to have a power all its own to bring the Holy Spirit down on the community. Let this passing remark suffice now, for we shall have an opportunity to insist on this again in the next chapter, in connection with the contemporary Charismatic Renewal.

It should also be noticed that the charism of tongues is given to the first disciples, men and women, gathered together and forming a unified fellowship: "All these with one accord devoted themselves to prayer...they were all together in one place" (Ac 1,14; 2,1). Not only were they in one place, but — much more important that the physical location — they were *with one accord.* There was unity of place and specially unity of minds and hearts. Unity and prayer seem to be the two arms with which we draw the Spirit down on the community. And, as often happens even today, the result of such a unified prayer was far beyond the expectations of those praying. For it is certain that none of those early disciples of Jesus in Jerusalem dreamt of asking for such a lavish outpouring of the charismatic gift of tongues, which is not attested anywhere in the Old Testament literary tradition. The gift of *glossolalia* was something totally new which burst upon the tiny Jerusalem church quite unexpectedly. It all goes to show that the Holy Spirit often gives more than he is asked for, the gift often surpasses the request.[7]

b) *The charismatic vitality of the infant Church*

As a consequence of their pentecostal experience, the Apostles were baptized, that is, plunged, immersed in the

7 Some authors speak of Pentecost as the beginning of the Spirit's indwelling in the Church. K. Rahner, for instance, is of the opinion that Pentecost was "the beginning of that indwelling of the Spirit permanently and enduringly... in the Church". Yet this is an arbitrary conclusion unwarranted by the biblical text, which speaks rather of charisms, not of the indwelling. These two realities need not necessarily go together, and Luke's narrative is concerned exclusively with the charismatic activity of the Spirit, not with the indwelling in the first Christians. Theological conclusions that go beyond the biblical premises will always remain somewhat precarious.

Spirit. And this pentecostal outpouring had a direct missionary thrust; the Spirit was given to them precisely to spread the message of Jesus: "You shall receive power when the Holy Spirit has come upon you; and you shall be my witnesses in all Judea, and Samaria and to the end of the earth" (Ac 1,8). The charismatic power of the Holy Spirit will eventually drive them out of the narrow confines of Palestine to scatter the seed of Jesus' Gospel — but not yet. The illusion seems to be still fairly widespread that soon after Pentecost and as an immediate result of the activity of the Spirit, the Twelve fanned out beyond the national frontiers of Palestine as the messengers of the risen Lord. However, the fact is that nearly two decades after Pentecost, at least some, perhaps most, of the Apostles were still present at the so-called council of Jerusalem. The outward missionary expansion had not yet started.

After Pentecost the Holy Spirit becomes the ruling principle of the Church through his charismatic activity. It is nothing short of astonishing to realise to what an extraordinary extent the infant Church was governed by the Spirit in her day-to-day life. In this connection there are two peculiar expressions used by Luke in Acts which are highly significant: to be "full of the Spirit" and to receive "the gift of the Spirit".

Full of the Spirit. Today's reader, especially in view of what we have seen above regarding the intensification and growth of the Spirit's indwelling, might be inclined to take the expression in the sense of a fullness of the indwelling, as the summit, as it were, of the sanctifying activity of the Spirit within the Christian. Yet, this is not at all the meaning of the expression as used in Acts. To be full of the Spirit refers to the Spirit's *charismatic* activity, not to his sanctifying presence, for the book of Acts is not directly concerned with the sanctification of the individual Christian as Paul was, but rather with the missionary expansion of the Church. The expression, which occurs often in Acts, refers always to a certain charismatic fullness. Thus Paul immediately after his Damascus experience, but before his baptism, was "filled with the Holy Spirit" (Ac 9,17), as an immediate preparation for his incessant missionary activity. Similarly, when the need for more collaborators arose in the Jerusalem church, the Twelve chose seven ministers "full of the Holy Spirit and of wisdom" (Ac 6,3). Barnabas, Paul's inseparable companion in his missionary journeys, was a man "filled with the Holy Spirit and with faith' (Ac 11,24). Stephen, the first Christian martyr, was "full of the Holy Spirit" (Ac 7,55), and the same expression is also used by Luke in the gospel about Elizabeth (Lk 1,41) and her husband Zechariah (Lk 1,67). It would seem, therefore, that many of the key figures responsible for the outward thrust of the early Church were charismatics ruled and controlled by the Holy Spirit.

It is worthwhile to point out, so as to dispel all doubt, that the expression "full of the Spirit" is always connected with some concrete charismatic gift, like that of tongues in the case of the Eleven at Pentecost. Similarly when Peter and John are released from prison they and their friends entreat God to give them the charismatic gift of boldness, and "they were all filled with the Holy Spirit and spoke the word of God with boldness" (Ac 4,31). At other times the expression is connected with the gift of prophecy, like in the case of Elizabeth and Zechariah, or with the courage necessary to bear witness to Christ, as it is said of Peter (Ac 4,8) and Paul (Ac 9,17). Tongues, boldness, witnessing, prophecy: four precious charisms given indiscriminately to the rulers and to the ruled. When they have received the gift, they are said to be charismatically filled, that is, full of the Holy Spirit. Some of the gifts mentioned seem to be only transitory, but at other times the expression rather signifies a permanent disposition, in which case it refers to a person who is "habitually governed and controlled by the Spirit".[8]

The gift of the Spirit. This is the second expression typical of Acts. It does not refer to a gift different from the person of the Spirit, it rather means the Spirit himself as a gift — and a charismatic gift. So Peter exhorts the first disciples: "Be baptized, everyone of you. . .and you shall receive the gift of the Holy Spirit" (Ac 2,38). It is not an internal and therefore invisible communication of the Holy Spirit; on the contrary, this charismatic bestowal of the Spirit can be observed

8 M. Green, *I Believe in the Holy Spirit* (London 1975), p. 152.

through the senses. Simon the Magician is a case in point: "Now when Simon *saw* that the Spirit was given through the laying on of the Apostles' hands..." (Ac 8,18). On another occasion the first believers were amazed when they "*heard* them speaking in tongues", for "the gift of the Holy Spirit had been poured out even on Gentiles" (Ac 10,45). The gift of the Holy Spirit bestowed on the Gentiles was as externally noticeable as that imparted to the Apostles on the day of Pentecost. In sum: "the gift of the Spirit" designates in Lucan language a charismatic effusion of the Spirit which is often detectable through the senses.

The infant Church was essentially a Church of the word, fired from its very inception with the need to impart, to communicate the Good News. She felt an irrepressible urge to preach from the housetops the message of salvation centered on Jesus. There was no other means for the Church to grow, except through the preaching of the word. Peter, the same timid and fearful Peter who caved in and denied Jesus when confronted by a servant girl, is now bold enough to face the Jewish authorities and justify his incessant preaching. He and John are under strict orders "not to speak or teach at all in the name of Jesus" (Ac 4,18). Yet, they refuse to be silenced, "for we cannot but speak of what we have seen and heard" (Ac 4,20).

Preaching the message is of the very essence of the Gospel, and therefore silence would amount to betrayal. Paul explicitly asserts that his preaching is done "in power and in the Holy Spirit" (1 Thess 1,5), namely, in the power imparted by the Holy Spirit. Peter also speaks of those who preached the Good News "through the Holy Spirit sent from heaven" (1 Pet 1,12). The Corinthian church, built by Paul's preaching, is said to be the result "of the Spirit of the living God" (2 Cor 3,3). When the preachers of the Gospel are really led and controlled by the Spirit they are said to be endowed with *parresia*, that irresistible boldness in the proclamation of the message. Akin to this gift is that of apostolic exhortation or consolation, as possessed to a high degree by Barnabas, "the son of *paraklesis*", controlled by the *Paraclete*.

The infant Church, ruled entirely by the Spirit, was not only a Church of the word, she was also essentially a missionary Church which very soon expanded into the Gentile world, as if unable to contain within herself all the vitality that she had received from the Spirit. And she grew and expanded at a very fast clip. Palestine was no longer sufficient for her, she had to make her presence felt in the rest of the Roman Empire.

And so, when the Corinthian community was gathered in prayer it often experienced the double gift of tongues and prophecy, and although prophecy was primarily meant for believers, for members of the congregation, "if all prophesy and an unbeliever or outsider enters...falling on his face he will worship God" (1 Cor 14,24-25). This shows that even the charismatic gift of prophecy has a missionary dimension. More explicitly yet, the Spirit directs Philip, one of the Seven, to queen Candace, ready for conversion (Ac 8,29). The same Spirit chooses Paul and Barnabas for their missionary journeys: "The Spirit said, 'Set apart for me Barnabas and Paul for the work to which I have called them' " (Ac 13,2). Years later they are "forbidden by the Holy Spirit to speak the word in Asia" (Ac 16,6); they try to reach Bythinia, "but the Spirit of Jesus did not allow them" (Ac 16,7). At a given moment Paul seems to be exercising his missionary activity in semi-darkness, he does not know exactly what the future holds for him: "I am going to Jerusalem, bound in the Spirit" (Ac 20,22). He is ready to walk into the dark, "except that the Holy Spirit testifies to me in every city that imprisonment and afflictions await me" (Ac 20,23). In the midst of this uncertainty it is the Spirit that leads him on. Similarly it is said of the prophet Agabus that he "foretold by the Spirit that there would be a great famine" (Ac 11,28).

In a word, it is as if the Holy Spirit, having taken the infant Church by the hand, was directing and guiding her at every turn. The Church is the child of the Spirit, constantly guarded and protected by him. Conscious of this protection the Church experiences a quiet, all-pervading sense of joy: "And the disciples were filled with joy and with the Holy Spirit" (Ac 13,52). "You received the word...with joy inspired by the Holy Spirit" (1 Thess 1,6). Acts 9,31 is a marvelous summary of this all-inclusive activity of the Holy Spirit: "And so the Church throughout all Judea and Galilee and Samaria had peace and was filled up; and walking in the fear of the Lord and in the comfort (*paraklesis*) of the Holy Spirit, it was multiplied".

I have mentioned above the four concentric circles or ripples of the Spirit's gradually expanding charismatic action: the community leaders, the promise of a future outpouring on the community itself, the actual fulfillment of this prophecy at Pentecost, when the community becomes the beneficiary of the Spirit's action, and lastly, as the outer circle, those who lie outside Christianity, the Gentiles. Now the process is complete and the Spirit has finally reached the outer fringes of the unbaptized, non-Christian world. There are no closed barriers, no frontiers before the irresistible outward expansion of the Spirit's charismatic acivity. The Spirit moves slowly through the centuries, but the general trend of his activity is unmistakable; his charismatic action embraces not only the Jewish or Christian communities, but also the rest of the world.

This is the remarkable teaching of the Cornelius episode in Acts 10. On a certain occasion Peter happened to be staying at the pretty little city of Joppa, on the Mediterranean coast, not far from the populous Caesarea Maritima, one of the strongholds of the Roman occupying forces in Palestine. At noon, as was customary among Jews, he retires to the terrace of the house to pray, and there receives the strange vision of the tablecloth full of supposedly unclean animals. The tablecloth vanishes and reappears three times, and Peter, as could be expected, is simply flabbergasted, he can make neither head nor tail of it all. It is only later, after receiving the messengers from Cornelius, the pious Roman centurion from Caesarea, that the meaning of the vision becomes suddenly clear to him: the Spirit makes no distinction between Jews and Gentiles. Finally Peter perceives clearly that "God shows no partiality, but in every nation anyone who fears him and does what is right is acceptable to him" (Ac 10,34-35).

Subsequently Peter makes a speech to quite a crowd around him, and gives an account both of his own vision on the terrace and of what he has heard from Cornelius' messengers, and "while Peter was still saying this, the Holy

Spirit fell on all who heard the word. And the believers among the circumcised who came with Peter were amazed, because *the gift of the Spirit had been poured out even on the Gentiles.* For they heard them speaking in tongues" (Ac 10,44-46).

And it is Peter himself who finally grasps and explains the extraordinary significance of this new outpouring of the Spirit. It is simply a repetition of the Pentecost experience in Jerusalem a few years earlier: "The Holy Spirit fell on them just as on us at the beginning. . . . God gave the same gift to them as he gave to us" (Ac 11,16-17). God truly makes no distinction, and pours out his Spirit on baptized Christians and unbaptized non-Christians alike, for it is only *after* having received the charismatic effusion of the Spirit that Peter "commanded them to be baptized" (Ac 10,48). The Holy Spirit had been charismatically bestowed on a group of righteous but unbaptized persons, showing thereby that charisms are meant for all, that the call to charisms is entirely universal. But in this connection it should be remarked that in the New Testament the Holy Spirit may be given to the unbaptized but never to unbelievers: faith is even more necessary than baptism to receive the charisms of the Spirit.

This remarkable episode will prove to be of the utmost importance at the subsequent council of Jerusalem, when, after a protracted and heated discussion, it was finally decided not to impose the observance of the Jewish Law on Gentile converts to Christianity. At the conciliar assembly, after arguments and objections have been going back and forth, Peter's moderate stand, based precisely on his personal experience with the Gentile Cornelius, will eventually carry the day: "And God who knows the heart bore witness to them, giving them the Holy Spirit just as he did to us; and he made no distinction between us and them" (Ac 15,8-9). This reasoning clinches the dispute: if the Spirit shows his good will towards Gentiles who have obviously not observed the Jewish Law, who are we to impose such an observance as necessary on Gentile Christians? The Cornelius episode has offered Peter on a platter the incontrovertible argument that will eventually prove decisive: the presence of genuine charisms from the Spirit among Gentiles is a clear pointer to

God's mind, a sure proof that the Jewish Law has had its day and is no longer to be imposed on new converts.

A modern reader cannot but look back with a certain sense of nostalgia on this Lucan account of the charismatic activity of the early Church. There is a freshness in it, a dynamism and vitality that makes one feel almost jealous. The Holy Spirit had certainly not limited his intervention to Pentecost day. Even after that, he led, guided, encouraged, restrained, forbade, urged, exhorted, consoled, coaxed the infant Church as she progressively spread out of Jerusalem into the most distant regions of the civilized world. When reading Luke's account one can almost sense, feel the Spirit's presence in the midst of the expanding Church: invisible and yet tangible; forcefully present and yet elusive; a self-effacing person, yet active everywhere; withdrawn and faceless, yet clearly discernible; remote in his transcendence, yet immanent in his proximity to man: this was the Spirit of Jesus present and active in the early Church.

3) A PROPHETIC CHURCH

The Pauline church of Corinth was in many respects a puzzling, fascinating church, witness at once to crude sexual misbehaviour and to the finest activity of the Holy Spirit; the place of sharp social divisions within the community and yet unified in the Spirit; wavering in fundamental articles of their Christian faith like the resurrection, yet proud of their charisms. A peculiar church if ever there was one, where light and shadows intermingled constantly, where the Spirit and the flesh fought fierce battles for the possession of man. That the Spirit should have poured out his choicest gifts on such an earthy community of raw Christians constitutes a phenomenon that defies all rational explanation.

Paul's arrival in his local churches of Asia Minor was often accompanied by an extraordinary profusion of charisms: "You are not lacking in any gift of the Spirit" (1 Cor 1,7). The Corinthians have witnessed themselves the power of the Spirit present in Paul: "My speech and my message were not in plausible words of wisdom, but in demonstration of the Spirit and power" (1 Cor 2,4). The neighbouring church of Galatia, too, has seen some extraordinary things. At the time of their Christian initiation its members "began in the Spirit" and later Paul will flash before their eyes "all the favours you have received....Does God give you the Spirit so freely and work miracles among you..." (Gal 3,3-5). It would seem that at the time of their baptism Paul's Christians in Galatia had been simultaneously endowed with both the indwelling of the Spirit and a lavish profusion of charismatic gifts. Paul's churches were simply drenched in charisms.

Paul seems to have attached an extraordinary importance to this charismatic dimension of the Church's life, if one is to judge from the fact that he mentions it in four different places, especially when writing to the Corinthians. He enumerates about twenty different charisms, but a complete, exhaustive list is both difficult and unnecessary. It is not so much their number as their profusion and rich variety that matters, and specially the fact that all these charisms, with hardly any exception, are directed to the upbuilding of the community. It is most unusual for Paul to devote so much space in his letters to one single topic. Even more important themes like the Eucharist and the resurrection do not rate so high as charisms, as far as space is concerned. No other subject deserves two full chapters as charisms do (1 Cor 12 and 14). The length of the treatment can partly be explained, no doubt, because of the peculiar circumstances in Corinth that demanded it, but this is probably not the only reason. Charisms are essential to the total structure of the Church and Paul knows it.

It is still disputed if Paul enumerates charisms in order of importance, but the fact is that he often places apostles and prophets right on top of the list. The apostolate is for him the first and foremost charism, but particularly Catholic readers should be careful not to hastily identify the Pauline charismatic apostle with the Twelve. This identification, current in Catholic spirituality and liturgy, is certainly not wrong, but it is due to Luke rather than to Paul. The Pauline conception of the apostle is broader, it embraces people like Paul himself and Barnabas, who were not members of the original Twelve. Briefly put, for Paul an apostle is a man who fulfills a twofold condition: he has seen the risen Christ and has received from him the commission to preach. Vision and commission, taken jointly, constitute a Pauline charismatic apostle.[9]

For Paul the apostle comes before all other charismatics, for even prophets are subject to the apostles: Paul lays down rules for the use of charisms, basing his authority on his personal possession of the Spirit and forcing other charismatics to acknowledge the legitimacy of these rules. The same Spirit who inspires the charismatics inspires also Paul to govern them; it is not an unbridled effusion of charisms that reigned in the Pauline churches; on the contrary, "all things should be done decently and in order" (1 Cor 14,39).

Important as he undoubtedly is, the Pauline apostle is a figure of the past, for presumably none of us now can claim to have received both a vision of the risen Lord and a direct commission from him to preach the Gospel. There certainly were in the early Church after Paul successors in the apostolate, but in them the double condition of authentic apostolicity was already considerably watered down, since none of Paul's successors could claim either vision or commission. But the Church of God is "built upon the foundation of apostles and prophets" (Eph 2,20). The Pauline apostle may be, in the strong and original meaning of the term, *passé*, but the prophet is certainly not.

After the gift of the apostolate, no other charismatic gift of the Spirit can match that of prophecy in importance and usefulness for the upbuilding of the Church. Prophecy places the mind of the charismatic into direct contact with God's thought and will, the prophet reads God's mind and his salvific or punishing designs, and communicates them to the community. For Paul the prophet is not a seer of the future, but an interpreter of the present. He is not a man of foresight but of insight, not a man who inquiringly peeps into the future, but a man who illumines the present. He is simply God's oracle, the proclaimer of his will and mind here and now. He exhorts and encourages, admonishes and

9 In the context of the present controversy concerning the ministry of women in the Church and the possibility of women priests, it is interesting to observe that Mary of Magdala fulfilled both the conditions laid down by Paul to be an apostle: she saw the risen Jesus and received from him the commission to announce the fact of the resurrection to the frightened disciples.

reproofs, comforts and consoles — and thereby builds the ecclesial community.

The preaching of the prophets is not accompanied by frenzied, ecstatic manifestations; they are rather level-headed, reasonable preachers of the word in the community. Alienation and raving are foreign to them. "The responsible personality of the prophet remains intact even though the whole man... stands under the operation of the Spirit".[10] The prophet is neither created nor commissioned by the community, but directly chosen by the Holy Spirit when it pleases him to do so. The election of the prophet has absolutely nothing to do with the general priesthood of believers, it rather belongs to a different realm of the Spirit. Whereas the apostle is subject only to the word he proclaims, the prophet is subject to the apostles. The community cannot judge the apostle, but it has the inherent right to test the alleged prophet: "Do not despise prophesying, but test everything" (1 Thess 5,20-21). Hence, the prophet occupies a special position, for in a way he stands between the Spirit who sends him and the community of believers who, helped by the charismatic sense of discernment given by the same Spirit, will pass judgement on his claim to genuineness. The prophet enlightens the community, but the community judges the prophet.

A few years after its foundation the church of Corinth was in turmoil. Possibly influenced by the non-Christian surroundings, and excessively attached to esoteric gifts of wisdom and personal enlightenment, the Corinthian Christians were apparently suffering from a momentary loss of true Christian perspectives. They tended to overvalue the secondary charismatic gift of tongues and undervalue the much greater gift of prophecy. Paul decides to set the record straight and correct the imbalance. Corinth seems to have experienced an unusual outburst of *glossolalia* or gift of tongues, accompanied by an exaggerated appreciation of the gift, and Paul's whole contention is to trim it down to size.

Tongues are undoubtedly an excellent charismatic gift of prayer of praise and thanksgiving: "For one who speaks in a tongue speaks not to man but to God" (1 Cor 14,2).

10 M. Friedrich, "Prophetes", *Theologicat Diotionary of the New Testament*, VI (Grand Rapids 1968), p. 851.

Yet this gift is directed primarily to the benefit of the individual, not of the community, for the tongue is unintelligible: "No one understands him, but he utters mysteries in the Spirit" (1 Cor 14,2). In order to render it understandable to those present, the gift of tongues should be accompanied by the concomitant gift of interpretation: "Therefore he who speaks in a tongue should pray for the power to interpret" (1 Cor 14,13). Paul certainly knew what he was talking about, for he himself spoke in tongues, and he can be pardoned for bragging about it: "I thank God that I speak in tongues more than you all" (1 Cor 14,18).

He is firm and perfectly clear: the gift of tongues should certainly not be despised, for it is good and desirable, but prophecy is definitely better: "Now I want you all to speak in tongues, but even more, to prophesy. He who prophesies is greater than he who speaks in tongues" (1 Cor 14,5). And the reason is plain: the gift of tongues remains unintelligible to the community, nobody in the assembly, not even the speaker himself, knows what he is saying, and therefore the community is not thereby built in any way; whereas the prophet's message is understood by all, light simply pours into the congregation through the channel of the prophet, and the ecclesial community is thereby built up. Prophecy carries light within itself, it is a transparent, luminous gift, whereas tongues remain opaque. "He who speaks in a tongue edifies himself, but he who prophesies edifies the Church....In church I would rather speak five words with my mind, in order to instruct others, than ten thousand words in a tongue" (1 Cor 14,3.19). Presumably his Corinthian readers were convinced of Paul's general contention regarding the superiority of prophecy over tongues. "So, my brethren, *earnestly desire to prophesy*" (1 Cor 14,39). Charismatic gifts of the Spirit are to be longed for and to be asked for.[11]

11 Certain details in this precious and exceedingly practical chapter (1 Cor 14) are debatable, but the general thrust of the argument is transparently clear. Paul does appreciate tongues, but is opposed to a public use of the gift that is not interpreted, just as he frowns on the use of tongues when they are simultaneous and uncontrolled. This is not an obsolete piece of advice: members of the present Charismatic Renewal could profitably keep these Pauline norms in mind. I shall return to this more at length in the next chapter.

In a way, the gift of prophecy is based on personal experience. The prophet speaks of God and his salvific grace, not like a learned theologian who has secured some abstract knowledge about him by dint of intellectual effort, but rather as an individual who has gained personal experience of God. Prophecy is an experiential gift. The prophet is a man who, with a kind of intuition, reads the signs of the times and interprets the facts of contemporary history from the vantage point of his personal experience of God. Light simply streams into the Church through him.[12] "Prophecy does not demand learning, or wisdom or experience. Prophecy is not a career. When prophecy is needed, the Spirit acts; and I believe that the Spirit calls to prophecy more frequently than we recognize. I believe that the Spirit calls many in vain".[13]

The prophet is a man with a vocation, who nearly always opposes dead ritualism and formalistic routine in favour of a reawakening of the Spirit. He runs the risk of being isolated and becoming unpopular on account of his constant and outspoken opposition to the received institutional forms. It is not always easy to draw the line of demarcation between genuine prophecy and obdurate obstinacy: purposefulness may be mistaken for stubbornness and hard-headedness may claim to be the power ot the Spirit....

In spite oi its obvious dangers, prophetism remains a very precious charismatic gift of the Spirit to his Church. Its suppression or disappearance would bring in its wake an impoverishment for the entire Church. "The prophets of

12 It is difficult to avoid sexist language in this area. Women readers will kindly note that all the above applies to prophets *and* prophetesses, who made their appearance already in the New Testament (Ac 21,10). Nobody will deny that considerable light has streamed into the Church through feminine channels also. Prophetic figures like St Teresa of Avila and even more St Catherine of Siena should not be overlooked, both of whom left an indelible mark on the Church of their time.

13 J. Mckenzie, *Authority in the Church,* p. 156. The same author aptly remarks that "the prophetic call is a great and fearful thing....His friends will all assure him (the prophet) that he should not rock the boat, wash dirty linen in public, foul his own nest or do any of the things which these homely old saws call imprudence. I suppose Amos must have known people who gave him this advice" (*ibid.*, p. 161).

old were sent to establish the faith and correct evil ways.... Today the faith is already established, but prophecy, which has for its aim the correction of evil ways, has not ceased and will not cease".[14]

4) THE UNIVERSAL CALL TO CHARISMS

The day of Pentecost seems to have been like the opening of the floodgates for the Church, which, as a consequence, was simply soaked in charisms. Especially some of the local churches of Pauline origin seem to have experienced an incredible profusion of charisms, and — this should be stressed — these charisms were definitely *not* confined to hierarchical channels, they were rather given to all, they were, in a way, "democratic". "You were enriched in him in every way...so that you are not lacking in any spiritual gift (*charismati*, in the Greek)" (1 Cor 1,5-7); "as you excel in everything..." (2 Cor 8,7); "and God is able to provide you with every blessing in abundance, so that you may always have enough of everything..." (2 Cor 9,8). The Corinthian church, so earthy and so uninspiring in certain respects, was however awash in charisms. In it the activity of the Spirit could be almost sensitively felt.

And nearly all of these charisms were both non-sacramental and non-hierarchical. As a matter of fact, since the only two passages dealing with a sacramental charism (ordination to the ministry through imposition of hands: 1 Tim 4,14 and 2 Tim 1,6) were almost certainly written by one of Paul's disciples, rather than by Paul himself, it would seem that Paul knew only non-sacramental charisms. And these charisms were open to absolutely all Christians. The Church of Corinth in particular seems to have been rather a democratic church with hierarchical structures reduced to a minimum.

14 *In Matthaeum* XI. It is within this general setting of prophetism that the typical case of *private revelations* (Margaret Mary, Lourdes, Fatima...) is to be judged. Through them God manifests the concrete course he wants to give to his Church at a given moment. They are certainly not additions to Christ's final, public revelation, but this does not render them superfluous either. They are like a new onrush of light and power from the Spirit of life who never abandons his Church. Suffice it to say that, as regards this particular form of prophetism in the Church, credulity would be as dangerous as scepticism.

Neither bishops nor presbyters nor priests nor deacons are ever mentioned in Paul's correspondence with Corinth. And yet that Church knew of a plethora, a veritable explosion of charisms.

A remarkable feature of this charismatic outpouring is that the call to charisms seems to have been absolutely universal, for Paul emphatically and repeatedly says that all share in the charismatic riches of the Church. "*Each* has his own spiritual gift (*charisma*) from God, one of one kind and one of another" (1 Cor 7,7, in a protracted discussion on virginity and marriage, both of which are considered to be charisms). "*To each* is given the manifestation of the Spirit for the common good" (1 Cor 12,7); "as *each* has received the gift (*charisma*) employ it for one another as good stewards of God's varied grace" (1 Pet 4,10). The stress in all these passages is on *each* one; no member of the Christian community seems to be excluded, the reason probably being that charisms are always connected with one's own vocation within the People of God. Christian vocation means a call to and within the Church, and when God calls, he also gives the necessary help to fulfil such a call — and the call together with the help constitute precisely the charism. Since the call is universal, applicable to all Christians, so are also the charisms connected with it. In which case, "where the Church or community thrives only on office-holders and not on all the members, one may wonder in all seriousness if the Spirit has not been thrown out with the charismata".[15]

After this exuberant profusion of charismatic activity that characterized some of the local churches, charisms rather mysteriously seem to have almost vanished from the field, and this strange phenomenon gave rise to the widespread misconception that charisms were like props needed to sustain the Church as long as she was in a state of infancy; that, once she reached the state of adulthood, all these temporary manifestations of the Spirit could be dispensed with, for she was already able to stand on her own two feet. To seek charisms today, therefore — this opinion runs — would be a

15 H. Küng, "The charismatic structure of the Church", *Concilium*, April 1965, p. 30.

sign of lack of faith, for Jesus had provided the Church with a firmly established hierarchy and whatever administrative structures she needed to fulfil her salvific function. In proportion as the Church outgrew the period of her infancy, the charismatic Spirit withdrew. Charisms would have been nothing but colourful fireworks which performed a useful but strictly temporary function. To clamour for charisms now would be a retrograde step, a return to the period of the Church's infancy.

This opinion, prevalent until fairly recently, is not only entirely false, but highly dangerous as well. For it seems to forget that, according to the New Testament, some of the charisms — prophecy, for instance — belong to the very heart of the Church, to her essential structure. Thus, convinced of this, Paul will not hesitate to state that the Church is "built upon the foundation of apostles and prophets" (Eph 2,20), and we have seen above that both of them, apostleship and prophecy, are charismatic gifts of the Spirit. Nothing else is mentioned as the foundation of the household of God except these two charisms. This, by itself, should be enough to dispel the wrong conception that charisms belonged exclusively to the early, undeveloped period of the Church, that now they can be dispensed with. Since when does the foundation of a building have only a temporary function to perform?

Yet this widespread misconception does have a grain of truth: it is true that after the second century the early charisms seem to be much less noticeable, but several convincing reasons can be adduced to account for this fact, without conjuring up the illusion that an adult Church needs no charisms. In the first place, the Spirit retains his supreme freedom, which he exercises when and as he pleases. A period of superabundance can be followed by a period of scarcity. Floods are at times followed by droughts, but the rains will eventually come back. Secondly, the Church in the course of her history has oftentimes showed herself unable to avoid the pitfall of overreaction, thereby temporarily losing her balance. And this is precisely what seems to have happened in the early third century, after the deplorable excesses of the Montanist heresy, which set up a false division and even conflict between the official, hierarchical Church and the "real", charismatic

Church. This confrontation was not only entirely arbitrary, it was extremely dangerous, and when faced with it, the Church understandably overreacted. From then onward she would look with almost instinctive suspicion on any display of charismatic activity, no matter how moderate and legitimate. Charisms had fallen on hard times. Fear of excesses put a constraint on the activity of the Spirit within the Church.

Thirdly, it is false to imagine that the Church passed from infancy to adulthood and maturity, in a kind of homogeneous growth. In reality, the transition was from infancy to partial decadence. Freedom from the fear of bloody persecution, and the official recognition of Christianity as the state religion, were but a mixed blessing. As a consequence of both, the spirit of the world, so pervasive and difficult to control at the best of times, made dangerous inroads into the structures of the Church. It was the Pauline flesh versus the Spirit once again, and this round in the old fight went to the flesh. The spirit of the world momentarily stifled the Spirit of God, and therefore his charismatic vitality suffered in the process.

And finally, we should not forget that the practice of adult baptism gradually gave way to that of infant baptism. According to the testimony of the New Testament (Galatians 3 is a case in point) adult baptism was often accompanied by extraordinary, even miraculous manifestations of the charismatic Spirit, the gift of tongues being only one of them. When infants began to be baptized the door was closed to any charismatic outpouring of the Spirit. Infant baptism may be a sign of the Spirit's impatience in entering and possessing the person of the new Christian, but at the same time any charismatic manifestation of the Spirit, which implies necessarily a sufficient psychological development in the faculties of the recipient, was thereby precluded. The cumulative effect of all these reasons was a considerable diminution in the charismatic vitality of the Church. As a consequence of this multifaceted evolution, the very name "charism" came to be almost banished from the theological vocabulary. Or rather, it came to have only historical importance, as a way of designating theological fossils of the past. Charisms became interesting, no doubt, but also unimportant and dated, something belonging to bygone ages.

And so it came to pass that charisms were relegated to the periphery of the Church as an object of only historical interest — until Vatican II, that is. In the course of the council Cardinal Suenens shocked the episcopal audience at St Peter's with his famous speech on charisms, which marked a turning point in the understanding of the Church. The Belgian Cardinal stated:

> Thus to St Paul the Church of the living Christ does not appear as some kind of administrative organization, but as a living web of charisms, of ministries. The Spirit is given to every individual Christian, the Spirit who gives his gifts, his charisms, to each and everyone.... '*In each of us* the Spirit is manifested in one particular way, for some useful purpose' (1 Cor 12,7)....*Each and every Christian*, whether lettered or unlettered, has his charism in his daily life, but — as St Paul says — 'All of these must aim at one thing: to build up the Church' (1 Cor 14,26)....Attention and reverence is due to those charisms and impulses of the Holy Spirit who very frequently breathes through Christian laymen who have no position of authority.[16]

The speech caused a sensation in the episcopal assembly. Ignoring the conciliar regulation which explicitly forbade applause in the basilica, hundreds of bishops rose spontaneously to their feet and signaled their enthusiastic approval through a thunderous, prolonged applause. Thanks to the intervention of Cardinal Suenens, charisms had reentered the portals of the Church.

No one who followed the Council closely was therefore particularly surprised to see that the final Constitution on the Church, *Lumen Gentium*, had largely incorporated the gist of the above speech. The Council says that "by this sense of faith which is aroused and sustained by the Spirit of truth, God's People...clings without fail to the faith once delivered to the saints, (Jud 3).[17] Absolutely all the faithful, men and women, young and old, are endowed with this subtle, mysterious, yet real and precious reality which is the "sense

16. Y. Congar - H. Küng - D.O'Hanlon, *Council Speeches of Vatican II* (London 1964), pp. 19-20, with emphasis added.

17 *Lumen Gentium*, 12: W. Abbott, *The Documents of Vatican II*, pp. 29-30.

of faith". It is a kind of supernatural instinct by which the faithful sense and detect what is genuinely Christian, what is in keeping with the Gospel, what clicks or clashes with the message of Christ. "It refers to the presence of a graced sensitivity in the faithful to the reality of sacred tradition".[18] It is a kind of intuitive grasp of what is consonant with the Christian truth, a sort of charism of discernment by means of which the simple, often unlettered faithful can tell truth from error. It is not only through hierarchical structures, but also through this intuitive, instinctual faith that the Holy Spirit maintains the Church in the truth.[19]

This instinctive faith of the entire People of God is a kind of universal charism that affects all the members of the Church. But Vatican II is yet more explicit when it comes to the universal call to charisms. The conciliar passage is worth quoting in full:

> Allotting his gifts 'to every one according as he will' (1 Cor 12,11) he (the Holy Spirit) distributes special

18 P. Granfield, "The *sensus fidelium* in episcopal selection", *Concilium*, Sept. 1980. p. 33.

19 As regards this instinct of faith, which is so difficult to handle well, history records both remarkable achievements as well as deplorable failures. At the time of the fierce christological controversies that rocked the Church in the 4th century, many of the bishops defected from the faith and lapsed into or at least dallied with, the heresy of Arianism, which denied the divinity of Christ. At that time of crisis it was the simple faithful that preserved the true faith, rather than their heretical bishops. Similarly, when Popes Pius IX and Pius XII defined respectively the Marian dogmas of the Immaculate Conception and the Assumption, they relied to a large extent on this instinct of faith of the Catholic laity. But there are also shadows in the picture: the same instinct of faith went badly off the track when it fancied and propagated in the Middle Ages — even down to very recent times!— fanciful notions concerning purgatory which have absolutely no foundation whatever in the Christian faith. In order to be genuine and reliable, this sense of faith should pass in each case through a fourfold stage of development: the faithful should be enlightened by their pastors, for the opinion of an unenlightened crowd is often worthless (communication); but this often leads to a confrontation of views (conflict); eventually agreement is reached (consensus), and this will foster internal unity in the Church (communion). Communication, conflict, consensus, communion: these four steps in various degrees of intensity are a must if the much vaunted faith-sense is to achieve its purpose of preserving and deepening the Christian faith; cf L. Sartori, "What is the criterion for the 'sensus fidelium'?" *Concilium*, Oct. 1980, pp. 56-60.

> graces *among the faithful of every rank*. By these gifts he makes them fit and ready to undertake the various tasks or offices advantageous for the renewal and upbuilding of the Church, according to the word of the Apostle, 'The manifestation of the Spirit is given to *everyone* for profit' (1 Cor 12,7). These charismatic gifts, whether they be the most outstanding or the most simple and widely diffused, are to be received with thanksgiving and consolation, for they are exceedingly suitable and useful for the needs of the Church.[20]

This crucial passage of Vatican II has chartered out a new course for the post-conciliar Church. It is like a solid bridge that, going over the abyss of the centuries-old neglect of charisms, links up again with the biblical shores. The conciliar document on the laity not only echoes the above passage, it goes even further in strengthening this universal call to charisms. "From the reception of these charisms or gifts...there arises in each believer the *right and duty* to use them in the Church and in the world for the good of mankind and for the upbuilding of the Church. In doing so, believers need to enjoy the freedom of the Holy Spirit".[21] It should be stressed, therefore, that according to the Church's official doctrine all the faithful have the right and the duty to make use of their charisms, for in a certain way these gifts of the Spirit do not belong to them as their individual property, they belong rather to the community of the Church, for whose sake they are granted. It is their God-given responsibility that they do not let these charisms stagnate and lie unused and unproductive. They owe it to the Church, not to themselves. If led by a false sense of humility, the faithful were to leave them unrecognized and untouched, they would be acting in a highly irresponsible manner and committing a serious sin of omission.

It is a marvelous web of charisms that covers the entire Church, not only at the time of Paul but also today: apostles, prophets, evangelists, teachers, miracle-workers, healers,

20 *Lumen Gentium*, 12: W. Abbott, *The Documents of Vatican II*, p. 30, with emphasis added.

21 Vatican II, *Apostolicam actuositatem*, 3: W. Abbott, *The Documents of Vatican II*, p. 492, with emphasis added.

helpers, leaders, speakers in tongues, interpreters of tongues... (cf 1 Cor 12,28-30); and many others, for Paul's list is in no way meant to be exhaustive. "The Church must cease to be afraid of charisms. They are essential characteristics of the Church".[22] We should all make a determined effort to disassociate charismatic from extraordinary, to cease to consider charisms as synonymous with quasi-miraculous. Most of the charisms enumerated by Paul are not at all extraordinary in appearance, though they are all exceedingly useful for the upbuilding of the Church.

> The charismata are not primarily extraordinary but common; they are not of one kind but manifold; they are not limited to a special group of persons, but truly universal in the Church. All this implies that they are not a thing of the past (possible and real only in the early Church), but eminently contemporary and actual; they do not hover in the periphery of the Church, but are eminently central and essential to it. In this sense one should speak of a *charismatic structure* of the Church which embraces and goes beyond the structure of its government....A Church order based on the charisma does not mean...enthusiasm, which degenerates into arbitrariness and disorder, nor legalism which hardens into... uniformity. Neither caprice nor uniformity...but order in liberty marks the charismatic Church.[23]

5) The discernment of charisms

It is true that "where the Spirit of the Lord is there is freedom" (2 Cor 3,17), but not unbridled charismatic freedom, for "all things should be done decently and in order" (1 Cor 14,40). The Pauline churches may have been rich in charisms, but they were certainly not whipped into charismatic frenzy by the Spirit. Nor does Paul or any other New Testament writer contend that all those who claim to be genuine charismatics are so in reality. For the existence of false prophets

22 A. Grillmeier, in H. Vorgrimler, ed., *Commentary on the Documents of Vatican II*, I (London 1966), p. 166.

23 H. Küng, "The charismatic structure of the Church", *Concilium*, April 1965, p. 32, with emphasis in the original.

has been a constantly recurring phenomenon in the history of the Church. Just as there is a true discernment of spirits, there should also be a necessary discernment of charisms, for in this area the danger of deception is great. Side by side with genuine charismatics inspired and moved by the Spirit, there have always been innumerable self-styled charismatics inspired only by their own fancy. From Jesus to Vatican II this has been a constant problem in the Church, how to recognize the true charismatic and how to unmask the false prophet. In the charismatic field of the Church the wheat and the darnel seem to grow always together....

Vatican II solved the problem of the discernment of charisms very drastically. "Judgement as to their authenticity and proper use belongs to those who preside over the Church, and to whose special competence it belongs, not indeed to extinguish the Spirit, but to test all things and hold fast to that which is good (1 Thess 5,12.19-21)".[24] This is certainly clear and precise: according to the Council, it is the bishop who has ultimately to pass judgment on the authenticity of the alleged charism, it is he who has the final word on a controversial charism. The difficulty with this norm, however, is that it is not directly biblical, and it is rather unfortunate that in order to butress its contention, the Council should have quoted Paul wrongly, making him say what in reality he did not say.

The problem of discernment is as old as the Church, and Paul had to grapple with it already in his very first letter, to the Thessalonians: "Do not quench the Spirit...test everything" (1 Thess 5,19-20). But this directive is given to the entire community, not to its leaders. The letter is addressed to the church at large, not to its bishop (bishops are never as much as mentioned in that letter), and consequently, those entrusted with the task of discernment are all the faithful to whom the letter is addressed, rather than their non-existent bishops to whom the letter is not directed. In other words, if the reality of charisms is universal, really meant for all, and therefore democratic, the criterion of discernment is equally democratic. We have to acknowledge that this

24 *Lumen Gentium,* 12:Abbott, *The Documents of Vatican II,* p. 30.

criterion may not be very practical in reality, but objectivity requires that Paul's thought be quoted faithfully, rather than distorted by attributing to him a meaning which is foreign to the text.[25]

For Paul the true judge of an alleged prophet is either the apostle (1 Cor 14,37), or another prophet (1 Cor 14,32), or the entire community (1 Thess 5,19-20). In the last case the function of discernment may create a certain tension within the Church but, as we saw above in a different context, there are tensions which are healthy and as such should not be suppressed. This particular confrontation between charismatics and those in authority was often transcended in the early Church by the Spirit himself: at times charismatics were chosen as office-holders, and conversely, office-holders were often endowed by the Spirit with a profusion of charismatic gifts, like the Twelve, Stephen, Philip, Barnabas, Ananias etc. Charismatic leaders, men of the Spirit, docile to his voice even when this voice comes from below: the Church can thrive only on such a foundation.

As for the criteria of discernment of charisms, they largely overlap those discussed above for the discernment of spirits. It is obvious and beyond dispute that the charism under scrutiny has to bear a strong christological colouring, for nothing opposed to Jesus and his Gospel can proceed from the Spirit. For the Holy Spirit is essentially the Spirit of Christ and therefore it is simply inconceivable that he should be the author and dispenser of "charisms" that lead the faithful away from Christ. A greater and deeper attachment to Christ will always be the genuine hallmark of a true charism.

All charisms are given "for the common good" (1 Cor 12,7), namely, they all have a second characteristic, which is the upbuilding of the Church, rather than the sanctification of the individual. It is obvious that acts of mercy, teaching, service (Rom 12,7-8), helping and administration (1 Cor 12,28) have all an ecclesial aim in view. The point is too clear to need further elaboration. But here a word of caution may

25 In order to justify Vatican II one can of course reason out that today's bishops are the successors of the Apostles, and that therefore today's charismatics have to be subject to their bishops as much as the early prophets were subject to Paul. Perfectly true, but this is not what Paul wrote to Thessalonika.

not be out of place, for a narrow and somewhat rigid use of this ecclesial criterion may at times result in the rejection of a perfectly genuine charism. Charisms come from the Spirit and the Spirit often delights in acting in a most unpredictable manner. There are no foreseeable blueprints and chartered paths for the Spirit; on the contrary he often acts in ways that are totally unexpected.

And so, for instance, it may happen that a prophet temporarily upsets the peace of his or her community (whether provincial, diocesan, national or ecclesial) in the name of God. An immediate, unenlightened use of this second ecclesial criterion might lead one to conclude hastily that such a prophet is no prophet at all, since he is upsetting the peace of the community. Such a way of proceeding may well display merely human judgment rather than supernatural wisdom. We should not forget that the Old Testament prophets frequently thundered against existing institutions and accepted forms of worship, thereby often upsetting the cart and rocking the boat — and yet they were genuine prophets, sent by Yahweh to awaken the community from its slumber. This occurrence in the Old Testament should sound a warning to us not to apply the ecclesial criterion of discernment in too rigid a manner, for a temporary disturbance in the community often leads to the infusion of new vitality and eventually to lasting peace.

Furthermore, besides its christological and ecclesial nature, a true charism should be detectable by simply scrutinizing the life of the charismatic. It is true that charisms are given to fallible and sinful men and women, and that, taken by themselves, charisms do not directly sanctify the individual. Nothing prevents God from making use of imperfect channels of transmission in furthering the life of the Church. Consequently, it would be foolish and unrealistic to expect canonizable sanctity from all charismatics. This simply does not happen. But, on the other hand, a lasting and glaring discrepancy between the life and the preaching of a "prophet" is already a clear indication that he is nothing but a fake. Even false prophets may confess Jesus Christ (Mt 7,22); hence, the christocentric character of their teaching, though indispensable, is not an absolute guarantee of genuineness. The prophet's life must be carefully scrutinized, for, as Jesus himself said, "you will know them by their fruits" (Mt 7,20). Protracted, consistent failure to practise what he or she preaches so vociferously is already a decidedly nagative sign. A prophet may be short-sighted and short-tempered, narrow and nagging, blunt and brutal — but he has to be entirely authentic and transparent to the light of the Spirit. Sincerity and complete authenticity will always characterize the true prophet. The Spirit does not choose fakes or hypocrites as his oracles, for he is, after all, the Spirit of truth, and he acts accordingly.

It has become fashionable nowadays to speak of "prophetic actions" and of taking a "prophetic stand" on various issues, whether theological or social. One may be permitted to doubt the legitimacy of some of these facile claims. The credentials of some of these self-styled prophets simply do not ring true, they carry no conviction. Loud, radical talk need not be a sign of genuine prophecy. Some of these alleged prophets seem to have forgotten that in the Old Testament all the authentic prophets were men of the word, certainly, and men of both strong convictions and daring action. But before that they were men who had a long, personal experience of God. They were men of prayer before being men of action. For the prophet is essentially an intermediary who draws light from the mind of God and sheds it on the community of men. And a sure, practically indispensable way to search the mind of God is to approach him in prayer. "Prophetic stands" taken by prayerless men and women are utterly worthless, they are nothing more than colourful, empty soap-bubbles that will disintegrate at the slightest pressure. It might be worth keeping this in mind, for claims to prophecy are always easy to make and not half as easy to authenticate.

6) Conflicts between the centre and the periphery

In contemporary spiritual literature, with its endless talk about charisms and charismatics, one often gets the impression that these two terms have of late undergone a subtle shift, and that, as a consequence, they are almost exclusively applied nowadays to persons under authority rather than to those in authority. This is a serious mistake, for, as pointed out above, in the New Testament some of the most outstanding charismatic figures are precisely men in authority. It is obviously wrong to assume gratuitously that the Spirit acts charismatically only in the periphery of the Church, ignoring the centre. An opposition and even confrontation between centre and periphery, as if the centre were always synonymous with structures, rigid and oppressive, and the periphery the privileged witness of the Spirits's charisms, free, flexible and unpredictable, would surely be entirely artificial and arbitrary. For the Spirit remains the master and guide of the entire Church, rulers and ruled, centre and periphery, and often shows his activity in both these spheres. Yet, the facts is that the Spirit does seem to have a certain strange predilection for the periphery, though predilection does not mean exclusivity.

It would be futile to imagine the early Church as one made up exclusively of charismatics, for the later writings within the New Testament itself bear witness to the transmission of the Spirit through sacramental means. So, for instance, Paul reminds his beloved disciple Timothy: "Fan into flame the gift that God gave you when I laid my hands on you. God's gift was not a spirit of timidity, but the Spirit of power, and love, and self-control" (2 Tim 1,7). Hence, it its not only the person of the office-holder, but in a certain way the office itself that must be acknowledged to be charismatic. And when the charism is transmitted this way, through institutionalized sacramental channels, it shows a certain permanence and stability which goes beyond a mere intermittent effusion or temporary outpouring. And so, in the later stages of the New Testament certain structures of government can already be detected, somewhat rudimentary and ill-defined, but true and real, for they are the creation of the Spirit.

Therefore, when confronted with the appearance of a charism in the community, authority, itself guided by the Spirit, must discern and accept it if genuine, and once accepted, authority should have the courage and ability to organize it, to lay down clear norms and supporting structures for its preservation. For history seems to show that even genuine charisms proceeding from the Spirit, when left unprotected and unsupported, often tend to melt away and disappear. It is the function and duty of authority to keep the true charism alive and take all the necessary measures to avoid its disintegration. The gift of virginity, for instance, is most certainly a true charism of the Spirit, yet subject in the Catholic Church to clear norms and definite regulations intended, not to stifle it, but to protect it. It would be foolish to leave pearls unprotected and gold biscuits unguarded.

But preservation presupposes acceptance, and acceptance implies a prior discernment. When a charism makes its first appearance in a community the right attitude on the part of those in authority ought to be liberty rather than repression. A nervous, hasty intervention on the part of authority on the ground that such a charism shows signs of being troublesome as opposed to traditional practices and accepted norms of conduct, could be very dangerous, for it risks throwing away the baby along with the bath water. In the initial stages — which may last for a fairly long time — tolerance should prevail over repression, and the freedom to which the charismatic is entitled should not be hastily suppressed as long as the spurious character of the charism has not been clearly and convincingly established.

But, on the other hand, weakness and undue hesitation on the part of authority could prove fatal and even self-destructive for the community. Courage to oppose widespread, popular tendencies and swim against the stream can well be part and parcel of the charism of those in authority. Weakness and timidity can masquerade as patience and Christian tolerance, when in reality the alleged prophet or prophetess should have been silenced long ago. Once the false origin of the "charism" has been clearly detected, it is the duty of authority to suppress it with a firm hand, or the community will suffer. Firmness in upholding a refusal can be simply stubbornness and a splendid means of quenching the Spirit, but it can also be the exercise of a true charism on the part of authority.

Despite all the above, however, one should acknowledge that nearly all the charisms mentioned in the New Testament have nothing to do with hierarchical channels, they are rather popular and, in a sense, democratic. Surely the office-holders can be true charismatics, but they certainly do not have the monopoly of the Holy Spirit. Y. Congar remarked wisely long ago that "all have the Spirit of God within them, and so are not like a flock of silly sheep whose understanding is all in the shepherd who looks after them". The Spirit surely vivifies also those in authority, but not only them. Nor is there any guarantee that the office-holder will always and everywhere enjoy a richer, more lavish effusion of the charismatic Spirit. For it would be dangerous to imagine that "the hierarchy is the only portal through which the Spirit enters the Church".[26]

The Holy Spirit retains an astonishing liberty of action and a fairly high degree of unpredictability. He simply cannot be curbed or "domesticated" into hierarchical or institutionalized channels. History shows, once again, that very often, especially in periods of crisis, he bursts the customary structures with the irrepressible force of a divine freedom which cannot be quenched. For the entire Church, rulers and ruled, is subject to Spirit and never above him.

Hence, the voice of the Spirit can be perceived both in the centre and in the periphery of the Church, it can come from above and from below. "Provision has to be made that bureaucratic routine, turning means into ends themselves, rule for the sake of rule and not for the sake of service, the deadwood of tradition, proud and anxious barricades thrown up against new tasks and requirements, and other such dangers, do not extinguish the Spirit".[27] That the voice of the Spirit can come from below has been sufficiently shown by contemporary history. We have only to cast a retrospective glance over the last eighty years or so to realize to what an extraordinary degree the Spirit seems to show his preference for the periphery over the centre. At least four remarkable trends or movements have characterized the Catholic Church this century: the biblical movement, the ecumenical movement, the liturgical movement and the contemporary charismatic movement. Nobody will contest today that these four waves that have swept throughout the Church bear the clear imprint of the Holy Spirit. On the other hand, it is a sobering

26 K. Rahner, *The Dynamic Element in the Church* (London 1964), p. 48.
27 K. Rahner, *The Dynamic Element in the Church*, p. 80

though to realize that *of all them*, without a single exception, began in the periphery of the Church. When confronted with a prevailing wave, the center showed itself either cold and unresponsive or definitely hostile and condemnatory. It was only later, much later, that the centre came to realize the genuineness of these movements.

One must acknowledge in all sincerity that, as far as detecting the voice and action of the Spirit is concerned, this century the centre has cut a very sorry figure, unable for long decades to feel the touch of the Spirit who was stirring the periphery. Every time it was the periphery, not the centre, that showed a heightened sensitivity to the action of the Spirit. There seems to be a certain undefinable stiffness in the centre that does not bend easily. Why does the Spirit show such a marked preference for the fringes of the Church as the privileged witness to his action?[28].

The charismatic stands in a position of disadvantage with regard to authority, for whereas authority can suppress the charismatic, the charismatic cannot suppress authority. True charisms are to be protected not only by authority, but also from authority. For a frequent feature of the charismatic is his desire for change and reform, and office-holders can mistake this genuine charism for insubordination and restlessness. A peaceful harmony between these two forces should prevail, but this harmony cannot be regulated and institutionalized, for it is itself charismatic, and therefore this unavoidable tension between authority and the charismatic can be transcended only by the Holy Spirit who moves both. Regularity and order can be an indication that harmony has been attained, but it can also be the sign that a troublesome charism and the Spirit who was behind it have been quenched. This

28 The theological field offers more examples of the same unresponsive attitude of the centre. Scholars of the stature of Lagrange, Teilhard de Chardin, Congar, Chenu, Rahner, de Lubac, Courtney Murray and others, were first frowned upon and silenced by Rome; yet, eventually some of them became the architects of Vatican II, and their "dangerous" theories became eventually the official doctrine of the Church. Their pardonable mistake was apparently to have had the audacity of thinking years ahead of their time. Why is Rome often so slow in detecting the voice of the Spirit? And why does Rome so often mistake progress for unorthodoxy and new insights for danger to the faith?

tension is not only real, it is healthy and necessary. Complete, undisturbed peace can be found only in the graveyard, where peace has been attained at the cost of life.

The roles of both the office-holders and the charismatic are absolutely essential for the welfare of the Church, to which all charisms are ultimately directed. A hasty, high-handed suppression of charismatic voices by authority would lead to a despotic and autocratic Church, contrary to the intention of Jesus; just as an unbridled upsurge of charisms regardless of authority would end in absolute anarchy. And, once again, history shows that both these dangers are far from theoretical.

A superficial observer might well think that a charismatic surely enjoys the glow of publicity and the glare of the media, especially if he takes a stand that substantially differs from that of authority. In reality, however, the reception of a charism for the service of the Church is a burdensome task, often associated with intense suffering. Apart from interference by legitimate authority, a charismatic may have also to endure the opposition of another man, subject of an equally legitimate charism. It is the same Spirit who arouses apparently conflicting forces in the Church to help her grow in vitality and service. Suppression of one of them in the name of order is no solution. "It is the one Lord who creates a force and resistance to it, the wine of enthusiasm and the water of sobriety in the Church, and has given to none of its servants singly the task of representing him".[29]

Long-enduring patience in face of protracted opposition is one of the qualities of the true charismatic. His obvious temptation will be to give up and thus avoid suffering, and even curse the day he was called to such a troublesome charismatic vocation, like Jeremiah of old. But this renunciation would be both an infidelity to the Spirit that moves him and a clear disservice to the Church for whose sake the charism is given. Once the true charism has been detected through the necessary process of discernment, it must be held on and firmly adhered to. To let the charism lie idle and untouched simply to avoid the suffering implied in its use, would be highly irresponsible and a subtle form of selfishness

29 K. Rahner, *The Dynamic Element in the Church*, p. 78.

under the cover of humility. If the Spirit gives charisms, fidelity to the Spirit demands that we make use of them.

Yet a genuine charism can be misused, as much as an internal inspiration of grace can be quenched and go unheeded. True charismatics are often suffering servants more than domineering lords. Vast movements of renewal in the Church have often been initiated by obscure charismatics, subject to the Spirit in patient fidelity.[30] And there is certainly no reason to think that today's Church is less rich in charisms than the early Church, even if they are possibly less striking and glaring.

We see, in conclusion, that charisms are given to the individual for the sake of the Church, but the Church cannot create charisms at will, she can only receive them with gratitude and use them with fidelity. Although the Spirit is *in* the Church and dwells in her, he is not the Spirit *of* the Church. as he is the Spirit of Christ. And so, a necessary tension will always exist between the Spirit and the Church, with the Church always living under the supreme direction of the Spirit. For the Spirit is domiciled in the Church but he cannot be "domesticated" by the Church. She can never curb the freedom of the Spirit, and if she has the certainty of communicating the Spirit through sacramental channels, it is because of God's fidelity and freedom to subject his grace to external signs, not because of any power inherent in the Church. Hence, this capacity to impart the Spirit will always remain a free, unmerited gift of God, to which the Church has no right and to which she can lay no claim. She will always remain the humble handmaid of the Lord who is constantly upheld and will eventually be saved by the strength of his unmerited love.

30 Founders and reformers of religious Orders were undoubtedly true charismatics who, always faithful to the Spirit, succeeded in bringing about enduring movements of reform within the Church. It has been correctly pointed out more than once that these fresh infusions of vitality in the Church (one has only to think of Benedict, Bernard, Francis of Assisi, Dominic, Ignatius of Loyola, Teresa of Avila...) always started in the periphery. There does not seem to be one single case in the history of the Church of a creation or reform of a religious Order that started in the centre. It is very difficult to give a convincing reason why this should be so, but it is simply a fact of history which goes to show, once again. that in certain respects the Spirit shows his preference for the periphery...

Bibliography

Rahner, K.: *The Dynamic Element in the Church* (New York 1964), pp. 42-83.

Küng, H.: "The charismatic structure of the Church", *Concilium*, April 1965, pp. 22-23.

McKenzie, J.. *Authority in the Church* (London 1965), pp. 151-162.

Friedrich, G.. "Prophets and Prophecies in the New Testament", *Theological Dictionary of the New Testament* 6 (1968) 828-861.

Lohse, E.. "Pentekosté", *Theological Dictionary of the New Testament* 6 (1968) 44-53.

Dunn, J.: *Baptism in the Holy Spirit* (London 1970), pp. 55-72.

Stuhlmüller, C.: "A community assesses its prophets", *Sisters Today* 45 (1973/74) 242-259.

Rahner, K.: "Observations on the factor of the charismatic in the Church", *Theological Investigations* 12 (1974), pp. 81-97.

Dunn, J.: *Jesus and the Spirit* (London 1975), pp. 135-156; 259-300.

Green, M.: *I Believe in the Holy Spirit* (London 1975).

"Charisma in the Church", *Concilium*, 1977/9.

McNamara, M.. "Discernment criteria in Israel: true and false prophets", *Concilium*, 1978/9, pp. 3-13.

Vogels, W.: "Discerner le prophète authentique", *Nouvelle Revue Théologique* 99 (1977) 681-701.

Dupont, J.: *The Salvation of the Gentiles* (New York 1979), pp. 35-59.

Dulles, A.: *A Church to Believe in* (New York 1982), pp. 18-40.

Vallin, P.: "Prophétisme dans l'Eglise", *Dictionnaire de Spiritualité* 12 (1986) 2434-2446.

Chapter Eleven

THE CHARISMATIC RENEWAL

The Holy Spirit is constantly present in the Church, but his activity within it resembles the ebb and flow of the sea, with exhilarating moments of high tide followed by others of low tide, when his activity is hardly noticeable. Today there seems to be strong evidence of an extraordinary charismatic activity of the Holy Spirit in the Christian Churches. The Charismatic Renewal (known also under the name of Pentecostal movement) is the fastest growing movement in Christendom. A typical trait of the movement is its spontaneity. As will be seen presently, it did not start as the result of a preconceived plan, for it was born quite unexpectedly and spread spontaneously. "The Pentecostal movement is comparable to a fire racing through a field of stubble. The burning stalks pass the fire on to one another, and this gives a continuity to the whole blaze, but not as though the grasses had deliberately joined forces".[1] Whatever be the final theological assessment of the movement one thing seems to be certain: that given its astonishingly rapid spread throughout the Churches (including the Catholic Church) the movement is a new form to be reckoned with. One can either approve or condemn it, but one can certainly not bypass it.

1) History of the movement

The generally recognized founder of Pentecostalism is the Methodist pastor Charles P. Parham. On the basis of the

1 E. O'Connor, *The Pentecostal Movement in the Catholic Church* (Notre Dame 1971), p. 34.

New Testament, particularly of the book of Acts, Parham and his students concluded that the only sure sign of the reception of the Holy Spirit was the gift of tongues. In keeping with this conviction, the group devoted days and nights to intense community prayer, asking the Holy Spirit for the gift of *glossolalia.* On New Year's day, 1901, a woman student received the gift after having been prayed over. A few days later Parham himself and most of the other students had the very same experience. The event took place at Topeka, Kansas, in the the U.S., and from there, after encountering initially much opposition, it spread unobtrusively throughout the southwest. In 1905 a new outburst occurred at Los Angeles in the course of ten days of prayer and fasting. It should be remarked, therefore, that in both the places, Topeka and Los Angeles, the beginning of the movement was clearly associated with prayer, as if this fresh charismatic outpouring were an answer to the intense petitionary prayer addressed to the Holy Spirit.

The Christian Churches, however, were not ready to accept this unexpected infusion of charismatic vitality in their midst. For, after all, charisms were almost universally judged to be a thing of the past, with only historical interest for the present. Consequently, those who accepted the new movement were soon driven out of their respective Protestant Churches. They were thereby forced to set up new Churches which came to be known as Pentecostal, usually considered as a third force in the Christian world, between Protestantism and Catholicism.

During the 1950s the movement entered a new phase, as charisms began to be received by members of the established Churches, who this time refused to withdraw and join a Pentecostal denomination. Thus the movement made deep inroads into the existing Protestant Churches. This is the phase known as the New Pentecostalism. Episcopalians (Anglicans) were the first to be affected by this new trend, but very soon Lutherans and Presbyterians followed. Many of these Protestant communities were, and to some extent still are, rent by internal divisions, and sharp differences of opinion over the issue whether a Pentecostal, and particularly one who has received the gift of tongues, could remain as a member of the original Church. By the 1960s Pentecostalism was already firmly entrenched within the structure of many Protestant Churches.

But it could not possibly be long before the Catholic Church, too, began to feel the impact of the movement. The fire was ignited for the first time within the Catholic enclosure in March 1967, in Pittsburgh, U.S. Yet long before this date regular meetings had been going on, which consisted of spontaneous prayer and Scripture readings. At a meeting of the Notre Dame community several of the participants received the gift of tongues, accompanied in some cases by deep sentiments of peace and joy: the Catholic Pentecostal movement or Charismatic Renewal had started. A remarkable sign of its present vitality is that the number of 34 countries represented at the International Leaders Conference in 1974 had grown to 94 by 1981. In the Catholic Church the features of the Charismatic Renewal have altered considerably: it has become more peaceful and quiet, less emotional and demonstrative, more orderly, and perhaps a little more structured. Yet, the main traits remain exactly the same. Many Catholic Episcopal Conferences have given the movement their cautious approval.

Pope Paul VI approved it explicitly in 1975. "You aspire at a renewal which is spiritual, authentic, Catholic, in the Holy Spirit. We detect the signs of such a renewal: love of prayer, of contemplation, of praise of God, receptivity to the grace of the Spirit, more assiduous reading of Scripture".[2] Six years later, in 1981, Pope John Paul II was equally warm and encouraging. "The Church has seen the fruits of your attachment to prayer in your deep dedication to the sanctity of life and love of the word of God. We have remarked with particular joy the manner in which the leaders of the movement have developed increasingly large ecclesial perspectives and have redoubled their efforts so that these perspectives may become a reality".[3]

2 Address of Pope Paul VI to the first International Congress, held in Rome in May 1975, cf *La Documentation Catholique* 72 (1975), p. 564.

3 Address of Pope John Paul II to the sixth International Congress, cf *La Documentation Catholique* 79 (1981), pp. 569-570. It is certainly remarkable that neither of the two Popes mentions the dangers inherent in the movement, as some of the Catholic Episcopal Conferences have done. The twofold papal assessment seems to be entirely positive.

2) THE MAIN CHARACTERISTICS

The main features of the Charismatic Renewal seem to be: prayer meetings, charisms (particularly the gift of tongues) healings and baptism in the Spirit.

a) *Prayer meetings* are for the members of the Renewal the natural, almost indispensable setting for the communication of the Spirit. It is clear from the history of the movement that it arose and spread in a deep atmosphere of communitarian prayer, and even today prayer seems to be like the required vehicle for the spread of the movement. This is surely consonant with the testimony of the New Testament, where the Spirit is often imparted to the believers when they are praying. So, for instance, at the moment of Jesus' baptism in the Jordan, when he "was praying the heaven was opened, and the Holy Spirit descended on him in bodily form" (Lk 3,21). Similarly, in the Cornelius episode already referred to above, Luke says that "Peter went up on the housetop to pray", and during that noon prayer he received the vision of the impure animals he would not touch; later, "while Peter was pondering the vision, the Spirit said to him..." (Ac 10, 9.19). This was also the experience of the first Pentecost: the Eleven "with one accord devoted themselves to prayer together with the women and Mary, the mother of Jesus" (Ac 1,14) — and the pentecostal effusion of the Spirit follows.

It is exactly the same mysterious but real connection between prayer and the Spirit that is observable at the meetings of the Renewal. For, as already remarked above, there seems to be an undefinable something in a prayerful atmosphere that brings the Holy Spirit down on the group. But these prayer meetings are kept flexible, without any fixed formula or pattern. Scripture readings alternate with spontaneous prayer and singing of hymns, in an atmosphere of peace, joy and felt presence of God.

b) *The gift of tongues*. Most classical Pentecostals believe that this is an indispensable sign to recognize if a person has really received the baptism in the Spirit. It would be entirely wrong, therefore, to imagine that the gift of tongues was something reserved exclusively to the early Church, for the very same gift seems to be abundantly present in our contemporary Church as well. According to Le Cossec "speaking in unknown tongues is the normal and biblical manifestation of the Holy Spirit, the external proof of an inner fulfilment". Jerusalem witnessed the first outpouring of the gift on the day of Pentecost, and the church of Corinth followed a few years later. Although the gift of tongues in both these cases seems to be substantially the same, the difference lies in the fact that in Jerusalem the tongues were understood by those present, whereas in Corinth they were ununderstandable.

In most meetings of the Renewal the tongues spoken remain unknown even to the speaker himself. According to the testimony of professional linguists the tongues are not real languages, either living or dead, but rather language-like sounds emitted in the course of prayer. But in any case there is no question of an ecstatic utterance, as if the speaker had lost control of his or her senses. The New Testament testimony in this regard is still the object of controversy, but exegetically it seems to be far more probable that in both the places, Jerusalem (Ac 2) and Corinth (1 Cor 14) there was a perfectly controlled use of the gift of tongues, and this is also borne out by the contemporary experience in the Charismatic Renewal. For nowhere does the New Testament describe the gift of tongues as an ecstatic utterance. It would seem that today those who have received this gift can make use of it just as they please; it is a permanent charism whose use is left to the discretion of the individual.

But just as it was the case at Corinth, the gift is directed to God, not to the neighbour, for speaking in tongues is primarily a gift of prayer rather than of preaching: "One who speaks in a tongue speaks not to man but to God" (1 Cor 14,2). In addition to the character of praise and thanksgiving, the gift of tongues can apparently be also used as a powerful form of intercessory prayer, particularly when the concrete needs to be prayed for are unknown to the individual. It is more than doubtful, however, that Paul's testimony in Romans 8,26 ("We do not know how to pray, but the Spirit himself intercedes for us with sighs too deep for words") can be used in this connection. The text is not precisely a model of clarity, and it would be hazardous to throw light on it by attributing to Paul a meaning which probably was not his.

The importance of this type of prayer seems to lie not in the gift of tongues itself but rather in its sign-value. Speaking in tongues "is only the superficial part of the charism, like the one-eighth of an iceberg that appears above water".[4] It is a tangible testimony that here and now the person is under the direct and immediate control of the Spirit working from within him and praying in him.

Akin to this gift is the so-called "message in tongues": at a meeting a particular person is inspired to speak out a certain message which is meant for others, but since the message is conveyed in an unknown tongue, it remains unintelligible until it has been interpreted. This gift is a sort of cross between tongues and prophecy, meant for the community, like prophecy, but couched in tongues. Obviously this charism cannot be used at will like the gift of tongues, for its nature is not permanent but transitory.

c) *Prayer for healing* is practiced at most meetings of the Charismatic Renewal. The participants display great trust and confidence in the power of God to heal all diseases, whether physical or psychological, whether considered curable or incurable. This deep faith and trust are usually the fruit of experience rather than the result of theological reflection. The person healed is usually (but not necessarily) prayed over by some other member of the group, whether priest or layperson, often with the accompanying imposition of hands. A fairly high number of such healings, especially of physical diseases, has been reported.

d) *Baptism in the Spirit.* This is the all-important reality of which the exteriorly perceptible gift of tongues is only a visible sign. Shortly before his ascension the risen Jesus had promised the Eleven: "Before many days you shall be baptized in the Holy Spirit" (Ac 1,5), namely, submerged, immersed in the person of the Spirit, like a sponge is soaked in water. The expression "baptism in the Spirit", therefore, which has become a veritable hallmark of the Renewal, refers to a personal *experience* of the Spirit filling and transforming the individual, like he transformed the Apostles at Pentecost. It is from the renewal of this pentecostal experience that the

4 E. O'Connor, *The Pentecostal Movement* p. 125

movement derived its original name and dynamism. Though concrete experiences vary from person to person, two different types of baptism in the Spirit seem to have emerged, the manifest type and the hidden type.

The manifest type. When a person is being prayed over, he may experience a deep, inexplicable sense of joy, love and peace welling up from within him and flooding his entire being. This feeling is not the result of some other experience that would then produce this joyful peace as a kind of a psychological reaction. He rather feels that this inner experience is directly communicated to him by God and, as a consequence, he is certain of its divine origin, for this peaceful joy as well as the certainty of its supernatural origin come together, as two different but inseparable facets of one and the same experience. This may be accompanied by the gift of tongues or by some other externally visible charism, but it need not always be so. It is a *deep sense of the presence of God experientially apprehended.*

The hidden type. At some other times the same experience of love, joy and peace comes to the individual, not suddenly like an avalanche, but rather slowly and gradually, like the waters of an imperceptibly rising tide. Nothing seems to happen after the person has been prayed over, but the effects begin to manifest themselves only after some time. It is the Spirit transforming the indididual over a certain period of time. And it would be an error to take this gradual growth in the experience of the Spirit as a sign that the experience itself is less intense and valuable. It definitely need not be so, for still waters run deep, and in the long run this hidden type of baptism in the Spirit may prove even more effective and specially more durable than the sudden, manifest type.

There may be other cases that fall somewhere between these two types, but all of them seem to be characterized by an experiential possession of the Spirit, usually conscious. It is the Spirit making his presence sensibly felt in man's psychological faculties. The first case of baptism in the Spirit recorded in modern history (Topeka, Kansas, in 1901) was described thus in Johannine language: "It was as though rivers of living water were proceeding from my inmost being".

It was simply the confirmation of the Pauline "let the Spirit fill you" (Eph 5,18).

Finally, it should also be noted that this baptism in the Spirit is generally transmitted through the laying-on of hands, as the vehicle for the communication of the Spirit. But there are exceptions to the rule. And the one imposing hands is normally a person who has already received the baptism in the Spirit earlier, whether priest or layperson, man or woman; a fact that points to the strongly ecclesial or communitarian character of this baptism. The transforming effects are received by the individual, but they are communicated to him through the instrumentality of the community.

Lest all the above remain somewhat theoretical, it might be now worthwhile to listen to real witnesses, people who have experienced in their lives the baptism in the Spirit:

> I was invaded by a new power of love.
>
> Before, I was on the bank of a river. Now I am in it.
>
> At the time nothing of which I was aware happened. I got up. I felt a bit put out. But very quickly I found inner peace and was quite sure that I had received the gift of God himself. During the time that followed. I experienced a deep certainty of faith, rather like Mary after she had been visited by the angel. It was as if I had discovered for myself the depths of my own heart, the spiritual centre of my being where God dwells. This intimate presence was like an intense but gentle fire.
>
> A new life, I felt, was beginning for me. It consisted above all of an intense consciousness of the presence of God but also of a new kind of prayer. At times I could hardly bear to tear myself away from that prayer. I found myself living in a climate of great trust and joy.
>
> This sense of concrete, factual presence is the perception of the nearness of Jesus as Lord, the realization at the personal level that Jesus is real and is a person.... With great frequency this sense of presence is accompanied by a sense of power, most specifically the power of the Holy Spirit....Another characteristic response to presence and power is an intensification of the whole prayer life, with a special love for the prayer of praise....

> The experience has a resurrection quality about it that is joyous and triumphant.[5]

3) The effects of the movement

This is the decisive issue, for the Renewal will finally have to be judged by the effects it has produced: "You will know them by their fruits" (Mt 7,20). This will always remain the touchstone of genuineness and reliability. A full enumeration of all the fruits the Renewal has produced is both difficult and unnecessary. But the most important can be reduced to the following:

Experiential knowledge of God. Before his baptism in the Spirit the pentecostal might have known about God, but now he knows God in the biblical sense, for God is no longer an abstraction dwelling up there, to be apprehended in dark faith; God has suddenly become a living person whose incredible proximity can be felt, relished and tasted. There is a ring of personal familiarity when a member of the Renewal speaks of God as a person he has actually encountered in his life. Often his experience is crystallized into a deep sense of God's fatherhood, which makes him or her realize the deep truth involved in the Pauline "Abba, Father" (Gal 4,6). Before the experience, God was the Creator, now he has become his Father, incredibly close to him, enveloping him in his love, care and solicitude. He experiences a transition from an abstract, intellectual form of knowledge to a personal, intimate relationship pervaded by intense love and quiet trust. For him God has suddenly sprung into life.

Prayer life. This deep experiential knowledge of God seems to be the root cause of many other effects, one of which is a deeper appreciation of the life of prayer. The pentecostal prays, and he prays long. It is not, however, the mere length of his prayer that is so characteristic, bnt rather the intimacy of its nature. The Renewal seems to be profoundly marked by the prayer of praise, too often neglected by other Christians. It may also be that baptism in the Spirit brings the pentecostal into the first, rudimentary stages of the prayer of quiet, at the very threshold of mystical life. At least the effects of quiet

5 Testimonies quoted by Y. Congar, *I Believe in the Holy Spirit*, II, pp. 196-197.

joy and deep peace are typical of the prayer of quiet. If sustained, this deepened life of prayer would be one of the most precious possessions of the Renewal.

Deliverance from sinful habits like drunkenness, fornication, drug addiction, etc. It is a sudden conversion effected by the Holy Spirit, and this seems to be one of the most frequently reported traits of the movement which is hardly subject to illusion. For these effects are often dramatic and always tangible. It is a remarkable confirmation of Paul's teaching on the Spirit of freedom, for those who have received the baptism in the Spirit feel often liberated, they experience in their personal life that the fetters of sin have snapped, and they are free to start a new life far removed from sin.

Peace and joy, which seem to be present practically in all the recorded cases. Deliverance from a sinful habit is often accompanied by this enveloping atmosphere of joyful peace as an unmistakable sign of the Spirit's presence. And it stands to reason that this should be so, for from New Testament times peace and joy have always been the trademarks of the Holy Spirit's action.

Other effects are no less characteristic, like a sudden enthusiasm for Scripture, a heightened sensitivity to the promptings of the Holy Spirit guiding the pentecostal from within, a renewed attachment to Mary, attraction to an intense sacramental life (among Catholics), particularly as regards the Eucharist; a deepened sense of sin and penance, consideratedness towards the unavoidable shortcomings and human failures of the hierarchy, and in general towards those in authority, etc.

The durability of these effects varies, but there seems to be a sort of inversed ratio between their intensity and their durability: it is not always the most sudden and intense that are the most durable. Some of them are transitory, whereas those involving a change of mentality and general attitude may be more permanent. But the lack of permanence observable in some of these effects need not necessarily be taken as a negative sign. Some of the effects of true mystical prayer are not permanent either, yet this is no reason to doubt their authenticity.

4) Theological assessment

In general, the theological judgment to be passed on the Renewal will largely depend on its fruits. And the fruits (at least among Catholics) seem to have been, by and large, positive. The movement has awakened a new consciousness of the Spirit's activity throughout the entire body of the Church, and this is certainly welcome. With the exception of the Orientals, who have always had a very refined and profound theology of the Holy Spirit, all the other Christian Churches have for centuries sorely neglected such a theology, but now they seem to be finally coming to the full realization that the Spirit guides the Church today no less than he did at the beginning.

The heart of the Renewal seems to be *the experience of the Spirit*, and there is nothing that can reasonably be objected against this. Paul implies that the Christian should normally experience the Spirit, and if this principle was valid in the early Church there is no convincing reason why it should not be valid now. Nor can it be objected that this experience is beyond the capabilities of the ordinary faithful. Probably many of the experiences they tend to dismiss as pure imagination or sheer sentimentality may well proceed from the divine source living and acting within them. In any case most of the striking testimonies given in this connection proceed from plain, ordinary faithful, men and women, married and single, young and old, and there is no reason to doubt their sincerity and authenticity. The grace of the Spirit enters so gently and unobtrusively into our psychic life that it often passes unnoticed and is difficult to detect. It may well be that more people than we imagine do experience the Spirit, but are not conscious that it is the Spirit that is moving them.

As regards charisms in general and specifically the *gift of tongues* haughty scepticism could be, once again, as dangerous as uncritical credulity. The Charismatic Renewal and the gift of tongues are so closely associated in the minds of many as to be almost interchangeable, and this is certainly not correct. In this area, too, the New Testament should retain its normative value. It is true that speaking in tongues seems to have practically disappeared from the Church after the second century, but no valid theological reason can be adduced to disprove its reappearance in the twentieth. The Spirit is the supreme master of his own gifts, which he bestows and withdraws as and when he pleases. Speaking in tongues cannot be glibly discarded as an unimportant psychic phenomenon of merely human origin. The considered opinion of one of the greatest specialists in the movement, K. McDonnell, is worth listening to: "After an examination of the pertinent literature on the subject of the gift of tongues, and after examining the testimonies of pentecostals themselves, it is my opinion that many of the cases of speaking in tongues are genuine. In a matter of this kind the possibilities of deception are great...but all (the effects) indicate that this is more than a psychic phenomenon".[6] But the claim that the tongues spoken are real languages remains unproved.

However, in several circles of the Renewal there seems to be an exaggerated appreciation of this gift, and this is not sound. Paul had to face exactly the same attitude in Corinth with regard to tongues, and his opinion should be normative even today: he does not forbid the use of the gift (1 Cor 14,39), only its uncontrolled and uninterpreted use (1 Cor 14,27). For, if there is no one endowed with the parallel gift of interpretation, the speaker in tongues should "keep silence in church and speak to himself and to God" (1 Cor 14,28). This is a perfectly clear norm given by Paul, yet it is at times neglected in meetings of the Renewal. Paul surely appreciates the gift and wishes that all should be endowed with it (1 Cor 14,18), but he judges it to be definitely inferior to prophecy; for it builds only the individual himself, not the community (1 Cor 14,19.39).

Charisms are undoubtedly a normal dimension in the life of the Church, but among them the gift to tongues is one of the least valuable. It impels the individual to prayer, but directly it does not build the Church. The danger of certain "charismania" among some members of the Renewal is far from theoretical, and constant and unguarded talk of charisms, far from being helpful, is rather detrimental, as it may lead to a certain discredit of the Renewal.

6 K. McDonnell, *Catholic Pentecostalism: Problems in Evaluation* (Pecos 1970) p.59.

Despite some recent criticism levelled against the expression "baptism in the Spirit", nothing of consequence can be objected against it, for the expression is substantially biblical: did Jesus not promise the Eleven that they would be "baptized with the Holy Spirit" (Ac 1,5)? Yet it cannot be denied that the expression at times covers a wrong baptismal theology. Baptism in the Spirit, to be genuine and legitimate, should imply only a new experience of the Spirit, not the bestowal of the Spirit. For it is not the baptism in the Spirit that confers on the Christian the indwelling of the Spirit, but rather the baptism of water that has preceded it. An appreciation of the baptism in the Spirit that would imply a corresponding depreciation of sacramental baptism would be clearly unsound. Sacramental baptism, in some form or other, is necessary for salvation, whereas baptism in the Spirit is not. The reception of the Spirit in the indwelling is far more important than the experience of his presence. However, this danger of devaluing water-baptism does not seem to be present among Catholic members of the Charismatic Renewal.

One obvious danger of the Renewal, just as of any such charismatic movement, is that of secession from the Church. Past history, from early Montanists to medieval spiritualists, all of them claiming a special guidance of the Spirit, sufficiently shows that the danger is not imaginary. In fact, some Protestant Churches have been plagued by fissiparous tendencies of this kind. Yet, this danger of breaking away from the established Church, though present in the Renewal, does not seem to be endemic to it. The defections from the Church among Catholic pentecostals have been very few. In fact, some have confessed that the Renewal acted rather as a brake against their tendency to cut themselves loose from the moorings of the official Church. If the movement is inspired by the Spirit, as seems to be the case, it cannot but lead deeper into the Church, rather than away from her, but single defections should not cast a slur on the entire movement, as long as they remain truly exceptional.

Though my assessment of the Renewal is on the whole positive, the *negative aspects* or dangers to be avoided should not be passed over in silence: a penchant for the striking and sensational, and a possible neglect of gifts which are less showy but more useful; a certain emotionalism which attaches excessive importance to feelings and personal experience when judging the fruits of the Spirit; elitism, which exaggerates the importance of belonging to the Renewal, and may even tend to despise those who do not belong to it; certain fundamentalism in the interpretation of scriptural passages, neglecting the results of scientific exegesis; false ecumenism, which tends to play down the doctrinal differences that are still keeping the Christian Churches apart; and a certain self-centredness which seems to neglect the social dimension in the Church's life.

In conclusion: An overall view of the fruits produced by the Renewal, specially among Catholics, seems to justify a cautious approval. Dangers and individual deviations there will always be, but this does not jeopardize the authenticity of the movement itself, for even genuine charisms are not always found in a pure, unalloyed state. Even when the Spirit is at work the channels of transmission are always sinful, fallible men and women. If the waters of a river are found to be less pure in a particular spot, this need not make the very spring suspect. On the whole the Renewal seems to be eminently suitable for a visual, pictorial culture like ours, dominated by the media, "one where the medium of communication — as in biblical times — is not definition but description; not pronouncement but story; not doctrine but witness; not the theological *Summa*, but the hymn; not the treatise but the television programme....".[7]

At the end one cannot but agree with E. O'Connor's considered opinion: "The pentecostal experience seems to correspond to authentic Christianity, and the lifeless patterns to which we have grown accustomed seem to be the sign, not of fidelity to authentic tradition, but of resignation to uninspired mediocrity which needs a new breath of the Spirit to stir it".[8]

Bibliography

Beare, F.: "Speaking with tongues. A critical survey of the

7 As quoted by Y. Congar, *I Believe in the Holy Spirit*, II, p. 159.
8 E. O'Connor, *The Pentecostal Movement*, p. 279.

New Testament evidence", *Journal of Biblical Literature* 83 (1964) 229-252.

Sweet, P.: "A sign for unbelievers: Paul's attitude to glossolalia", *New Testament Studies* 13 (1966/7) 240-257.

Ranaghan, K.: *Catholic Pentecostals* (New Jersey 1969).

Bruner, F.: *A Theology of the Holy Spirit. Pentecostal Experience and the New Testament Witness* (London 1971).

O'Connor, E.: *The Pentecostal Movement in the Catholic Church* (Notre Dame 1971).

Sullivan, F.: "The Pentecostal Movement", *Gregorianum* 53 (1972) 237-265.

Montague, G.: "Baptism in the Spirit and speaking in tongues", *Theology Digest* 21 (1973) 342-360.

McNutt, F.: *Healing* (Notre Dame 1974).

McDonnell,K.: "The distinguishing characteristics of the charismatic pentecostal spirituality", *One in Christ* 19 (1974) 117-128.

Theological and Pastoral Orientations on the Catholic Charismatic Renewal (Malines document: Notre Dame 1974).

Scanlom,M.: *Inner Healing* (New York 1974).

Sullivan,F.: "Baptism in the Holy Spirit", *Gregorianum* 55 (1974) 49-68.

Suenens, Card.: *A New Pentecost?* (London 1975).

"The Catholic pentecostal movement: creative or divisive enthusiasm?", *Pro Mundi Vita*, n. 60 (1976) 1-36.

Kelsey, M.: *Healing and Christianity* (New York 1976).

Laurentin,R.: *Catholic Pentecostalism* (London 1977).

Suenens, Card.: *Ecumenism and Charismatic Renewal* (London 1978).

McDonnell,K.: ed., *Presence, Power, Praise. Documentation on the Charismatic Renewal*, 3 vols. (Collegeville 1980).

Congar, Y.: *I Believe in the Holy Spirit*, II (New York-London 1983), pp. 145-212.

Sullivan F,: "Pentecôtisme", *Dictionnaire de Spiritualité* 12 (1984) 1036-1051.

ENNIS AND NANCY HAM LIBRARY
ROCHESTER COLLEGE
800 WEST AVON ROAD
ROCHESTER HILLS, MI 48307